T0140127

Human–Computer Interaction Series

The Human–Computer Interaction Series, launched in 2004, publishes books that advance the science and technology of developing systems which are effective and satisfying for people in a wide variety of contexts. Titles focus on theoretical perspectives (such as formal approaches drawn from a variety of behavioural sciences), practical approaches (such as techniques for effectively integrating user needs in system development), and social issues (such as the determinants of utility, usability and acceptability).

HCI is a multidisciplinary field and focuses on the human aspects in the development of computer technology. As technology becomes increasingly more pervasive the need to take a human-centred approach in the design and development of computer-based systems becomes ever more important.

Titles published within the Human–Computer Interaction Series are included in Thomson Reuters' Book Citation Index, The DBLP Computer Science Bibliography and The HCI Bibliography.

Charlie Hargood · David E. Millard ·
Alex Mitchell · Ulrike Spierling
Editors

The Authoring Problem

Challenges in Supporting Authoring for
Interactive Digital Narratives

 Springer

Editors
Charlie Hargood 🆔
Bournemouth University
Poole, Dorset, UK

David E. Millard 🆔
University of Southampton
Southampton, UK

Alex Mitchell 🆔
National University of Singapore
Singapore, Singapore

Ulrike Spierling
Hochschule RheinMain
Wiesbaden, Hessen, Germany

ISSN 1571-5035   ISSN 2524-4477 (electronic)
Human–Computer Interaction Series
ISBN 978-3-031-05216-3   ISBN 978-3-031-05214-9 (eBook)
https://doi.org/10.1007/978-3-031-05214-9

Contents

The Authoring Problem: An Introduction

Charlie Hargood, David E. Millard, Alex Mitchell, and Ulrike Spierling

Abstract The title of this book is 'The Authoring Problem: Challenges in Supporting Authoring for Interactive Digital Narrative'. For a reader new to this emerging field, while the title must have been intriguing enough to attract them to start reading this introduction, there may be a number of questions in their mind. What exactly is the 'authoring problem'? Or more generally, what is 'authoring', and what do we mean by 'interactive digital narrative'? In this introduction, we, as the editors of this volume, will try to provide some preliminary answers to these questions. The rest of the chapters in the book will then proceed to investigate and problematise these answers and raise questions and directions for further research. While many writers' guides exist for game narrative, hypertext and other forms of interactive digital narrative (IDN), guiding authors through solutions to the problems of authorship, that is not the focus of this book. Here we are collecting unsolved research problems—challenges yet to be overcome and questions unanswered which have accumulated over many years in the broad range of research communities connected to IDN.

C. Hargood (✉)
Bournemouth University, Poole, UK
e-mail: chargood@bournemouth.ac.uk

D. E. Millard
University of Southampton, Southampton, UK
e-mail: dem@soton.ac.uk

A. Mitchell
National University of Singapore, Singapore, Singapore
e-mail: alexm@nus.edu.sg

U. Spierling
Hochschule RheinMain, Wiesbaden, Germany
e-mail: ulrike.spierling@hs-rm.de

© The Author(s), under exclusive license to Springer Nature Switzerland AG 2022
C. Hargood et al. (eds.), *The Authoring Problem*, Human–Computer Interaction Series,
https://doi.org/10.1007/978-3-031-05214-9_1

1 The Authoring Problem

The 'authoring problem' has long been seen as an issue in the field of IDN. According to Theng, Jones and Thimbleby, writing in 1995 in the context of hypertext (one particular type of IDN):

> Creating hypertexts is complex because of the richness of interconnectivity that exists among nodes and links in hypertexts. As such, the demands placed on hypertext authors in authoring hypertexts cannot be underestimated. [1]

These concerns are perhaps even more important given the many and varied types of IDN that authors are faced with today, including those that make use of intelligent narrative technologies (see Thue's chapter in this volume), emergent narrative (see Kreminski, Mateas and Wardrip-Fruin's and Kybartas's chapters) and those that tackle difficult topics (see Koenitz, Barbara and Bakk's chapter).

More generally, there have long been recognised a wide range of authoring issues 'beyond tools', due in part to the difficulties that the field has faced defining what exactly it is we mean by 'authoring'. As Spierling and Szilas have argued:

> …it is hard to clearly define what steps of creation fall within the scope of authoring, and where the boundaries of so-called authoring tools are located. This is because on one hand we assign a co-creation role to the user regarding the resulting story experience, and on the other hand we cannot precisely distinguish between authoring a dynamic storyworld and programming the engine. [2]

These early discussions of the 'authoring problem' led to much research, including a number of workshops exploring this topic [3–10]. However, it is still a central problem in the IDN field, as can be seen by recent work in this area [11, 12]. It is the ongoing and central nature of the authoring problem to IDN research and practice that motivates this book.

2 What Do We Mean by 'Authoring for Interactive Digital Narratives'?

So, what exactly do we mean by 'authoring for interactive digital narratives', and why is there an 'authoring problem'? As is often the case in this field of IDN, first we need to unpack this phrase, and define some of the key terms that make up the concept, namely: 'interactive digital narrative', 'authoring' and 'problem'.

The name of the field itself is something that tends to reflect the multiplicity of the types of interactive digital narratives: Interactive fiction, interactive stories, hypertext fiction, storygames and playable stories are just some examples. For this book, we have decided to use the term 'interactive digital narrative', or IDN, as this seems to be the broadest term, which is increasingly used across the various communities that discuss this new form of storytelling.

The idea of what makes something '**interactive**' is at once immediately and intuitively obvious, and simultaneously difficult to pin down accurately in an agreed definition. One simple way to think of this is to use Crawford's definition of interactivity as 'a cyclic process in which two actors alternately listen, think, and speak' [13], where the two 'actors' are either two humans or potentially a user and a computer. This suggests that interactivity requires some form of input (listen), some output (speak) and some consideration for how to go from input to output (think). For a user (or an 'interactor' to use Murray's [14] terminology), thinking involves understanding what is happening in a given situation based on previous output and then deciding what choice to make. For the computer, this involves making use of some rules or procedures to map the input to the output. Missing here is some notion of how this changes over time. For this, we can use Rafaeli's definition of interactivity as 'an expression of the extent that in a given series of communication exchanges, any third (or later) transmission (or message) is related to the degree to which previous exchanges referred to even earlier transmissions' [15]. This suggests that, in the context of IDN, a work is interactive if there is an ongoing relationship between what the interactor is doing, and how their experience of the work progresses.

The adjective '**digital**' is perhaps the easiest concept to define: something is considered digital if it is represented in terms of discrete rather than continuous values, often in the form of binary numbers, or ones and zeros. Most likely the material support for this will be electronic (although this need not necessarily be the case). Of course, even something seemingly simple can be complicated on closer examination. The implications of a work being created using digital media have been widely discussed. Murray proposes four properties of digital media: procedural, participatory, spatial and encyclopaedic [14]. While these are all very helpful when thinking about IDN, the first two are most relevant. The procedural nature of digital media means that it is possible to encode rules and procedures within a work which will be executed without the involvement or presence of the person who wrote those rules. This suggests that the 'thinking' portion of the interactive cycle can be automated. The second property, participatory, directly supports interactivity—the medium itself enables input and output and incorporates the interactor's actions into the way that the medium behaves.

So far, we have defined the terms 'interactive' and 'digital', suggesting that an IDN work allows (or even requires) input from an interactor, is able to contain automated rules that determine how that input affects the state of the work and then provides output as a result, with current changes of state-dependent not only on the current input, but also previous input. This brings us to the third concept, '**narrative**'. For this term, we take a cognitive narratological perspective, considering narrative to be 'a forgiving, flexible cognitive frame for constructing, communicating, and reconstructing mentally projected worlds' [16]. This is rather broad, so we follow Herman by further considering narrative to involve 'situatedness, event sequencing, worldmaking/world disruption and what it's like' [17], where 'situatedness' implies the narrative takes place in some form of 'world', 'event sequencing' requires something to change or 'happen' within the narrative, 'worldmaking/world disruption' implies that those events cause some disequilibrium within the constructed world, and 'what it's like' suggests that the process of experiencing this narrative conveys something of the experience of those within that constructed world as they undergo the process of encountering that disequilibrium.

Putting it all together, we can consider an **interactive digital narrative**, or IDN, to be a work that evokes the construction of a mentally projected world (narrative) in the mind of the interactor, at least in part as the result of some actions taken by an interactor combined with the history of those actions (interactive), represented in a discrete, electronic medium (digital).

Having defined IDN, we can now specify what we mean by **'authoring'**. This can be seen as the complete process of going from an idea for an IDN through to the creation of the artefact or experience to be engaged with by the interactor. As Kitromili, Jordan and Millard suggest, this can involve a number of stages, including ideation, training and support, planning, visualising and structuring, writing, editing, compiling and testing and publishing [18]. This covers a wide range of activities, and as the chapters in this volume will explore, there are many different skills and abilities required of an author to carry out this process in the context of interactive digital narratives.

This brings us to our final definition—what do we mean when we say that there is an authoring problem? A **'problem'** is, according to the Oxford English Dictionary, '[a] difficult or demanding question; (now, more usually) a matter or situation regarded as unwelcome, harmful, or wrong and needing to be overcome; a difficulty.' [19] This suggests a number of ways of thinking about authoring in the context of IDN—what is it here that is difficult or demanding, or that may be unwelcome, harmful, wrong or in need of overcoming? Why should the combination of 'Interactive Digital Narrative' and 'authoring' be a problem?

One way to think about this, focusing on the notion of authoring being difficult or demanding, is to consider what it is about this particular process or activity that might create difficulties. Difficulty implies the presence of some obstacles or challenges—so what are the challenges presented by this situation? How might authors engage with or possibly overcome these challenges? And how can we, as researchers and practitioners, help authors with these challenges? This is what this book is about—understanding the research questions underlying the authoring problem, and how researchers and practitioners are currently thinking about and trying to overcome these problems.

3 Where Did This Book Come from?

The present volume has emerged from a series of workshops, 'Authoring for Interactive Storytelling' (AIS), first held at the International Conference on Interactive Digital Storytelling (ICIDS) in 2017 in Madeira, Portugal, in 2018 in Dublin, Ireland, and 2020 in Bournemouth, UK (held online due to the COVID-19 pandemic). This series of workshops in turn was preceded by a number of workshops organised separately by the editors, including Spierling's earlier workshops and tutorial at ICIDS

2008–2010 [3, 4, 9, 10], Mitchell and Spierling's ICIDS 2014 workshop [5], Mitchell et al.'s ICIDS 2016 workshop [6] and Hargood and Millard's ongoing Narrative and Hypertext workshop series at ACM Hypertext [20]. The editors come from across the various communities involved in IDN research, including ICIDS/ARDIN, ACM Hypertext, ELO, DiGRA and others. Part of the motivation behind these workshops has been to bridge and bring together these communities.

Most directly, many of the chapters in this volume largely started as position papers presented at the AIS 2020 workshop.[1] With the aim of collecting together the challenges, issues and unanswered questions of IDN authorship research scattered across multiple communities, participants were asked to submit contributions as potential chapters for a book. Following the workshop, we invited authors of selected submissions to revise their papers and submit them as chapter proposals and approached selected experts in the field to author chapters covering any gaps. Once these proposals had been compiled, they were submitted together with the manuscript proposal to Springer, where the book proposal was peer-reviewed. On acceptance by Springer, we asked the chapter authors to expand their proposals to full chapters. The submitted chapters were put through a single-blind reviewing process, with each chapter receiving two reviews from other authors in the same book section. Chapters were then revised by authors based on reviewers' comments, and the editors worked with the authors to polish their chapters, leading to the final versions included in this volume.

4 What is the Structure of the Book?

The resulting book is organised into four sections: authors and processes, content, form and research issues. Each section was handled by one editor and is intended to focus on specific aspects of the authoring problem.

4.1 Authors and Processes

The first section, *authors and processes*, provides a focus on the author, and very broadly what the author does when creating an interactive story. Sofia Kitromili and Maria Cecilia Reyes begin the section by proposing a general model of the IDN authoring process, which they see as consisting of ideation, pre-production, production and post-production. This model emerges from a synthesis of both Kitromili and Reyes' previous work, and also draws on elements of Koenitz's four-step design process [21]. The model describes the authoring process from idea through to published product as a series of steps but acknowledges that, although the process is

---

[1] http://narrativeandplay.org/ais/2020/.

presented in the order that the steps are most likely to occur, there is also the possibility for variation and iteration throughout the process. One key point that Kitromili and Reyes mention is that it is worth looking beyond the notion of an 'author' and instead consider the 'IDN creator' as a broader role that cuts across the various stages in the IDN authoring process.

Following on from this, Sam Brooker explores the genealogy of the field of interactive digital narrative. Brooker begins, much as we did in this introduction, with a brief attempt to define key concepts, such as 'interactive', 'digital', 'narrative' and 'author', although he perhaps wisely leaves these as sketches and quickly moves on to a survey of several threads that together form the fabric of the field. The most obvious way to trace these threads back to their origin is through the connections between pioneering digital works, such as *ELIZA* [22, 23] and *Colossal Cave Adventure* [24], hypertext fiction such as *The Patchwork Girl* [25] and *afternoon, a story* [26], through to contemporary IDN works such as *80 Days* [27] and *Heaven's Vault* [28]. Brooker pushes beyond this, considering literary antecedents, influences from theatre and cinema, and equally important input from games and computer science, each of which brings its own specific contributions. In the process, the chapter manages to touch on many of the key developments in the field, although as Brooker admits, IDN is a complex field, and one in which it is easy to omit or overlook works or academic contributions.

After this overview of the field, Joey Donald Jones provides a deep dive into the notion of 'authorial burden', exploring in detail the various ways in which the authoring problem is, indeed, a challenge to authors. Ways in which IDN authoring can present a burden for authors include the 'explosion of content' created by branching choices, the complexity involved in maintaining and tracking changing state and the many decisions involved in deciding on the final form of the work. Jones then provides an overview of a number of possible ways in which authors can reduce, or at least manage, this burden, including reducing or limiting scope, reusing existing content, decoupling dependencies of upcoming content on the previous content, taking a more generative approach, and perhaps most controversially, embracing the authoring burden as part of the process. Many of these approaches to tackling the authoring burden are echoed throughout the rest of the volume.

Perhaps another way to reduce the authoring burden, at least indirectly, is through the formation of communities of practice, often around specific authoring tools. This is what Daniel Cox explores in his chapter, investigating the communities that have arisen around three different IDN authoring tools: Bitsy [29], ink [30] and Twine [31]. As Cox suggests, while there have been literally hundreds of authoring tools created over the years, those that continue to survive tend to be the ones that have attracted a community of users, who in turn create documentation and learning resources, which form a feedback loop for the further growth of the community and continued use of the tool.

In the final chapter in the first section, Mark Bernstein takes a different perspective on the authoring problem, arguing that the authoring problem is, in fact, a publishing problem. Bernstein suggests that in addition to the various factors discussed so far, the literary economy and the practices of the book trade have also influenced the development of the field of IDN. Drawing on his own rich experiences over the past several decades as owner of Eastgate, a publisher of literary hypertexts, Bernstein argues that we have failed to create an audience for 'thoughtful interactive narratives', and that we can learn from the experience of the book publishing world to address this problem.

5 Content

This is followed by the second section, *content*. Although the distinction between content and form can be somewhat problematic, and we acknowledge that the boundaries between this and the next section are somewhat fuzzy, here we have tried to include chapters that focus on what an author is trying to say and how they are trying to say it through the creation of an IDN work.

David Thue begins the section by exploring the different ways in which authors can think about actions in an IDN. Thue argues that as a narrative progresses, what usually changes is the state of the narrative world. In an IDN this usually involves the interactor taking action either to impact the state of the world or discover more about the state of the world. In an attempt to encourage a broader perspective on actions within IDN, the chapter describes the Interactive Process Model (IPM), a generalised model for how interactor states change as the result of user interaction. This includes transition functions (how actions change states), observation functions (how these state changes are conveyed to the user) and action functions (how observations by the user lead to them taking subsequent actions). Thue then describes how this model can be used both to analyse an existing IDN and as a way to explore possible types of actions during the authoring process.

In addition to considering the actions an interactor can take within an IDN, an author must also consider how an interactor will both trigger and see the outcome of those actions. The question of narrative interaction design, often overlooked in the field, is something that Ulrike Spierling explores in detail. The chapter argues that there are essentially two ways of thinking about interaction in IDN: as navigation, either by clicking on links or through spatial navigation; or through 'natural' interaction, which tries to emulate physical participation in a virtual story world beyond simple spatial navigation. Spierling argues that what has been discovered in the move towards 'natural' interaction is that there is nothing natural about this form of interaction and that, in fact, the attempt to create something natural and invisible leads to additional problems, as users need to learn the bounds of the interaction—the expectation that the interaction will be natural actually becomes a barrier to use. In fact, except in some situations where the difficulty of the interaction is deliberate, the interaction can compete for attention with the narrative. This suggests an additional burden for authors of IDNs, that of designing the interaction with the narrative.

An underlying assumption in most IDN is that interactors can go back and re-experience a work, as a way to explore different paths or see the story from different perspectives. Despite the centrality of replay to IDN, little work has been done to explore this. Alex Mitchell's chapter explores the issues involved in authoring what Janet Murray calls a 'replay story', where the author deliberately wants to encourage or require the interactor to replay their work, focusing specifically on how authoring tools can support the additional authoring burden this imposes. This involves considering how authors can be helped both to think about and implement this type of IDN. A key issue that arises is whether the degree to which a tool embodies a particular approach to replay will be too constraining for authors, who may have different perspectives on how to encourage replay. This tension between providing support for authors and allowing flexibility, particularly at the tool level, is one that comes up across a number of chapters in this volume.

Following on from this, the question of how to help authors think about how to structure their work is often viewed from the perspective of patterns. In his chapter, David E. Millard, investigates the notion of 'strange patterns', arguing that even in a post-structuralist world, patterns can be a useful way to think about IDNs. The chapter describes how patterns manifest in an IDN at the micro, macro and meso levels, drawing on concepts from structural and formalist approaches to narrative, and the use of patterns in other fields, including architecture and software engineering. The chapter then provides more details about the different levels of patterns. Micro-level patterns include structures such as links and storylets. Meso-level patterns, formed from combinations of micro-patterns, are perhaps the most commonly discussed across the IDN literature. Finally, macro-level patterns provide a broader way of considering the structure of an IDN. The chapter ends by questioning the role of patterns in a post-structuralist world, suggesting that the notion of 'strange patterns' may be a way to move beyond what could otherwise be seen as a conservative approach to authoring.

John Murray and Anastasia Salter provide another perspective on this issue, considering the ways that the presentation or visualisation of IDN structures in an authoring tool relates to the process of authoring an IDN, focusing on five tools that are both widely used and have a strong user community: Inform 7, Adventure Game Studio, Twine, StorySpace 3 and inklewriter/freeinklewriter. In addition to providing an overview of the approaches these tools use to visualisation, the chapter also classifies and catalogues the ways in which these visualisations attempt to address the authoring burden. As with patterns, one issue that arises here is the tension between providing a specific way of visualising an IDN and enabling the author to create the work that they really want to make. As the authors argue, 'the lowering of the authoring burden is not necessarily a matter of more information'— instead, it is providing the appropriate information at the appropriate stage in the process, suggesting a need for customizable, flexible tools. This echoes the call in Millard's chapter for support for 'strange' patterns unique to a particular IDN.

In the final chapter in this section, Mark Bernstein explores the relationship between category fiction, such as mystery, science fiction, fantasy and horror. In doing so, he is drawing attention to a different type of pattern, perhaps at a higher level than Millard's macro-patterns, that of categories of (non-interactive) fiction, and how the frameworks on which these categories are built can help inform the craft of IDN. As part of this discussion, Bernstein draws parallels between games and kitsch, arguing that games tend in this direction as the result of a focus on a mass audience. From here, the chapter surveys a number of categories of fiction, including fantasy, science fiction, horror, romance and the western, suggesting ways that these categories are amenable to use in IDN. This leads to a discussion of the possible limits to what type of stories can be told in IDN. The suggestion is that some 'common story frameworks are... hostile to interactive agency', a suggestion that can perhaps be seen as yet another form of the authoring burden, one which authors are challenged to work to overcome.

6 Form

The third section of the book focuses on *form*, in which the chapters explore the issue of authoring across a range of different manifestations of IDN ranging from emergent and locative narrative, to hypertext fiction, games and intelligent narrative technologies.

One area where the notion of 'the author' and authoring is particularly interesting is that of emergent narrative. Max Kreminski, Michael Mateas and Noah Wardrip-Fruin discuss the notion of a *story sifter*, a system that is designed to identify 'compelling' stories within the masses of narrative events generated by an emergent narrative simulation such as *Dwarf Fortress* [32]. They describe two types of authoring—the authoring of story sifting patterns for identifying which events to highlight in an emergent narrative, and the authoring of the simulations themselves such that they are 'siftable'. Here, authoring is taking on a very different manifestation than in some of the other chapters in this volume.

Another increasingly common form of IDN is that of locative narrative. In her chapter, Valentina Nisi explores the ways in which place and space can form the basis for interactive digital narrative and the role of the author in this context. She argues that this type of authoring can be seen from three perspectives: author as storytelling facilitator, author as the architect of spatially distributed drama and authors that gamify narrative. These approaches to authoring again further stretch the demands on the author, requiring additional expertise in areas such as spatial design and game design.

The question of form is central to Stuart Moulthrop's discussion of the tensions between the tools that authors of IDN have to work with, the ways that these tools visualise the structures of the works being created, and the complex relationships that authors often try to create in their stories. The idea that visualisations of hypertext structure can be both empowering and limiting is central to the authoring problem, something that echoes Murray and Salter's discussion of visualisation, Millard's strange patterns and Mitchell's consideration of the impact of tool design on how authors think about replay. Moulthrop connects these ideas to a detailed discussion rooted in a consideration of two classic hypertext fictions, Larsen's *Marble Springs* [33], and his own *Victory Garden* [34].

While the IDN works discussed in Moulthrop's chapter are hypertexts, in which the main 'action' taken by the reader is to click on a link (with all the complexities that can entail in terms of reading and interpretation), Alex Mitchell discusses the ways that game mechanics can be seen as a narrative mode. This chapter describes and makes connections between two key approaches to the use of game mechanics in IDN, mechanics as metaphor and poetic gameplay, arguing that effective use of metaphor often depends on the interactor's expectations for the use of metaphor being undermined, forcing them to work to make sense of the meaning of the game mechanics. Mitchell argues that the combination of metaphor and poetic gameplay can be a powerful tool for creating IDNs.

The section on form ends with David Thue's discussion of the challenges that authors face when working with intelligent narrative technologies, which here refers to the application of artificial intelligence (AI) in the context of narrative. This provides particular challenges to authors, as authors not only need to have the technical skills to work with AI but also have some degree of understanding of both how the AI system behaves, and how they can, as an author, influence that behaviour so as to get the type of narrative experience they desire for their audience. Thue proposes that there are two ways an author can approach this: By experimenting with the system, and by examining the behaviour of the system. Using Jones' terminology, the use of intelligent narrative technologies involves embracing and becoming comfortable with certain aspects of the authorial burden.

7   Research Issues

Finally, the book wraps up with a discussion of the various *research issues* involved with authoring in the field of interactive digital narrative. One area that has not been given enough attention is that of authoring issues that arise in the context of multi-disciplinary teams. Nicholas Szilas and Ulrike Spierling explore the ways that the nature of interactive digital narratives creates particular challenges for interdisciplinary teams, beyond those faced by such teams in other areas, and specifically how these challenges relate to authoring. Although large interdisciplinary teams work in similarly complex areas, such as game development and film, the exploratory and experimental nature of much IDN work introduces additional complexities. The tension between developing new technologies and making those technologies accessible to authors, as discussed in Thue's chapter on intelligent narrative technologies, adds to this complexity. Szilas and Spierling identify a number of additional challenges, including dealing with change, sharing a vision, dealing with a range of data representations and fighting opacity. All of these continue to be issues facing teams working in the field of IDN.

A central approach to helping authors deal with the authoring problem has been the creation of authoring tools, which often take the form of software designed to be used by authors to create IDN works. In their chapter, Charlie Hargood and Daniel Green examine the problem of evaluating these tools. Surveying previous work on authoring tools, they suggest that, while most tools demonstrate thier functionality, they could be evaluated in a more systematic and rigorous manner. This is, however, not easy, as many of the problems discussed in the other chapters in this volume come to a focus in the design and development of authoring tools, and present additional challenges when it comes to evaluating those tools. The chapter suggests a number of ways that this issue can be addressed, and calls for more attention to be given, not only to the reader's experience but also to the author's experience.

As discussed in Kreminski, Mateas and Wardrip-Fruin's chapter, emergent narrative presents particular challenges to authors. Quinn Kybartas provides a survey of a number of ways to consider the use of quantitative evaluation of emergent narratives as part of the authoring process. As Thue suggested in his chapter, understanding AI-driven storytelling can be challenging for authors, something that is particularly true for emergent narrative. Authors can begin to understand the behaviour of an emergent narrative system by analysing the rules that drive the system, analysing the simulation itself and analysing the interactor's experience. Kybartas discusses four ways that quantitative analysis can help authors overcome this challenge, namely benchmarking, comparisons, verification and classification. The challenge remains as to how to make these tools accessible to authors.

The section concludes with a discussion of the ethical dimensions of authoring IDN, in which Hartmut Koenitz, Jonathan Barbara and Agnes Karolina Bakk explore the particular issues that arise in a work that allows for user interaction based on processes and systems created by the author(s) of the work. The authors of an IDN create the context for interaction, but the interactor also contributes to the experience, making choices as to how the story progresses, which aspects of the story are seen, and possibly what meaning they take away from the work. What happens when the IDN work is dealing with possibly sensitive or controversial issues? If, for example, a character in an IDN makes a morally questionable choice, who is responsible for this? Koenitz, Barbara and Bakk argue that, although interactivity seems to shift some burden of responsibility to the interactor, ultimately it is up to the authors to take responsibility for any ethical issues. This can be seen as an additional authorial burden, beyond those discussed in the earlier chapters. In this final chapter, a set of ethical guidelines are suggested, to help authors take on this responsibility and act ethically as they tackle the authoring burden.

8   What Next for the Authoring Problem?

The authoring problem has been part of the field of IDN since its early days. In part, this book is a call for more attention to this problem, across the various communities involved in IDN research and practice. At the same time, as can be seen in these chapters, the authoring problem cuts across many different areas, from interaction design to intelligent narrative technologies, from the economics of the publishing industry to game mechanics and metaphors. We hope that the chapters in this volume inspire more researchers and practitioners to engage with not just the *product* of authoring in IDN, but also the *problem* of authoring, in the hope that this leads to a deeper understanding not only of authoring but also of IDN more generally. We look forward to seeing how you make use of the insights from this volume to take steps towards addressing the authoring problem in IDN.

References

1. Theng YL, Jones M, Thimbleby HW (1995) Designer tools for hypertext authoring. In: IEE colloquium on authoring and application of hypermedia-based user-interfaces. IET
2. Spierling U, Szilas N (2009) Authoring issues beyond tools. In: ICIDS '09: Proceedings of the 2nd joint international conference on interactive digital storytelling Springer, Berlin, Heidelberg. pp 50–61. https://doi.org/10.1007/978-3-642-10643-9_9
3. Spierling U, Iurgel I (2008) Workshop and panel: the authoring process in interactive story-telling. In: Spierling U, Szilas N (eds) Interactive storytelling (ICIDS 2008). Lecture notes in computer science, vol 5334. Springer, Berlin, Heidelberg. https://doi.org/10.1007/978-3-540-89454-4_43
4. Spierling U, Iurgel I, Richle U, Szilas N (2009) Workshop on authoring methods and conception in interactive storytelling. In: Iurgel IA, Zagalo N, Petta P (eds) Interactive storytelling. Springer, Berlin Heidelberg, pp 356–357
5. Spierling U, Mitchell A (2014) Story modeling and authoring. In: Mitchell A, FernandezVara C, Thue D (eds) Interactive storytelling (ICIDS 2014). Lecture notes in computer science, vol 8832. Springer, Cham, pp 262–263
6. Chen F, Kampa A, Mitchell A, Spierling U, Szilas N, Wingate S (2016) Exploring new approaches to narrative modeling and authoring. In: Nack F, Gordon AS (eds) Interactive storytelling (ICIDS 2016). Lecture notes in computer science, vol 10045, Springer, Cham, pp 464–465
7. Hargood C, Mitchell A, Millard DE, Spierling U (2017) Authoring for interactive storytelling. In: Nunes N, Oakley I, Nisi V (eds) The tenth international conference on interactive digital storytelling (ICIDS 2017). Springer International Publishing, Cham, pp 405–408
8. Mitchell A, Spierling U, Hargood C, Millard D (2018) Authoring for interactive storytelling: When, why, and do we actually need authoring tools? In: Lecture notes in computer science (including subseries Lecture notes in artificial intelligence and lecture notes in bioinformatics), pp 544–547. https://doi.org/10.1007/978-3-030-04028-4_63
9. Spierling U, Szilas N, Hoffmann S, Richle U (2010) Tutorial: introduction to interactive story creation. In: Joint international conference on interactive digital storytelling. Springer pp 299–300
10. Spierling U, Szilas N, Hoffmann S, Richle U (2010) Workshop: education in interactive digital storytelling. In: Aylett R, Lim MY, Louchart S, Petta P, Riedl M (eds) Interactive storytelling. Springer, Berlin Heidelberg, pp 289–290
11. Kitromili S, Jordan J, Millard DE (2019) What is hypertext authoring? In: Proceedings of the 30th ACM conference on hypertext and social media. Association for computing machinery, New York, NY, USA, pp 55–59. https://doi.org/10.1145/3342220.3343653
12. Short AE. What does your narrative system need to do? https://emshort.blog/2022/04/09/what-does-your-narrative-system-need-to-do/, last accessed 10 April 2022
13. Crawford C (2002) The art of interactive design: a euphonious and illuminating guide to building successful software. No Starch Press
14. Murray JH (1998) Hamlet on the holodeck: the future of narrative in cyberspace. The MIT Press
15. Rafaeli S (1988) Interactivity: from new media to communication. Sage Annu Rev Commun Res: Adv Commun Sci. 16:110–134

16. Herman D (2002) Story logic: problems and possibilities of narrative. University of Nebrask Press
17. Herman D (2011) Basic elements of narrative. Wiley
18. Kitromili S, Jordan J, Millard DE (2020) What authors think about hypertext authoring. In: Proceedings of the 31st ACM conference on hypertext and social media. Association for computing machinery, New York, NY, USA, pp 9–16. https://doi.org/10.1145/3372923.340 4798
19. Oxford English Dictionary: "problem, n." https://www.oed.com/view/Entry/151726?result= 1&rskey=7Hnuwt&
20. Hargood C (2018) The narrative and hypertext workshop series and the value of workshops to research communities. SIGWEB Newsl 2:1–2:6. https://doi.org/10.1145/3266231.3266233
21. Koenitz H (2015) Design approaches for interactive digital narrative. In: Interactive storytelling. Springer, Cham, pp 50–57. https://doi.org/10.1007/978-3-319-27036-4_5
22. Weizenbaum J (1966) ELIZA
23. Weizenbaum J (1966) ELIZA—a computer program for the study of natural language communication between man and machine. Commun ACM 9:36–45
24. Crowther W, Woods D (1976) Colossal Cave Adventure [Computer game]
25. Jackson S (1995) The Patchwork Girl. Eastgate
26. Joyce M (1990) afternoon, a story. Eastgate systems, Inc
27. Inkle (2014) 80 Days
28. Inkle (2019) Heaven's Vault [Computer game]
29. Le Doux A (2017) Bitsy
30. inkle studios (2017) Ink
31. Klimas C (2009) Twine [Computer software]
32. Kitfox Games (2006) Dwarf Fortress [Computer game]
33. Larsen D (1993) Marble Springs [Hypercard stack]. Eastgate
34. Moulthrop S (1992) Victory Garden. Eastgate systems, Inc

Authors and Processes

Understanding the Process of Authoring

Sofia Kitromili⬤ and María Cecilia Reyes⬤

Abstract The process of authoring an interactive digital narrative has been one of the main issues in our field of studies. Throughout the history of the field, considerable attention has been given to the development and usage of authoring tools, very often disregarding the authoring process as a creative activity. In this chapter, we transcend the discussion around authoring tools, to delve into several models that describe the authoring process of different kinds of interactive digital narrative artifacts from ideation to publishing, identifying common practices across them. Subsequently, we propose an iterative and inclusive authoring process that is open to any form of interactive digital narrative artifact. The process consists of four stages: ideation, pre-production, production, and post-production. Finally, we discuss our thoughts on the understanding and acknowledgment of the interactive digital narratives' creator and their role.

1 Bringing an Interactive Digital Narrative into Existence

Since the early beginnings of the field, the study of the Interactive Digital Narrative (IDN) authoring process, and the development of IDN authoring tools that enable such a process, have been central issues constantly evolving alongside digital technology and society. The study of the authors' creative process allows for the development and improvement of authoring tools and prototyping methods, but furthermore, it creates a dialogue between artistic practice and research. When addressing authoring in computer-mediated creations, the IDN community has focused on the technical issues of the authoring process (systems, agents, supports, tools, etc.), while the IDN field would benefit from an "author-focused" perspective that goes "beyond the tools" [1]. In 2014, Koenitz [2] highlighted the lack of interactive digital narrative

S. Kitromili (✉)
Bournemouth University, Fern Barrow, Poole BH12 5BB, UK
e-mail: s.kitromili@soton.ac.uk

M. C. Reyes
Vilnius University, Saulėtekio al. 9 10222, Vilnius, Lithuania

© The Author(s), under exclusive license to Springer Nature Switzerland AG 2022   17
C. Hargood et al. (eds.), *The Authoring Problem*, Human–Computer Interaction Series,
https://doi.org/10.1007/978-3-031-05214-9_2

creators and the lack of a shared perspective to study authors' processes: "we should neither concentrate only on how existing technology can be better exposed to authors nor solely investigate how authors use existing systems." These claims acknowledge that bringing an IDN into existence is a complex creative process that transcends the usage of technology, as an artistic and communicative operation.

Due to the wide variety of technologies, multimedia supports, themes, and topics that the creation of an IDN experience can involve, the authoring process is an endeavor that very often cannot be carried out by one person only but needs an interdisciplinary team that can be as large as the scope of the project. Regardless of the collective or individual nature of authorship, the type of technology that runs the IDN, or its themes, needs to be a unified authoring process, one in which different types of authors can see their contributions reflected. It is here where we find that there is a miscommunication between the creative conception of the author and the use and development of authoring tools, which shows how we as a field still fail to understand the creative process of IDN authoring itself and what it entails.

In this chapter, we propose a general model of the IDN authoring process, understanding it from an artistic point of view, both narratological and digital. We delve into each stage of the authoring process, from the mental work of the author in creating a complex story world up to the publishing of the IDN experience, covering both narrative and interactive authoring tasks, as well as planning and production activities. The proposed authoring process is intended to be a universal process to which any kind of IDN creator can relate. Establishing and validating a unified IDN authoring process model will allow developers to reflect on what tools they should create, or which features to improve, and will allow artists, designers, and researchers to develop methodologies and techniques to foster interactive narrative design, storyboarding, worldbuilding, among other creative tasks, to accomplish a better result.

In the same way that we do not fully understand the authoring process, we also do not fully understand the IDN author either. After presenting a further understanding of the authoring process, we delve into the profile of the IDN author. An author-focused perspective needs to recognize the evolution of the IDN author and its transformation into a maker of experiences rather than just a storyteller. Authors and IDNs have evolved together: from text-based, to cinematic/performative, to ludic/experimental [3]. With the current pace of development and improvement of technology, the awakening of IDN creators and their relevance to the current media landscape will keep growing, and now is the time to understand their spirit. In the following sections, we aim to take a detailed look at the authoring process of an IDN, and the profile of the IDN creator.

2   The Authoring Process

It is a critical acknowledgment in our field that the process of authoring interactive digital narratives is difficult, making it part of the generic authoring problem. Lubart

[4], who has worked on conceptions of the creative process through the years, defines the creative process as "the sequence of thoughts and actions that leads to a novel, adaptive production." As such, when we refer to the creative process of bringing an IDN to existence as the *authoring process*, we mean the interactive narrative structure and content that an author must put through one or more tools to come out with a final product, including the thoughts and actions that the author must follow to design such content.

2.1 Tools Make It Possible, Authors Make It Real

One of the most commonly mentioned authoring barriers is the technical complexities of authoring tools authors must use to create IDNs. We, however, consider that this assumption is not entirely valid. It is not simply that a creator must deal with a complex tool to create—thus potentially experience artistic limitations—it is also that the tool a creator chooses, and its attached hermeneutics, may not be the right fit for their intended purpose. Authors by no means lack ample tools. Shibolet et al. [5] have identified over three hundred IDN tools and classified them in a repository so that scholars and other interested parties, can learn about the tools and their effects on the creative artifacts. For a creator, this repository is a priceless list of what kinds of tools are out there, and what IDN possibilities the tools possess. Nonetheless, every creator has their own needs, and it is often the case that the tools available might not be entirely what they seek. There is no perfect tool for a creator because every creator sets out to do something different, and as such tools may forever seem complex to creative minds regardless of technical skills. In the case that among these creative tools one is the perfect tool for a particular creator, there is no knowing how the interaction between creator and tool will develop. There is no way to predict what issues will arise in that agreement, and it is often the case that one simply cannot communicate successfully with the other because when the tool was developed, the narrative creator had no part in the design of how the tool would be experienced.

To surface some of the issues maintaining a gap in this communication, a framework of issues was developed in previous work relevant to the creative process, based on feedback from IDN authors. Among many issues, it is suggested that the most difficult to address is a potential conceptual misalignment between the mind of the creator and the purpose of the tool. This can be caused either because an author fails to understand which tool works best for the narrative they want to create or because the tool fails to convey its narrative purpose [6]. Part of the satisfaction that should be delivered to the IDN author is the pleasure of achieving the desired product. The other part is for their readers to appreciate their creation. If the tool of choice is the wrong one, then the creation might be misconceived, and the creator might be disappointed.

It is only in recent years that research in IDN has approached the design of authoring tools by methods commonly used in User Experience (UX) research [6–8]. As we are improving authoring tools and enabling a cohesive relationship between creator and tool of choice, it stands to reason that UX research should be at the forefront of this task. We are building these authoring tools because we want and need to see more IDN artifacts out there. This is what will inspire and transform research in the field, and it is what will help us expand this magnificent storytelling form that we have been nurturing for over 30 years.

The process of creation, which is strongly dependent on the tools, has never been properly conceptualized or examined in terms of how things work between authors and tools, and what happens when the two communicate. We think of the interactive element in IDN artifacts as a process that exists but not many have tried to identify what it entails, or how authoring tools can accommodate that element. Research acknowledges that the state of creation comes with its issues, technical and otherwise [1, 9–11]. Not a lot of work has been done to explore what those issues mean for the author and how they relate to their authoring process, aside from the framework developed in Kitromili et al. [6], where issues were identified and matched to the creative process. The work examined issues relevant to the misalignment between author and tool, the documentation available for creative development, the complexity of the authoring tools, the tools' programming environment and the general creation lifecycle. The identification of this framework had set out to establish an initial steppingstone to components tool developers should consider if they wish to predict and account for problems that might arise during the creative experience.

The creative experience, which we refer to as "the authoring process," has been discussed but so far there is no one unified model available for the IDN discipline, and the process until recently was not clearly conveyed. The general agreement among researchers who have attempted to demystify this process is that there is not just one step accommodating it, but several.

2.2 *Approaches to the IDN Authoring Process*

Kampa [12] has identified 15 steps to the creative process of locative interactive narratives, classified under creative, technical, and scientific actions. An influence on the development of our own process model is the four-step design process developed by Koenitz [3], based on his experience teaching IDN, which involves the following steps: *Paper phase* (idea to treatment to flow diagram), *Prototype phase* (check interaction and flow without (final) assets), *Production phase* (create (final) assets, structure, and interaction), and *Testing phase* (beta user testing, final adjustments). Specific to the hypertext fiction domain, Pohl and Purgathofer [13] have identified a series of actions recorded by authors using their hypertext tool and classified those actions into categories to develop a process. The resulting categories were text editing (writing and deleting text and node titles), node actions (creating and deleting nodes), moving (positioning nodes in the overview map), link actions (creating and deleting links), and other actions.

In other art and design disciplines, the four-stage model presented in Lubart [4] is widely adopted. It consists of (1) problem or task identification, (2) preparation (gathering and reactivating relevant information and resources), (3) response generation (seeking and producing potential responses), and (4) response validation and communication. Lubart's [4] model, which is suggested as an improvement on the default creative process used over the years in the arts, was developed by recruiting professionals and questioning them on their creative process. There are other examples of approaches where researchers tried to develop creative models by examining the experience of professionals. Sawyer [14] describes a studio model developed by conducting ethnographic studies and interviewing professors on the pedagogical practices they use in art and design courses, to teach students how to create. Botella et al. [15] recruited art students to identify the stages of the creative process based on the actions mentioned by students in their creative experiences. In the literary discipline, Doyle [16] examined the creative process in fiction by interviewing a small sample of contemporary writers of the time.

To construct our new authoring process model, we combined ideas from our previous work, which amalgamates approaches from multiple interactive narrative forms. Our previous work includes

1. Reyes's [17] proposal of an authoring process for interactive cinematic virtual reality (VR) movies, integrating the cinematographic production pipeline with the specificities of Interactive Fiction (IF) and VR. She identifies four stages: (1) Development: which is based on the system design of the System–Process–Product (SPP) model [11], comprising both interactive and narrative design. She proposes a screenwriting framework for interactive fiction in cinematic VR [18] that includes the writing of the screenplay as a mind map and the connection of the narrative units (NU) through diegetic and extradiegetic hotspots. (2) Pre-Production: this stage comprises storyboarding, scripting, and scouting, as well as preparing all the resources (human, financial, technical, etc.) needed for production. (3) Production: this stage includes the shooting of the cinematic NUs, the recording and mixing of the soundtracks, and the production of any other asset needed for the experience (images, 3D models, 2D videos, etc.). (4) Post-Production: this is an iterative stage that comprises the editing of the linear NUs and the interactive structure editing, together with testing and troubleshooting needed to finally launch a successful experience.

2. Kitromili et al.'s [19] process model is based on the work of various researchers in the field of IDN about their authoring process. The process model has been verified by a group of IDN authors, academics and narrative designers that were invited to interviews, to reflect on their experiences and discuss their process during the creation of an IDN [6]. They identified eight stages in the authoring process: (1) Ideation, (2) Training & Support, (3) Planning, (4) Visualizing & Structuring, (5) Writing, (6) Editing, (7) Compiling & Testing, and (8) Publishing. The process model was initially inspired by the development of text-based IDNs, but we consider it adaptable and relevant to other forms of IDN, as it is staged in a format that bears similarities to literary publishing, game development, and film production [20–22]. These authoring model's results are particularly relevant to

the field as they emerge from in-depth interviews with creators. It is an author-focused model rather than a technology-focused one while addressing authoring tool developers.

3   The IDN Authoring Process Model

Based on the process model in Kitromili et al. [19], we identified the need for extending the model so every type of IDN can be included, and all kinds of IDN creators can relate. Thus, we propose an IDN authoring process model (Fig. 1) that expands on the four-stage processes seen in Koenitz's [3] and Reyes's [17] models. The resulting process comprises an ideation stage, followed by pre-production, production, and post-production. Each stage is broken down into a series of actions that can be adapted to any type of IDN (text-based, cinematic, performative, ludic, spatial, etc.).

We present the steps in our creation process, from the idea to the published product, in the most likely order to be followed. However, this is a flexible and iterative order as each author is expected to work on their creative vision and utilize actions from each step at any point, as it suits them. It is also more than likely that several steps will be repeated throughout the authoring lifecycle, and there is no prediction of how many times, or in which order the author will conduct them. In the same way, there might be actions that are unique to a specific type of IDN that can be added to any of the stages. In this sense, the four-stage model that we propose aims to be inclusive and iterative, being open to the addition of new actions into each stage and to the repetition of actions to accomplish the desired result.

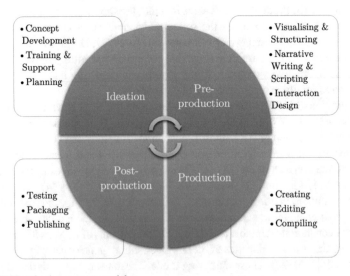

Fig. 1   IDN authoring process model

The breakdown of each stage into actions allows researchers and tool developers to have a detailed overview of the process to develop methodologies, techniques, and tools that can address specific steps of the authoring process while being mindful of the other actions and stages of the process.

3.1 Ideation

Creators see connections where nobody else sees them. The realization of these connections is what historically has been called an epiphany, or a "*eureka!*" moment: that time in which authors identify within themselves an idea, a message to convey, or a creative impulse. The ideation stage is the birth of ideas [23], where the story world with narrative content takes form in the mind of the author and it is the author's work to define the narrative foundation of an IDN.

Concept development. Envisioning the interactive digital narrative, how the inter-actor will access that narrative space; what the relationships are between inter-faces and the story world, the types of interaction and plot lines of the potential experience.

Training and Support. Guiding the author on how to implement the IDN through the chosen interfaces; how to innovate in the development of the assets; how to use the chosen authoring tool(s) via examples, guides, or tutorials.

Planning. Sketching the overall interactive structure with the possible plot(s), creating characters, drafting events, and making notes for the next stage.

3.2 Pre-Production

With a clear concept, enough research and training, and an initial narrative structure creators start to develop early prototypes. Pre-production is the stage of creating the backbone of the IDN and developing the necessary assets, materials, and resources to go into production. It comprises the development of the blueprint of the overall system and narrative design.

Visualizing/Structuring. Graphically creating, studying, and revising the struc-ture of a story (meaning the relationships between events, characters, chapters, or scenes) and granting an overview of the whole.

Narrative Writing & Scripting. Writing of the main narrative line(s) that traverses the experience, and that will guide the development of the IDN structure, environments, materials, and assets. It comprises the scripting of the *mise-en-scène* by virtual or human actors and their dialogues, as well as the development of any content that is part of the narrative presented directly to the interactor (text or audiovisual) considering any specialized language of the tool.

Interaction Design. Planning of the interaction modalities and rules based on the narrative content and chosen interfaces, shaping how the interactor is going to experience and affect the IDN.

3.3   Production

Whatever the artifact a creator is bringing to life, following their initial sketches of interconnected nodes and first drafts of narrative content, eventually, the separate constructs they imagined must become one complete product. Production is the stage where pieces of the IDN come together and the IDN takes shape.

Creating. Developing moving images, sounds, texts, photographs, 3D spaces, and other assets. Inputting this content or other material that is part of the narrative presented directly to the interactor into the authoring tool.

Editing. Assembling the different assets, and materials, into the tool. Revising, augmenting, and modeling the content and structure of the story, for example, embedding media in the text, composing behaviors for the interactive assets, changing stylesheets, keeping a revision record, or updating the structures or relationships between narrative units.

Compiling. Checking that the design is complete and error-free, for example without any loose ends or empty nodes. Also, in the case of using a tool with its own vocabulary, the language was used without syntactical errors or any other coding faults.

3.4   Post-Production

When the artifact is complete, the creator will need to refine it, make sure it behaves as intended, and prepare it for distribution to an audience. Ultimately, the creator will want their creation to be viewed and experienced by others. They will want their work out there in the world. Post-production is the stage where the IDN is tested, packaged, and released to the public.

Testing. Proofreading, debugging, and playtesting the IDN to make sure content and mechanics work as intended and that it is ready to be presented to the public.

Packaging. Preparing and exporting the IDN into a presentable and disseminative format so that the public can interact with it.

Publishing. Making the IDN available and distributing it where people will be able to access and interact with it.

Even though several of these tasks can be automated by the authoring tool, the breakdown of the process shows that the creative labor spans across all the stages: from the concept development, the narrative writing and the interaction design, the creation of the narrative units that are perceived by the interactor, all the way to publishing and distribution strategies. Such a complex endeavor, that is both imaginative and practical, needs a deeper understanding of the mind and skills of the IDN creator.

4   The Awakening of the Interactive Digital Narratives Creator

As IDN authors create technological artistic expressions, they are both artists and engineers of their medium: "we cannot precisely distinguish between authoring a dynamic story world and programming the engine" [1]. In the same way, it is difficult to categorize the Lumiere brothers as engineers or artists. The variety of interfaces, electronic supports, and assets that are used for the creation of IDN experiences requires a complex technological setup that presupposes a great challenge for creators when it comes to translating mental images into sensory stimuli on a digital system. On one hand, creators must master the technologies and tools they are using and the techniques to compose an artistic text on specific platforms. On the other hand, media involving different perceptive stimuli usually require a dialogue between different experts. Complex artworks such as films, video games, and IDNs often require a multidisciplinary team to develop the project, which questions the role of the author.

In *Enactive Cinema: Simulatorium Eisensteinense*, Pia Tikka [24] refers to the authoring process as "the hypothetical imagery aspects of the author's mental working process. This set-up implicitly excludes the other potential agencies of authorship, and the collaborative teamwork [...] it is understood to converge into a single holistic embodiment of expertise, as exemplified by Sergei Eisenstein's own use of the word 'author' or 'creator'." Both Eisenstein's and Tikka's positions transcend craftwork and technicalities to refer to the imaginative work of creating a story world, and the labor of coding these mental visions and sensations into a concrete text to be decoded by another human being. At the same time, these positions locate the owner of the creative labor into only one figure despite the multiple workers that a single film may need.

Video game production also requires a large interdisciplinary group of artists and technicians, making it difficult to confer the authorship into a single name and often leading to creators opting for distributed authorship or authorship concentrated under a studio or team name [25]. Richard Rouse III [26] suggests that this is part of a strategy of the video games industry to avoid giving too much recognition to the names behind the work: "devaluing the creative visionary to prevent them from leveraging recognition into more creative control or higher pay either at that company or another." In contrast, Rouse III [26] points out that other members of the team can understand the role of a single author as "egotistical and somehow diminishing their own contributions," opting for a long credit list so every single member of the team is accountable for the creative work. Rouse III also highlights that "only a creative leader can make something that has character, identity, and an opinion, that goes off to truly uncharted territory" [26]. Such a statement brings us back to our effort of granting creative authority in IDNs to a single author, regardless of whether this authorship is individual or collective.

The need for character and identity in the artwork was already made clear by Aristotle [27] in his *Poetics* when he wrote that "the poet is a poet because they create myths, and not so because they make lyrics," stating here that an author is deemed as such, not because they write the words of a story, but because they are behind the process of creation [28]. Foucault [29] has also supported the concept of detaching a writer from the term "author," simply because they are subjected to the action of writing. In his essay, the meaning of authorship went beyond just the act of creating words, rather he suggested that authorship projects creatorship. Barthes [30] on the other hand decided to "kill" the author and established that the art of authoring is dependent on the reader's open interpretation or perception of the work. His approach "foregrounds the idea of the author as a conduit for ideologically charged discourses rather than as an individual responsible for her/his text" [31]. With the expansion of the digital medium, "Barthes's famous prediction [...] has come to pass, not because the author is nowhere, but rather because she is everywhere" [32]. Indeed, this "rebirth" of the author is fundamental from the current critical theory perspective, as we should care about who is speaking and from where the author speaks. In this regard, concentrating authorship on one figure (individual or collective) is also a matter of responsibility. It means to clearly establish who is the sender of specific messages within the communication act and the ethical implications it entails.[1]

When we refer to the IDN author, it is not entirely clear to whom we are referring, what the role of that author is, or what actions the author is performing while creating. This lack of understanding of the author and their creative process has been critical in the long-term authoring problem that the IDN discipline has been facing since its uprising. The main trait that distinguishes the IDN author from authors referred to in other disciplines, is that the IDN author, whatever form the artifact they are building takes, must account for the element of interactivity between interactor and plot. The IDN author "uses an entirely new medium of storytelling, built to accommodate interactivity via complex mechanisms specially designed to do things other mediums are not capable of" [33]. The IDN author becomes a writer and a designer of digital space [34] and often, that digital space requires a creator to possess a certain level of coding skills that not all creators possess. To identify the role of the IDN author, we agree with Foucault and Aristotle that the IDN author (or authors) is not just someone who puts words into a system but rather one or more people who either solely or collaboratively put an idea through a system and deliver a creative interactive product. This is a process that resembles the one in the successful industry of games [35].

Authoring in IDN is a procedural process [36], which means writing rules that will govern the components in a story. The process of authoring a story depends heavily on the use of an appropriate authoring tool. Authors then must master the tool to effectively deliver the complex structures conceptualized by them, into a meaningful

---

[1] See the final chapter in the current volume for more on ethics in IDN authoring.

interactive experience for the interactor [28]. IDN authors must be prepared to think in a non-sequential way, they need to consider the possibility of multiple plots existing in their story [33], and they need to be able to create appropriate actions and responses for the interactor during narrative navigation [37]. They must be willing to forfeit enough control to interactors, to allow interactors to explore the narrative as they will, and make sure it is both well developed and well functioning to avoid the risk of interactors encountering dead ends or losing interest in random choices [38].

Considering that IDNs are based on the creation of complex story worlds and that nowadays IDNs can be audiovisual, geo-localized, and tridimensional, it is even harder to find a specific term to refer to the person that imagines, designs, and directs the narratological and technological development of such a work that is no longer "a fixed output" [11] but an experience. If the ultimate purpose of an author is to immerse its receiver into the story world and to build not a work that can be "read" but instead an experience that involves interactivity and bodily perception, we can refer to the author as an *experience-designer*, or *experience-maker*. From a spatial point of view, one can call them *space-makers*, *architects*, and *designers*; from a hypertext angle, we refer to *hyperwriters*; from a technological point of view, we can speak of *developers*, *programmers,* or *coders*. Janet Murray called this new type of interactive narrative authors *cyberbards* or *hackerbards*. Hybrid beings that are poets and hackers, that can write stories while coding specific programs for their characters to live. A new kind of author that will awake amid the "cacophony of cyberspace" [36].

Even today, more than 25 years after Murray's [36] declaration, we are still expecting IDN authors to tell us something "more real than reality." This is a desire that spatial storytelling accomplishes by imprisoning human cognition through a head-mounted display. The *cyberbard*'s task is no longer *to tell*, but literally *to immerse*: to transport others into the digital fictional universe, not only cognitively but perceptually. In this sense, a holistic term that transcends the craftwork and embraces an ulterior meaning is *creator*. To refer to any kind of narrative author, including the IDN author, as "creator" has intrinsic religious connotations that equate the author with a sort of God that has created a very complex space for the human to follow their own paths and through their non-transferable experience and interpretations. The term "creator" comprises both conceptual and pragmatic work: it goes beyond a specific task of any stage of production and comprises the labor of envisioning the final work and directing the team towards that vision.

Based on Koenitz's SPP model [11], we refer as "author" to the *creator* of the IDN system, its narrative, components, and interaction design, independently from the medium, authoring tool, and scope of the IDN project. The creative effort puts together the whole system that allows the interactor to perform an interactive process and create a unique product. By locating authorship in the creation of the IDN system, we distance ourselves from the debates that acknowledge the interactor as co-creator and co-author, and under this premise, we place any interactor's authorship on the SPP stages of "process" and "product." This distinction is also aligned with Barthes' separation of "work" and "text" used by Jennings [24] to analyze authorship in video games: "text implies the act of interpretation, and thus implies the presence of an interpreter. [...] A work, on the other hand, is that which has been authored; it is material, tangible [...] It is the static container of the authored contents, while the text is the ever-flowing plurality of interpretive potentialities" [24].

We thus disagree with the notion of interactors owning any creative rights to the container of authored contents that is the IDN system. Specialists in the field have established that IDN works, even in their simplest form, will be compiled from a series of predetermined interconnected events by the author, which an interactor can only influence [39]. As such, the IDN interactor is not considered an author, something that Murray [36], and Aarseth [40] also support, nor does the power invested in them render them responsible for the artifact. This responsibility rests with the creator of the IDN, the author [33].

5   Conclusion and Further Research

In this chapter, we have presented a four-stage IDN authoring process model that describes the phases and steps of the creation of an IDN, spanning from the time of ideation to the final point of publishing. The presented model aims to unify the process model that comprises the creative and technical labor behind the complex operation of building an IDN. We shifted our point of view on the authoring process away from an authoring tool-oriented approach toward an author-centered one. Such a change of focus led us to an understanding of the in-depth relationship between author and process. The proposed model is based on work that was compiled with input from a variety of IDN creators. It considers different types of IDNs, and it is meant to be flexible enough to be both inclusive and iterative. After decoding the authoring process, we also decoded the profile of the IDN author. We distance ourselves the traditional concept of "author" to introduce the rise of the "IDN creator" as an open invitation to dive deep into the essence of the IDN's creative practice and by doing so, into the essence of interactive narratives themselves.

It is not to be neglected that while heavily dependent on the digital inventions of our time, and therefore products of technology, IDN artifacts are artistic products that mandate the same creative requirements as traditional forms of art. In this regard, our discipline needs to include in its research developments and inspiration from beyond the computer sciences and focus on issues other than the everlasting effort of creating the perfect authoring tool. More importantly, we need to talk more to the creators themselves, and learn about their creative processes. Only then will we be able to fully conceptualize the relation between creator, process, tools, IDN work, and interactors.

Further research on an author-focused approach to IDN authoring studies would benefit from understanding IDN authoring as both an artistic-aesthetic process, and a communicative act. These approaches to the study of the authoring issue empower the author and facilitate the comprehension of meaning-generation processes and the evaluation of the interactor experience of IDN works. In contrast, a method-focused vision of authoring –be it technological, narratological, or both—excludes context, motivations, and expectations from both sides of the creator-interactor communicative relation. Questioning how creators envision, experience, and develop their IDN ideas in the first place would allow us to have a better grasp on how they assemble the IDN works, and subsequently how interactors experience and interpret the resulting IDN products.

References

1. Spierling U, Szilas N (2009) Authoring issues beyond tools. In: Iurgel IA, Zagalo N, Petta P (eds) Interactive storytelling, LNCS. Springer, Berlin Heidelberg, pp 50–61
2. Koenitz H (2014) Five theses for interactive digital narrative. In: International conference on interactive digital storytelling. Springer, Cham
3. Koenitz H (2015) Design approaches for interactive digital narrative. In: Schoenau-Fog H, Bruni LE, Louchart S, Baceviciute S (eds) Interactive storytelling, LNCS. Springer International Publishing, pp 50–57
4. Lubart TI (2001) Models of the creative process: past, present and future. Creat Res J 13:295–308
5. Shibolet Y, Knoller N, Koenitz H (2018) A framework for classifying and describing authoring tools for interactive digital narrative. In: International conference on interactive digital storytelling, ICIDS. Springer, Cham, pp 523–533
6. Kitromili S, Jordan J, Millard DE (2020) What authors think about hypertext authoring. In: Proceedings of the 31st ACM conference on hypertext and social media, HT'20. Association for Computing Machinery, USA, pp 9–16
7. Green D, Hargood C, Charles F (2020) A novel design pipeline for authoring tools. In: Bosser A-G, Millard DE, Hargood C (eds) Interactive storytelling. Springer International Publishing, Cham, pp 102–110
8. Revi AT, Millard DE, Middleton SE (2020) A systematic analysis of user experience dimensions for interactive digital narratives. In: Bosser A-G, Millard DE, Hargood C (eds) Interactive storytelling. Springer International Publishing, Cham, pp 58–74
9. Green D, Hargood C, Charles F (2018) Contemporary issues in interactive storytelling authoring systems. In: Rouse R, Koenitz H, Haahr M (eds) Interactive storytelling. Lecture notes in computer science. Springer International Publishing, pp 501–513
10. Spierling U (2018) Tools and principles for creation in interactive storytelling: the issue of evaluation. In: Workshop "Authoring for Interactive Storytelling 2018" at ICIDS 2018. Online Proceedings http://www.narrativeandplay.org/ais/2018/proceedings.html
11. Koenitz H (2010) Towards a theoretical framework for interactive digital narrative. In: Aylett R, Lim MY, Louchart S, Petta P, Riedl M (eds) Interactive storytelling. Lecture notes in computer science. Springer, Berlin Heidelberg, pp 176–185
12. Kampa A (2018) Authoring tools: saving effort in the authoring process for interactive digital storytelling experiences. In: Workshop "Authoring for Interactive Storytelling 2018" at ICIDS 2018. Online Proceedings http://www.narrativeandplay.org/ais/2018/proceedings.html
13. Pohl M, Purgathofer P (2000) Analysis of the authoring process of hypertext documents. In: Proceedings of the eleventh ACM on hypertext and hypermedia, HYPERTEXT'00. ACM, New York, NY, USA, pp 240–241
14. Sawyer RK (2018) Teaching and learning how to create in schools of art and design. J Learn Sci 27:137–181
15. Botella M, Zenasni F, Lubart T (2018) What are the stages of the creative process? What visual art students are saying. Front Psychol 9:2266
16. Doyle CL (1998) The writer tells: the creative process in the writing of literary fiction. Creat Res J 11:29–37

17. Reyes MC (2019) Interactive fiction in cinematic virtual reality: epistemology, creation and evaluation. https://iris.unige.it/handle/11567/945937
18. Reyes MC (2017) Screenwriting framework for an interactive virtual reality film. In: 3rd immersive research network conference. iLRN 2017
19. Kitromili S, Jordan J, Millard DE (2019) What is hypertext authoring? In: Proceedings of the 30th ACM conference on hypertext and social media, HT'19. Association for Computing Machinery, Hof, Germany, pp 55–59
20. Clark G (1994) Inside book publishing, 2nd ed. Routledge
21. Dunlop R (2014) Production pipeline fundamentals for film and games. Routledge
22. Guynn W (2010) The stages of the film production process. In: Guynn W (ed) The Routledge companion to film history. Routledge, pp 53–77
23. Graham D, Bachmann TT (2004) Ideation: the birth and death of ideas. Wiley
24. Tikka P (2008) Enactive cinema: simulatorium eisensteinense. Aalto University
25. Jennings SC (2016) Co-creation and the distributed authorship of video games. In: Valentine KD, Jensen LJ (eds) Examining the evolution of gaming and its impact on social, cultural, and political perspectives. IGI Global, pp 123–146
26. Rouse III R (2013) Game design. In: Wolf MJ, Perron B (eds) The Routledge companion to video game studies. Routledge, pp 109–116
27. Aristotle (2008) Poetics. Zitros, Thessaloniki
28. Millard DE, West-Taylor C, Howard Y, Packer H (2018) The ideal ReaderBot: machine readers and narrative analytics. In: NHT'18, July 2018, Baltimore, USA. http://nht.ecs.soton.ac.uk/2018/proceedings.htm
29. Foucault M (1969) What is an author? Bulletin de la Societé Francais de Philosophie 73–104
30. Barthes R (1967) The death of the author. Aspen 5–6
31. Fludernik M (2009) An introduction to narratology. Routledge
32. Rombes N (2005) The rebirth of the author. CTheory 28(3)
33. Kitromili S (2021) Authoring digital interactive narratives. https://eprints.soton.ac.uk/455723/
34. Coover R (1999) Literary hypertext: the passing of the golden age. Keynote in: Digital arts and culture 1999 conference
35. Ramadan R, Widyani Y (2013) Game development life cycle guidelines. In: International conference on advanced computer science and information systems. ICACSIS 2013
36. Murray JH (2017) Hamlet on the holodeck: the future of narrative in cyberspace. The MIT Press, Cambridge, Massachusetts
37. Riedl MO (2009) Incorporating authorial intent into generative narrative systems. In: AAAI spring symposium: intelligent narrative technologies II, pp 91–94
38. Kolb D (2009) Hypertext structure under pressure. In: Bernstein M, Greco D (eds) Reading hypertext. Eastgate Systems, MA, USA, pp 194–210
39. Spierling U (2009) Conceiving interactive story events. In: Iurgel IA, Zagalo N, Petta P (eds) Interactive storytelling, ICIDS 2009. Lecture notes in computer science, vol 5915. Springer, Heidelberg, pp 292–297
40. Aarseth EJ (1997) Cybertext perspectives on ergodic literature. The John Hopkins University Press, United States of America

Interactive Digital Narrative: The Genealogy of a Field

Sam Brooker

Abstract *A gifted young storyteller, orphaned at birth, has traced their origins to the city of knowledge. Fascinated by the youth's potential, the scholars each lay claim.* The cinematographer maps their filmic features, a vocabulary of edits and frames; the actor cites their own history of interactivity and dynamic audiences; the author notes the storyteller's obvious place in the illustrious family of narrative convention; the computer scientist, present at the birth, is keen to ensure their place is recognised; the ludographer, youngest of the scholars, denies such reliance on any family history, instead seeing them as the start of a new, illustrious line—and encouraging the storyteller to define a new way of thinking. This chapter charts the intertwining, dynamic and interdisciplinary history of interactive digital narrative. Drawing on the breadth of scholarship, it provides a convenient primer for the convoluted, often-contradictory genealogy of the field and its complex relationship with authorship, along with open questions to consider.

A gifted young storyteller, orphaned at birth, has traced their origins to the city of knowledge. Fascinated by the youth's potential, the scholars each lay claim.

This chapter charts in broad strokes the intertwining, dynamic, and interdisciplinary history of interactive digital narrative (IDN). Drawing on the breadth of scholarship, it hopefully provides a convenient primer for the convoluted, often-contradictory genealogy of the field. From these origins emerge common concerns about authorship which this volume seeks to address.

Even the name *interactive digital narrative* betrays the complex strands that converge within it. *Digital* is there to distinguish the expressive potential of digital computers [1] from analogue forms of interactive narrative, a definition that will suffice for this chapter. The same cannot be said of *interactive* and *narrative*.

Writing in 1989, scholar Michael Moore [2] was already describing *interactive* as carrying "so many meanings as to be almost useless." Do I interact with my cats in the same way as I interact with people, for example, or with computers in the

---
S. Brooker (✉)
Richmond, The American International University, London, UK
e-mail: sam.brooker@richmond.ac.uk

© The Author(s), under exclusive license to Springer Nature Switzerland AG 2022
C. Hargood et al. (eds.), *The Authoring Problem*, Human–Computer Interaction Series,
https://doi.org/10.1007/978-3-031-05214-9_3

same way as a novel? Is all interaction equal? "Just as chlorophyll was used to sell toothpaste in the 1950s", wrote George Landow [3], so *interactivity* is often assigned incredible, universal properties that are not reflected in every (or even any) specific form of interaction.

Narrative, too, is a term with a multitude of meanings. Describing the period between the early 1990s and mid-2000s, a period which coincides with the flourishing of early IDN, Marie Laure Ryan argued that few other words have "enjoyed so much use and suffered so much abuse" [4] within academic communities.

Behind these terms, we have another problematic notion, the one upon which this volume is focussed: *author*. Apparently simple definitions like that of Alexander Nehamas [5]—"the actual historical agent causally and legally responsible for the text"—are undermined when we learn that Nehamas' definition comes from an article that, following pioneering critic Michel Foucault, seeks to separate this definition of *writer* from the notion of *author.* Does my intention as a writer override your interpretation as a reader? Why can you *write* a shopping list but not be said to *author* one? What happens when a work is the product of many collaborators, a group that may include the reader themselves?[1]

For now, let's pin these slippery terms,[2] and first provide a brief outline of significant developments in IDN, and how they affect our understanding of authorship.

"To my mind," wrote pioneering scholar of humanities computing Janet Murray in 2018, "digital interactive narrative practice can be traced to 1966—a little over 50 years ago—when Joseph Weizenbaum's *Eliza* program introduced the first interactive digital character to the world" [6, 7]. Developed at the MIT Artificial Intelligence Laboratory, this computer program simulated a conversation between a Rogerian psychotherapist (whose echoing back of the patient's language leant itself to the technological limitations of the time) and the user. A decade later (1976), computer programmer Will Crowther developed *Adventure,* a text-based game in which the user explores a cave system by typing in short commands [8]. This experiment would provide the basis for subsequent similar games like Infocom's 1979 *Zork,* which expanded on the affordances of Crowther's earlier work [9].

Even these early experiments bring our understanding of authorship into question. Writing in 1976, Weizenbaum reports one user sending him out of the room during a session, while others were incensed at his monitoring of their chat logs [10]. Who is the author in this situation, the source of meaning in these conversations? Has the creator been usurped as author, with the user entering into dialogue with the machine? In an analysis of Crowther's work, Steven Levy [11] notes that *Adventure* was "expressive of the personality and environment of the authors", commenting on the attempted recreation of real-world cave environments Crowther enjoyed.

These preliminary text-based experiments in interactive storytelling were complemented by later developments in branching narrative. Michael Joyce's 1987 work *afternoon, a story* [12] arguably defined the initial formal qualities of what became

---

[1] For more on the "author", see the chapter by Kitromili and Reyes in this volume.

[2] For another attempt to define these terms, see the introduction of this volume.

known as hypertext fiction: "more than one entry point, many internal branches, and no clear ending" [13]. Composed of short passages (Lexia) connected by links, hypertext fiction works like Judy Malloy's *Uncle Roger* (1986), Shelley Jackson's *Patchwork Girl* (1995), or Stuart Moulthrop's *Victory Garden* (1991) were literary experiments that gave readers a measure of control over the order in which they encountered story elements [14–16]. Their DNA can be found in games like Inkle Studios' *80 Days* and *Heaven's Vault* (2014 and 2019 respectively), and in platforms like Chris Klimas' interactive fiction writing tool *Twine* (initially launched in 2009)—though these later works favour the single point of entry and exit typified by linear works [17–19]. Whether offering one place to start and finish, or many, these works proceed by navigational choices made by the user.

While they have the virtue of historical "firstness", text-based IDNs were soon augmented by developments in computer graphics. This expansion in the aesthetic potential of IDN saw new innovations in storytelling. Successful video game series like *Monkey Island* (1990–present), *King's Quest* (1980–2016), or *Myst* (1993–2020) built on the puzzle-solving work of pioneers in text-based narrative, establishing conventions both narrative and technical that are still explored today [20–22]. The ambiguous moral choices of *King's Quest* are echoed in the branching paths found in the work of Telltale Games or Supergiant Games, while the humour and puzzle-solving of *Monkey Island* and *Myst* respectively can be found in Valve's *Portal* or Jonathon Blow's *The Witness* [23, 24]. Similarities with cinema can be seen in IDNs like Hazelight Studios' 2018 *A Way Out* [25], while works by Quantic Dreams (founded in the late-1990s) attempt to emulate their cinematic forebears—to mixed effect. The "highbrow" of hypertext fiction and its antecedents has at times been contrasted with the "low-brow" of the more commercially successful, populist genre of video games. Today we distinguish less between these forms, as IDNs rise to become a dominant form of expression and amalgamate these strands beyond the point of a useful distinction.

Histories of interactive digital narrative tend to speak in terms of waves or phases or trajectories [1, 6, 26] rather than straightforward avenues. This language is at least partly due to their overlapping periods of technological development. With each new development, existing scholarly communities saw echoes of their own disciplines, their own theories. How much of the cinematic, literary, or theatrical approach to authorship can be detected in each emerging form of IDN?

As a young field, IDN has accumulated many more questions than it has answers. At the end of each section in this chapter, you will find some indicative questions worth considering as you move through the rest of this volume.

First to speak—indeed, first to arrive—was the keeper of the scriptorium. A family tree already lay before them, along with lists of ancestral traits that proved indisputably the artist was their child.

"Opening Hamlet at a certain point," wrote Jill Patton-Walsh in her 1994 novel *Knowledge of Angels* [27], "will always reveal him eternally bracing himself to murder his uncle." This passage represents the guarantee of linear media: that however active the audience may be, however differently they may react to story events, the work itself remains the same. Older readers may recall the episode of the

TV sitcom *Friends* in which Joey, reading about a character's increasing sickness, asks that the 1868 novel *Little Women* be placed in the freezer. Active or passive, engaged or deeply bored, a reader cannot affect the content of a linear print work—only their interpretation of it. Once defrosted, *Little Women* will always conclude in the same way. The writer deemed it so.

Literature has always strained against the limitations of print. The index, for example, permits connection between thematically linked passages of a linear print work, while religious works often offer criss-crossing commentaries, as scholars grapple with the work's meaning (and one another) across the centuries. Vladimir Nabokov's 1962 novel *Pale Fire* [28], a 999-line poem festooned with interlinking fictitious commentary, looks very much like a hypertextual network when presented as such by Professor Simon Rowberry [29], with nodes and links between ideas.

Further examples abound. Saporta's 1963 *Composition no.1* [30] offers 150 pages which can be rearranged and read in any order, while Stuart Moulthrop [31] describes Deleuze and Guattari's *A Thousand Plateaus* [32] as an "incunabular hypertext" because its book sections can be read in any order, going on to describe it as "a matrix of independent but cross-referential discourses." In Kurt Vonnegut's 1969 novel *Slaughterhouse Five,* the main character becomes "spastic in time" [33], moving uncontrollably back and forth between the events in his life; Martin Amis' 1991 *Time's Arrow* [34] presents its narrative in reverse, the reader only gradually realising the story is that of an Auschwitz scientist; the reverse structure renders atrocity mercy—and kindness cruelty.

Such structural experiments often require the reader to reconstruct the chronology of each experience, a process recalling the *fabula* and *sjuzhet* of Russian formalism. Terms widely employed within the structuralist study of narrative, *fabula* (roughly equivalent to *story*) describes the full range of potential narrative elements (characters, locations, situations) within a narrative world, and their inclusion or exclusion from the work. *Sjuzhet* (roughly equivalent to *discourse*) refers to the selective presentation of narrative elements and their relationship to one another. Vonnegut's playful reorganisation of events reflects this, but what if the order of events were in some fashion the reader's decision? In his analysis of Raymond Queneau's 1961 work *Cent Mille Milliards de Poeme* [35], which offers ten pages of fourteen-line paper strips which can be flipped to produce 10^{14} combinations, Espen Aarseth [36] wondered who it was that created each combination: The work? The author? The reader?

As we can see, it is not that digital media *invents* the notion of navigating and experiencing the printed work nonlinearly, or uniquely owns the consequences of such approaches for our understanding of authorship. Instead, digital media offers tools that move such nonlinear navigation from a complex analog process to a comparatively trivial digital one.

"What is unnatural in print," argued Jay Bolter [37], "becomes natural in the electronic medium." Professor Johndan Johnson-Eilola [38] similarly argued that the physical stability of books rendered them "machines for transmitting authority," an authority which the flexibility of IDN may diminish. This is a common claim: Koenitz et al. make the argument that interactive digital narrative "promises to dissolve the division between active creator and passive audience and herald the advent of a new triadic relationship between creator, dynamic narrative artifact and audience-turned-participant" [1] just as theorist Stuart Moulthrop had argued that hypertext fiction cannot have authors "in the old-fashioned sense" [31] two decades earlier.

Describing hypertext fiction, Jane Yellowlees Douglas argued that it "consists of words, characters, plots—all the constituents of the Great Novel—and seems to present itself as narrative fiction's next leap" [39]. Electronic literature represents a partial continuity with the existing concerns of literary theory—audience, interpretation, matters of structure and device—that interactivity might illuminate.

What happens if we do grant the reader some control over the structure of the narrative? What is the author's role in this new environment? "The relationship between narration and interactivity," wrote Eku Wand [40], "would appear to be antithetical." If narration is about organising the events of a story in such a way as to produce a particular effect, then what happens when the reader has some control over that organisation?

This tension between interactivity and narrative coherence, in which increased player choice results in more opportunities to harm the progression of the plot, has been given various names: chiefly the narrative paradox [41] or boundary problem [42]. If we define narrative as "a perceived sequence of non-randomly connected events" [43] then permitting readers to alter that sequence changes the nature of their experience. Interactive narratives, wrote Marie Laure Ryan [4], demand choices "sufficiently broad to give the user a sense of freedom, and a narrative pattern sufficiently adaptable to those choices to give the impression of being generated on the fly." This sentiment echoes Janet Murray's 1997 challenge: to invent formulaic scripts "flexible enough to capture a wide range of human behaviour" [13].

But is the boundary problem really a *problem*? Do readers use interactivity to evade the author, or to encounter their creations on different terms? Seen in this way, interactivity simply expands the storytelling toolbox—much like any other new medium. "After the celebrated deaths of the author, the work, and reading," wrote Aarseth in 1994, "the text is now giving up the spirit" [36]. We could instead consider this a rebirth—a renewed textual space for readers and authors to explore.

- How does control over sequence affect other literary structures?
- Is the relationship between reader and author really about power?
- What new literary structures are possible in an interactive medium?

In a voice rich with a lifetime's training, the theatre director made their case.
Brazilian theatre director, writer, politician and activist Augusto Boal (1931–2009) was frustrated. Theatre as he saw it was too passive, almost fascistic. Terrible violence and gut-wrenching tragedy would play out on stage, as we in the audience sit obediently and just let it happen. What was this teaching us about our responsibilities as spectators—as people? And who was the author to impose such horrors upon us?

Inspired in part by educationalist and close friend Paulo Freire, who argued that "if the structure does not permit dialogue the structure must be changed" [44]), Boal began experimenting with interactive techniques for both rehearsal and performance. The audience, previously mere spectators to the action, now became *spect-actors,* occupying a dual role as both spectator and actor. *Actor* here means something other than *performer*—it refers to a wider ability to *take action*. The events were no longer fixed—performances and rehearsals can be paused at any point by any participant, allowing changes to be made in a process called *Simultaneous Dramaturgy*.

In addition to Boal's political approach, this collapse of the fourth wall between audience and performers has been exploited for any number of other reasons: to solicit votes on the outcome of an unfinished story, as in the 1985 musical *The Mystery of Edwin Drood;* to disorient and confuse, as in 2004's *You Me Bum Bum Train*; to situate you as hostage within an experience, as in 2012 kidnap drama *66 min in Damascus* [45–47]. In each case, audiences bear some degree of control over the narrative. In gaining control they enjoy *agency*, "the satisfying power to take meaningful action, and see the results of our decisions and choices" [13]. At the same time, the actors and director (traditionally the authors of the theatrical experience) enter into a dialogue with their audience, relinquishing some of their control over the performance.

In some respects, the computer has more in common with the theatre than it does any other pre-digital medium discussed here. Both represent a framed space within which another world exists [48]; both offer (at least in interactive theatre) the potential for real-time feedback and frictionless revision to the narrative. Brenda Laurel's seminal 1991 work *Computers as Theatre* explores this relationship, arguing that human–computer interfaces share much with Aristotlean drama. "Designing human–computer experience isn't about building a better desktop," she concludes. "It's about creating imaginary worlds that have a special relationship to reality— worlds in which we can extend, amplify, and enrich our own capacities to think, feel, and act" [49].

In the theatre of the screen, events are no longer set—instead, we occupy another dual role, which this time we call *the user*. Such ideas form the backdrop to Michael Mateas and Andrew Stern's influential 2005 IDN work *Façade* [50].

Façade takes the form of a simulated evening spent in the company of a feuding couple, with interaction via simple movement controls (for navigating their apartment) and a text box into which users can type statements. Within the limited character recognition parameters of the text box, anything can be entered: users may ask about a nearby sofa, where the protagonists buy their shirts, or what they have to drink; equally, they may ask who first walked on the moon, or how many people perished in London's great fire. Writing in the paper that accompanies their project, Mateas and Stern [51] expressed concern that "players cannot yet speak in natural language to the game" and must rely on "contrived, restricted forms" of communication like the branching conversation menu found in games like Interplay's 1997 *Fallout* (amongst numerous others) [52]. To achieve their full expressive potential, they reasoned, games should aspire to give users a full range of expression.

Façade was not an entirely new direction for interactive storytelling. Poet Robert Pinsky's 1984 work *Mindwheel* [53] is an early example of this kind of interactive fiction, what theorist Nick Montfort [54] describes as "a program that simulates a world, understands natural language text from an interactor, and provides a textual reply based on events in the world". An almost identical logic appears in Ocelot Society's 2016 video game *event[0]*, in which the player can talk to a computer called Kaizen [55]. Anything can be typed into the computer terminal, to which Kaizen will attempt to reply.

Taken on its own terms, as a research project that "pushes the formal boundaries of participatory drama" [56], *Façade* feels like a valuable transitional step that both tests and recognises the limitations of digital storytelling. "A player in an interactive drama becomes an author," wrote Mateas [57], continuing that "these contributions are constrained by the material and formal causes (viewed as affordances) provided by the author of the interactive drama." Joseph Weizenbaum's earlier chatbot *Eliza* "relied upon the user's imagination to make the conversational inferences that would lend coherence to the exchange" [10], while *event[0]*'s malfunctioning AI provides narrative justification for the narrow range of text inputs players can use. *Façade* instead relies upon the player to meet it halfway, treating awkward pauses where input cannot be interpreted as part of the awkward fabric of the drama.

Theatre represents perhaps the ultimate ambition for one branch of IDN: seamless communication, unhampered by technological or material restrictions, in which the asymmetry between creator and audience is fully dissolved. For others, the peculiarities of the medium, and its restrictions, were (and are) precisely what makes IDN interesting—and worthy of study. Before giving the latter group a chance to speak, we should swing the spotlight over to a group who inherited some of theatre's conventions—and a fair slice of its audience.

- How closely can a digital space simulate dialogue?
- Does an asynchronous relationship always disadvantage one party?
- How do digital narratives break out of the frame?
- How does a collective narrative experience differ from an individual one?

Next to speak was the cinematographer. Though related to scribes and actors, they heard in the artist's speech their own unmistakable grammar of edits and frames.

Like the printed novel, film has often strained at the limitations of its medium. In Kurosawa's 1950 *Rashomon,* for example, we find various characters recounting the story of a samurai's murder [58]. Through each retelling, the audience is introduced to different versions of the same story, in turn being asked to reflect on their bias toward one version or another.[3] As with earlier linear print experiments, we see cinema testing certainties in the contract between author and reader.

Other works have experimented with cause and effect, sharing with literary theorists a preoccupation with notions of sequence and our understanding of reading. In Gaspar Noé's controversial 2002 film *Irréversible,* for example, fourteen scenes are presented in reverse chronological order [59]. This decision (echoing Christopher Nolan's *Memento* [60] from two years earlier) resulted in the audience encountering Mick's violent murder before the assault that turns his killing from a random act of violence to a grim revenge tragedy. The reversal of events withholds the "pleasure" of genre convention from the audience.

---

[3] *Rashomon* itself was adapted (largely faithfully) from Ryunosuke Akutagawa's short story *In a Grove,* which also experiments with the impact of multiple competing retellings of the same story.

Cinema as an interactive medium has its own distinct history. A collaborative project under director Radúz Činčera, *Kinoautomat* (1967) placed its audience in a small, customised cinema [61]. Each seat was equipped with a red and green button, and at key points during the film audiences voted on where the story would lead. Twin projectors ensured the chosen section could be played. While movies like 1995's *Mr. Payback* allowed audiences to vote where the story would go using joysticks in the theatre's armrest, the cost of customising theatres for such novelty experiences was usually prohibitive [62].

Depicting in real-time the lives of a Los Angeles ensemble as they prepare to shoot a movie, Mike Figgis' 2000 film *Timecode* attempts to achieve a similar effect without the need for such technical paraphernalia [63]. In its original theatrical version, the film is presented as four continuous 93-min takes occupying the four corners of the screen. Control over point of view—"one of the most important means of structuring narrative discourse and one of the most powerful mechanisms for audience manipulation" [64]—shifts to an extent from the filmmaker to the audience, as we determine which quarter we want to watch.

While an interesting experiment, the poster's tagline—*Who Do You Want To Watch?*—does not reflect the reality of the experience (in theatres at least). The audio mix amplified whichever story was considered most significant at that moment, and dialogue sequences in one quadrant were often accompanied by extended periods of silent contemplation in the others. While in principle the audience was free to focus on whichever section they chose, in practice, the limitations of the medium still presented one dominant narrative line.

Despite such formal experiments, it was primarily with the move from theatrical spaces to the home console and computer that interactive cinema gained some prominence. *Timecode*'s DVD release had an interactive mode that allowed users to switch audio tracks in real-time, for example—a marked improvement on its theatrical predecessor. Following the success of such full motion video (FMV) games as 1992's *Night Trap* and the *Wing Commander* series, the genre largely fell out of favour until the independent game revolution of the mid-2000s, when developers began experimenting with the integration of video into game experiences [65, 66].

Sam Barlow's 2015 *Her Story* takes the form of the Graphical User Interface (GUI) for a mid-1990s Police computer [67]. On it are stored numerous short video clips, ostensibly from a series of police interviews with the chief suspect in a murder case. Transcripts for each clip are included as metadata, meaning typing *murder* will bring up clips including this word.

"Hypertext presupposes an experiential world in which the goal is always potentially but one jump or link away" [3] and so too does *Her Story*. In an essay discussing his own hypertext murder mystery, Professor Chris Willerton [68] argued that "a hyperfiction reader's wish for control is not absolute. It is subordinate to the wish to be interested and entertained." Here we again encounter the reader as enjoying rather than rejecting asymmetry, an important distinction sometimes lost in discussions which position the reader and author as antagonistic toward one another.

"Interactive Cinema reflects the longing of cinema to become something new, something more complex, and something more personal, as if in conversation with an audience" [69]. One final lesson from interactive cinema is not technical, but philosophical. The structural conceits above were approached by critics as intentional devices, to be interrogated more for their intellectual rather than technological affordances. Films featuring multiple intersecting narrative lines (Rodrigo Garcia's 2005 *Nine Lives*, for example, or Altman's 1993 *Short Cuts*) were discussed for the way these techniques illuminate the nature of experience or the complexity of human relationships, rather than as spectacle alone [70, 71]. Radúz Činčera ensured that no matter what, *Kinoautomat* would conclude with the protagonist's apartment burnt to the ground—a satirical comment on the weakness of democracy—while Grahame Weinbren's seminal 1995 essay *Navigating the Ocean of Streams of Story* questions above all what interactivity affords audiences as an experience [72]. Perhaps the more restrictive vocabulary presented by the limitations of linear filmmaking (and its comparatively lengthy history) has permitted more emphasis on the *why* of such experiments than has at times been found in IDN.

- Should form or content be the focus of analysis for IDN?
- Does interactivity create a more intimate relationship between creator and audience?
- Why are cinematic approaches so prevalent in video games?
- Like cinema, how should we evaluate the authorship of games created by large, interdisciplinary teams of people?
- Consider a version of *Irreversible* produced in the correct chronological order. If I saw this version and you saw the other, did we see the same film?

The ludographer, the youngest of the scholars, begged the artist to deny their family history and break with tradition.

In late 2001 games scholar Ian Bogost produced a poster depicting an upcoming boxing match: Janet Murray on the left, Espen Aarseth on the right. Above them in heavy type are the words *LUDOLOGY* and *NARRATOLOGY*. The conflict between the two would, it seems, be resolved that year.

"The politics of the university are so intense because the stakes are so low."[4] A kinder formulation, perhaps, is that within small and passionate communities there can be great, fierce debate about matters which from the outside seem comparatively trivial. To understand the importance of stressing the *interactive* or the *narrative* part of IDN, we should return to our scholars of the scriptorium. Like carpenters embarking on a new project, they brought to the study of IDN their own set of analytical tools. Better to have it and not need it, as the saying goes, than need it and not have it. Perhaps literary giants like Richards, Barthes, Iser, and the rest would have no bearing on interactive digital narratives, or perhaps their thinking might have new relevance. Better to have it, and not need it.

Others disagreed. "Even if simulations and narrative do share some common elements," wrote Gonzalo Frasca [73], "their mechanics are essentially different."

---

[4] Often ascribed to Henry Kissinger in his speech to Ashland University, this quip is most likely the work of Professor Wallace Stanley Sayre. He is commonly considered to have articulated it as early as 1950.

Having previously cited the underdeveloped nature of games studies as a reason for its consideration through the inadequate lenses of traditional narrative and drama [74], Frasca now joined other young scholars in seeking to define what they called *Ludology*: the discipline that studied games as games.

The antagonistic relationship between narratology and ludology is somewhat overstated—Frasca's 2004 essay doesn't actually *reject* the importance of studying narrative structure, only its emphasis over analysing games as a distinct medium. Nonetheless, there was a considerable effort in the early years of the twenty-first century to distinguish how games should be studied from the approaches of other disciplines. "Games are not part of the narrative media ecology formed by movies, novels, and theatre," wrote Jesper Juul [75], arguing that the apparent continuities in storytelling found in the latter are fundamentally different to those of the former. The emphasis on description and aesthetics, for example, did not reflect the more rules-oriented world of video game. "The dimensions of Lara Croft's body,' wrote Aarseth [76], "already analysed to death by film theorists, are irrelevant to me as a player, because a different-looking body would not make me play differently." A rebuttal by Stuart Moulthrop, pointing out that *Mr Bean: Tomb Raider* would be unlikely to sell as well, was rejected by Aarseth on the grounds that it tells little about the actual *gameplay*.

This distinction—between what video games theorist Jesper Juul [77] calls *rules* and *fiction*—is an important one. *Rules* govern what players can do, while the *fiction*, the surrounding narrative elements, are beyond the user's control. Juul cites early point-and-click adventure games like LucasArts' 1997 *The Curse of Monkey Island*, in which the user may be presented with a spectacular tavern scene containing only two interactive elements, but we might consider *Detective Vision* instead. Found in a diverse range of games, Detective Vision highlights interactive world elements in bright colours, removing colour from other elements. While the normal view may show a fully populated world of consoles, doorways, and switches, Detective Vision highlights only those elements which have interactivity: see Klei Entertainment's 2015 *Invisible Inc.*, Rockstar's *2015 Arkham Knight*, Bethesda Softworks' 2012 *Dishonored,* and Suspicious Developments' 2013 *Gunpoint* [78–81].

These illuminated elements show us the rules that govern the world, so we can determine what possibilities exist within it. Users are "free only within the boundary of those rules", to quote Roger Caillois [82]; more positively, we may echo George Landow in describing such works as "rule-governed possibilities" [83]. A proper understanding of the way these rules function is valuable for a user, as this determines those areas over which they *do* have control. Irrational Games' 2007 game *BioShock* [84] highlights all interactable elements in gold—would the experience be improved if the user had to try and interact with every inanimate mop and non-functional briefcase?

"No one has been interested in making the argument that there is no difference between games and stories," wrote Janet Murray, in a 2005 keynote preface that largely closed the debate, "or that games are merely a subset of stories" [85]. So how should we approach this brief but important antagonistic episode in IDN history? Here a film scholar raises her hand, offering an illuminating story from the early twentieth century. Louis Bunuel's 1928 film *Un Chien Andalou* [86] arose when the narrative conventions of silent film (both mainstream and avant-garde) seemed to have concretised [87]. Bunuel's subversive use of offbeat intertitles as temporal markers and jarring juxtapositions [88] encourages us to engage with what is unique about film, rather than focussing on narrative convention. We might try to consider the ludologists in the same way: keen to emphasise the *differences* in this exciting medium over similarities and continuities. If we are going to study IDN, shouldn't we place at least equivalent emphasis on the form as the content?

- What are the fundamental differences (and surprising similarities) between IDN and its precedents?
- When studying IDN, should we begin with the *rules*, the *fiction*... or something in-between?
- What are the advantages and disadvantages of becoming an IDN specialist?

Despite being present at the birth, the computer scientist wasn't sure if they would be welcome—or if they wanted to be there.

Hypertext fiction writing environment StorySpace was collaboratively created in 1987 by literary theorist Jay David Bolter, writer Michael Joyce, and Professor of Computer Science John Smith. In an interview with Belinda Barnet, Smith clarified the brevity of his involvement by explaining that he was "not interested in prose, in fiction" [89].

How important is it to study the code that underpins IDN? In their 2009 book *Racing the Beam*, Professors Nick Montfort and Ian Bogost noted that "little work has been done on how the hardware and software of platforms influences, facilitates, or constrains particular forms of computational expression" [90], which echoes Manovich's earlier conclusion that "excited by all the rapid transformations cultural computerization was bringing about, we did not bother to examine its origins" [91]. Should programmers be considered co-authors?

The importance of underlying code has not gone unnoticed. Literary theorist Myron Tuman mentioned in 1992 that the author is present both whilst writing the work and "through manipulation of the software controlling the degree of 'freedom' the reader experiences" [92], an argument which has been adopted by the various new and emerging fields that have made digital textuality their subject.

Critical Code Studies (which focuses on the cultural significance of computer *code* rather than explicitly its functionality) was initiated in 2006 by new media scholar Professor Mark Marino: "The history of the program, the author, the programming language, the genre, the funding source for the research and development (be it military, industrial, entertainment, or other), all shape meaning" [93]. In his review of Critical Code Studies' first four years, however, Marino notes that "the lines of code that appear in these discussions are precious few and their role in the argument is often minimal, a mere passing example, an illustration that the software does in fact have code" [94].

The last decade has seen significant change in this area, however, with MIT's *Software Studies* series and journals like *Computational Culture* underscoring the importance of platform and software. Despite this, code itself arguably remains an underexplored and fruitful object of study.

- How important is it to study the code that underpins IDN?
- Should programmers be considered co-authors?
- How do we ensure that the platforms on which IDN were created survive?
- What are the assumptions underlying the way software is designed?

At a nearby table an impatient merchant was listening in. The sooner this was resolved, the sooner the artist would get back to work.

Concerns about the "parochialism and imperialism" of disciplinarity have a long history [95], as emerging fields struggle to align with, and differentiate themselves from, existing modes of thought. Dismissing the study of English literature, historian Edward Freeman argued that "we cannot examine tastes and sympathies" [96]; Film Studies emerged in a hostile environment which asked whether "academic oversight was pertinent or wholesome" [97]; the early days of game studies were rife with concern about "intrusions and colonisations from the already organised scholarly tribes" [77, 98].

"The great stake-claiming race is on," wrote Espen Aarseth in 2005 [76]. "As with any land rush, the respect for local culture and history is minimal, while the belief in one's own tradition, tools, and competence is unfailing." The origins of interactive digital narrative are an ultracrepidarianist minefield, and no doubt the preceding chapter offers at least one infuriating omission for every reader who navigates it. If nothing else, this should demonstrate how deeply and intricately these various fields intersect with developments in the interactive digital narrative. One significant omission in this chapter worth noting is the plurality of hobbyist or small-scale independent IDN that represent the majority of works produced in any given year. Such works represent both IDN's leading edge (the extensive community that sprung up around *Twine*, for example, or various Game Jams producing novel work on a given theme) and its long tail (the still-active modding scenes for often decades-old games, for example, and those maintaining active support for platforms otherwise abandoned by their original creators).

At the time of writing Statista places the value of the global video games market at 138.4 billion dollars. This extraordinary proliferation of distribution platforms, genres, and modes of expression grants IDN an enormous amount of commercial and cultural capital. Unpicking its impact requires a group effort by scholars, one that crosses traditional disciplinary boundaries. The indicative questions outlined above represent collective problems, which can be addressed from within any formal discipline—or none.

The history of IDN is one of intellectual histories colliding, of communities meeting on unstable ground; of territories not to be conquered, but to be explored and nurtured, together. The Authoring Problem is one such territory; this book is your guide.

References

1. Koenitz H, Ferri G, Haahr M, Sezen D, Sezen T (2015) Interactive digital narrative history, theory and practice. Routledge, New York
2. Moore M (1989) Three types of interaction. Am J Distance Educ 3(2):1–6
3. Landow G (2006) Hypertext 3.0: critical theory and new media in an era of globalization. Johns Hopkins University Press, Baltimore
4. Ryan ML (2006) Avatars of story. University of Minnesota Press, Minneapolis
5. Nehamas A (1986) What an author is. J Philos 83(11):685–691
6. Murray J (2018) Research into interactive digital narrative: a kaleidoscopic view. In: Rouse R, Koenitz H, Haahr M (eds) ICIDS 2018 interactive storytelling. Springer, Cham, pp 3–17
7. Eliza (1966) Developed by J Weizenbaum. [Software programme]
8. Adventure (1975) Developed by W Crowther. [Video game]
9. Zork (1979) Developed by Infocom. [Video game] Infocom
10. Weizenbaum J (1976) Computer power and human reason. W. H. Freeman and Co, New York
11. Levy S (1984) Hackers: heroes of the computer revolution. Anchor Press, New York
12. Joyce M (1987) afternoon, a story. Eastgate Systems, Watertown
13. Murray J (1997) Hamlet on the Holodeck. MIT University Press, Cambridge
14. Malloy J (1986) Uncle Roger. https://people.well.com/user/jmalloy/party.html. Accessed 15 June 2022
15. Jackson S (1995) Patchwork girl. Eastgate Systems, Watertown
16. Moulthrop S (1992) Victory garden. Eastgate Systems, Watertown
17. Days (2014) Developed by Inkle. [Video game] Inkle
18. Heaven's Vault (2021) Developed by Inkle. [Video game] Inkle
19. Twine (2009) Klimas C. https://twinery.org/. Accessed 15 June 2022
20. Monkey Island (1990–2010) Developed by Lucas Arts. [Video game series] LucasArts
21. King's Quest (1980) Developed by Sierra on-line. [Video game series] Sierra Entertainment
22. Myst (1980) Developed by Cyan. [Video game series] Broderbund
23. Portal (2007) Developed by Valve. [Video game] Valve
24. The Witness (2016) Developed by Thekla, Inc. [Video game] Thekla, Inc.
25. A Way Out (2018) Developed by Hazelight Studios. [Video game] Electronic Arts
26. Bell A (2010) The possible worlds of hypertext fiction. Palgrave Macmillan, London
27. Patton-Walsh J (1994) Knowledge of angels. Houghton Mifflin, New York
28. Nabakov V (1962) Pale fire. G.P. Putnam's Sons, London
29. Rowberry S (2011) Pale Fire as a hypertextual network. In: Proceedings of the 22nd ACM hypertext conference, Eindhoven, Netherlands June 06–09. ACM, New York, pp 319–324
30. Saporta M (1962) Composition No.1
31. Moulthrop S (1994) Rhizome and resistance: hypertext and the dreams of a new culture. In: Landow G (ed) Hyper/text/theory. Johns Hopkins University Press, Baltimore, pp 299–322
32. Deleuze G, Guattari F (1980) A thousand plateaus. Midnight Press, Paris
33. Vonnegut K (1969) Slaughterhouse-five, or, the children's crusade: a duty-dance with death. Random House, New York
34. Amis M (1991) Time's arrow. Jonathon Cape, London
35. Queneau R (1961) Cent mille milliards de poèmes. Gallimard, Paris
36. Aarseth E (1994) Nonlinearity and literary theory. In: Landow G (ed) Hyper/text/theory. Johns Hopkins University Press, Baltimore, pp 1–86
37. Bolter J (2001) Writing space. Routledge, London
38. Johnson-Eilola J (1994) Reading and writing in hypertext: vertigo and euphoria. In Cynthia L, Hilligoss Selfe S (eds) Literacy and computers: the complications of teaching and learning with technology. Modern Language Association, New York, pp 195–219
39. Douglas JY (2001) The end of books, or books without end? University of Michigan Press, Ann Arbor
40. Wand E (2002) Interactive storytelling: the renaissance of narration. In: Rieser M, Zapp A (eds) New screen media: cinema/art/narrative. British Film Institute, London, pp 163–178

41. Aylett R (1999) Narrative in virtual environments: towards emergent narrative. Technical report, working notes of the narrative intelligence symposium
42. Magerko B (2007) Evaluating preemptive story direction in the interactive drama architecture. J Game Dev 2(3):25–52
43. Toolan M (2001) Narrative: a critical linguistic introduction. Routledge, London
44. Freire P (1996) Pedagogy of the oppressed, 2nd edn. Penguin Books, London
45. The Mystery of Edwin Drood (1985) Directed by R Holmes. [Interactive theatre] MTI Europe
46. You Me Bum Bum Train (2004) Directed by Bond K and M Lloyd. [Interactive theatre] Performed in London, 2008
47. Minutes in Damascus (2012) Directed by L Bourjelly. [Interactive theatre] Performed at Shoreditch Town Hall, June 23 2012
48. Manovich L (1998) Towards an archaeology of the computer screen. In: Elsaesser T, Hoffmann K (eds) Cinema futures: Cain, Abel or cable? Amsterdam, Amsterdam University Press, The Screen Arts in the Digital Age, pp 27–43
49. Laurel B (2013) Computers as theatre. Addison-Wesley Professional, Boston
50. Façade (2005) Developed by Procedural Arts. [Video game] Procedural Arts
51. Mateas M, Stern A (2003) Façade: an experiment in building a fully-realized interactive drama. In: Game developer's conference: game design track, San Jose, California, March 2003. http://homes.lmc.gatech.edu/~mateas/publications/MateasSternGDC03.pdf. Accessed 15 June 2022
52. Fallout (1997) Developed by interplay. [Video game] Interplay
53. Mindwheel (1984) Developed by Synapse software. [Video game] Brøderbund Software
54. Montfort N (2004) Interactive fiction as 'Story,' 'Game,' 'Storygame,' 'Novel,' 'World,' 'Literature,' 'Puzzle,' 'Problem,' 'Riddle,' and 'Machine.' In: Noah W-F, Harrigan P (eds) First person: new media as story, game, and performance. MIT University Press, Cambridge, p 310
55. Event[0] (2016) Developed by Ocelot Society. [Video game] Ocelot Society
56. Murray J (2004) Janet Murray responds in turn. Electronic Book Review. http://www.electronicbookreview.com/thread/firstperson/artifactual. Accessed June 15 2022
57. Mateas M (2004) Michael Mateas responds in turn. Electronic Book Review. http://www.electronicbookreview.com/thread/firstperson/bestyled. Accessed June 15 2022
58. Rashomon (1950) Directed by A Kurosawa. [Feature film] RKO Radio Pictures
59. Irreversible (2002) Directed by G Noé. [Feature film] Mars Distribution
60. Memento (2000) Directed by C Nolan. [Feature film] Newmarket
61. Kinoautomat (1967) Directed by R Činčera. [Interactive film] Screened at Expo 67, Quebec, Canada
62. Mr. Payback (1995) Directed by B Gale. [Interactive film] Sony New Technologies
63. Timecode (2000) Directed by M Figgis. [Feature film] Screen Gems
64. Stam et al (1992) New vocabularies in film semiotics: structuralism, post-structuralism and beyond. Routledge, London
65. Night Trap (1992) Developed by digital pictures. [Interactive film] Sega
66. Wing Commander (1990–2007) Developed by origin systems. [Video game series] Electronic Arts
67. Her Story (2015) Developed by Sam Barlow. [Video game] Sam Barlow
68. Willerton C (2000) Structure problems in hypertext mysteries. In: Proceedings of the ACM 2000 conference, San Antonio Texas, May 30–June 4 2000. ACM, New York, pp 234–235
69. Davenport G, Agamanolis S, Barry B, Bradley B, Brooks K (2000) Synergistic storyscapes and constructionist cinematic sharing. IBM Syst J 39(3–4):456–469
70. Nine Lives (2005) Directed by R García. [Feature film] Magnolia Pictures
71. Short Cuts (1993) Directed by R Altman. [Feature film] Fine Line Features
72. Weinbren G (1995) In the ocean of streams of story. Millenn Film J 28:15–30
73. Frasca G (2004) Simulation versus narrative: introduction to ludology. In: Wolf M, Perron B (eds) The video game theory reader. Routledge, London
74. Frasca G (1999) Ludology meets narratology: similitude and differences between (video)games and narrative. https://ludology.typepad.com/weblog/articles/ludology.htm. Accessed 7 Jan 2021

75. Juul J (2001) Games studies 0101: games telling stories? Game Stud Int J Comput Game Res 1(1)
76. Aarseth E (2004) Genre trouble. First person: new media as story, performance, and game. MIT Press, Cambridge, pp 45–55
77. Juul J (2007) Half-real: video games between real rules and fictional worlds. MIT University Press, Cambridge
78. Invisible Inc. (2015) Developed by Klei Entertainment. [Video game] Klei Entertainment
79. Batman: Arkham Knight (2015) Developed by Rocksteady studios. [Video Game] Warner Bros. Interactive Entertainment
80. Dishonored (2012) Developed by Arkane studios. [Video game] Bethesda Softworks
81. Gunpoint (2013) Developed by suspicious Developments. [Video Game] Suspicious Developments
82. Caillois R (2006) The definition of play. In: Salen K, Zimmerman E (eds) The game design reader. MIT University Press, Cambridge, pp 122–155
83. Landow G (1994) What's a critic to do? Critical theory in the age of hypertext. In: Landow G (ed) Hyper/text/theory. Johns Hopkins University Press, Baltimore, pp 1–50
84. Bioshock (2007) Developed by 2K. [Video game] 2K Games
85. Murray J (2005) The last word on ludology v narratology. Inventing the medium. https://inventingthemedium.com/2013/06/28/the-last-word-on-ludology-v-narratology-2005/. Accessed 15 June 2022
86. Un Chien Andalou (1929) Direct by L Buñuel. [Feature film] Classiques
87. Thiher A (1977) Surrealism's enduring bite: 'Un Chien Andalou.' Lit/Film Q 5(1):38–49
88. Powrie P (2006) The cinema of France. Wallflower Press, London
89. Barnet B (2013) Memory machines: the evolution of hypertext. Anthem Press, London
90. Montfort N, Bogost I (2009) Racing the beam: the Atari video computer system. MIT University Press, Cambridge
91. Manovich L (2013) Software takes command. Bloomsbury Academic, New York
92. Tuman M (1992) Word perfect: literacy in the computer age. University of Pittsburgh Press, Pittsburgh
93. Marino M (2006) Critical code studies. https://electronicbookreview.com/essay/critical-code-studies/. Accessed 15 June 2022
94. Marino M (2010) Critical code studies and the electronic book review: an introduction. https://electronicbookreview.com/essay/critical-code-studies-and-the-electronic-book-review-an-introduction/. Accessed 15 June 2022
95. Sayer A (1999) Long live postdisciplinary studies! Sociology and the curse of disciplinary parochialism/imperialism. In: British sociological association conference. British Sociological Association Conference, Glasgow
96. Trent W (1904) The teaching of literature. Sewanee Rev 12(4):401–419
97. Andrew D (2009) The core and the flow of film studies. Crit Inq 35(4):879–918
98. Eskelinen M (2004) Towards computer game studies. In: Wardrop-Fruin N, Harrigan P (eds) First person: new media as story, performance, and game. MIT Press, Cambridge, pp 36–44
99. Moulthrop S (1995) Traveling in the breakdown lane: a principle of resistance for hypertext. Mosaic 28:55–77

Authorial Burden

Joey Donald Jones⬥

Abstract Limits that emerge out of the interactive nature of interactive digital narrative make authoring it challenging. These limits include exponential branching, where branches in the narrative increase the amount of content needed to be written progressively throughout the work; combinatorial explosion, where increasing combinations of possible game states makes writing additional content complex, as well as programming scope problems that are seen in any digital project, wherein the range of features or game interactions that could be implemented is infinite but development time finite. These limits place on the authors of interactive digital narrative an authorial burden, increasing the amount of content needed to be written, states managed or features programmed. Multiple strategies exist for tackling the burden, from reducing or reusing content, to decontextualising and generating content.

1 Introduction

Any creative endeavour has its difficulties, many of which arise out of their respective mediums. Painters mix paints; filmmakers must control the lighting in their shots. Interactive narrative similarly has its own creative challenges. Allowing interaction—especially choices which lead to alternative content—can require a great deal of additional content to be created. This content can be increasingly complex to the author. This has been referred to as the authorial burden.[1] This isn't meant to be pejorative: the act of writing doesn't need to feel burdensome. Rather, the authorial burden refers to the workload cost of authoring incurred by making interactive design decisions.

---

[1] The first appearance of this term appears to be by Mateas and Sterne in 2002 when discussing the authoring of their story-game, *Façade*, [38] though the problem clearly predates the term. This term has appeared regularly in the literature since then [16, 19, 28, 42, 44, 49, 50, 53–56, 62].

J. D. Jones (✉)
University of Southampton, Southampton, England
e-mail: j.d.jones@soton.ac.uk

© The Author(s), under exclusive license to Springer Nature Switzerland AG 2022
C. Hargood et al. (eds.), *The Authoring Problem*, Human–Computer Interaction Series,
https://doi.org/10.1007/978-3-031-05214-9_4

Content can be slow to write because there is a great deal of it to produce, or it can be slow to write because each new bit of content is complex to the author: Garbe refers to these limits as the 'authoring wall' and the 'complexity ceiling' [22]. Authoring interactive digital narrative is not just writing, but rather a range of complimentary activities including planning, visualisation, structuring, testing and so forth [34]. If content is difficult to visualise or test, then it will be slower to write and have a greater concomitant burden.

1.1 Authoring Wall

If you have a branching story with two equal length paths, then you'll need to write twice as much; if you have a story with content displayed differently based on combinations of different game states, then adding more states exponentially increases the content required; if you give the player a great deal of freedom of action, i.e. if the scope is particularly large, then a greater amount of content needs to be written.

The simplest structure of interactive narrative is the branching story, in which choices split the plot and the separate paths do not converge. This tree structure is sometimes known as the broomstick (especially with regards to endings) [8] or the Time Cave (after the Choose-Your-Own-Adventure novel of the same name that had this structure) [2]. Time Caves most quickly run into the problem of exponential branching. Without merging branches, any kind of branching work faces the limit of exponential writing. To date, the longest complete branching work which has no merging is *Girth Loinhammer's Exponential Adventure* [63]. This is only ten passages long, with each complete playthrough having nine choices with exactly two options each. This leads to 512 separate endings. If the author, Damon Wakes, were to write one extra choice for every possible playthrough, he would have to write 1024 additional passages. Another choice on top of that would be 2048 additional passages. With this simple structure, the authorial burden doubles every time the average game length is increased by one choice. The limit on how long a narrative of this type can be is quickly reached.

1.2 Complexity Ceiling

The authorial burden can be large because of the amount of content that needs to be written, but it also can be large because the content that needs to be authored is difficult to write due to state complexity. This can take the form of multiple different plot-states that need to be kept in mind while authoring, or trying to author snippets of content where the final presentation is unclear, or attempting to account for combinations of states. Scenes become more difficult to write the more alternative states there are. For example, an author might have to take into account whether two characters in a scene had already met, or what they know about each other, and if they had already met what happened between them.

Classic authoring problems from literature, like avoiding writing oneself into a corner, or maintaining continuity in a long work are compounded in an interactive piece if multiple possible plot-states can be true for any given scene, or if certain choices must be disallowed to ensure continuity later on in the story. For instance, a character dying can incur an authoring burden for future scenes in which that character could appear, requiring extensive additional writing; and the act of making sure that any given scene isn't incurring an undue burden is itself an additional factor that increased can slow down authorship.

The simple branching structure has only one game state at any given time. A common way to manage choice in interactive fiction is through tracking multiple states. This allows any choice to have an effect on branching the story without requiring that every choice immediately creates a hard fork. However, works that rely on combinations of states run into a different problem of unmanageable combination sets. When each new state added can be combined with a number of existing states and new content needs to be written for this combination, the author eventually runs into a limit of complexity that they can handle [23].

1.3   Forms

Interactive narrative can take many different forms with varying authorial burdens. Long-form branching narrative, whether text-based, filmed or animated, where the player selects from choices, will be created differently to classic text adventure with a parser where players type commands. Compare this with agent-based simulationist works where a narrative emerges from interaction with virtual actors requires different skills, or database fiction where a player explores some body of content in order to make their own connections, or games like walking sims where the player explores a 3D environment. Some narratives require tactical decision-making from the player or puzzle solving, others have purely kinetic interaction. Nevertheless, the underlying interactive nature of these various forms generates a need for authors to write additional content which, if not properly managed, can expand exponentially. As such, many of the broad approaches for managing the authorial burden apply to multiple different forms of interactive narrative and many of these different forms can themselves be understood not only as aesthetic decisions but also as means of overcoming the constraints associated with authoring content which varies.

The intended length of experience is intertwined with the chosen form. Some works are intended to be played through once to completion, others are designed as repeatable experiences. Of those repeatable experiences, some might allow short iterative playthroughs, others (like *Fallen London* [20]) may be designed to come back to repeatedly over long periods of time and perhaps never reach an ending. These different intended lengths have their own concomitant burden; a work which is designed to be experienced once may employ approaches that wouldn't be as satisfying in a work designed for repeat experience.

The form of a digital work a player may experience doesn't necessarily reflect its coded structure. A well-written loop with expansive use of textual variation might be experienced by a player as a linear series of similar but distinct events. A branching section can be experienced as linear by a player who is unaware that variations were possible. It is the creative decision about the work-as-written rather than the work-as-experienced that incur an authorial burden.

1.4   Strategies for Unburdening

There are strategies for reducing the authorial burden that can be deployed to reduce or re-use content, decouple or generate segments of content, or otherwise improve the process of authorship.

  i **Reducing** Authors can seek to cut the authorial burden by reducing the amount of possible content, such as by limiting scope or merging branches.
 ii **Reusing** Existing content (such as backgrounds, animations and even scenes) can be repurposed, thereby avoiding the need to create additional content. The same representation can be repeated (e.g. having the same scene occur in two branches) or the same assets, text snippets or animations may be reused to represent different things (e.g. using the same library of responses for different non-player characters).
iii **Decoupling** New content can be harder to write the more it needs to be continuous with existing content. Making sections more context-independent can reduce the writing complexity, allowing more to be written. Structuring works into distinct episodes can be a form of decoupling.
 iv **Generating** Content can be procedurally generated, allowing a great deal of possible novel combinations. This may reduce the writing burden while increasing other forms of workload (e.g. testing and programming).
  v **Embracing** Rather than changing the form of an interactive narrative itself, the ability of authors to write can be improved. These approaches embrace the authorial burden by increasing the capacity of authors to tackle it.

These kinds of strategies can be seen instantiated in the various approaches to tackling the authorial burden. It should be noted that there are other reasons for making design choices beyond their effect on the total workload. Managing authorial labour is only one of several reasons an author might use a specific structure of interaction or set of tools. Different plot types, such as the epic plot-based or the dramatic character-based form may fit better or worse with different modes of interaction [57]. Narrative structures expressed through choices offered to the player, or actions possible, are also poetic gameplay devices for evoking specific emotions in the player [10]. Interactivity is deployed for different purposes, depending on the experience the creators intend. Interactive elements can have multiple functions, even within the same work. For instance, puzzles might be included for challenge, humour, or to gate progress based on the player's understanding of the story. A loop might be present to establish a theme of repetition or return. Clickable text links may be used for pacing, or to develop a sense of complicity.

Nevertheless, given the untenability of compounded branching, any story with alternative content will necessarily be authored with some strategy for managing the authorial burden. Strategies aren't mutually exclusive, and the categories can overlap. Reusing content is at the same time reducing possible content.

2 Reducing

The most straightforward way that a digital project can involve a great deal of writing is by having a large scope. Indeed, one way of conceiving of the authorial burden is as under-managed scope. All completed projects necessarily limit scope to some extent: decisions always have to be made about what not to include. Scope limitation comes in different forms. In interactive narrative, scope is limited along at least these two axes: objects and verbs.

2.1 Limiting Objects

Implementing a large range of objects in a digital work (locations, characters, items, musical scores, etc.) incurs a burden of content creation for all things implemented. A typical way of reducing scope is to simply cut planned or possible content. In multimedia (animation, acting, illustration, etc.), keeping the range of assets used manageable can be important for keeping costs down and not just for time reasons. This has been called the 'economics of building' [47]. Diegetic constraints are often employed, grounding the limitation of elements in the fiction: aside from reasons of plot and atmosphere, this is why there is a plethora of closed houses, isolated islands and small casts in interactive narrative. As in a novel, in a purely textual work with minimal state-tracking and no visual assets, new locations and characters do not pose the same limitations.

2.2 Limiting Verbs

In an interactive work, the player is typically able to undertake various actions. This can range from choosing between links to click, all the way up to simulating a virtual environment. The range of verbs allowed then might range from one to many hundred (in the case of some parser-based games). For these games where the player might type anything, some authors have chosen to supply a very curtailed list of accepted words, but then implement bespoke responses for every valid combination. CEJ Pacian employs this approach in several of his works and calls the approach 'shallow but broad' [46]: in *Superliminal Vagrant Twin*, [46] the player can travel to a large range of planets, allowing a great sense of openness, but this is achieved by tightly limiting the possibility space on each planet to less than a dozen options.

2.3   Primacy of Text or Dialogue

Assets range considerably in cost and development time. Next to animation, live filming, illustration and so forth, text is comparatively cheap. Works can contain a great deal of text in descriptions and dialogue in a highly scalable way, in that adding more lines of text does not typically require new capabilities. This primacy isn't absolute: while a line of unique dialogue may typically appear once in a work, the experience of many games is made up of performing repeatable actions in a virtual space.

Similarly, lines of dialogue don't necessarily require unique animations or assets (though in some productions they may be voiced), and so by centring the exchange of words as the primary experience, the authors save on having to produce and program animation that would be required in a more physically expressed experience. This is a common strategy in computer roleplaying games which can have tens of thousands of lines of dialogue [60].

2.4   Existing Tools

Creating bespoke engines is programming labour which can have a huge time cost, and so using existing narrative engines, programming languages, visualising tools, etc. can save a lot of possible work, with the compromise that what can be made will be limited to what is possible within those tools. For example, the walking sim *Dear Esther* [52] was originally written as a modification for the Source game Engine [47]. This allowed the game to be made using a ready-to-use existing tool that the developers were familiar with, although until its remake, this limited what could be achieved both in the structure of the island and in the visual art style.

2.5   Abstraction

Abstracting away realist elements is a common scope management technique. Players of games in general, including narrative games, will accept a great deal of abstraction and repetition which might break the suspension of disbelief in film or literature; the player can cultivate a playing stance which allows them to separate the gamelike elements from their understanding of the work's narrative [33]. For example, choice-based conversations will often happen outside of real time, or may be repeated word-for-word without breaking immersion. Players accept game conventions, such as not being able to scale trivial obstacles, or having numerical stats represent aspects of their protagonist, just as the theatre-goer accepts when stage-hands and the audience are ignored by the actors of a play.

2.6 Gauntlet

A classic solution to writing reasonably lengthy stories with choices but without compounded branching is the gauntlet structure [2]. In the gauntlet, the story has one core path with many short endings off of this path. In gamebooks, this would often be represented by premature deaths. This structure only suits certain kinds of stories, though it still can be seen in contemporary works such as in large parts of the interactive film Bandersnatch [7]. A variant of the gauntlet is the 'friendly gauntlet' in which there are no premature endings: all side branches fold back onto the main path (see Merging Branches below). Most episodes of the choice-based videogame *Life is Strange* [17] follow a friendly gauntlet structure.

3 Reusing

Reusing the same element (a scene, a piece of art, a sign-off in a conversation, etc.) can be economical. This reaches its limit if it becomes prohibitively difficult to write content using existing elements or to cohere with pre-decided plot points.

3.1 Merging Branches

Branching and then merging is the most fundamental strategy for managing interac-tive narrative. Across a whole work, it has been referred to as a 'branch and bottleneck' structure, for the way, paths can branch out in a story and then return at bottlenecks [2]. Hargood and Crawford have separately referred to this as a foldback [15, 27], in which the branches of the story bend back on themselves. Similarly, Bernstein refers to this pattern as the Split/Join [4]. Most other hypertext patterns are versions of this at different scales. This can be conceived of as a way to reduce possible content by sending the player back to a central trunk of content.

Branches can be merged instantly or after divergent content. The breadth and form of divergent content can vary from an inconsequential minor variation, to fully developed parallel branches.

3.1.1 Empty Choice

The purest merge is to offer a choice and redirect the player to the same subsequent content regardless of their pick, with no states tracked. Here the choice might be functioning as a pacing device or to offer the player a different sense of the story or protagonist. This has little concomitant burden beyond the labour involved in conceiving of the non-choices. This technique has been called Illusory Agency, [19], and the offering of False Choices [39]. Such a strategy may genuinely save labour, but players (especially on replay) may see through the device, especially if consistently or overwhelmingly employed.

3.1.2 Recognised Choice

A player's choice can be recognised with a small divergence such as some differing text or dialogue. This creates some writing burden, but the burden isn't compounded as the story continues the same regardless of what is chosen. Mawhorter et al. call this a Flavor Choice [39].

3.1.3 State Changes

A choice may have a delayed effect, [39] with outcomes tracked by the narrative. A relationship might change, or an item may be gained, etc. These states can then be used later in the narrative without the requirement to branch immediately. Choice of Games, a publisher of interactive novels, refers to this as Delayed Branching [18].

3.1.4 Parallel Branches

A more authorially taxing form of splitting and merging branches is having substantial branches run in parallel, which then might merge at choke-points within the story. Ashwell refers to this structure as the Quest, [2] and it can be seen in works like *80 Days* [31] where multiple different parallel paths are possible for traversing the narrative at any given time.

3.2 Loops

Structurally, loops are a way of re-using the same content or set of choices offered. In a loop, the player is returned to a point in a scene or location which they have experienced before. Large narrative games like *Fallen London* make extensive use of this structure, with most content capable of being re-experienced. Time travel stories such as *Elsinore* [24] are based around this core idea, allowing large swathes of the game to be re-experienced, often with a separate player agenda on replays, allowing for continual agency despite repeated content [43].

3.2.1   Hub Nodes

The hub node is one use of a loop. It is a node of an interactive story which can be returned repeatedly in a cycle pattern until some condition is met to move forward [4]. These hubs can appear in an otherwise unidirectional structure. At a hub, a list of choices are offered. After exploring one of these choices (which may have its own sub-choices), the player returns to the hub. Each time they return, used choices may be removed and new choices may be added. This is often the way conversation systems are implemented. Clusters of hub nodes can be used to implement a location structure in a choice-based work that is more commonly seen in parser fiction (see for instance, *16 Ways To Kill A Vampire At McDonalds* [13], or *With Those We Love Alive* [9]). The hub node is an effective way of structuring narrative segments in which there are multiple smaller scenes that could coherently be experienced in any order.

3.3   World Modelling

Many of the strategies discussed are based on a choice branching structure. Moving away from this going further than the loop is implementing a world model of persistent locations, objects and characters. Text adventure games are distinguished by their use of world models. As models become more richly implemented, they create their own authorial burden (for instance, in implementing different verbs and accounting for various combinations of objects). Still, modelling a persistent set of locations and objects is very common in fully illustrated works, as creating artwork for a location is costly, so it often makes sense to re-use places as much as possible (this is a common feature of narrative adventure games, such as *The Secret of Monkey Island*, [35] where the same locations and characters are returned to repeatedly).

3.4   Cumulative Variables

A straightforward way of lowering complexity in tracking narrative states is to use cumulative variables instead of, say, multiple Boolean values. For example, the interactive space opera, *Mass Effect*, [6] tracks how 'Renegade' the protagonist is. Instead of checking a list of every possible time they acted in a renegade way, the player's Renegade score accumulates at such occasions, and when relevant the single variable is checked. This principle is used extensively in the works of Choice of Games [30].

4   Decoupling

Decoupling is a way of reusing content, or rather by allowing scenes to appear regardless of previous content. The more self-contained segments of content are, the easier new sections can be written without having to write lots of variations depending on the world-state. This structure lends itself to narrative genres such as the picaresque in which the protagonist might embark on a series of loosely connected adventures. Conversely, agent-driven simulations and tightly plotted dramas may be harder to decouple.

4.1   Storylets

The storylet structure is a clear example of decoupling. The term was coined by the writers of the massive multi-million word browser-based text game, *Fallen London* [20] to refer to the chunks of content that can be experienced in many different possible orders. When these storylets are displayed based on conditional triggers, this is referred to as Quality-Based Narrative, [58] or Sculptural Hypertext [5]. Storylets in Fallen London work on a principle that has been referred to as the 'fires in the desert' approach: the writers create self-contained chunks of story (the well-lit 'fires'), leaving it up to the reader to infer the linkage between these chunks (the dark 'desert' between these bright spots of story) [21]. This strong context independence asks more from the reader than in traditional storytelling where events have much clearer causal links.

4.2   Modularisation

Modularising interactive narrative is to separate it into relatively self-contained segments. This is the same concept as 'levels' in videogames more broadly. To take an example: most long-form interactive novels published by Choice of Games[2] adhere somewhat to their stylebook, a set of guidelines for content and structure. The content guidelines ensure that content is in line with the values of the publishers (inclusive choices, no hate speech, etc.). The structural guidelines are a set of 'best practices for game management'. One of the guidelines is that works should be comprised of approximately ten vignettes that occur in sequential order. This ensures that the games are of sufficient length to meet their expected standards, but it also manages branching. It ensures that on a macro-scale across the whole interactive novel, no matter how many internal branches in a chapter, and no matter how any of them may end, they each must lead on to the next chapter in sequence. This modular design prevents the stories from sprawling out to an unmanageable number of parallel branches.

---

[2] Such as *Choice of Robots*, [25] *Créme de la Créme*, [48] *Trials of the Thief-Taker* [32] and so on.

Essentially this approach is a more formal application of the 'branch and bottleneck' structure, but in other works, modules might be even more independent.

4.3 Episodes

Full modularisation into distinct episodes can allow for episodic release in much the same manner as television shows, a technique used by Telltale Games for many of their narrative games. Episodic release has the benefit of allowing the creators to make and receive feedback from manageable chunks, as well as develop more of a prolonged event around the release of a work. Fully decoupled episodes, such as those that comprise *Kentucky Route Zero* [12] allow players to jump directly into any of the released episodes, as very few states are tracked between episodes. Brendan Patrick Hennessy's *Known Unknowns* [29] goes a step further, allowing players to jump into any chapter within any of the episodes, allowing scenes to be re-experienced in the same manner a reader might return to a favourite scene in a novel.

5 Generating

Generating content combines the approaches of reusing and modularising content, most often allowing the same elements to be recombined in a wide variety of contexts. Combining elements can happen at various different scales. It can happen at the level of the individual collection of pixels (as in procedural animation) or environmental elements such as rooms or objects, but also at the level of the sentence, word or letter. For words, tools like Tracery allow word lists to be recombined to create a huge variety of grammatical sentences according to simple iterative rules [11].

5.1 Procedural Content Generation

Procedural Generation is a strategy for creating content with many possible states instead of hand authoring unique state combinations. Sufficient content is required to populate generative lists and testing is needed to make sure the output is of sufficient quality. Narrative designer Cat Manning once quipped that procedural generation means 'generating twice the content in twice the time'.[3] Creating variations with the same quality and variety as equivalent hand-authored content may require different authoring skills but isn't necessarily less work.

---

[3] See https://twitter.com/catacalypto/status/1470893540964134913.

5.2 Supplementary Generation

Rather than generating core narrative content, supplementary elements can be generated. Reed has presented a system for reducing the authorial burden of writing by procedurally generating satellite sentences for pacing and context [50]. Ryan has demonstrated recombinant conversation generation for creating filler conversations [55]. Neither of these approaches produce content as satisfactory as bespoke-authored content, but they could be used to supplement such content. For instance, by giving variations of greetings and goodbyes and other formulaic conversation elements.

5.3 Natural Language Processing

Natural language processing is a set of tools for parsing user input. Rather than create bespoke responses to every possible useful input (as would be common in normal parser fiction), this approach seeks to dynamically 'understand' user input to decide what content should be shown next.

This technique is demonstrated in *Façade* which takes the player's written input and interprets it into various viable responses [37]. Responses depend on the current story beat being played through, so the same player input can be interpreted in different ways throughout the story (e.g. if the player continually says the word 'no', what they are saying it in response to and how the other characters might respond will vary considerably throughout the narrative). For any given beat, the parser will channel the player's response into one of around eight different interpretations. These can further the current story beat or trigger a new beat. In theory, this approach could negate much of the need for hand-authoring parser interpretations, but in practise the authors ended up creating many ad hoc phrases for specific beats.

5.4 Simulated Agents

While not necessarily a way of reducing labor, creating simulated agents pushes the authorship into a different domain, that of writing patterns of behaviour [3]. With the right tools, this approach can allow the creation of a great deal of novel situations that emerge out of the simulation.

Works like *Prom Week* [40] involve simulating characters, with a narrative coming through the player's interaction with these characters and their simulated behaviour amongst themselves [41]. Martens and Iqbal have made Villanelle, a story-engine for the creation of these kinds of narratives [36]. Among commercial works, agents can be seen in highly procedural games like *Dwarf Fortress*, [1] and more tightly authored experiences like *Elsinore*.

6 Embracing

Rather than seek to design it away, Stern has argued that we ought embrace the combinatorial explosion [61]. The authoring wall is only high in comparison to the capacity of the authors of an interactive narrative. Embracing the burden is the final strategy.

6.1 More Hours

One common method of overcoming the authorial burden is allotting more time to it. This can either mean taking longer to create the work, or more controversially, it can mean crunch: packing more working hours into a short period of time, typically before product launch. While this approach is often baked into the habitus of game creation, extended over-work leads to exhaustion and burnout [14].

6.2 More Writers

One paradigm of interactive narrative is the solo-authored piece, product of a single vision. But the other paradigm is that which is common in videogame companies: to have several writers, often in large teams. While this approach has diminishing marginal returns, if you have more writers, under the right conditions more content can be written.

6.3 Developing Craft Knowledge

Access and education for authors has been highlighted as an important area for developing interactive narrative; [59] being able to think and write interactively is a skill that writers of other media don't automatically possess. The more acquainted authors are with common interactive patterns, and familiar they are with their tools, the more ambitious projects they will be able to complete. It is perhaps no surprise that the most popular narrative text engines, such as Inform 7, Twine and Ink all have extensive documentation.

6.4 Developing Better Tools

It has been argued that improving the 'user experience' of authoring tools can help authors attain greater competency with tools and unlock deeper affordances, [51] as well minimising interruptions to authoring flow [26]. This approach is taken up elsewhere in this volume.

Tool creation itself can be unproductive if the tools are never utilised or re-create the affordances of existing engines. However, for some story-structures, the right kinds of visualisation and testing tools can have a huge effect. Emily Short described such an 'author-friendly toolset for writing Versu stories... that sped up content production by a factor of at least ten and meant that we could produce much bigger, longer stories than previously released' [45].

7 Conclusion

The most basic form of interactive narrative, the pure branching story, creates a large writing burden, sharply curtailing the possible length of such a story. As greater levels of state tracking and content structuring are introduced, the complexity of writing new content increases. Ways of ameliorating this twin burden of the volume of content and difficulty of production can in themselves create new challenges, requiring different skills from authors. Strategies don't necessarily alleviate work, so much as change the form it takes.

When faced with an ambitious idea, the author of an interactive work has many paths to realising it. They may pare back the scope; they may employ structures like merging and loops to keep branching under control; they could make use of more advanced forms, using salience to decide what to display, or procedurally generating a large number of variations. They might take their time, improve their skills or work with others to see the idea through.

The authorial burden then isn't a hard limit on what can be achieved, but a malleable border that shifts. It is the point at which an author is willing to compromise between their vision, and what tools, time and their own powers allow them to achieve.

References

1. Adams T, Adams Z (2006) Dwarf Fortress
2. Ashwell SK (2015) Standard patterns in choice-based games. https://heterogenoustasks. wordpress.com/2015/01/26/standard-patterns-in-choice-based-games/
3. Badler NI, Reich BD, Webber BL (1997) Towards personalities for animated agents with reactive and planning behaviors. In: Trappl R, Petta P (eds) Creating personalities for synthetic actors: towards autonomous personality agents. Lecture notes in computer science. Springer, Berlin, Heidelberg, pp 43–57. https://doi.org/10.1007/BFb0030569

4. Bernstein M (1998) Patterns of hypertext. In: 9th ACM hypertext and hypermedia. HYPER-TEXT '98, Association for computing machinery. New York, NY, USA, pp 21–29. https://doi.org/10.1145/276627.276630

5. Bernstein M (2001) Card shark and thespis: exotic tools for hypertext narrative. In: Proceedings of the 12th ACM conference on hypertext and hypermedia. HYPERTEXT '01, Association for Computing Machinery, New York, NY, USA, pp 41–50. https://doi.org/10.1145/504216.504233

6. Bioware: mass effect (2007)

7. Brooker C, Slade D (2018) Bandersnatch. https://ifdb.org/viewgame?id=dh7kphu7nmjt1ia5

8. Bruckman A (1990) The combinatorics of storytelling: "mystery train interactive". The MIT Laboratory

9. Charity Heartscape P, Neotenomie B (2014) With those we love alive. https://ifdb.org/viewgame?id=445d989vuwlh4cvz

10. Chew EC, Mitchell A (2019) Bringing art to life: examining poetic gameplay devices in interactive life stories. Games and culture. SAGE Publications, p 1555412019853372. https://doi.org/10.1177/1555412019853372

11. Compton K, Kybartas B, Mateas M (2015) Tracery: an author-focused generative text tool. In: Schoenau-Fog H, Bruni LE, Louchart S, Baceviciute S (eds) Interactive storytelling. Lecture notes in computer science. Springer International Publishing, Cham, pp 154–161

12. Computer C (2013) Kentucky Route Zero

13. Corfman A (2016) 16 ways to kill a vampire at mcDonalds. https://ifdb.org/viewgame?id=s8oklhvdqoo5dv4l

14. Cote AC, Harris BC (2021) 'Weekends became something other people did': understanding and intervening in the habitus of video game crunch. Convergence 27(1):161–176

15. Crawford C (2020) Flawed methods for interactive storytelling|interactive storytelling tools for writers. http://www.erasmatazz.com/library/the-journal-of-computer/jcgd-volume-7/flawed-methods-for-interact.html

16. Domínguez IX, Cardona-Rivera RE, Vance JK, Roberts DL (2016) The mimesis effect: the effect of roles on player choice in interactive narrative role-playing games. In: Proceedings of the 2016 CHI conference on human factors in computing systems. Association for Computing Machinery, New York, NY, USA, pp 3438–3449. https://doi.org/10.1145/2858036.2858141

17. Enix S (2015) Life is strange

18. Fabulich D (2011) By the numbers: how to write a long interactive novel that doesn't suck. https://www.choiceofgames.com/2011/07/by-the-numbers-how-to-write-a-long-interactive-novel-that-doesnt-suck/

19. Fendt MW, Harrison B, Ware SG, Cardona-Rivera RE, Roberts DL (2012) Achieving the illusion of agency. In: Oyarzun D, Peinado F, Young RM, Elizalde A, Méndez G (eds) Interactive storytelling. Lecture notes in computer science, Springer, Berlin, Heidelberg, pp 114–125

20. Games F (2009) Fallen London

21. Games F (2010) Echo bazaar narrative structures, part three. https://www.failbettergames.com/echo-bazaar-narrative-structures-part-three/

22. Garbe J (2020) Increasing authorial leverage in generative narrative systems. PhD thesis, UC Santa Cruz. https://escholarship.org/uc/item/4dq8w2g9

23. Garbe J, Kreminski M, Samuel B, Wardrip-Fruin N, Mateas M (2019) StoryAssembler: an engine for generating dynamic choice-driven narratives. In: 14th international conference on the foundations of digital games. FDG '19, Association for Computing Machinery, New York, NY, USA, pp 1–10. https://doi.org/10.1145/3337722.3337732

24. Glitch G (2019) Elsinore

25. Gold K (2014) Choice of robots. Choice of Games

26. Green D, Hargood C, Charles F (2018) Contemporary issues in interactive storytelling authoring systems. In: Interactive storytelling. Lecture notes in computer science. Springer International Publishing, Cham, pp 501–513

27. Hargood C, Hunt V, Weal MJ, Millard DE (2016) Patterns of sculptural hypertext in location based narratives. In: Proceedings of the 27th ACM conference on hypertext and social media.

HT '16, Association for Computing Machinery, New York, NY, USA, pp 61–70. https://doi.org/10.1145/2914586.2914595

28. Harrison B, Ware SG, Fendt MW, Roberts DL (2015) A survey and analysis of techniques for player behavior prediction in massively multiplayer online role-playing games. IEEE Trans Emerg Top Comput 3(2):260–274. https://doi.org/10.1109/TETC.2014.2360463

29. Hennessy BP (2016) Known unknowns

30. Hill JS (2017) A taxonomy of choices: axes of choice. https://www.choiceofgames.com/2017/12/a-taxonomy-of-choices-axes-of-choice/

31. Inkle: 80 days (2014)

32. Jones JD (2017) Trials of the thief-taker. Choice of Games

33. Karhulahti VM (2012) Suspending virtual disbelief: a perspective on narrative coherence. In: Interactive storytelling, vol 7648. Springer, Berlin, Heidelberg, pp 1–17

34. Kitromili S, Jordan J, Millard DE (2019) What is hypertext authoring? In: Proceedings of the 30th ACM conference on hypertext and social media. HT '19, Association for Computing Machinery, New York, NY, USA, pp 55–59. https://doi.org/10.1145/3342220.3343653

35. LucasArts: The secret of Monkey Island (1990)

36. Martens C, Iqbal O (2019) Villanelle: An authoring tool for autonomous characters in interactive fiction. In: Cardona-Rivera RE, Sullivan A, Young RM (eds) Interactive storytelling. Lecture notes in computer science. Springer International Publishing, Cham, pp 290–303

37. Mateas M, Mateas M, Stern A (2003) Façade: an experiment in building a fully-realized interactive drama. http://130.203.136.95/viewdoc/summary;jsessionid=72514A39F6B5D5F3EC79C74A537960DA?doi=10.1.1.14.6176

38. Mateas M, Stern A (2002) Architecture, authorial idioms and early observations of the interactive drama Façade

39. Mawhorter P, Mateas M, Wardrip-Fruin N, Jhala A (2014) Towards a theory of choice poetics, p 8

40. McCoy J, Treanor M, Samuel B (2012) Prom week

41. McCoy J, Treanor M, Samuel B, Mateas M, Wardrip-Fruin N (2011) Prom week: social physics as gameplay. In: Proceedings of the 6th international conference on foundations of digital games. FDG '11, Association for Computing Machinery, New York, NY, USA, pp 319–321. https://doi.org/10.1145/2159365.2159425

42. Mehta M, Ontañón S, Ram A (2008) Adaptive computer games: easing the authorial burden

43. Mitchell A, Kway L (2020) How do I restart this thing? repeat experience and resistance to closure in rewind storygames. In: Bosser AG, Millard DE, Hargood C (eds) Interactive storytelling. Lecture notes in computer science. Springer International Publishing, Cham, pp 164–177 (2020). https://doi.org/10.1007/978-3-030-62516-0

44. Méndez G, Hervás R, Gervás P, Martín A, Julca F (2019) Dynamic emphatical narration for reduced authorial burden and increased user freedom in interactive storytelling. Connect Sci 31(1):33–59. https://www.tandfonline.com/doi/full/10.1080/09540091.2018.1454891

45. Nutt C (2014) The end of Versu: Emily short looks back. https://www.gamedeveloper.com/business/the-end-of-versu-emily-short-looks-back, section: business

46. Pacian C (2016) Superluminal vagrant twin. https://ifdb.org/viewgame?id=5xzoz5wimz4xxha

47. Pinchbeck D (2008) Dear Esther: an interactive ghost story built using the source engine. In: Spierling U, Szilas N (eds) Interactive storytelling. Lecture notes in computer science. Springer, Berlin, Heidelberg, pp 51–54

48. Powell-Smith H (2019) Créme de la Créme. Choice of games

49. Reed A, Samuel B, Sullivan A, Grant R, Grow A, Lazaro J, Mahal J, Kurniawan S, Walker M, Wardrip-Fruin N (2011) A step towards the future of role-playing games: the SpyFeet mobile RPG project. In: Seventh AAAI conference on artificial intelligence and interactive digital entertainment

50. Reed AA (2012) Sharing authoring with algorithms: procedural generation of satellite sentences in text-based interactive stories. In: Proceedings of the the third workshop on procedural content generation in games, PCG'12. Association for Computing Machinery, New York, NY, USA, pp 1–4. https://doi.org/10.1145/2538528.2538540

51. Revi AT, Millard DE, Middleton SE (2020) A systematic analysis of user experience dimensions for interactive digital narratives. In: Bosser AG, Millard DE, Hargood C (eds) Interactive storytelling. Lecture notes in computer science. Springer International Publishing, Cham, pp 58–74

52. Room TC (2012) Dear Esther

53. Ryan J (2020) Generating natural language retellings from prom week play traces. Procedural content generation in games. https://www.academia.edu/15396431/Generating_Natural_Language_Retellings_from_Prom_Week_Play_Traces

54. Ryan J, Fisher A, Owen-Milner T, Mateas M, Wardrip-Fruin N (2015) Toward natural language generation by humans. In: 8th workshop on intelligent narrative technologies

55. Ryan JO, Barackman C, Kontje N, Owen-Milner T, Walker MA, Mateas M, Wardrip-Fruin N (2014) Combinatorial dialogue authoring. In: Mitchell A, Fernández-Vara C, Thue D (eds) Interactive storytelling. Lecture notes in computer science. Springer International Publishing, Cham, pp 13–24

56. Ryan JO, Mateas M, Wardrip-Fruin N (2015) Open design challenges for interactive emergent narrative. In: Schoenau-Fog H, Bruni LE, Louchart S, Baceviciute S (eds) Interactive storytelling. Lecture notes in computer science. Springer International Publishing, Cham, pp 14–26

57. Ryan ML (2008) Interactive narrative, plot types, and interpersonal relations. In: Spierling U, Szilas N (eds) Interactive storytelling. Lecture notes in computer science. Springer, Berlin, Heidelberg, pp 6–13

58. Short AE (2016) Beyond branching: quality-based, salience-based, and waypoint narrative structures. https://emshort.blog/2016/04/12/beyond-branching-quality-based-and-salience-based-narrative-structures/

59. Spierling U, Szilas N (2009) Authoring issues beyond tools. In: Iurgel IA, Zagalo N, Petta P (eds) Interactive storytelling. Lecture notes in computer science. Springer, Berlin, Heidelberg, pp 50–61

60. Staff G (2008) Star wars: the old republic revealed. https://www.gamespot.com/articles/star-wars-the-old-republic-revealed/1100-6199726/

61. Stern A (2008) Embracing the combinatorial explosion: a brief prescription for interactive story R&D. In: Spierling U, Szilas N (eds) Interactive storytelling. Lecture notes in computer science. Springer, Berlin, Heidelberg, pp 1–5

62. Talbot C, Youngblood GM (2012) Spatial cues in Hamlet. In: Nakano Y, Neff M, Paiva A, Walker M (eds) Intelligent virtual agents. Lecture notes in computer science. Springer, Berlin, Heidelberg, pp 252–259

63. Wakes D (2017) Girth Loinhammer's most exponential adventure. https://damonwakes.wordpress.com/books/girth-loinhammers-most-exponential-adventure/

We Make How We Learn: The Role of Community in Authoring Tool Longevity

Daniel Cox

Abstract Since 1979, hundreds of authoring tools have been created. While many factors contribute to the survival of a tool beyond its initial introduction, the largest factor for an authoring tool lasting more than a publication or initial experiment is the active involvement of a community. Authoring tools survive by those who use them. Active community involvement in projects extends their lives, and the resources created by communities around a tool help new users learn to use it. This chapter examines three different open-source projects, authoring tools, *Bitsy* and *Twine*, and scripting language, *ink*, with a focus on how their communities have played a role in their perception and longevity.

1 Who Survives? Who Tells Your Story?

The interactive digital narrative (IDN) community has lost much of the history of authoring tools. New research on older tools is rarely shared across the community because of a lack of a shared vocabulary across different journals and conferences [1]. What might be recognized as an authoring tool can also differ across academic disciplines, with disagreement on a standard definition of the term [2]. Some parts of the larger community actively discuss certain authoring problems and may work on their own solutions, while other parts consider these same problems to be solved. This is further compounded by organizational restrictions limiting access to source code and new ideas not finding an audience. This problem of the IDN community "forgetting what has already been addressed," as Koenitz and Eladhari [1] explain the issue, has had a major effect on authoring tools and their history. While new tools are frequently being invented or revised as part of student projects, funded graduate research, or as part of more commercial experiments, very few last beyond their initial introduction. Even fewer live beyond their inclusion as an academic paper, hobbyist project, or doctoral publication.

D. Cox (✉)
University of Central Florida, Orlando, FL, USA
e-mail: dancox@knights.ucf.edu

In their research of authoring tools starting from 1979, Shibolet et al. [3] have collected evidence of more than 300 authoring tools being created across nearly 40 years of the field. Yet, the number of tools under active development is relatively small. Even accounting for a very loose definition of development, an update anywhere from every few months to once across multiple years, the number of active projects remaining since 1979 consists of roughly half of the 300 projects found by researchers [3].

Why do some authoring tools survive when others do not? In some cases, for those created as part of funding sources in academic settings, the answer may be straightforward. Once the funding runs out, the project can no longer be maintained, or there might not be interest in continuing the work. For more commercial ventures, the reason might also be funding or changes to internal organization or interests. For projects with public code and contributions, the answer might also be as simple: community support. In their research on 1,932 GitHub projects, Avelino et al. [4] provide an answer for why some open-source projects survive and others are abandoned: active investment. As a project faces possible abandonment by its original creators, new core developers can extend its life [4]. Those projects with active communities around them are also more likely to survive multiple years as improvements are suggested and new code is contributed [5]. For communities of active users and contributors, their work around a project can often lead to a higher quality of code and much longer lives than smaller projects with less active people involved in its development [6]. Based on the research on open-source projects, one major factor for longevity becomes obvious. For an authoring tool to survive, it needs an active community around it to contribute new ideas and updates. Without this influence, the fate of any tool is to be abandoned and ultimately forgotten by the larger IDN community, as many others have before it.

This chapter examines three examples of open-source projects and the roles their communities have played in supporting and influencing their development. The first is *Bitsy* [7], the youngest authoring tool of the set, but one whose community actively contributes resources to help new users learn to use the tool based on the work of mostly a single developer. The second is the narrative scripting language *ink*. Maintained by a small team of people inside a commercial company, Inkle, many code contributions come from its larger community. Inkle has recently taken a new move to publish its own resources in competition with those from its community. The last authoring tool examined is *Twine* [19]. While often praised as being easy to use, it now faces an uncertain future as parties within its own community have presented different, conflicting views of the path forward for the authoring tool.

2   *Bitsy Game Maker*

Introduced in 2017, *Bitsy Game Maker* (*Bitsy*) was created by Adam Le Doux. The project repository on GitHub describes itself as an authoring tool to "make tiny games, worlds, and stories" [7]. Presenting an online editor, authors can use multiple panels to edit the position, color, and text of player interactions on a 2D grid of pixel squares. Once finished with their work, authors can then publish their work as HTML files for others to play in web browsers.

In the five years since its introduction, thousands of artifacts have been created with *Bitsy* [8]. It has increasingly seen usage in classrooms, workshops, and in public art projects [9]. *Bitsy* has seen coverage in online media outlets such as Wired [8], Rock, Paper, Shotgun [10], and PC Gamer [11]. It also has a robust set of modifications for creating different types of experiences for players and for expanding the visual presentation beyond a flat, mostly textual 2D interaction into 3D and other hybrid media forms [12]. As a primarily online authoring tool, it has attracted many with the promise of quickly creating a story and publishing it as HTML for others to easily experience.

Despite this seeming popularity, there is no official documentation. No tutorials are published with the project, and it has no introduction beyond the interface of its editor. Anyone wanting to learn to use *Bitsy* beyond trying different things in the authoring tool itself must first find one of the many tutorials, videos, or previous workshops published online. This is explained by an online fan collection of such materials by different authors: "As there are no officially-written tutorials for how to use *Bitsy*, the community relies on its other members for help" [12]. Learning to use *Bitsy* means looking beyond the authoring tool itself.

An examination of the code contributions for *Bitsy* on GitHub shows the work of primarily a single developer with occasional code from other parties [7]. Yet, the longevity and growing popularity of the project across five years comes not from this mostly solo development work, but from its community and the labor around creating resources for new and returning users. Extensive guides and step-by-step explanations have been created for those wanting to use the tool across different websites and social platforms while the tool continues to have no materials for learning how to use it beyond its description.

3   Narrative Scripting Language *ink*

The narrative scripting language *ink* (starting with a lowercase 'i') exists in two forms. The scripting language form allows authors to write dialogue and describe player interactions in a plain-text form designed for human audiences to read and edit the code. This is then processed into a second form of compiled JSON, designed for use with game engines such as Unity [14] and Unreal [13]. While some users prefer tools such as Visual Studio Code for editing *ink* when working with languages like JavaScript [14] not officially supported, most users experience *ink* in an editor named Inky, where the human-readable code can be entered on the left-hand side and its runtime output can be viewed on the right-hand side (Fig. 1).

From its public introduction in late 2015 until early 2022, the official documentation for *ink* consisted of a few pages as part of its GitHub repository with one central page titled "Writing with ink", covering its major concepts and how to use

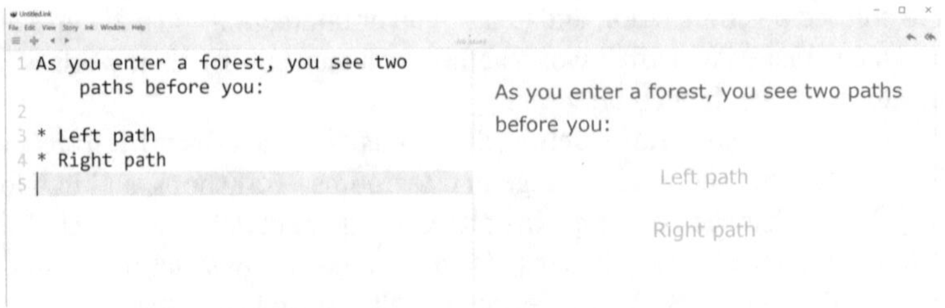

Fig. 1 Screenshot of Inky editor interface

them [15]. New users of the language often learned from guides, tutorial videos, and other resources created by members of its community. These materials ranged from short examples posted on its official Discord server to a much more comprehensive "unofficial cookbook" collection created for classroom usage [16]. Despite this issue, *ink* has seen continued growth, including the writing of a textbook explaining its concepts and how to use it for more advanced projects with the game engine Unity published in late 2021 [17].

Alongside this growth and interest in the language, Inkle and the community around *ink* have had a strained relationship at times. Many users seeking to learn the language have found themselves dependent on community resources and guides with occasional support from developers at Inkle via their Discord server when they encountered problems. In early 2022, this occasional tension between the creator of the language, Inkle, and its community took a new turn when Inkle announced its own book as a direct competition with resources from its community [20]. For the first time, Inkle had taken a much more direct hand in how *ink* was taught to others. It was officially labeling certain patterns of the language, found previously across numerous sources created by members of the community. While this is not unheard of for an authoring tool, as Inform 7 had its "Recipe Book" [21] while Aaron Reed's [18] book on creating projects with the language existed at the same time, Inkle's new work has created a dividing line between what was previously community-accepted materials and its own, internally-created work.

As an older project, *ink* and its community are now facing a tension soon to come for the younger *Bitsy* and its community. For most of its lifetime, like with *Bitsy*, the popularity and expansion of *ink* to new audiences was driven by its community resources. However, for the first time, new audiences have a choice between what Inkle considers official and those resources found in its community. While the popularity of *ink*, like with *Bitsy*, owes much to its community labor and influence, this new turn has yet to play out in how it shapes the willingness of the *ink* community to generate new resources it may find ignored or overridden by what Inkle states is official or not in the future.

4 *Twine*

Created in 2009 by Chris Klimas, what would eventually become *Twine* began its life as a plain-text scripting language, *Twee*, for creating stories, and a command-line tool interpreter program based on the wiki tool *TiddlyWiki* for generating compiled HTML others could experience [19]. This morphed over a decade from a binary executable for editing *Twee* named *Twine* into a later primarily online version named *Twine 2* featuring a much more visual interface showing connections between parts of a story to an author when editing a story (Fig. 2).

Throughout its lifetime, *Twine* has been closely associated with the terms "easy to use" and "accessible." In many published articles, the word "accessible" appears in the same sentence introducing the authoring tool [20–23]. In their introduction on the history of *Twine*, Salter and Moulthrop [19] also describe it as having a "beginner-friendly learning curve." There is an obvious perception of *Twine* as being easy to use. Yet, this perception originates not from the tool itself, but with how its community has described the authoring tool to others over many years.

One of the earliest community-driven tutorials on using *Twine* is from Anna Anthropy and highlighted the ability to quickly tell personal stories with little code [24]. At the time, the official documentation for what was then called *Twee* focused on using code with a header of "Adding Code to your Stories" featuring prominently [25]. Later in 2012, Anthropy included a chapter on *Twine* in her book, *Rise of the Videogame Zinesters*, again emphasizing how easy it was to use with little to no programming knowledge [26]. This was followed by one of the first academic conference presentations on *Twine*, noting its ease of use because of how its interface matched "common brainstorming techniques" [20]. In her book, *Writing Interactive*

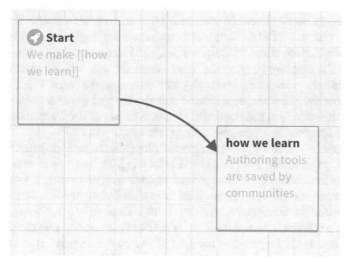

Fig. 2 Screenshot of *Twine 2* interface

Fiction with Twine, Ford (2016) then made the same connection Anthropy did a few years before: a focus on the personal rather than programming aspects of storytelling possibilities in *Twine* [27]. Despite some of the earliest documentation focusing on code, the dominant narrative quickly became one on how *Twine* "distinguishes itself for beginners and those uninterested in the arduous process of learning to program" [28] and how it "does not require knowledge of even basic programming concepts" [29]. This perception led to its role in a rise in personal storytelling as part of a "Twine revolution" of new projects from marginalized creators [30].

The perception of *Twine* not requiring programming has often been at odds with its own internal presentation. The official collection of examples named the "Twine Cookbook" explains in-depth on how to use HTML and CSS with projects. It also includes many entries with twenty or more lines of JavaScript code per example based on community patterns and possible solutions to common questions from authors on how to use or implement certain functionality with the tool [31]. The most used story formats in *Twine* 2, options for how an author can compose stories and how its content will be presented to readers, include the word "code" dozens of times in their own official documentation [31, 32]. Newer resources on Twine also feature this same focus with a book on "coding activities" with *Twine* [33] existing alongside education resources for learning programming explicitly using *Twine* [34].

5   We Make How We Learn

Authoring tools survive by their communities. This is driven by how those communities create materials and maintain a perception of the authoring tool for itself and new users. For *Bitsy*, now going into its sixth year of ongoing development, it is nearing a point where a decision must be made about how it is taught from official channels. Currently, with no official documentation, new users are taught based on how others figured out and made things on their own. Inkle and its community are now facing an issue with the scripting language *ink* where there are unofficial resources, some of which have existed for years, competing with new, official materials. For *Twine*, the oldest of this set, its earlier perception of an authoring tool where an author does not need to write code seems increasingly at odds with newer documentation focusing on using programming languages to create stories with the tool.

Communities remember. If the greatest challenge for an authoring tool is in being "forgotten" as presented by Koenitz and Eladhari [1], the best way an authoring tool can survive into the future is through how its community describes it to new users. Over the course of a decade, *Twine* went from a hobbyist project to being part of a creative revolution. On a smaller scale, the same is also true of *ink*, which progressed from a set of GitHub pages serving as its official documentation to the publishing of two books on the language in the span of five months nearly seven years later. As for *Bitsy*, it might also see the same fate as *ink* and *Twine* as its community tries to collect and preserve resources for those learning the authoring tool for the first time. The deciding factor for all of these and more is in how the community makes new resources for users to learn. In shaping the perception of the authoring tools, the communities around an authoring tool serve to keep it in living memory and prevent it from being lost alongside too many others.

References

1. Koenitz H, Eladhari MP (2019) Challenges of IDN research and teaching. In: Cardona-Rivera RE, Sullivan A, Young RM (eds) Interactive storytelling. Springer International Publishing, Cham, pp 26–39. https://doi.org/10.1007/978-3-030-33894-7_4
2. Green D, Hargood C, Charles F (2018) Contemporary issues in interactive storytelling authoring systems. In: Rouse R, Koenitz H, Haahr M (eds) Interactive storytelling. ICIDS 2018. Lecture notes in computer science, vol 11318. Springer, Cham. https://doi.org/10.1007/978-3-030-04028-4_59
3. Shibolet Y, Knoller N, Koenitz H (2018) A framework for classifying and describing authoring tools for interactive digital narrative. In: Rouse R, Koenitz H, Haahr M (eds) Interactive storytelling. Springer International Publishing, Cham, pp 523–533. https://doi.org/10.1007/978-3-030-04028-4_61
4. Avelino G, Constantinou E, Valente MT, Serebrenik A (2019) On the abandonment and survival of open source projects: an empirical investigation. In: 2019 ACM/IEEE international symposium on empirical software engineering and measurement (ESEM). IEEE, Porto de Galinhas, Recife, Brazil, pp 1–12. https://doi.org/10.1109/ESEM.2019.8870181
5. Kaur R, Kaur K (2022) Insights into developers' abandonment in FLOSS projects. In: Nagar AK, Jat DS, Marín-Raventós G, Mishra DK (eds) Intelligent sustainable systems. Springer Nature Singapore, Singapore, pp 731–740. https://doi.org/10.1007/978-981-16-6309-3_69
6. Aberdour M (2007) Achieving quality in open-source software. IEEE Softw 24:58–64. https://doi.org/10.1109/MS.2007.2
7. Doux AL (2022) Bitsy. GitHub. https://github.com/le-doux/bitsy. Accessed 18 Jun 2022
8. Finley K (2019) You too can make these fun games (no experience necessary). Wired. https://www.wired.com/story/you-make-fun-games-no-experience/. Accessed 18 Jun 2022
9. Reed E (2020) From tool to community to style: the influence of software tools on game development communities and aesthetics. In: Clarke MJ, Wang C (eds) Indie games in the digital age. Bloomsbury Academic, London, pp 99–122. https://doi.org/10.5040/9781501356421.0010. Accessed 18 Jun 2022
10. Dixon A (2018) How small game makers found their community with Bitsy. Rock, Paper, Shotgun. https://www.rockpapershotgun.com/how-small-game-makers-found-their-community-with-bitsy. Accessed 18 Jun 2022
11. Kelly A (2020) People are making amazing, tiny games with this free tool, and I can't get enough of them. PC Gamer. https://www.pcgamer.com/people-are-making-amazing-tiny-games-with-this-free-tool-and-i-cant-get-enough-of-them/. Accessed 18 Jun 2022
12. LeBlanc SS (2022) Bitsy hacks. GitHub. https://github.com/seleb/bitsy-hacks. Accessed 18 Jun 2022
13. Colson D (2022) Unreal ink. GitHub. https://github.com/DavidColson/UnrealInk. Accessed 18 Jun 2022
14. Lohse Y (2022) y-lohse/inkjs. GitHub. https://github.com/y-lohse/inkjs. Accessed 18 Jun 2022
15. Writing with ink. inkle. GitHub (2022) https://github.com/inkle/ink/blob/master/Documentation/WritingWithInk.md. Accessed 18 Jun 2022
16. Cox D, Howard T (2020) Unofficial ink cookbook. GitHub. https://github.com/videlais/Unofficial-Ink-Cookbook. Accessed 18 Jun 2022
17. Cox D (2021) Hands-on dynamic story scripting with ink: create dialogue and procedural storytelling systems for unity projects. Packt Publishing

18. Reed A (2011) Creating interactive fiction with Inform 7. Course Technology, Cengage Learning, Boston, MA
19. Salter A, Moulthrop S (2021) Twining: critical and creative approaches to hypertext narratives. Amherst College Press
20. Jane F (2014) Untangling Twine: a platform study. In: DiGRA 2013—Proceedings of the 2013 DiGRA international conference: DeFragging game studies. http://www.digra.org/digital-lib rary/publications/untangling-twine-a-platform-study/
21. Tran KM (2016) "Her story was complex": a Twine workshop for ten- to twelve-year-old girls. E-Learn Digit Media 13:212–226. https://doi.org/10.1177/2042753016689635
22. Salter A (2016) Playing at empathy: representing and experiencing emotional growth through Twine games. In: 2016 IEEE international conference on serious games and applications for health (SeGAH). IEEE, Orlando, FL, USA, pp 1–8. https://doi.org/10.1109/SeGAH.2016.758 6272
23. Barbara J (2020) Twine and DooM as authoring tools in teaching IDN design of LudoNarrative dissonance. In: Bosser A-G, Millard DE, Hargood C (eds) Interactive storytelling. Springer International Publishing, Cham, pp 120–124. https://doi.org/10.1007/978-3-030-62516-0_11
24. Anthropy A (2012) How to make games with Twine. http://www.auntiepixelante.com/twineInte rnetArchive, https://web.archive.org/web/20120920233553/, http://www.auntiepixelante.com/ twine. Accessed 19 Feb 2022
25. Klimas C (2012) Writing with Twee. http://gimcrackd.com/etc/doc/InternetArchive, https:// web.archive.org/web/20120901011337/, http://gimcrackd.com/etc/doc/. Accessed 03 Mar 2022
26. Anthropy A (2012) Rise of the videogame zinesters: how freaks, normals, amateurs, artists, dreamers, dropouts, queers, housewives, and people like you are taking back an art form. Seven Stories Press, New York
27. Ford M (2016) Writing interactive fiction with Twine. Que, Indianapolis, Indiana
28. Bernardi J (2013) Choose your own adventure-maker: Twine and the art of personal games. Vice. https://www.vice.com/en/article/xyyp9a/twine-and-the-art-of-personal-games. Accessed 06 Oct 2022
29. Harvey A (2014) Democratization, depoliticization, and the queering of game design. G|A|M|E. 3/2014. https://www.gamejournal.it/3_harvey/
30. Ellison C (2013) Anna Anthropy and the Twine revolution. The Guardian. https://www.thegua rdian.com/technology/gamesblog/2013/apr/10/anna-anthropy-twine-revolution
31. Arnott L (2022) Harlowe 3.2.3 manual. https://twine2.neocities.org/. Accessed 03 Mar 2022
32. Edwards TM (2021) SugarCube v2 documentation. https://www.motoslave.net/sugarcube/2/ docs/. Accessed 03 Mar 2022
33. Rauf D (2020) Coding activities for writing stories in Twine. Rosen Publishing, New York
34. Kirilloff G (2021) Interactive fiction in the humanities classroom: how to create interactive text games using Twine. Programming Historian

The Authoring Problem is a Publishing Problem

Mark Bernstein

Abstract Publishers connect readers and writers. The literary economy with its diverse currencies—cash, attention, academic tenure—is not an inescapable natural phenomenon, but is continually reshaped by editors, manufacturers, booksellers, and critics. Central aspects of today's literary economy would have been unexpected and even astonishing a few decades back, while customs and practices that we take for granted arose from temporary policies adopted almost a century ago. Fashion, talent, and critical success all enter into the story, but so, too, do details of the accounting practices of booksellers and the real-estate expenses of local pharmacies and neighborhood newsstands. This chapter examines how the literary economy and the practices of the book trade have shaped interactive media through the course of 35 years and considers what aspects of that economy are now most liable to transformation.

1 The Publishing Problem

Publishers connect writers and readers [24]. The authoring problem that confronts interactive digital narratives is a publishing problem: we do not yet know how to connect these interactive creations to the readers who need them.

There are many works and many readers; matching works and readers is hard work.

Beginning in the 1980s, my firm Eastgate Systems began to publish "serious hypertexts"—interactive digital fiction, nonfiction, and poetry. Ours was arguably the first commercial enterprise to explore literary interactive narrative, and we considered this effort, at first, a service to the research community; by making available a body of "standard" hypertext works, we would free research groups from the necessity of writing their own hypertexts—each tailored for each laboratory's system. Some of the work we published attained significant critical success [14, 15, 26, 39, 29].

M. Bernstein (✉)
Eastgate Systems, Inc., 134 Main Street, Watertown, MA 02472, USA
e-mail: bernstein@eastgate.com

The published titles were profitable, albeit on a small scale (cf. [59]); sales depended primarily on direct mail marketing to an audience of adventurous literary tastes [19].

I assumed from the start that the best metaphor for interactive digital narratives was the book. Other early publishers of digital literature looked to different models. Bob Stein, at Voyager, thought the promising metaphor was cinema. Eastgate had editors, Voyager had producers. Voyager saw new media through the prism of "expanded books"—books with an admixture of illustration and apparatus—and assumed that the film industry's model of specialized craftspeople would most efficiently facilitate their production. Though he never fully embraced the cinematic parallel, Robert Coover found this approach persuasive [16]. Stein also assumed that new media would share a core affliction of the film industry: a narrow distribution channel. Films needed theaters to reach an audience; Voyager worked hard to gain distribution and to generate the sort of buzz that would convince retailers to pay attention.

Jaime Levy's Electronic Hollywood, on the other hand, saw the music business (as it existed in the 1980s) as a better model for emulation. There was only one Hollywood, but music was thoroughly Balkanized, divided into numerous discrete spheres that were separated by race, class, region, politics and style. Anyone in 1987 might see *Platoon* or *The Last Emperor*, but the audiences for Michael Jackson, Cher, Stevie Wonder, Elton John, Bruce Springsteen, Madonna, U2, Def Leppard, and Whitney Houston were largely disjoint. All these musicians had best-selling singles around the time of the first ACM Hypertext Conference. Moreover, it was possible in music (though seldom in film) to make money from a small segment even if that segment seldom or never put your artists at the top of the charts: Motown, Memphis, and Blues were just a few of many examples. Music, like film, was driven by buzz, but that buzz was generated in small communities of enthusiasts [11, 31, 62]; Levy saw an opportunity to build an audience through retail influencers.

Each of these efforts saw notable successes. In the generation since, we have seen great technological leaps and made important conceptual strides. Considerable creative work has expanded our vision of interactive literature. Yet we have not constructed an audience for thoughtful interactive narratives: the authoring problem is a publishing problem.

2 Book Publishing

My expectation that the world of publishing interactive digital narratives would reflect core aspects of the book world was not based on a desire to slavishly imitate every aspect of contemporary trade publishing, and still less by nostalgia for an imaginary past in which our ancestors enjoyed the smell of fine, leather-bound volumes beside the manorial fireplace [3]. Rather, the core problems of book publishing seem likely to become the core problems of any economy in which digital narratives are produced and consumed. Such economies are neither divinely ordained nor immutable: they are created by people and can be changed, intentionally or otherwise [2].

First: there are lots of books [49, 67]. We have—and we want—stories about fathers and sons, sons and lovers, good sons, prodigal sons, wayward sons, sons of witches, native sons, and all my sons. Tomorrow, we may want a different sort of narrative, one that describes how to assemble your new bicycle, how to get your schooner back to shore, or how to make friends and influence people. Worldwide, about a million titles appear each year [67], a quantity astronomically greater than was produced in the third century BCE when Ecclesiastes complained that "of making many books there is no end."

The cost of writing, manufacturing, and marketing a book is modest. Many books take a year to write, and we expect the first-time writers we call "doctoral students" to research and write a demanding work in two or three. A publisher can earn a profit on a book that sells a few thousand copies. Other media are not equally fortunate. Before it can reach an audience, a film must be exhibited in theaters—expensive, dedicated real-estate investments—in cities and towns around the world. Since a film must bear these real-estate costs, an additional investment of vast fixed costs in development and production is easily justified [2]. Books are not like that: for several centuries, the retail price of a book has tracked the price of a restaurant dinner.

Most books reach a modest audience: a Harvard librarian observed that "as a librarian I am conscious that perhaps the majority of the books ever printed have rarely been read." [1] The expense of purchasing a book is typically dwarfed by the labor cost of reading it. The value that readers receive from a book, moreover, will often greatly exceed what readers pay for the privilege. Three or four textbooks will take you to the frontiers of human knowledge in physics or computer science [47]. The right book at the right moment can change everything and often has: consider *Common Sense, Capital, The Interpretation of Dreams, The Lives of Black Folk, Catch-22,* or *Our Bodies Ourselves.* Hannah Arendt's *The Origins Of Totalitarianism,* Rachel Carson's *Silent Spring,* and John Hersey's *Hiroshima* changed the course of nations.

Finally, just as books are numerous, so are readers and their needs. Many people read only a few books a year, and a few read more than two hundred. Readers must choose with care. It can be difficult for a good book to find the readers it deserves.

This combination of factors—the plenitude of books and their variousness—creates unusual economic challenges. Indeed, the experience of contemporary shopping was first defined by the bookstore, a place where you personally examined packaged and branded merchandise that was displayed on shelves, rather than instructing a shop clerk to fetch what you require from the storeroom. Supermarkets were designed to emulate early modern bookstores [51].

3 Book Worlds

We are inclined to think that books are an ancient technology that gradually has been brought to perfection, and that the book world has always been as it is. This is a mistake: books change constantly, and the economies that surround them change as well. Interactive digital stories are a far cry from the books that Gutenberg knew, and farther still from the book world described in Jeremiah 36:32.

> Then took Jeremiah another roll, and gave it to Baruch the scribe, the son of Neriah; who wrote therein from the mouth of Jeremiah all the words of the book which Jehoiakim king of Judah had burned in the fire: and there were added besides unto them many like words.

Books have changed over the generations as new technologies provide new opportunities for making and receiving them. The size of the book in antiquity—for example, the "book of Jeremiah" mentioned above—was limited by the size of a scroll that would be comfortable to hold [9]. The size of scrolls meant that large works—Pliny's *Natural History* runs to 37 books, and Livy's *From The Foundation Of Rome* once spanned 142—were difficult to store and inconvenient to access. This shaped the design of ancient libraries [52]. The replacement of scrolls by the codex book was accelerated because Jews and Christians created a demand for their libraries of canonical writing. The size of books changed as readers gained access to interior light, and then to eyeglasses, and as they found it useful to carry some books about with them either for reference or for display [1]. Changes in print technology, paper production, and bookbinding facilitated larger print runs [34], freer use of illustration [65], and most recently, electronic distribution of e-books [56].

The way readers acquire books has changed dramatically as well. When I was young, one bought serious books—real books—at a bookstore: in Chicago, either from Kroch's and Brentano's, which was big and downtown, or from Stuart Brent [5], which was smaller and smarter. You could buy paperback best-sellers and science fiction at the pharmacy, too: magazine distributors called "rack jobbers" rented retail space in established stores and stocked their racks with whatever titles they thought might sell at the moment. If someone bought a copy, the jobber collected a share. If not, the jobber would replace the stock with fresher stock [24, 55].

This was still the book world of Harvard Square in the late 70 s: you had Booksmith and Wordsworth, The Coop (which was loosely connected to Harvard), and Harvard Books (which was not but was the brainiest store in the neighborhood). You had Grolier (poetry) and Schoenhoff's (foreign languages). You had tons of used bookstores [66].

In the 80 s, I got my degree and wound up in Wilmington, Delaware, where you bought your books (and nearly everything else) in a mall of chain stores. Chain stores were efficient for bookselling because large chains actually had enough aggregate volume to know what was selling [55]. Sales results of one day in one store seldom generate reliable statistics, but chains had scores of stores, reporting daily. Still, the trends you could see were simply the trends happening everywhere. The chains made Oprah Winfrey a vast influence over literary taste because she had a television audience and occasionally mentioned a book.

In time, the little mall stores, which had outcompeted many individual booksellers, were themselves overcome by big Borders outlets and even bigger fortresses of Barnes and Noble. Then, Amazon clobbered everyone. Today, Amazon alone accounts for about half of all trade book sales [56].

4 Other Worlds

Other book worlds exist alongside the world we know. Book worlds in other languages predate our Anglophone world and continue outside it.

The rate at which new works appear has a terrific impact on the way people think about books. If a new novel in your language appears a few times a year, then you and your fellow readers might read pretty much everything and still find yourself without enough to talk about. If there is a new book every week, it is a different matter: it may be hard to read everything, but there is plenty to discuss—if only what you need to read next [49].

Other book worlds are separated by specificity of interest, which often corresponds to an audience addressable by an efficient but separate sales channel. A book world of particular importance to interactive narrative, and one very much in our minds in Eastgate's early years, is literary publishing. Literary publishers accept that the audience for the most sophisticated and serious contemporary writing may be small—not least because avant-garde work addresses other avant-garde work and the medium itself. It demands a reader who already knows a lot [28]. Knowing that they cannot hope for hugely profitable best-sellers, literary writers and publishers strive instead to acquire intellectual and symbolic capital. Paying their authors little and their staffs poorly, literary publishing hopes to reward pioneers while finding enough cash to pay printers and the post office [37].

Different traditions and regulatory forces change other book worlds. In the U.S. and Great Britain, most authors are represented by agents; in France, agents are uncommon [41]. The U.S. Commercial Code requires manufacturers (like publishers) to offer the same prices and trade terms to all comparable buyers, but in Britain a publisher may offer preferential or exclusive terms to specific supermarkets [60]. Discounting became the core value proposition of U.S. bookseller chains in the 1990s; in France and elsewhere in Europe, discounting of books was outlawed.

Eastgate's hope had been to create a book world conducive to and enthusiastic for interactive digital narratives [19]. The rewards of changing the literary landscape are themselves not always what they are cracked up to be.

Nobody really wants to be James Joyce, though, when it comes down to it. Totally inaccessible and publishing poison, forced to self-publish with the help of two (inadequately-celebrated) lesbians, thought to be a madman, and still cursed to this day. No one really wants to be James Joyce, living in borderline poverty with an insane daughter and a layabout son, quietly changing the world. [17]

Indirect rewards do matter. Teaching jobs are nice; so is tenure. Prizes can buy groceries [40]. Indirect economies are inefficient and generally undesirable, but at times indirect rewards are the rewards that can be won.

Alternate book worlds are sometimes cultivated by publishers or generated by aesthetic movements, but they may also emerge simply because some group of potential customers is easily addressed in a particular place. The growth of newspapers was intimately tied to London and Edinburgh coffee houses, because that was where you could find people with the time and money to support newspapers and the need for news [32]. The growth of computer games was spurred by the discovery that groups of preadolescent boys across the U.S. had a habit of spending after-school hours at a specific chain toy store, and could be persuaded to buy computer games if they were packaged to appeal to preadolescent boys. Girls congregated in different stores; those stores had no interest in selling computer games and even a dedicated effort to reach girls ultimately failed [42].

Book worlds are often separated by place, by topical interest, or by aesthetics, but they may also be organized along other lines. In 1843, Charles Dickens published the very popular (and profitable) novella, *A Christmas Carol.* Its strong sales encouraged Dickens to craft Christmas books annually through 1848. (In 1843, Dickens was living from month to month; by 1848, the success of *Dombey and Sons* had relieved this pressure and the Christmas stories were no longer essential to the household budget.) The subsequent Christmas books did not receive the same critical acclaim as *A Christmas Carol,* but they sold very well: people liked the idea of getting a Christmas story in December. Dickens had created a book world built on a seasonal habit [61]. The Icelandic *Jólabókaflóðið* (Christmas book flood), a tradition that grew out of World War II rationing, is a book world with its own customs and dynamics.

5   Finance

Let us pause for a moment to consider finance. An interactive narrative is to be published: money will be required to do that. How much money is needed, and where is it to be found?

The work that is to be published may not yet be complete. The author might require money for travel, research, and to purchase groceries. Even if the work is complete, it may require revision. If the work is a book, it must be typeset, printed, and bound. An interactive digital narrative may not require cloth covers, but might need retail packaging, promotional materials, documentation, and Web and social media support. Review copies must be delivered to publications that commission and publish reviews. Advertising may need to be created and booked. Author tours— an important promotional innovation in the late twentieth century [25]—require planning and funding.

A publisher can seldom borrow the funds needed to publish an interactive narrative. This is not new: a peculiar fact of the book world of the seventeenth and eighteenth centuries was that printers had little or no access to bank financing. First, printers were mechanics who worked with their hands; they were not gentlemen and not worthy of credit. Indeed, the first John Murray went to considerable expense to purchase a costly West End house specifically to assert a tenuous claim, if not to gentility, at least to a sort of presentability [44].

Second, the nature of the book trade made the publisher's inventory worthless as collateral. If a debtor failed to repay a loan on a house, the bank knew that it could readily sell that house to recover the remaining debt. If a cloth merchant defaulted, the bank could be reasonably confident that the local market could absorb a warehouse of silks and satins. But local markets have limited capacity to absorb any one specific book; even in a world where almost anyone might want *some* book, hardly anyone wants any specific book.

Printers acquired manufacturing facilities sufficient to meet peak production needs; if they failed so to do, they would be forced in busy times to turn away business, sending it to their competitors. At less busy times, they used slack equipment and idle staff to print things they might sell to customers who visited their shop. Printing benefits from scale; the first copy is very costly and additional copies cost far less. It made sense, then, to print editions of hundreds or even thousands of copies, because even if the immediate market was modest, it might prove possible to sell additional copies at a later time or a greater distance. This slow, long-distance selling relied on professional contacts and took lots of time: it was not something a banker could expect to do [27].

These business practices might be thought to be of merely antiquarian interest, but they continue to shape publishing today. A bookseller stocks thousands of individual titles; a large store might stock 70,000 [56]. But throughout much of the world, most of these titles may be returned for credit; bookseller inventory is held on consignment and stays on the balance sheet of the publisher, not the bookseller. This practice kept many U.S. booksellers afloat through the Great Depression, but it persists a century later. Given this arrangement, booksellers naturally want to stock books most likely to sell rapidly while also ensuring sufficient variety to meet the requirements of shoppers, and these factors have far-reaching impact on the length of time that books remain available in stores [55, 59]. The same considerations shape the environment that interactive digital narratives must inhabit.

5.1   Finance and Interactive Digital Narratives

Interactive digital narratives are stories, and as we have already noted, the capital needed to tell a story in print is modest and fairly predictable. You need to fund a writer for a period that might range from a few weeks to a few years, and you need to pay for the preparation and production of an economically viable press run. Modern publishers, large and small, are in the business of making investments on this modest scale to put stories before audiences.

But interactive digital narratives are also software. The capital required to design and implement software is sometimes modest, and much of our most-admired software was originally crafted by individuals or small teams over a short span of years [6]. The management of software projects, however, is notoriously tricky, and bad (though sensible) early decisions sometimes lead to late and unexpected failure. Partly in consequence of this risk, software development is typically funded through risk capital: individual investors and firms jointly risk modest sums on a portfolio of attractive proposals. Many projects will fail, but investors trust that the success of others will cover these losses [64].

The viability of this investment model depends, in turn, on each product's ability to establish a barrier to entry. Absent such a barrier, predatory competitors could simply wait for a software developer to complete their design, and then mimic the completed design. Various barriers can be found. For example, if the product can be patented, the originator has exclusive rights to its use for a number of years. If the product is very large and complex, the originator's expertise may be a sufficient barrier: if your firm already employs all the leading experts in generating convincing images of explosions, it may be difficult for a competitor to build a team to duplicate your computer graphics. Customers themselves can form a barrier to entry: if you can secure most of the potential marketplace before competitors have time to enter, little will be left for your competitors.

Unfortunately, none of these barriers are likely to be available to an interactive narrative. The software development effort may require funding by the author or the publisher [53], or the use of whatever tools are already available [54].

6 Acquisition

Sachez que sur près de trois mille manuscrits reçus chaque année par notre maison, nous n'en retenons que deux ou trois.—Antoine Laurain Le Service des manuscrits (2020)

   You should know that out of nearly three thousand manuscripts received each year by our house, we acquire only two or three.—Antoine Laurain, The Readers' Room (2020)

The first challenge facing a trade publisher is, and has always been, finding something to publish. In practice, an acquisitions editor identifies work they wish to publish. Typically, the acquiring editor must secure the support of more senior editors or of an editorial committee. At this point, the editor and the author (or their agent) negotiate terms of a publishing contract—primarily, the size of an advance against royalties, the rate of royalty, and the disposition of such subsidiary rights as foreign language rights, film rights, and serial rights. In selecting work to publish and in setting terms, it is essential that the publisher typically pay enough to keep the author afloat, and that typical works sell well enough to keep the publisher afloat [24].

A century ago, it was entirely possible to earn a living, often a good living, from writing. A writer could travel extensively and pay for the journey with a bit of writing [18, 23]. Nancy Mitford, daughter of Lord Redesdale, was able to escape genteel poverty and patronize Chanel after the publication of *Love In A Cold Climate* [48]. Raymond Chandler, having lost an aircraft company in the Great Depression, salvaged his finances by rewriting Erle Stanley Gardner until he understood the bones of the mystery [12].

Today, few people make their living primarily by writing trade books, a fact with broad societal and aesthetic ramifications. "The supply of fiction far outpaces the demand," reports editor Donna Shear [57]. To be a well-regarded novelist carries more cachet than to be a writer of appliance instruction manuals, but the technical writer is likely to earn more, and have a more stable income. Many writers receive salaries for serving as university writing instructors, and writing programs were in fact the homes of many early electronic writers.

This situation creates an indirect economy. To be published—and well published—grants prestige, and prestige leads in turn to desirable teaching jobs. New titles secure one's position, and their absence endangers academic tranquility [10].

In the twentieth century, literary competitions became an important route to publishing and to recognition [40]. The centrality of competition got started in 1919 with the Yale Series for Younger Poets, which offered publication as a prize. Such competitions have been an important route to recognition for poets and avant-garde writers; selection by a prominent judge (and the subsequent publicity) focuses attention on a writer who might otherwise be obscure. Notable awards include the Robert Coover Award, given by the Electronic Literature Organization, whose winner receives $1000, and the Interactive Fiction Competition, sponsored by the Interactive Fiction Technology Foundation, whose winner currently receives about $250. The prestige of winning, of course, may be worth substantially more than the cash prize.

Publishers of interactive digital narratives face several handicaps in dealing with the indirect economy of prestige and promotion. First, legacy players—whether commercial publishers, universities, or foundations—inherit the prestige of age, where a new entrant must establish themselves in the minds of potential contributors and judges. Second, indirect economies are inefficient: dollars may be converted to fame or to tenure credit just as dollars can be converted to euros, but the latter is faster, more reliable, and more predictable.

7 Production

The finished work must fit the constraints, tacit as well as explicit, of the sales channel. If an interactive story is to be sold by booksellers, it must be the sort of thing that booksellers sell, or can imagine themselves selling. At present, a trade book typically costs $30 or less, is rectangular, and can be identified and examined by shoppers while it is on the shelf. These are all familiar affordances of the modern codex book, but none of these properties are necessities of interactive digital stories.

For example, a digital story might be priced much less than $30. In that case, the bookseller will consider the shelf space it occupies. If that were devoted to a conventional $30 book, the bookseller would expect to keep perhaps 60% of the sales price, or $18. If, on average, the store turns over its stock three times a year, that space represents $54 in annual revenue. If the digital story costs $5, the bookseller is going to have to sell a lot of them. If the digital story retails for $100, the bookseller only has to sell one of them a year to pay for the space it occupies on the shelf, but may be anxious about the potential loss should it be damaged or stolen. The higher price point would be no deterrent to retailers accustomed to more costly merchandise, and *Agrippa: The Book Of The Dead* did establish that art galleries could sell new media successfully.

Above all, bookstores need a spine if they are to sell interactive narratives. Book-sellers today sell lots of non-book merchandise—coffee, postcards, and games—but their vocation is the book. At Eastgate, we made prodigious efforts to develop a package that was sufficiently book-like for stores to accept, but did not appear to be a simulacrum of a book. Provision for efficient display, either face-out (if the bookseller wants to feature it) or spine-out (as almost all books in the store will be displayed) was indispensable. Developing short-run packaging for hypertexts that could withstand customer handling and that had a spine was indispensable to the book channel. We never found an ideal solution, but marketing through booksellers was probably impractical from the start; booksellers in the 1990s were either huge chains (for whom we could do little) or struggling independents. We could help stores by arranging signings and readings, workshops and demonstrations, but it was never going to make a crucial difference to any store's survival.

What worked for Eastgate was direct sales to our own customers, and to people who read about hypertext and were willing to call a toll-free number to order a copy sight-unseen. For direct sales, durability was crucial. Packability mattered as well: life was far easier if the hypertexts people wanted to buy were all the same size and fit into the same box.

8   Distribution and Marketing

Once the work has been produced and packaged, it must be made available for purchase, and people who might want to purchase it must be made aware of its avail-ability. In the U.S. and the U.K. in the late twentieth century, when Eastgate began to sell hypertexts, trade publishers sold books to booksellers at a 40% discount. Distrib-utors received a modestly larger discount, and offered booksellers an opportunity to combine orders from several publishers in one shipment, reducing their paperwork. Booksellers expected to return unsold books for credit.

Readers learned of new books from reviews in newspapers and magazines. Through the 1950s, American publishers advertised in magazines, newspapers, mass transit placards, and billboards. Later, advertising lost traction [25], and late in the century it was understood that book advertising was aimed at booksellers, not readers [55].

These arrangements had existed since the Great Depression and seemed eternal. They would not last, and matters were quite different at other times and in other places. But just as the constraints of production shapes book worlds, the needs of distribution and marketing matter.

8.1   Subscriptions

In the early modern era, it was common for prospective authors to solicit advance subscriptions, committing buyers to purchase a new book on publication. Subscriptions were particularly important to expensively illustrated titles like Audubon's *Birds Of America*. The subscription model has been revived with great success by Kickstarter and similar firms. In 2020, Kickstarter contributors pledged $25.6 M to fund new titles. Subscriptions ameliorate or remove the publisher's risk and capital requirements, shifting some of the burden of advance marketing to the author. Subscription sales work best when the audience can easily anticipate the work and foresee how useful it will prove—both difficult assertions for innovative works to make. This is not always an insuperable obstacle: *Lady Chatterly's Lover* was published by subscription. Convincing people to commit to purchasing a work they cannot examine can be a difficult proposition. Nevertheless, this model has been attractive to authors and prospective publishers in need of capital.

8.2   Binding and Branding

Early modern booksellers sold books unbound; readers would bind books to match their decor, taste, and budget. Buying books in sheets and having them bound could be more convenient for the buyer, and because binding did not enjoy great economies of scale, custom binding did not cost much more. The English-language book trade shifted to mass-produced, uniformly bound editions not from the efficiency of manufacture, but from the efficiency of shipping. When most of your books were sold over the counter at the front of your print shop, custom binding made sense; as an increasing share of your print run would be dispatched to distant cities, the protection afforded by a binding and dust cover became increasingly important. This tension remains in digital narratives: do we want to bear the cost of creating an attractive artifact, or is our product to be disembodied bits on the wire?

A further tension in binding and cover design is that between the desire to sell a specific volume and the desire to build the publisher's brand. Ideally, publishers have always wanted to be associated with particular excellence in the minds of their audience—ideally excellence sufficient to recommend their books of whatever kind. This has always been a difficult proposition: readers in 1841 knew and cared that *The Old Curiosity Shop* was written by Charles Dickens, but few made a point of noting that it was published by Chapman and Hall. They looked for "the next Dickens," not "the latest Chapman and Hall," just as a later generation would keenly discuss the merits of Charlie Chaplin or Alfred Hitchcock without caring greatly who worked for Warner and which films came from Metro-Goldwyn-Mayer.

Yet some publishers have, for a time, created a recognizable and profitable brand—often by means of adopting a recognizable visual style. Harper Bros., for example, built its business in the 1820s by offering American editions of selected British writers in uniform bindings [8]. A library, school, or avid reader could order a selection of books from Harper that would fit together on a shelf and shared a common recommendation—an important factor for small-town buyers trying to build a library in the wilderness.

In the 1950s, Barney Rosset's Grove Press worked to establish a reputation for publishing daring work that others could not understand or were too intimidated to publish: Lawrence, Brecht, Kerouac, and Henry Miller [45]. Grove Press covers adopted a minimalist graphic vocabulary that was instantly recognizable on the shelf. In the 1980s, category publishers Soho—a specialist in mystery—and O'Reilly—specializing in technical documentation—each built brands on the basis of uniform editorial standards and uniform cover design. Branding has sometimes been achieved in interactive digital narratives, most notably by Infocom, but the decline of retail software businesses and the growth of electronic delivery have made visual branding difficult.

8.3 Books in Backwaters

The production of English-language books was long focused in London, and indeed in a single neighborhood adjoining the churchyard of St. Paul's. Provincial readers had to send for books, sight unseen, or to rely on the taste and acumen of local booksellers, who were seldom numerous [22]. What was inconvenient to Jane Austen's England, however, was an insuperable obstacle through much of the new United States. The prosperous farms of the Chesapeake, for example, though convenient to navigable bays and rivers, were, in the early nineteenth century, at the outer limit of the Philadelphia trade zone. There was plenty of money to buy books, but there was no population center in which a store might thrive.

Faced with an imprudent overrun of Oliver Goldsmith's *History Of The Earth And Animated Nature,* Philadelphia publisher William Carey struck a deal with an itinerant Methodist minister, Mason Weems [27]. If prosperous families had no bookstore to visit, Weems would bring the books to the families—taking orders as he went, and delivering books on his next call. Weems also arranged for storekeepers to accept a selection of inexpensive books on consignment, again accepting payment for sales when he next visited. This business model did not ultimately succeed—the costs of travel exceeded the revenues that could be obtained—but it showed how a reading culture could be cultivated outside the great cities. Similar promotional efforts have been important throughout the history of interactive digital narrative: Jamie Levy's Electronic Hollywood, the circle of Interactive Fiction fans surrounding Emily Short and Graham Nelson, and the Twine community are all examples.

The inaccessibility of bookstores to small-town and rural readers lent prominence to direct mail book clubs in American publishing. Harry Scherman's "Book Of The Month Club", launched in 1926, gave hundreds of thousands of readers access to cutting-edge books. Its Doubleday competitor, The Literary Guild, was equally successful in telling America what it needed to read [20]. This influence was not always sound, as being named "Book Of The Month" became a sort of lottery ticket for new titles, capable of making careers at the whim of a small panel of "judges". It might have been preferable to be able to browse books and to select those you wanted, but being told what was hot in the big cities did connect small-town intellectuals with the nation—an influence not to be underestimated for shaping taste [43].

Book clubs and other forms of direct marketing are able to spend less on the physical characteristics of the work, and on non-captive marketing, because the consumer purchased the product before receiving it. The works must ultimately please the recipient, but the recipient also wants to be pleased, much as the theater audience at the start of the performance wants the production to validate their decision to spend time and money on attending this show and not another. This was, for Eastgate, a great attraction: our short-run titles could not look as good as those produced by game publishers, but we believed an audience for serious hypertext fiction could be found, and that it would be receptive to pretty much any title of merit. This was true—on a small scale, at least—until the World Wide Web became ubiquitous. After that, there really was too much to read.

9 Tilling the Field

An editor's job does not end when the revised text is sent for production, or when the galley proofs go out to reviewers. There is always the next book, and it is never too soon to consider what that book might be.

9.1 Big Names

Through much of his legendary career at The New Yorker, editor Harold Ross became known for an unending quest to find a manager or successor who would solve all his problems. This obsession was strange because, to a first approximation, Ross had no problems: his New Yorker was a perfect fit for the upper-middle-class readers his publisher addressed and to which his advertisers clamored for access [45]. Insecure and shy, he knew how to edit for an audience that was terrified of being found out. Pleasing this audience required tact; it was important to explain everything that might be unfamiliar to a middle-aged banker or to the high-school dropout, but never to suggest that any explanation was needed.

From the very beginning of my work publishing digital narratives, people advised me to seek a writer who would compel the audience's attention, a big name who would set the new medium aflame. This is not really how new media have succeeded historically [4]: cinema, for example, created its own stars. So did the Elizabethan theater. Anyway, our chronic shortage of capital meant that we never came close to a hot property.

Others tried harder, but their success was mixed. Stephen King self-published an electronic novella, *Riding The Bullet,* in 2000 with initial sales of 600,000 copies and revenues of $1.5 million [60, 63], but this was an ebook, not a hypertext, and Stephen King has one of the most loyal reading audiences ever assembled. William Gibson published *Agrippa: The Book Of The Dead* in a very limited Deluxe Edition at $1500, which erased itself after it was read; Agrippa was performance art, or perhaps gallery work, rather than interactive narrative. Paul La Farge proposed [38] that the problem was simple incompetence: "the early hypertextualists just weren't good enough writers to carry off such a difficult form."

One important facet of the book world is that, while many people have a good sense of what can be made into a good book and what cannot, no one is able to predict which books will sell and which will not [60]. Agents and editors find books unexpectedly [41]. Experience is far from infallible: Tom Clancy's first best-seller, *The Hunt For Red October*, was published by a small specialty press, and *Catch-22*, the great novel of the Second World War, was turned down repeatedly [25]. Few readers know which books, once purchased, they will eventually read: Nick Hornby published monthly lists of "books bought" and "books read" in *The Believer,* but the two seldom coincided [30].

9.2   An Awkward Conversation

Books converse with other books. A novel reacts to the author's previous work, and also to novels written in response to that work, or that respond to the tradition in which the writer is working. Publishers are well placed to shape that discussion, to guide it toward interesting and productive channels while avoiding acrimonies and disputes that are mere distractions [7, 20]. Indeed, the historical literary worlds we recall most fondly are characterized by clusters of people who strove against each other: fifth-century Attic drama and philosophy, Julio-Claudian scholarship and poetry, and Tudor-Stuart drama come to mind. Compact clusters can be extraordinarily interesting, whether located in the center of things (Victorian London, Paris between the Wars) or in the middle of nowhere (Concord, Massachusetts). Publishers are well situated to assuage the scrapes and bruises to which any vigorous discussion is prone.

Because new media are new, curating this conversation can be extraordinarily difficult. Digital storytellers who met with some unexpected success sometimes dismissed it as an accident. (Storytellers who met with unexpected setbacks were inclined to blame their publisher [36]). In effect, this placed writers in tension, on the one hand, with other writers, and on the other hand, with the medium. The openness of hypertext to intertextuality, and the fondness of late Modernism for intertextual intrusions, tended to place the dialogue between writer and medium in the center of the work. The dialogue between writers took place elsewhere, over late-night glasses of wine or in tenure-committee deliberations. There, it was far harder for a mere publisher to smooth things over.

As interactive digital narrative began to gain audience and critical attention, the dictates of time and biology scheduled a generational dispute. This was hard to see at the time, in part because the intertextuality of early fictions (and their concern with structure) were also under challenge. In 1994, critic Sven Birkerts was chiefly hoping to keep the ramparts of the codex book from being overrun by the barbarian electronic horde [3], but by 1997 the ground had shifted and Janet Murray would argue not that hypertext fiction was barbaric, but that it was over, already old-fashioned [50]. In 2001, Markku Eskillinen [21] viewed it all in the past tense, boasting that "The golden age of media essentialism—confusing readers with writers, links with intertextuality and texts with rhizomes…—has been over for a while now, along with some careers, and if that's the end of the world as we know it, I feel fine."

The hostility of this essay is characteristic of its moment, as was the centrality of career in this discussion of esoteric literary theory. Eskillinen's essay appeared a month before the dot-com collapse and the start of a global recession that would sour what was already a very bad academic job market. There were ripostes, of course, and counter-ripostes, battling over terminology that was obscure even to a specialist. Once the dinner guests began to exult in ending the careers of their fellow guests, the after-dinner conversation was likely to prove an ordeal.

9.3   The Next Book

Fiction writers build an audience not just from a single success, but also by developing a following over the course of numerous books [46]. In his memoir, Robert Gottlieb observed that, while he continues to write and edit nonfiction, he no longer edits novels because, at his age, he is not confident of his ability to shape not just a book but a career [25]. The rhythms of academe do not always fit easily into this pattern [10, 35], but the most early writers of interactive narrative have worked within, or aspire to entire, the academic orbit. This mismatch has exerted a number of deleterious effects. In particular, the key audience for much new media criticism has been university tenure committees, whose interests and judgment may not coincide with that of the reading world.

As a comparatively young publisher in a very young field, I gave far too little thought to each author's next work, and for their eighth or eighteenth. I was not alone in this, but it was a mistake.

10   The Problem of Publishing

The first generation of digital narratives failed to construct a literary economy that supports the work to which we aspire [2]. Such failures are not uncommon or excep-tional. These failures (or, charitably, limited and circumscribed successes) do not mean that we cannot succeed, but suggest the difficulty of the underlying task, which is to match readers with the work they need.

Looking back, it now seems clear that the audience for the earliest interactive digital narratives, the audience of the 1990s, was the wrong audience. That audience was deeply conflicted: it wanted high modernism, it wanted postmodern theory, and it wanted to have fun. It wanted all this simultaneously, and without too much effort and expense. These were incoherent desires and unsatisfiable longings, but every time is *sui generis* and the aftermath of Reagan, Thatcher, and AIDS was perhaps not conducive to literary consensus or even literary reflection. Our literature may indeed have been coping with the end of the world since the late eighteenth century [13], but at the end of the twentieth century nobody was feeling terrific about it.

The early audience was incoherent in its desires, and that incoherence fractured the field into myriad schools and disciplines, each with its own borders—self-imposed but rigorously policed: literary hypertext, digital storytelling, interactive digital narrative, visual novels, adventure games, interactive fiction, codewerk, Netzkunst, literary games, and many more. This fragmentation—and further segmentation by age and language—has complicated audience formation. If you liked early Hemingway and wanted to know what else to read, you could ask Gertrude Stein or stop by Shakespeare & Company. If you were an Elizabethan who liked Marlowe, it's likely that any Southwark barkeep could advise you that ticket to see young Shakespeare would not be a waste. But today, a devoted reader (or author) of Japanese-style visual novels might well find it difficult to find allied work from another community.

The work of building a new literary economy is not only finding an audience, but also working with that audience to create shared expectations of the work. Criticism of interactive digital narratives has focused narrowly on whether the work is worth buying, without much attention to what the work is trying to do. As a result, critics often wind up praising well-crafted kitsch with broad appeal, rather than taking the trouble to understand challenging work that addresses topics of specific interest. The developments of the Interactive Fiction world [58] and of the Twine community [54] are useful exceptions to this general rule[1]; in each case a small but dedicated cadre developed a critical apparatus sympathetic to their audience's specific concerns—dialogic storytelling and queer fiction, respectively. In contrast, literary hypertext and narrative games have received derisory and dismissive readings from distinguished critics who did not know how to approach the work [33] or who dismissed a body of work based on a selection ill-suited to their taste [3]. To know what the work asks, and what it requires, is consequential.

The early audience was the wrong audience. The publishing problem is, simply, the work of creating the right audience.

Acknowledgements I am grateful for advice from numerous colleagues, of whom I would particularly like to thank John Clute, Kathryn Cramer, Andy van Dam, Sarah Smith, Sally Starrels, and Adam Zehner for their patient assistance.

---

[1] For more on authoring communities, see Cox's chapter in this volume.

References

1. Amory H (1986) The trout and the milk: an ethnobibliographical talk. Harv Libr Bull 7(1):50–65
2. Bernstein M, Greco D (2008) Designing a new media economy. Genre 41(3/4):59–82
3. Birkerts S (1994) The gutenberg elegies. Faber and Faber
4. Bolter JD (1991) Writing space. Lawrence Erlbaum Associates
5. Brent S (1962) The seven stairs. Houghton, Mifflin
6. Brooks FP (2010) The design of design: essays from a computer scientist. Addison-Wesley
7. Brooks P (1986) Two park street. Houghton Mifflin
8. Casper SE (2010) Case study: Harper & Brothers. In: Gross RA, Kelley M (eds) An extensive republic: print, culture, and society in the new nation, 1790–1840. Published in association with the American Antiquarian Society by The University of North Carolina Press
9. Casson L (2001) Libraries in the ancient world. Yale University Press
10. Chabon M (1995) Wonder boys. Villard Books
11. Chabon M (2012) Telegraph avenue: a novel. Harper
12. Chandler R, MacShane F (1981) Selected letters of Raymond Chandler. Columbia University Press
13. Clute J (2011) Pardon this intrusion: fantastika in the world storm. Beccon Publications
14. Coover R (1992) The end of books. New York Times Book Rev 1
15. Coover R (1993) Hyperfiction: novels for computer. New York Times Book Rev 1
16. Coover R (2000) Literary hypertext: passing of the golden age. Feed Mag
17. Crispin J (2016) The self-hating book critic. In: Kurowski T, Miller W, Prufer K (eds) Literary publishing in the twenty-first century. Milkweed Editions
18. Delafield EM (1934) The provincial lady in America. Harper Bros
19. Ensslin A (2022) Pre-web digital publishing and the lore of electronic literature. Cambridge University Press
20. Epstein J (2002) Book business: publishing past, present, and future. W.W. Norton & Co.
21. Eskillinen M (2001) Cybertext theory: what an english professor should know before trying. Elect Book Rev
22. Fitzgerald P (1997) The bookshop. Houghton Mifflin
23. Fussell P (1980) Abroad: british literary traveling between the wars. Oxford University Press
24. Ginna P (2017) What editors do: the art, craft, and business of book editing. The University of Chicago Press
25. Gottlieb R (2016) Avid reader: a life. Farrar Straus and Giroux
26. Grant R (1993) Beyond books: never the same text twice. Washington Post Book World, pp 8–9
27. Green JN (2010) The rise of book publishing. In: Gross RA, Kelley M (eds) An extensive republic: print, culture, and society in the new nation, 1790–1840. Published in association with the American Antiquarian Society by The University of North Carolina Press
28. Greenberg C (1939) Avant-Garde and Kitsch. Partis Rev 34–49
29. Hayles NK (2005) My mother was a computer: digital subjects and literary texts. University of Chicago Press
30. Hornby N (2004) The polysyllabic spree. McSweeney's, Believer Books
31. Hornby N (1995) High fidelity. Riverhead Books
32. Johns A (1999) The nature of the book: print and knowledge in the making. University of Chicago Press
33. Kakutani M (1997) Never-ending saga. New York Times Mag 40–41
34. Kilgour FG (1998) The evolution of the book. Oxford University Press
35. Korelitz JH (2021) The plot. Celadon Books
36. Kunkel T (1995) Genius in disguise: Harold Ross of the New Yorker. Random House
37. Kurowski T, Miller W, Prufer K (2016) Literary publishing in the twenty-first century. Milkweed Editions
38. LaFarge P (2011) Luminous airplanes. Farrar, Straus and Giroux

39. Landow GP (1997) Hypertext 2.0: the convergence of contemporary critical theory and technology, 2nd edn. Johns Hopkins Press
40. Larimer K (2016) A culture of competition: some notes on writing contests & literary publishing. In: Kurowski T, Miller W, Prufer K (eds) Literary publishing in the twenty-first century, Milkweed Editions
41. Laurain A (2020) Le service des manuscrits. Flammarion
42. Laurel B (2001) Utopian entrepreneur. MIT Press
43. Lewis S (1919) Free air. Harcourt, Brace and Howe
44. McClay D (2018) Dear Mr Murray: letters to a gentleman publisher. John Murray
45. Menand L (2021) The free world: art and thought in the Cold War. Farrar, Straus and Giroux
46. Michener JA (1991) The novel. Random House
47. Misner CW, Thorne KS, Wheeler JA (1973) Gravitation. W. H. Freeman
48. Mitford N, Waugh E, Mosley C (1996) The letters of Nancy Mitford and Evelyn Waugh. Hodder & Stoughton
49. Moretti F (2007) Graphs, maps, trees: abstract models for a literary history. Verso
50. Murray J (1997) Hamlet on the holodeck: the future of narrative in cyberspace. The Free Press
51. Nash R (2016) What is the business of literature? In: Kurowski T, Miller W, Prufer K (eds) Literary publishing in the twenty-first century. Milkweed Editions
52. Packer JE (1997) The Forum of Trajan in Rome: a study of the monuments. University of California Press
53. Pears I (2016) Arcadia. Alfred A. Knopf
54. Salter A, Moulthrop S (2021) Twining: critical and creative approaches to hypertext narratives. Amherst College
55. Shatzkin L (1982) In cold type. Houghton Mifflin Company
56. Shatzkin M, Riger RP (2019) The book business. Oxford University Press
57. Shear D (2016) The view from a literary press. In: Kurowski T, Miller W, Prufer K (eds) Literary publishing in the twenty-first century. Milkweed Editions
58. Short E (2016) Beyond branching: quality-based, salience-based, and waypoint narrative structures. Emily Short's interactive storytelling
59. Stadler M (2016) The ends of the book: reading, economies and publics. In: Kurowski T, Miller W, Prufer K (eds) Literary publishing in the twenty-first century. Milkweed Editions
60. Thompson JB (2012) Merchants of culture: the publishing business in the twenty-first century. Plume
61. Tomalin C (2011) Charles Dickens: a life. Penguin Press
62. Ward E (2019) The history of rock & roll. The Beatles, the Stones, and the rise of classic rock. Flatiron Books
63. Wasserman S (2012) The amazon effect. The Nation
64. Wiener A (2020) Uncanny valley: a memoir. MCD/Farrar, Straus and Giroux
65. Wilson-Lee E (2019) The catalogue of shipwrecked books: Christopher Columbus, his son, and the quest to build the world's greatest library. Scribner
66. Young DW (2018) The booksellers (film)
67. Zaid G (2003) So many books: reading and publishing in an age of abundance. Paul Dry Books

Content

Getting Creative with Actions

David Thue

Abstract The goal of this chapter is to help refine and broaden how authors think about actions in the context of Interactive Digital Narrative. An action is generally something that a player can do to affect the progression of an interactive story, but the elements that actions can change are often limited to the state of the narrative world. Examples include moving the player's avatar through the narrative world because they typed "go north", or recording that the player has accepted a given quest. While a rich and diverse set of interactive stories has been made using only actions of this kind, we will see in this chapter how using other kinds of action can broaden the author's repertoire and enable new opportunities for player interaction.

1   Introduction

As more and more Interactive Digital Narratives (IDNs) become available to play, it becomes increasingly important for authors to differentiate their new works from those that came before. While differences in topic, tone, or visual presentation are common, the kinds of actions that players can perform have varied less, and their variation has been less frequent. More specifically, while most IDNs offer player actions that change the state of a narrative world, little or nothing else can be changed. What would it mean, though, to change something other than a narrative world's state? What might those other targets for change be? The open-ended nature of these questions makes them rather difficult to answer (where should one even start?), and a lack of answers might explain why so many IDNs rely on changing the narrative world state as the only way for players to act. In this chapter, we examine a concrete way to approach and answer these questions, while still considering the unique context of each author's IDN.

D. Thue (✉)
RISE Research Group, School of Information Technology, Carleton University, Ottawa, Canada

Department of Computer Science, Reykjavik University, Reykjavik, Iceland
e-mail: david.thue@carleton.ca

2   Actions as Instruments of Change

To gain a deeper understanding of actions in IDN, it is useful to think carefully about how interactive stories *progress*, i.e, what things change over time and what causes those things to change. To help with this sort of thinking, we will use Interactive Process Modelling (IPM), a framework for reasoning about interactive systems that works well for narratives and games [1, 2]. We will cover the ideas of IPM gradually as this chapter proceeds.

Usually,[1] only one thing can change as a story progresses: the state of the narrative world. Abstractly, a *narrative world state* describes the narrative world at a single moment during a story's progress. It does so using a collection of two elements: (i) the attributes of all of the world's entities at that moment and (ii) a set of information that summarizes the story's progress, up until that moment. The entities might consist of characters and objects, and attributes might include the position and orientation of every character and object, the goals and opinions of characters, the value or ownership of objects, and more. The information that describes the story's progress could include which quests the player has discovered, accepted, declined, or completed (if the IDN has quests). It might also include *flags*—unique markers which, when set, indicate that some particular happening has occurred in the story (e.g., the player's first time meeting a particular character). The first element describes the contents of the narrative world, while the second element describes extra-world information that is useful for tracking player progress.

One of the goals of Interactive Process Modelling (IPM) is to model how states change as a result of player interaction. Modelling this process of change is useful because the model can help designers reason carefully about several important facets of an IDN. These include how each state change is mediated, what can change, who (if anyone) can change it, how they can change it, how they perceive it, and what they perceive.

2.1   Preliminaries

Before we proceed, we will clarify what we mean by "action" with respect to some prior work. We will also situate the chapter's topic in the context of a popular framework for IDN: Koenitz's System, Process, Product model [3].

2.1.1   On the Meaning of "Action"

In 1976, van Dijk discussed the notion of action in the context of narrative as an intentional sequence of *doings* [4, 5]. For example, the action "open door" might consist of this sequence of doings: (reach for the doorknob, grasp it, turn it, and pull

---

[1] We will see some alternatives in Sect. 3, but delay them until later for the sake of simplicity.

back on it). In distinguishing between actions and doings, van Dijk's work helps us clarify the level of abstraction that we find appropriate for discussing actions. The abstraction level of doings is too low (too specific) to capture the actions that we wish to discuss, but considering each action to be a *sequence of doings* (which is a more abstract construct) suits our purposes well.

Although van Dijk considered interaction that might happen between the characters of a story, the notion of user or player interaction was not discussed. Later, however, Rafaeli defined "interactivity" as something that includes person-to-system communication, saying that what happens next must depend on what has already happened [6]. This dependence of future happenings on past happenings is modelled by IPM in the way that one or more states change as a result of agent interaction, as we will explain further in the sections that follow. While we primarily consider actions as being performed by the players of an IDN, it can also be useful to consider how the non-player characters of an IDN might perform actions as well (e.g., as part of a social simulation [7]).

In 2007, Zagal et al. defined an action in the context of a game as being the manipulation of one or more entities in the game's world [8]. This notion of action corresponds well with how actions commonly work in IDNs, in that they change the state of the narrative world. For example, "open cellar door" could be an action that manipulates the entity "cellar door", changing part of the game's narrative world state from "cellar door closed" to "cellar door open". The goal of this chapter, however, is to demonstrate that this kind of action is only one of several kinds that authors could choose to offer in IDNs.

2.1.2 The System, Process, and Products of an IDN

In this chapter, we follow Koenitz's System, Process, Product (SPP) model [3]. An *IDN system* is a combination of art assets, program code, computing platform, and input devices that offers the potential for someone to have one of the (typically many) experiences that might result from interacting with the system. An *IDN process* characterizes what occurs while a person interacts with an IDN system to have one of the experiences that it offers. Each such experience is an *IDN product*. When we refer to "an IDN system's process", we mean the general IDN process that will occur for any person who interacts with that system. Working within the SPP model, we use Interactive Process Modelling (IPM) to model what happens during an IDN system's process, which we relate to both the program code of the IDN system and the IDN product that results. As we will see in the following sections, sometimes an IDN system can be usefully modelled as a *collection* of separate processes, each of which offers opportunities to change a different part of an IDN system.

In the remainder of Sect. 2, we introduce the core concepts of Interactive Process Modelling one by one, and we combine them in Sect. 2.5 for a complete presentation. In Sect. 3, we explain how IPM can be used in an analytical mode, to distinguish between different kinds of action in existing IDN systems and identify how players might reason about what to do. In Sect. 4, we explain how IPM can be used in a more exploratory mode, prompting authors to consider different kinds of action that they could offer to their players.

2.2   Transition Functions: How Actions Change States

What causes the narrative world state to change? Every such change is caused by a sequence of two steps:

1. the player performs an action (which might just be to wait), and
2. the IDN system responds by changing the state.

A common player action that changes the narrative world state is "move"—players use it to change the position of their avatar (if they have one), or of objects, within the narrative world. Another is the "choose dialogue option" action that players often perform during conversations with story characters. A record of their choice is often kept, either to unlock later dialogue or to trigger variation if the conversation is repeated. This information is stored in the narrative world state, and updating the record thus requires changing that state.

The way that the IDN system responds to each player action is governed by a collection of functions, each of which carries out some author-given instructions to determine what should happen next. For example, in a story made with Twine, the author must describe which node of content should appear next, for each available link that appears in any node. Put another way, they must describe how the narrative world state (including what node to display) should change, given the current world state and an available player action. When the Twine story is played, the player will perform actions (e.g., by selecting links), and the system must respond to each action in a way that carries out the instructions that the author provided.

Interactive Process Modelling (IPM) refers to these response-governing functions as *transition functions*, because they help to transition some *target object* from one configuration to another (Fig. 1). The target object of one transition function might be the narrative world state, while other transition functions might target other elements of an IDN system. Note that the player's ability to affect change through actions is thus *indirect*—it is mediated by the IDN system's transition functions (Fig. 1). In an IDN system, the transition functions typically exist as program code that is *executed automatically*, meaning that their results are determined through digital computation. This is in contrast to Choose Your Own Adventure books (e.g., *The Cave of Time* [9]), where the narrative world state (which is described by the current scene) only changes if the book's transition function is executed *manually* (by flipping to the page indicated alongside a chosen action).[2]

---

[2] A demonstration of how IPM would model the (analog) system and process of a Choose Your Own Adventure book can be found in our prior work [1].

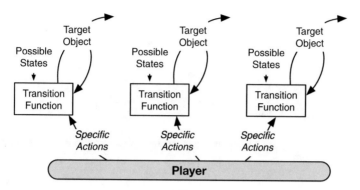

Fig. 1 An IDN system's different transition functions mediate how a player's actions are able to change different target objects within the system

2.3 Observation Functions: How States are Conveyed to Players

Thus far, we have described the narrative world state in the way that an omniscient oracle might know it, with clear and perfect knowledge of everything it contains. While this perspective can be useful for design-focused reasoning, it offers a poor representation of any player's likely perspective, because some aspects of the world state are usually obscured. For example, parts of the world state might be purposely hidden for dramatic effect (e.g., concealing the identity of a criminal to build suspense), or until some condition is met (e.g., a player might remain unaware of a quest until they find the character that offers it).

Understanding the player's perspective is important for understanding actions because players typically decide how to act based on what they observe. So, what determines a player's observations? Similarly to how a transition function determines what aspects of a target object should change as a result of a player's action, an IDN system's *observation functions* determine what parts of a state the player should get to observe (Fig. 2).

Fig. 2 An IDN system's observation functions mediate how the state of each target object can be observed by any player

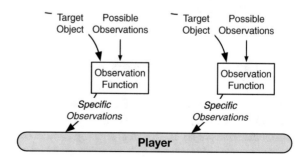

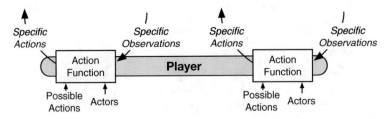

Fig. 3 An IDN system's action functions represent how a player uses their observations to decide what actions to perform

For example, the observation functions of an IDN system made in Twine are responsible for rendering a page of content that displays the current node of the story and what player actions are available from that node. When the player performs one of the available actions, the authored transition functions are executed to update the narrative world state (e.g., changing the current node to display), and the observation functions are then executed to produce new observations for the player, rendering the current node to the screen.

Like transition functions, the observation functions of an IDN system usually exist as program code that is executed automatically by the system.

2.4   Action Functions: How Observations Lead to Actions

Having received one or more observations, a player must decide what to do next. IPM models this decision-making work using a third kind of function: the action function. An *action function* represents how a player considers (or ignores) their observations and then chooses an action to perform (Fig. 3). Unlike how transition functions and observation functions are executed by the IDN system, action functions are executed by players (i.e., each player does the work to determine their desired action). Continuing our example in Twine, an action function would model the player's reasoning about what they observe (e.g., the text, links, and other content displayed on screen) as well as how they should behave as a result (e.g., they might choose to open an available door).

2.5   The Interactive Process

Having explained each of IPM's three primary functions, we can now describe how a transition function, an observation function, and an action function can be connected to model how a player changes a given target object over time. According to IPM, the state of a target object (such as a narrative world) changes as a result of one or more

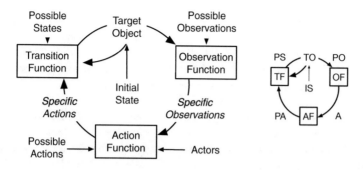

Fig. 4 Left: An interactive process. Boxes represent functions, while labeled arrows represent data. Italics show data that only arises while the process executes. Right: A minified version of an interactive process

agents performing actions. We use the term "agent" as a generalization of "player", to additionally include both simulated, non-player characters in a game or narrative world (e.g., those in *Prom Week* [7, 10]), as well as Artificial Intelligence-driven "managers" that steer how story events progress [11, 12]. While an IDN system's process is underway, an *agent* does two things: it observes aspects of some target object, and it performs specific actions that might change that target object.

The left of Fig. 4 shows an *interactive process* (IP), which models how the actions of one or more agents can change the state of a single target object. We begin our consideration in the middle of the diagram and address each element in turn.

- **Initial State**: The *initial state* describes the state of the IP's target object when the IDN system's process begins. For a narrative world, the initial state would describe the configuration of that world at the beginning of a player's story.
- **Time**: In an interactive process, execution proceeds clockwise around the circular shape of the figure, and time advances in a discrete way, by one *time step* each time the transition function determines the (next) state of the target object. Note that modelling time in discrete steps (instead of as a continuous value) is not restrictive in practice, because even player experiences of IDNs that *seem* continuous (e.g., playing a modern computer role playing game) have discrete time steps. Such experiences only seem continuous because the time steps pass by faster than most players will notice (e.g., 60 times per second or more).
- **Observation Function**: When the observation function is executed, it uses the current state of the IP's target object to produce a specific observation for each agent that can perform actions in the IP (those in the *set of actors*).
- **Set of Actors**: Any agent who can observe some aspects of an IP's target object and attempt to change it through actions is a member of that IP's *set of actors* ("Actors" in the bottom right of the diagram).
- **Set of Possible Observations**: A *set of possible observations* describes all of the observations of the target object that an actor in the interactive process might receive. This set can easily be very large (e.g., imagine all of the ways of rendering

a player's view of a complex 3D world). Nonetheless, it can be convenient to think of these possibilities all at once, as a single set of observations.

- **Action Function**: Each actor in the IP executes the *action function* by choosing a specific action to perform. To make this decision, an actor might consider observations that they have received from the observation functions of multiple IPs (as shown in Fig. 3).
- **Set of Possible Actions**: A *set of possible actions* describes all of the actions that an actor in the interactive process is able to perform as they attempt to change the target object. When the target object is a narrative world state, the possible actions are determined by the author(s), and might include "talk to character", "move", "pick up object", "use object", and more.
- **Transition Function**: A *transition function* takes in all of the IP's actors' actions as well as the current state of the target object, and produces a (potentially different) state, which becomes the new current state as the *time step* advances.
- **Set of Possible States**: A *set of possible states* describes all of the possible configurations of the target object. For example, when the target object is the state of a narrative world, the set of possible states describes (i) all possible ways of setting the attributes of the entities in that world as well as (ii) all of the possible records of story progress that might be recorded. Note that this set can easily be *very* large. As a simple example, consider a small narrative world with only five characters, each with ten attributes (hair color, favorite sandwich, etc.), where each attribute has its own set of eight different values that it might take on (black, brown, etc.; tuna, peanut butter & jam, etc.). The number of possible states in this world is $8^{(5 \times 10)}$, which is a number so large it takes 46 digits to write down. Fortunately, an author never needs to write down all of the possible states one by one, and for this chapter, it is enough to understand that it can be convenient to consider all of the possible configurations of a target object abstractly, all at once, as a set of possible states.

Using Interactive Process Modelling, an IDN is modelled as a connected collection of one or more interactive processes—one for each element of the IDN's system that can be changed by agent actions. Modelling an IDN via IPM can be useful to authors because it offers a way to manage and better understand IDN designs that offer a wider variety of ways for players to interact, beyond changing the state of the narrative world. In the following sections, we consider other elements of an IDN's system that might be changed and explain how a model containing multiple connected IPs can be built.

3 Understanding Kinds of Action

To help fulfill the goals of this chapter, we distinguish between different kinds of action based on how they aim to change different parts of an IDN system. An action that seeks to change the narrative world state is thus one kind of action, but what might other kinds be? Put differently, what elements of an IDN system might be changed, other than the narrative world state? Reed offered some examples in his 2017 dissertation [13], two of which we highlight here.

In a mode of interactive narrative that Reed calls "sculptural fiction", players can change the ways in which the state of a narrative world might progress. Reed explains that instead of performing actions to traverse a pre-connected web of narrative content, players of sculptural fiction must decide how to connect together a given set of narrative content, to define how the state of a narrative world could potentially progress. For example, consider *The Ice-Bound Concordance* [14], an IDN co-created by Reed. While playing, the player reads excerpts of several stories that are generated during gameplay, each of which takes place in its own narrative world. Some of the player's actions, however, do not manipulate the state of these narrative worlds—they instead manipulate a collection of dramatically charged symbols, whose configuration affects how the game's stories are generated. A single edit of the available symbols can affect multiple events in a generated story, such as how highlighting the symbol "afraid of the dark" can trigger later events including nightmares or ghosts ([13], pp. 157–159). By editing these symbols, the player can change the ways in which *Concordance*'s narrative worlds progress. Interactive Process Modelling gives us a way to analyze how the symbol-editing actions in *The Ice-Bound Concordance* are different from actions that change the state of a narrative world, as we will see in Sects. 3.1, 3.2, and 3.3.

Reed also discussed a second mode of interactive narrative, which he called "collaborative storygames"; *Dungeons & Dragons* [15] is an example of such a game.[3] Reed found that players of such games often engage in an activity he called *generation*. Generation refers to the creation of new content, such as inventing a new character and adding them into the narrative world. An action that generates new content is different from an action that changes the narrative world state, because generation redefines what states the world could possibly be in. For example, many digital games support the inclusion of player-created modifications ("mods"), which can add entirely new characters, items, or locations to a game's narrative world. By including such elements, the player expands the set of states that the narrative world can be in. We consider how player actions that perform generation can be analyzed using IPM in the following section.

3.1 Different Kinds of Action have Different Target Objects

Interactive Process Modelling offers a way to model how a transition function, a set of possible states, or other elements of an IDN system can be changed as a result of player actions. To do so, one sets the desired target for change (e.g., the transition function of some interactive process) as the target object of an *additional* interactive

---

[3] Although *Dungeons & Dragons* and similar games are not digital, they nonetheless served (and continue to serve) as inspiration for an entire genre of IDN systems: Computer Role-Playing Games.

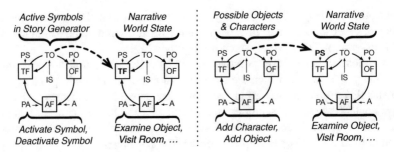

Fig. 5 Left: a partial interactive process model involving Reed's sculptural fiction [13]. Right: a partial interactive process involving Reed's idea of content generation. Both: The target object of each process is labeled across the top, and some possible actions in each process are labeled across the bottom. The thick dashed arrow shows a *target object link* (to be explained in Sect. 3.2)

process. This is possible because IPM's notion of a target object is quite broad. In particular, the term "object" should be understood both abstractly and flexibly—a target object could potentially be any part of an IDN system, so long as that part can be changed as a result of one or more agents' actions. The primary purpose of an interactive process is to model how its target object can be changed by the actions of one or more agents. As an example, Fig. 5 shows partial interactive process models for both sculptural fiction (Left) and generation in a collaborative storygame (Right), continuing from our discussion of Reed's work above. We consider each in turn.

Sculptural fiction allows a player to change how the state of a narrative world progresses, and IPM models the way that a state progresses as the transition function of an interactive process that targets that state (recall Sects. 2.2 and 2.5). An IP that targets a narrative world state in *The Ice-Bound Concordance* [14] appears second from the left in Fig. 5. To model how sculptural fiction allows a player to change this IP's transition function, we create an additional IP (first from the left, in the figure), setting its target object as the original IP's transition function (shown by a dashed arrow pointing to TF). When a player activates a symbol via an action in the left-most IP, their action changes how the game's story generator will behave from that point forward, as it transitions the game's narrative world to new states over time.

Content generation allows a player to change the possible states that a narrative world might be in. IPM represents these possible states as the *set of possible states* of an IP that targets the narrative world state (PS in the right-most IP of Fig. 5). To model how content generation allows a player to add characters or objects to the narrative world, and thereby change its set of possible states, we create an additional IP (second from the right, in the figure), setting its target object to the right-most IP's set of possible states, PS. When a player adds a character or object into the world via the new IP, the set of possible states of the narrative world changes.

Both models in Fig. 5 have one IP whose target object is a narrative world state, plus a second IP whose target object is an element of the first IP. Taken together, the two models offer three different kinds of action to players: one kind that seeks to change the narrative world state, a second kind that seeks to change the transition function that governs a narrative world state, and a third kind that seeks to change the set of possible states of a narrative world.

Distinguishing between actions based on their different target objects is helpful partly because it can disentangle elements of the IDN's system that are useful to consider separately during design. For example, the fact that the model at the left of Fig. 5 has two observation functions (OF) highlights that even once a method of rendering a narrative world state has been established, one must also consider how the active symbols of the story generator will be rendered for the player to see and understand. Section 3.3 offers another way in which IPM can be helpful.

3.2   Building an Interactive Process Model

While Reed identified a few changeable elements that are different from a narrative world state [13], he did not offer any general method to identify other potential elements. Interactive Process Modelling offers such a method, by modelling an IDN system's process and relating it to both the system's program code and the IDN's product [1]. In this section, we discuss a set of steps for building a model using IPM. Given a sufficiently complex transition function, observation function, and representation of the narrative world's state, it is possible to model any IDN system (even those with more than one kind of action, as we discuss them in this chapter) using a single interactive process (IP). Nevertheless, we argue that it is *valuable* to model an IDN system using multiple IPs because it allows an author, analyst, or designer to understand the system using a "divide and conquer" strategy, while splitting the system's elements along lines that reveal important considerations for interaction design. These considerations include questions such as "how will an agent learn about the element that they seek to change?", "which agents should have the power to change this element?", and more that we cover further in Sects. 3.3 and 4.

The *interactive process model* of an IDN system is a collection of one or more interactive processes, each of which represents how some element of the system or its process can change. The model begins empty (containing no interactive processes) and grows incrementally across the following sequence of steps.

3.2.1   Step 1: Identify Agents and Initial Objects

The first step in building such a model is to identify two things: (i) which agents should be considered as potential actors, and (ii) an initial set of objects that they can observe or change. Across very many IDN systems, the answers to these questions are the same: (i) a single player, and (ii) they can observe and change the narrative world state. As a more complex example, consider Reed's analysis of sculptural fiction [13] through the lens of IPM. We identify that (i) a single player should be considered an actor and (ii) two objects can be observed and changed: the narrative world state, and the transition function of an interactive process that targets the narrative world state.

3.2.2   Step 2: Build the Initial Model

Once one has identified the agents to consider and an initial set of n objects to be observed or changed ($n \geq 1$), the next step is to create and add n interactive processes to the model. Since each identified object can be observed and/or changed in some particular way, the goal is to use a unique interactive process to model how that change happens. We do this by setting the target object of each interactive process to one of the identified objects, until every identified object is the target of exactly one interactive process. Applying this step can lead to the partial models shown in Fig. 5. For sculptural fiction [13], we would need two interactive processes: one with the narrative world state as its target object, and a second process with the transition function of the first process as its target object (Fig. 5: Left). For a collaborative storygame where players can create new narrative world states (which Reed called "generation" [13]), we would also need two interactive processes: one process to target the narrative world state, and one to target the first process's set of possible states (Fig. 5: Right). When the target object of one interactive process is an element of another, we say that the target object of the first process is connected to the element of the second process by a *target object link*. These links appear as dashed arrows in Figs. 5 through 8.

3.2.3   Step 3: (Potentially) Expand the Model

Once we have an interactive process for each of the target objects that were identified in the previous step, the next step is to check whether other observable and/or changeable objects might have been missed. One way to do this is to recursively examine the existing model's elements, asking the question "can any agent observe or change this element?" for each one. By "element" we mean any function or set that is part of the current model's interactive processes. Whenever the answer for any element is yes, a new interactive process is added to the model with that element as its target object. The examination is recursive because for each new interactive process that gets added along the way, one must eventually examine all of *its* elements and consider whether or not each of them can be observed or changed. Eventually, the answers for all remaining elements will be "no", and the recursive analysis will end. The full model for the *The Ice-Bound Concordance* ultimately contains 17 IPs, as explained in a previous paper by the author of this chapter [1].

Note that although IPM can reveal many potential targets for change, it does not claim to fully cover every possible element of an IDN system and its process. As a result, the recursive analysis might not find some elements that were missed in the first step of modelling. Such an element can nevertheless be added to the model as soon as it is discovered, by creating a new interactive process with the element as its target object and performing a recursive analysis of the new process's elements.

3.2.4   Step 4: Assign Actors

Given m interactive processes with their target objects assigned to different, change-able elements of the IDN system or its process, the next step is to add one or more agents to each interactive process's set of actors. We do so by asking a simple question of every interactive process in the model, considering each of the agents that were identified in the first step above: can this agent observe or change this process's target object? When the answer is "yes", the agent is added to that process's set of actors. The sets of actors will be complete when every pair of interactive process and agent has been considered.

Each addition or omission of any agent to these sets will ultimately describe which target objects that agent is or isn't able to observe or try to change. For example, in some games of Dungeons & Dragons, observing and changing the set of possible world states is only be available to a player who has a special role (e.g., the "Game Master"); this means that only the Game Master would be added to the set of actors for the interactive process that targets the set of possible world states.

3.3   Influence Paths: How Actions Affect Narrative Experiences

A completed interactive process model will have m interactive processes, and each of these will allow its actors to perform a different kind of action than any other process in the model allows. These actions are different because they each offer the player a different way to exert influence over the IDN's potential narrative experiences, via different sequences of mediating elements across the IDN system. We call these different ways of exerting influence *influence paths* [2], because they can be traced across an interactive process model to show how an agent's actions can ultimately influence their narrative experience.

As a concrete example, consider *The Ice-Bound Concordance* once again, and how activating a symbol can affect the player's narrative experience. The effect is mediated across two influence paths, as shown in Fig. 6.

Along the path that remains within IP B (shaded dark grey in Fig. 6), the player's influence is mediated by the following elements of the IDN:

1. First, IP B's transition function mediates the effect of the player's action on the state of B's target object. This TF ensures that the player's symbol activation or deactivation is valid, as some of the generator's symbols cannot be deactivated. If the player's action is valid, this TF modifies the story generator's symbols accordingly; otherwise, the symbols remain unchanged.

2. Next, IP B's observation function mediates the immediate effect of this state change on the player's experience: it produces an observation that informs the player that the desired symbol has been activated. In *The Ice-Bound Concordance*, this is shown visually by rendering a spotlight effect over an image of the symbol.

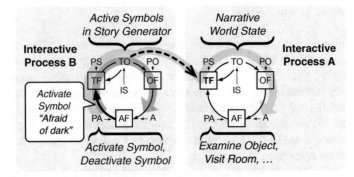

Fig. 6 A demonstration of how influence paths can be traced within and across the processes of an interactive process model. Two influence paths are shown—one in dark grey (fully contained within interactive process B), and one in light grey (which crosses from B to A). The example comes from *The Ice-Bound Concordance* [14], which uses Reed's sculptural fiction [13]

While this path of influence does not affect a narrative world state, it nonetheless affects the player's narrative experience, because it redefines their understanding of the narrative importance of the activated symbol.

The second influence path (shaded light grey in Fig. 6) crosses from IP B to IP A via B's target object link to A. This link exists because B's target object is A's transition function; activating or deactivating a symbol in IP B will change how the story generator in IP A's transition function works. When the player performs the "Activate Symbol" action in B, the effects of that action are mediated along this second influence path as follows:

1. First, IP B's transition function mediates the effect of the player's action on the state of B's target object, as in the first influence path explained above.
2. Next, the path crosses the target object link from IP B to IP A, because A's transition function is now different than it was before (because B's transition function just changed the story generator's active symbols). From this point in time onward, A's transition function will mediate the effect of any actions performed in A differently than it did before. As a result, activating the "afraid of dark" symbol in B will have a potentially lasting effect on how A's target object (the narrative world state) changes.
3. Next, as the story generator operates and the narrative world state changes, the effects of these changes will be mediated by A's observation function: it will produce observations (textual story excerpts) that inform the player about what changes have happened in the narrative world.

By examining the influence paths of an interactive process model, authors can better understand how different kinds of action might affect not only the operation of various parts of an IDN system, but also the various observations that a player could receive as they interact within that system's process.

3.3.1 Finding a Model's Influence Paths

To enumerate a given model's influence paths, one begins at the action function of each interactive process in the model. For each action function, a new influence path extends clockwise, first to the transition function of the same process, and then to its target object. If the target object is linked to an element of another interactive process via a target object link, then the influence path is duplicated. One copy carries on within same the process, first to the observation function and then to the action function from which it started. The other copy crosses the target object link to the element of the interactive process at the other end. It then carries along clockwise across the elements of the process, duplicating as needed to both carry on within the same process as well as cross any target object link that it encounters. Every influence path ends as soon as it reaches any of the model's action functions.

4 Exploring the Landscape of Different Kinds of Action

Section 3 explained how Interactive Process Modelling can be used in an analytical mode, to gain an understanding of what different kinds of action are made available by an IDN system and how they relate to players' experiences therein. In this section, we discuss how IPM can be used in an *exploratory* mode, toward discovering and making sense of kinds of action that go beyond what IDN systems typically offer.

To explore different kinds of action using IPM, we modify Step 3 of the modelling procedure (Sect. 3.2) as follows: instead of asking "can any agent observe or change this element?", we ask "should any agent be able to observe or change this element?" Whenever the answer is "yes", we create a new interactive process with the identified element as its target object. Unlike in the analytical mode, where the elements of each new interactive process represent existing parts of an IDN system, the elements of new processes that are created in the exploratory mode might not yet exist. For example, consider answering "yes" to the question "should any agent be able to observe or change the set of possible actions that players can use to modify the narrative world state?" While our question is about an existing element of an IDN system (the set of possible actions highlighted in Fig. 7), our "yes" answer prompts the creation of a new interactive process (C, in the figure) whose elements do not yet exist. By building the Interactive Process Model, the author is prompted to consider several important questions:

- Which agents should be able to observe or change A's set of possible actions? (C's set of actors)
- How should observations of A's set of possible actions be produced for each of C's actors? (C's observation function)
- What actions (in C) should C's actors be able to perform? (C's set of possible actions)

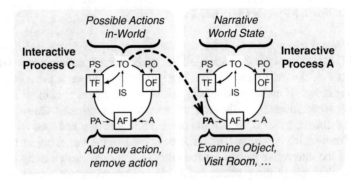

Fig. 7 When we answer "yes" to "should any agent be able to observe or change the set of possible actions that players can use to modify the narrative world state?", we create Interactive Process C to model how Interactive Process A's set of possible actions (PA) can change

- How should A's set of possible actions be allowed to change via C's transition function? (C's transition function)
- How should A's set of possible actions be when the story starts? (C's initial state)

After creating a new interactive process in response to each "yes" answer to our modified question, we continue with the recursive part of Step 3, asking the same question of every element of every new interactive process, until no new elements remain to ask about.

An author who answers "yes" many times during this recursive analysis will be prompted to consider a wide variety of potential kinds of action—each of which seeks to change a different (and perhaps not-yet-existent) element of an IDN system. Figure 8 shows one potential interactive process model that could result from such an exploration.

As an example of a longer chain of target object links, consider IPs X, Y, and Z as shown in the figure. IP X targets the narrative world state, and IP Y targets X's set of possible actions (PA). This means that Y's actors can observe or change the set of actions that are possible for X's actors to perform in the narrative world. This is a circumstance that arises commonly in pen-and-paper role-playing games, when players are welcomed to suggest courses of action that were not previously thought of or planned for (making them actors in IP Y, in addition to IP X). While the pre-programmed nature of IDN systems makes it more challenging to support this kind of player freedom, existing systems have allowed it by adding an additional, simultaneous player who can facilitate the required flexibility, much like the game-master of a pen-and-paper role-playing game. Examples include *Sleep is Death* [16], *Bad News* [17, 18], and *Kassinn / A Box in the Desert* [19]. Actors in IP Z can perform yet another kind of action: they can act toward changing IP Y's set of actors (A). To consider a potential purpose for doing so, imagine a platform for IDNs like *Sleep is Death*, where the (non-facilitating) player is able to "phone a friend" to get suggestions for new possible actions that might be added to IP X. Enlisting a

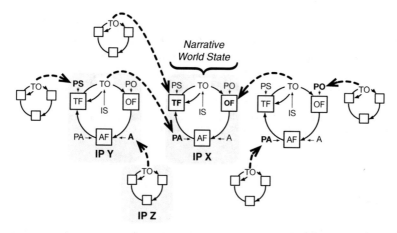

Fig. 8 An example of an exploratory interactive process model that could be generated by answering "yes" to the question "should any agent be able to observe or change this element?" for each of the elements shown in bold (and "no" for all other elements). Each of the eight interactive processes in the model allows a different kind of action. IPs X, Y, and Z are used as an example in the text

friend's help in this way would amount to adding the friend to IP Y's set of actors, and performing this addition would require the player to perform an action in IP Z.

Despite the title of this section, our aim is not to explore the landscape of different kinds of action ourselves in this chapter. Instead, we consider Interactive Process Modelling as a tool that enables authors and narrative experience designers to perform this exploration themselves. It is necessary to perform this exploration in the context of one's own project, because the answers to the core question "should any agent be able to observe or change this element?" depend fundamentally on that context. By considering this question for the elements of an interactive process model and following up with "and what might it mean for the answer to be *yes*?", authors will be prompted to imagine a wide range of potential kinds of action.

5 Summary

Interactive Process Modelling (IPM) allows an author to distinguish between different kinds of action in a particular way: based on which part of an IDN system they aim to change. By modelling an existing IDN system and examining its influence paths, authors can better understand how each of the different kinds of action that players can perform might ultimately affect their experience. Distinguishing between different kinds of action in this way is useful for innovation; the vast majority of IDN systems only allow the state of their narrative world to change, and they restrict themselves to offering only one kind of action as a result. By modelling an IDN system using IPM as the system is being designed, authors can explore a broad range of potential targets for player-affected change, and be guided through key decisions about how that change should happen. Actions in IDNs offer new opportunities for innovation, and IPM offers a structured way to explore, understand, and exploit that potential, while still remaining grounded in each author's specific work.

Acknowledgements The author acknowledges the support of the Natural Sciences and Engineering Research Council of Canada (NSERC), Grant #2020-06502.

References

1. Thue D (2020) What might an action do? Toward a grounded view of actions in interactive storytelling. In: Proceedings of the 13th international conference on interactive digital storytelling (ICIDS'20). Lecture notes in computer science, vol 12497. Springer, Cham, pp 212–220. https://rise.csit.carleton.ca/pubs/Thue_ICIDS_2020.pdf
2. Thue D (2021) Supporting the design of flexible game systems. In: Extended abstracts of the 2021 annual symposium on computer-human interaction in play, CHI PLAY'21. Association for Computing Machinery, New York, NY, USA, pp 216–221. https://doi.org/10.1145/3450337.3484223
3. Koenitz H (2010) Towards a theoretical framework for interactive digital narrative. In: Aylett R, Lim MY, Louchart S, Petta P, Riedl M (eds) Interactive storytelling. Springer, Berlin, Heidelberg, pp 176–185
4. van Dijk TA (1975) Action, action description, and narrative. New Literary Hist 6(2):273–294. http://www.jstor.org/stable/468420
5. van Dijk TA (1976) Philosophy of action and theory of narrative. Poetics 5(4):287–338. https://doi.org/10.1016/0304-422X(76)90014-0. www.sciencedirect.com/science/article/pii/0304422X76900140
6. Rafaeli S (1988) Interactivity: from new media to communication. Adv Commun Sci: Merging Mass Interpersonal Process Sage Ann Rev Commun Res 16:110–134
7. McCoy J, Treanor M, Samuel B, Reed A, Mateas M, Wardrip-Fruin N (2013) Prom week: designing past the game/story dilemma. In: Proceedings of the 8th international conference on the foundations of digital games (FDG 2013). Chania, Crete, Greece
8. Zagal JP, Mateas M, Fernández-Vara C, Hochhalter B, Lichti N (2005) Towards an ontological language for game analysis. In: DiGRA '05 proceedings of the 2005 DiGRA international conference: changing views: worlds in play. http://www.digra.org/wp-content/uploads/digital-library/06276.09313.pdf
9. Packard E (1979) Choose your own adventure: the cave of time. Crossroads Press
10. McCoy J, Treanor M, Samuel B, Reed AA, Mateas M, Fruin NW (2012) Prom week. https://promweek.soe.ucsc.edu/
11. Riedl MO, Stern A, Dini D, Alderman J (2008) Dynamic experience management in virtual worlds for entertainment, education, and training. Int Trans Syst Sci Appl Special Issue Agent Based Syst Human Learn 4(2):23–42
12. Thue D, Bulitko V (2018) Toward a unified understanding of experience management. In: Proceedings of the 14th AAAI conference on artificial intelligence and interactive digital entertainment (AIIDE'18). AAAI Press
13. Reed A (2017) Changeful tales: design-driven approaches toward more expressive storygames. PhD thesis, UC Santa Cruz
14. Reed A, Garbe J, Apostol N (2013) The ice-bound concordance. www.ice-bound.com
15. Gygax G, Arneson D (1974) Dungeons & dragons. Tactical Studies Rules, Inc

16. Rohrer J (2010) Sleep is death (Geisterfahrer). http://sleepisdeath.net/
17. Ryan JO, Summerville AJ, Samuel B (2015) Bad news. https://www.badnewsgame.com/
18. Ryan JO, Summerville AJ, Samuel B (2016) Bad news: a game of death and communication. In: Proceedings of the 2016 CHI conference extended abstracts on human factors in computing systems (CHI EA'16). Association for Computing Machinery, New York, NY, USA, pp 160–163. https://doi.org/10.1145/2851581.2890375
19. Agustsson A, Gunnars N, Hindley O (2017) Kassinn/a box in the desert. http://huldufugl.is/kassinn-a-box-in-the-desert

Authoring Interactive Narrative Meets Narrative Interaction Design

Ulrike Spierling

Abstract Authoring stories and designing interactions are often discussed separately, within differing communities. At the same time, it would be useful to regard these two tasks as actually one integrated process for the creation of interactive narratives. With a focus on non-standardized interaction styles, this chapter discusses the authoring challenges involved in conceiving IDNs for location-based and immersive experiences with novel technologies, one example being Augmented Reality. These challenges include the necessity to understand technologies and their users, as well as potential gaps between the platforms and circumstances of creation and experience. This chapter suggests approaches to these authoring problems, placing an emphasis on the integration of the story with repeatable interaction patterns.

1 Introduction: Towards Natural Interaction in Interactive Digital Narrative

Creating artworks and applications in Interactive Digital Narrative (IDN) means not only inventing a story or a storyworld with its elements, but also the form of interaction with this narrative content. While it is important to discuss the narrative rules or algorithms that decide what happens next in the flow of events, in this chapter, I will focus on creating the conditions for users to interact with advanced technology, making use of smart sensors and recognition software. The emphasis here is on the authoring problem of including interaction design considerations into the creation of a holistic experience with an interactive narrative.

After setting the frame regarding "natural interaction", I will focus on Augmented Reality (AR) and location-based storytelling, because these fields offer a particularly fertile ground for technological innovation in interactive narrative, and are also becoming increasingly popular. Drawing from experiences with location-based

U. Spierling (✉)
Hochschule RheinMain, Wiesbaden, Germany
e-mail: ulrike.spierling@hs-rm.de

© The Author(s), under exclusive license to Springer Nature Switzerland AG 2022
C. Hargood et al. (eds.), *The Authoring Problem*, Human–Computer Interaction Series,
https://doi.org/10.1007/978-3-031-05214-9_8

AR and storytelling projects, specific challenges for designers and authors will be discussed and recommendations summarized.

1.1 Beyond the Navigation Metaphor in Interactive Digital Narratives

In many discussions on interactive digital narrative, the role of interaction design as a discipline has been underexplored. Before presenting some of the related authoring challenges, I want to suggest a possible reason for this lack of attention. In many IDN forms, a navigational structure, in the sense of "navigation" as an interaction metaphor, is prevalent. The navigation metaphor, ubiquitous in our everyday contact with the World Wide Web, refers to an abstract spatial model of nonlinear narrative content. It implies that authors, who are breaking away from a linear timeline by which the story unfolds, think of creating paths through nodes—a spatial metaphor for traversing a designed structure. If more than one path is possible, or forking paths are included, it means that players can choose at certain authored points what path direction to take. It is one of the authors' many creative tasks to decide on the amount and quality of such choices.

Navigation by selection of hyperlinks is one of several conceptual models to approach thinking of interactions and variations in the story. In the authoring of a narrative hypertext, when we think about how to design these choice options as changes in the story, we often do not mention how—physically—players are performing these. This is because many or even most read or play interactions in this context are fully transparent or even invisible in the sense of Norman's "invisible computer" [1]. They have been designed to be performed at some screen-based device, such as a PC or laptop with a mouse, or a handheld touch interface. By clicking, tapping, or swiping, links can be followed to navigate a path in the hypertext. From a point of view within the diegetic story, these "actions" are invisible and even hardly noticed by most end-users (readers or players). The physical pressing of a button is a standardized action performed with the hardware (see the "lexical" level in Fig. 1). Not only standardized, but also trained with many repetitions, this action is part of the unconscious repertoire of humans handling a computer, and it has probably become fully internalized in muscle memory by many.

Of course, screens, keyboards and mouse can provide more complex interactions than following links, something which also is ubiquitous in computer games that allow real-time walking or flying, jumping, ducking, shooting, fighting, and so on, by linking hardware-bound physical commands to a semantic level of actions that make sense in a certain narrative domain. Thus, besides choices of predefined alternative outcomes or merely at the narrative discourse level, players can engage in active roles that become part of the story, affecting more complex world states. Actions like moving left or right, turning around or shooting work by hitting arrow or WASD keys, in a way that has to be learned once as a beginner, but later is repeated as a pattern that becomes second nature.

For the rest of this chapter, I will deliberately look beyond these "desktop"-based interaction styles and instead focus on areas with less established interaction conventions. In the areas discussed, the choice of an interaction style may become part of the whole interactive narrative design, gaining an importance for the overall narrative experience.

1.2 The Quest for Natural Interfaces

Since the beginnings of research in IDN, there have been projects that have tried to raise the potential of physical participation in a narrative world by inventing or employing novel, more human-like interactions. Instead of pressing buttons, humans interact with language and gestures, and they use their legs to walk and jump. In particular, telling stories is actually a language-based endeavour, going beyond movements through spatial information structures. Interactive drama and action on a real stage involve whole-body movements. With *Façade* (2005) [2], a milestone was set that not only integrated natural language in IDN but also included a staged setup with possible actions, drama management and a progressing conversation. Technically, *Façade* was also an experiment testing the limits of the state-of-the-art algorithms in natural language processing [3]. The designers of *Façade* documented their experimental authoring concepts [2] and finally extended the experience to an Augmented Reality play [4]. Authoring conversational interactions posed several problems, especially that of catching unforeseen user input. In that same decade, more projects with experiments in structuring language-based interactions followed [5].

Early examples using immersive virtual reality for storytelling started from the 1990s, including theme park entertainment projects such as *Aladdin* by Disney Imagineering [6], and mainly military simulations and training that included speech-based conversation and interaction with virtual humans [7]. An immersive example of interactive narration from the latest decade that combined dialogue interaction with a volumetric immersive setup was the nearly natural conversation with a filmed Holocaust survivor [8].

Another important development path of interface innovation has been mobile computing, bringing computers and/or interfaces into physical reality for storytelling. This chapter will lay its emphasis here. Combining physical and virtual reality leads to Augmented Reality (AR). These concepts have inspired narrative ghost hunts but also documentary storytelling on location. Early examples include *Geist* [9], *Voices of Oakland* [10], *Haunted Planet* [11], and *Spirit* [12], the last of which will be used as an example later. Tangible interfaces included playful objects that seamlessly connect board games to virtual content [13]. The most recent immersive AR interfaces are head-mounted displays with advanced sensing of their environment, enabling spatial recognition. *Fragments*, running on the first version of the Microsoft HoloLens [14], offers an immersive investigation experience that stages a detective game in the private homes of users, placing all game elements on the walls, floors and furniture of the scanned real environment. Players interact with the game by speech, gestures and moving around in their own room. Jin et al. [15] developed *The AR Journey* as an immersive narrative HoloLens experience. They compared graphical (GUI) with natural user interface (NUI) approaches, based on the hypothesis that "training to control a NUI is not required"—with mixed results.

1.3 Natural Interfaces Are Not Natural

Against all early hopes that natural interfaces would be the breakthrough for better interaction of the masses with high-end technology, this has not yet been the case [16]. Essentially, there is no ultimate "human-like" quality (yet) in human–computer communication, and computers are far from "understanding" the intentions of their users. This results in increased challenges inflicted on users to understand the capabilities and limitations of the ever-changing technology. I want to emphasize three of these as specific challenges for IDN.

The first challenge is reduced accessibility, as a consequence of presenting a non-standard interface for interactive narratives. We have to count in an "onboarding" phase that is longer than in general, in which new users need to get acquainted with specific interaction modalities, sometimes even learn new paradigms if they are confronted with a novel device for the first time. There are situations in which this is feasible, such as either in a professional environment in which workers get training, or for gamers who can and will spend the necessary time to master special intricacies and gain skills in their free time. However, there are situations especially in the location-specific domain, in which it is less acceptable for users to have to work through a long tutorial, such as in a museum, theme park or exhibition. At the very least, designers should be aware of the necessity for onboarding.

The second challenge is that interface modalities using speech, gestures or location and position sensors are imprecise, and at the same time promise too much fidelity and improvements concerning intuition. In contrast to these promises, users cannot expect to have full control, which results in a mismatch between expectations and outcome. This is less about controlling the resulting story, as it is more about making conscious choices and connecting the outcome with the user's own actions. If users are not aware of how they triggered a certain move in the story, this can result in uncertainty and finally in frustration.

Third, there might be a competition for attention between the narrative and the interaction. This may be fully intended by the design, as the way of interacting can tell us something through its mechanics. For example, if the intention is to create a feeling of unconfident movements and searching, because the goal is to simulate sensations of visual impairment, as in *Beyond Eyes* [17], then the implemented design of tentative interaction perfectly matches the narrative goal. However, if the story is not about failure experiences, these kinds of challenges at the interface level may distract from the actual story.

2 Authoring IDN for Augmented Reality

In the following, we will look at the interactive narrative authoring problem of integrating a novel interaction paradigm with narrative content. The main emphasis is set on interacting with location-based Augmented Reality—using a variety of potential sensors in state-of-the-art mobile hardware. These systems with novel smart sensors challenge the design by moving away from the affordances of classic interfaces, but on the other hand, they offer a great potential for narrative innovation.

2.1 Authoring Tools in Virtual and Augmented Reality

Authoring for Virtual and Augmented Reality applications has been a widely discussed problem area for many years [18]. However, the history of defining and solving these authoring problems has little overlap with the history of authoring in interactive narrative. While in both fields, it has frequently been argued that authoring tools shall free authors from the burden of programming, allowing them to focus on the content [19], it is that content which (mostly) differs.

Researching the reference lists of papers in AR or VR authoring will reveal not much overlap with those of authoring papers in interactive storytelling. It is a different professional culture, with a different meaning of "authoring", as the predominant industries for VR and AR have been engineering and production. Also today, for the head-mounted device "Microsoft HoloLens 2" that leads the current technical state of the art in immersive Mixed Reality, the main customer areas being addressed are the engineering, construction, manufacturing, medical, and higher education industries [20].

This difference becomes apparent when the foremost challenge discussed for authoring seems to be the import of CAD models and making them interactable as objects, by which is meant, to grab, modify, assemble, and disassemble them, and to place them in their virtual contexts. This affords the design of 3D interfaces for handling and navigating in virtual environments. Another implementation challenge is the technical connection to special periphery hardware, be it spatial displays or input devices. This explains why authoring in this domain is still seen as a technical challenge to application development rather than as a creative endeavour [21].

Recently, there have been research projects to make VR/AR platforms easier to author by reducing the demand for programming [21], for example by using ready-made components that fit the communication models of certain domains. One example is the "nuggets" concept [22] that lets authors simply exchange default placeholder elements of a given structure. This has been tested with standardized educational tasks, such as showing an object and filling labels that explain its parts. Since this process of editing templates limits the author's creativity, the challenge for the creative tool builder is to provide a long list of available nuggets that represent various elementary interaction patterns.

Some overlapping areas of engineering and storytelling included the development of educational and training scenarios, such as for military or employee training purposes [6, 23]. Only recently, with the integration of VR in games and the spread of game engines as VR/AR authoring platforms, for example Unity3D [24], have these cultural domains converged. The main common denominator is the conceptual model built upon a 3D space, expressed through the content format of a hierarchical scene graph to be constructed in the authoring tool. This scene graph, containing spatial relations of 3D objects, camera, and lighting, is an important influence on the mental model of authors, as thinking of creation in these tools starts with objects and a user interaction metaphor of navigating a space and handling these objects. Comparing this starting point to the "interactive writing" problems addressed in hypertext tools, we see that conceptual models of creation have to exist at several levels. In VR/AR authoring tools, the creation obviously starts with stage design. This stage—which forms the content of an interactive application—is also considered part of the interface, at a lower level.

In my 2015 article [25], I applied the concept of four levels of computer dialogue from a 1995 Computer Graphics book [26] to the practice of interactive storytelling (see Fig. 1). Regardless of whether the number of abstract levels is four (or three or five), the suggestion is to divide the larger task up into several analytic considerations for design decisions. The story level works as the top "conceptual" level, containing global goals including the overall interaction metaphor and user experience, while the lowest or "lexical" level is concerned with authored decisions about hardware-bound input styles, as well as visual and audio primitives. In between are levels that contain the "semantic" mappings to story-related actions and events, as well as "syntactic" patterns of possible interaction sequences.

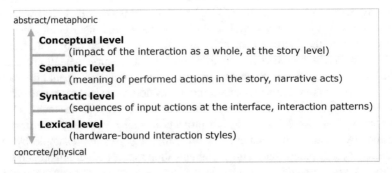

abstract/metaphoric

Conceptual level
(impact of the interaction as a whole, at the story level)

Semantic level
(meaning of performed actions in the story, narrative acts)

Syntactic level
(sequences of input actions at the interface, interaction patterns)

Lexical level
(hardware-bound interaction styles)

concrete/physical

Fig. 1 Four levels of interaction design (analogue to [25])

2.2 Augmented Reality and Location-Based Storytelling

For the main focus of this chapter, we now concentrate on such user interactions at the lower levels of Fig. 1 that are not (yet) standardized. For these areas, the hypothesis is that authors of an interactive narrative experience cannot be indifferent towards the interaction style, just the same way as they deeply care about "how" to tell a story. For the inclusion of examples of non-standardized interactions, we put an emphasis on Augmented Reality (AR) and its prerequisites for interaction with and in stories.

A main characteristic of AR is that a perception of virtual content exists above or within the real physical world that we experience at the same time. It is an ideal medium for storytelling if that told or shown narrative has something to do with the real surroundings of the viewer or audience during the experience [21]. Thus, for the interest of storytelling, AR is often employed for content that explains something physically present, such as for cultural heritage scenarios. Augmented Reality therefore is also inherently location-based.[1] This location can be either unique, in the sense of one distinct geographic coordinate, or it can be bound to movable or static objects, to specific images for recognition, or to general defined qualities of a real environment (such as for example, bound to any recognized horizontal plane).

In any of these cases, digital content assets (text, images, audio sequences, film, 3D objects) are attached as AR assets to a so-called "target" in the real world that serves as the background of that content. In many cases, users experience AR by looking through a device (see-through glasses or a video camera) into their real surroundings—then this "target" may also serve as a visual backdrop, the stage for storytelling. Complex image processing enables the illusion that the digital content becomes part of the environment. Computer Graphics researchers have been working on shading and lighting methods to make the digital visualization indistinguishable from reality. Other approaches deliberately play with abstract styles differing from reality [27, 28].

As AR binds stories into the environment of their audience, it is often a good idea to begin thinking about a new narrative from the point of view of the target environment. Making a cultural heritage story happen in a museum, a common start is to experience that museum environment first, and to determine what "targets" it would offer for storytelling, in the sense of visual backgrounds, points of interest, and places for stopping and reflection. Are there themes to serve as a framing narrative? Are there certain threshold objects that can be portals or entry points between the real and the narrative worlds? These targets may provide meaningful boundaries to a possible story, even if they are more general and not dependent on a specific location. For example, what stories can happen on any desk, in a picture book, at my vertical wall or hanging down from a ceiling? Is the shape of that environment predetermined and given, or is it part of the authors' creation, such as in a dedicated AR exhibition or in a picture book, custom-fit for the story?

When thinking about interactive story ideas for AR, it is also important to consider how and in what situation end-users will experience the content. If people are in a

---

[1] For more on the applications of Locative Narrative, see Nisi's chapter in this volume.

public environment, they may not be happy to have to use voice commands. If they are holding up a heavy tablet looking through the camera or if they wear a head-mounted display that could make them dizzy, the duration of each interactive story encounter should probably be short, rather than too long. If visitors are walking on a tour outdoors or in a museum, they may get tired and undergo distraction by other visitors or their peer group. Adapting to these circumstances influences the suitable depth of a narrative. Consequently, story ideas and the general modes of interacting with the elements of that story are two parts of one whole conception, which need to be integrated for optimum results. This can also increase communication needs between disciplines within an authoring team.[2]

3   Challenges and Recommendations for IDN Authoring with Interactions in Augmented Reality

While working in an interdisciplinary team may have the advantage to separate the different specialist tasks of narrative from interaction design and distribute the burden, there are strong dependencies between them. In the following, I will highlight the main challenges for interactive story authors, which stem from the demand to integrate their narrative ideas with the constraints and conditions of novel interactive forms. These challenges have been experienced in the applied research projects "Spirit" and "presentXR". In each AR project, we, the research teams, explored and developed authoring tools together with narrative interaction examples. Spirit re-enacts a fictional personal drama based on historic knowledge found within the mural remains of a Roman fort [29] and is experienced by means of hand-held tablets. presentXR supports guidance and exploration for visitors of a natural history museum with immersive head-mounted displays, in this case the MS HoloLens 2 [30].

In the following, I discuss the main challenges for story authors. First, these are demands to understand the targeted technology, as well as the audience as users of this technology. Concerning the development process, further challenges lie in the usual gaps between creation platforms and the ultimate experience platform. The main recommendations are to design repeatable interaction patterns that provide framings for the narration, and to set up prototyping environments during the development process, shortening the necessary iterative design cycle for testing the results of the design.

---

[2] For further discussion on the challenges of communication between disciplines in an authoring team, see the chapter by Szilas and Spierling in this volume.

3.1   Understanding the Technology

AR technology is fascinating for its possibilities and constraining at the same time. AR hardware and built-in software work with several types of sensors and with several stages of complexity in image processing for identifying the positioning of the device. A simple smartphone, for example, may provide GPS sensors for location recognition (maybe also gyroscope and accelerator sensors) and a camera, and run simple image recognition software for spotting QR markers. In contrast, simple tablets have fewer positioning sensors in general, and their configuration needs special attention, as often there is no gyroscope. Modern high-end smartphones may have fast processors for image processing and include depth recognition using Time-of-Flight or Lidar sensors, making sense of spatial features. The latest MS HoloLens2, a head-mounted display, additionally even constantly scans obstacles in the environment, as well as hand position and eye gaze of its wearer, to recognize user gestures. SLAM (Simultaneous Localization and Mapping) can convert keypoints in sequences of camera images to 3D landmarks, producing spatial maps in relation to the device. Sound and speech recognition is another option for catching user commands with most devices.

These technologies, summarized as "sensors", can all be options for triggering content and thus, adapt a narrative to specific situations that end-users may or may not be aware of. Mobile IDN apps could be designed for special hardware (e.g., rentals in a museum), which allows full authorial control over the available functions. In contrast, aiming for any consumer device ("bring-your-own-device") means having to focus on a reduced number of options, to make the desired triggers work reliably for everybody.

As story authors, it is probably not necessary to fully understand the algorithms and details of every technology when we consider using them for interaction with the narrative. However, the more these sensors and algorithms appear to provide us with almost natural interaction, the more it is this "almost" that can cause trouble. For example, the MS HoloLens recognizes hand gestures only if they are performed within its field of view, and the field of view is narrower than that of a human. A gyroscope has no absolute sense of direction as it only measures rotation differences based on movements, with some tolerance, so-called "drift". So, if a user turns around 90 degrees 4 times in a row, it does not mean that they end up with the same view direction as they started. Some compasses only work when the device is in the horizontal position, and not when the device is used upright with a camera. GPS (satellite navigation) works outdoors and is inexact depending on other nearby high objects, such as buildings or trees. Image recognition of landmarks in the environment depends on illumination and on unique features, making it easier to distinguish a significant portal of a castle than the bushes next to it. As this chapter is being written, the state of the art may progress fast, and novel or better interaction possibilities will evolve, especially those based on Artificial Intelligence. Still, it is unlikely that it will become easier for authors to estimate what kinds of triggers for story content they can safely employ.

To sum this up, I suggest that authors as interactive narrative designers do need to know at least the general constraints, imprecision, and uncertainties of the technology they are aiming at, because fitting the story to the limitations (including some work-arounds) is crucial.

3.2 Understanding Users

In an interactive narrative, members of the audience are either participants in a story who are granted agency to influence parts of the resulting narrative, or they are at least agents at a playback stage who co-define the details of the discourse of events. In location-based or AR storytelling, they become users of a system that waits for them to unlock or trigger content by moving around, pointing the camera at things, or performing other input actions based on the technology mentioned above.

From the authorial point of view, writing and building narrative content includes determining the conditions for its appearance. For example, with the "Spirit" system [29], users walk about the outdoor area of a Roman fort and need to trigger the appearance of a "ghost" scene in front of a specific building. The technical precondition for starting that scene is that users arrive within a given radius of the correct GPS position and point the camera of their handheld device at this building. Then, if they turn left and right, panning the device, they find more ghost scenes to the left and to the right. However, how do end-users know what they must do to unlock parts of the story? Do we need to first provide them with a long tutorial to learn how to handle the equipment, making use of the camera and gyroscope? Then, does every place in that area offer ghost scenes, or is this restricted to only a few defined spots? How does this search for content look like? Is it frustrating if not every corner has some ghosts? This type of interaction frames the stories as kind of a search game, inviting the audience to look for special places, which can also be fun.

At first, the design team of "Spirit" was fully in favour of having a mostly "natural" interaction. The initial vision was just to meet virtual ghosts in the real environment: we wanted users to see them through our magic equipment (the handheld device) [31] that lets us communicate with them if we apply magic energy, we would listen to what they tell us, and we did not want a screen full of ugly interface buttons.

In general, avoiding "too much" in terms of interface elements is a great idea, if we can find ways to give users hints as to what to look for and what to do—which refers to the interaction principle of providing "affordances" [32]. Further, users need to feel in control, and get a safe feeling that their actions are effective—which is the interaction principle of "feedback" [32]. In the end, having no button-like interface elements was a naïve idea, because "magic" was only a metaphor, while participants were already used to handling the devices in a certain way. We then provided a menu with a map for GPS navigation, with graphical "memory" stencils as building outlines, to give visual hints on what to search for [31], and we included left/right arrows in situations when it was worthwhile to look sideward for more content. Giving feedback is even more important when some steps are not performed consciously, as they would be after pressing a button, but in cases where they occur automatically, such as just after arriving at a certain geographic area of interest.

Another problem was that users could not pay proper attention due to the outdoor environment—they wanted some ghost dialogue to repeat, or wanted to fast-forward a scene to progress faster. In user tests, it turned out that it was helpful if a ghost video showed a display indicating its duration at playback. As a general advice for mobile interaction design, snippets of time-based media (such as video or audio) should be short. Showing a progress bar that confirmed to users what (short) time a sequence would take, resulted in increased motivation to watch it to the end.

The conclusion here is that while interfaces may vary with the technology, interactive narrative designers as authors benefit from a broad and general understanding of the principles of interaction design, including Norman's concepts of affordance, feedback, error handling, mapping, and constraints [32]. There is a wide range of books on human–computer interaction principles [33], but the main point here is to gather experience with integrating story and interaction. Any screen space or viewport space needs to be shared by narrative content elements and interface elements. Ideally, these interface elements are integrated to tell parts of the story.

3.3 Interaction Patterns

When humans interact with systems, they often follow patterns or scripts, such as sequences that feel natural. Humans learn these patterns through a specific cultural context, a famous example being the restaurant script that defines sequences of interaction when dining out [34]. Another sequential pattern lies in the steps we have learned to use a supermarket—a pattern of logical steps that meanwhile is also prevalent as a metaphor in online shopping: view a series of products, place selected products into a basket without a commitment to purchase, and then move on to the checkout to perform the purchase transaction.

In interaction design, patterns can exist at several levels [35]. As technical design patterns [36], they help developers to reuse existing code elements of a library instead of having to program new elements at every instance. However, in this chapter, the focus is not on software development solutions. Patterns in general also help endusers, as they can recognize familiar things and reuse them in established sequences, which may vary in "naturalness" but need to be learned only once. In short, patterns define what user interface components exist in a product and reusing these patterns leads to consistency in the interface. This design level refers to the abstract, secondlowest level depicted in Fig. 1, defining also syntactical or sequential aspects of input/output. In IDN, the goal could be to avoid making people think about things that are unimportant for the interactive story experience. Another goal could be to use patterns that fit or integrate well with narrative metaphors at the higher levels of Fig. 1. Thus, in an authoring team, some lower-level design tasks could indeed be seen as independent of a story idea and therefore left for a team member specializing in UI design. However, this depends on the way these lower levels integrate with conceptual levels of the interactive narrative, or the narrative interaction. In our Spirit example, the main fictional character recalled visual memory outlines, which henceforth were displayed as a graphical interface for searching locations – which was a design that made interface elements depend on the occurrence of narrative assets.

Well-established guidelines or patterns should not be violated, to meet familiar structures as much as possible. In this regard, design success partly depends on environmental factors that are beyond the authors' control. For example, in the middle of the research on the Spirit project, the mobile game Pokémon GO [37] was released worldwide, and a big leap in acceptance of location-based AR suddenly happened. This increased the familiarity of the associated kinds of interaction, which also eased the accessibility in our project.

To introduce novel or more uncommon interaction patterns, especially with less established paradigms such as in AR, it is necessary to include an "onboarding" phase for novice players to get acquainted with them. In a museum, visitors do not want to spend a long time for tutorials, so onboarding must be short. This implies that the patterns should also not contain too many different novel elements. For example, it is not wise to force users to learn several different hand gestures or spoken commands, especially if there is no implicit relation of the story content to learning such signs or terms. Otherwise, it will end up being predominantly a training game for new sign languages, which could be a nice aspect, if the story goal is about learning to communicate with aliens, but otherwise may be a distraction.

In part, knowledge from game design patterns, which have started to be collected after an initiative by Björk et al. [38], can also be applied. A similar concept in games to patterns at a higher level is that of a simple "core game loop", referring to a repetitive global goal-action-outcome principle. Basic usability needs that are likely to come up as requirements include a general way to get back, or simply undo an action, and to reach safe spots during the experience (either repeatedly returning to a point of rest, or knowing how to enable one), and to be able to start over. These safety points appear to be especially useful in immersive environments, such as with a head-mounted display that separates the user from the familiar environment.

Looking at the plethora of sensors that can be used as triggers for narrative elements in AR, it therefore becomes obvious that it is best to not try out all of them in one piece. Instead, the recommendation is to deliberately select a few and integrate them into a looping experience that aims at consistency at the interface level, while the interactive narrative progresses. In the Spirit project, we first tried several interaction and game styles, such as conversation models, or adventure game loops, which included quests and overcoming obstacles. Finally, we discarded many options and selected a narrative interaction pattern that started with a walk to search for locations that represented memory images of the main character (the ghost of a Roman soldier's daughter). The camera image then triggered a complex spatial scene, made up of a sequence of several transparent ghost videos that could be experienced by looking around and pointing the camera in sideward directions. At the end of the scene, the next memory images were presented, and the pattern could be repeated. After we established this pattern idea as a design rationale in the team, it was easier for the writer to adapt all scenes to the same spatial structure.

The end-user evaluation in this project [29] showed that the majority of users, who all had no previous training in using the app, could interact with the prototype after a short tutorial. However, as expected, all users considered the tutorial as highly necessary. It is fair to mention that one group of users had general difficulties, as it was their first contact with the concept of Augmented Reality.

The takeaway for authoring here is that authors or the team of authors are advised to come to a point in the design process, at which an integrated interaction pattern is established that will henceforth guide all ideas for interactive narrative content. However, the choice of interaction pattern can conversely depend on the narrative content or genre, underlining the importance of iterative design.

3.4 Iterative Design and Gaps Between Creation and Experience Platforms

Since iterative design is predominant in interactive media design, as is also the case in game design, it is certainly no surprise that we emphasize this way of work here as well. In all sorts of interactive narrative, the creative process and implementation are not a one-way street and need to include cycles of prototyping, testing, and improving. This means technical debugging as well as potentially adjusting interaction and story concepts after inspecting their partly unforeseeable outcomes.

Hence, when interactive narratives at a conceptual level need to be perfectly integrated with novel technical input possibilities and physical environments, it cannot be predetermined what authoring step needs to be undertaken first. The story may depend on a path to locations or immobile objects, their distances and features. It may also depend on ideas for multimodal interaction. The choice of locations, objects or their deliberate physical design may depend on the story, or on researched knowledge and existing material, as described above. It is crucial to take a spiral path across all design parameters [39], opening up in the beginning to consider many possibilities and combinations. In these phases, a kind of sandbox metaphor of work can lead to several playful prototypes that allow answering partial interaction design questions, and at the same time test narrative ideas. It is crucial that end-users are involved as testers in these cycles of prototyping and testing. All design possibilities must be filtered according to intermediate evaluations and project goals, and then narrowed down to a feasible interaction pattern. After a general pattern is established, more "bulk" narrative content can be written. This is usually the point that the sandbox phase ends and an implementation phase starts, in which it becomes more difficult to make changes at the conceptual levels.

A key experience feature of augmented reality and virtual worlds is the ability for immersion. Beyond concepts of mental immersion in a story, here we talk about a technically induced immersion (by immersive technology) that allows or supports the experience of "presence". While VR presence has to do with a believable imagination that the virtual surroundings look, sound, and feel real, AR means the integration of virtual content into a physical environment. There must be a shared perception of the physical reality being present together with the digital elements of the story.

One specific resulting authoring problem of interactive narrative in location-based AR is the typical distance between the end-user target environment and the ideal authoring environment. Content research, writing, creating assets as well as using a complex tool such as Unity are tasks that lean towards office work at a well-equipped desk. However, the location of the experience, such as a museum, an exhibition or even an outdoor path is often far away from that office. In a phase in which designers need frequent user tests, it is a challenge to have to move between these environments quite often. The iterative design cycle needs to be as short as possible.

There are two solutions to this problem: First, the real environment needs to be simulated close to the authors' office desks [21]. For example, poster images of a real environment could be hung on walls, as we did in the Roman fort project [31]. These images were used as triggers to test parts of the interaction, while of course, GPS had to be turned off, because this would have needed the real location to work. A pseudo exhibition can also be physically built representing a certain museum interior, modelled with cardboard ("brownboxing" [40]). The second solution is that, at least partially, certain authoring tool functions need to be extracted from a stationary tool (like Unity) and implemented on the final mobile test device [41, 42]. While the full authoring suite might not work on the mobile device, it is important to have some authoring parameters changeable right on the spot, when tests and final authoring adjustments are made at the real location.

This is increasingly important the more the end-user experience differs from the authoring perception, for example with the target hardware of a head-mounted display. Authoring for the HoloLens 2 needs to be performed mainly at a high-level desktop workstation in Unity with appropriate plug-ins. However, it is necessary to obtain a spatial scan of the physical target environment for placing augmentations more or less accurately. For presentXR, the authoring of assets and of the conditional progress of the experience was done in Unity. Then, the spatial setup of the assets were directly arranged within the museum environment, while wearing the HMD in an authoring mode with appropriate customized tools that had to be developed within the project [42]. After saving positions and sizes, iterative tests needed to be run to adjust timing and durations as narrative conditions. The need to partially design and test at a remote place away from the desktop is a time-consuming burden. It is also a special kind of "authoring problem", which needs to be taken into account in a project plan.

4 Conclusion

In this chapter, we have looked at general and specific IDN authoring challenges that come along with using novel technologies and novel interaction styles and paradigms, such as location-based Augmented Reality and other non-standard interaction styles. Therefore, the emphasis has been on interaction design, especially on the ways in which interactive narrative authors need to think and care about interaction design. Some of the issues mentioned are also relevant in the more traditional interaction paradigms of pointing and clicking.

The main points are:

- **Repeatable interaction patterns**. Natural and invisible interfaces lead to the problem that users need to learn the bounds of the interaction. Therefore, keep the interaction as simple as possible, and think of a repeatable interaction pattern. This is a general advice for all forms of IDN, albeit for standard interaction styles, this is easier to accomplish than with immersive media. In addition, after a repeatable pattern sequence (similar to a core game loop) is defined, it is also easier for writers to follow this structure.
- **Integrated art and design**. In an ideal world, this interaction pattern would be well integrated with the overall narrative design, so that it fits the 'gist' of the interactive narrative. This underlines the point that this design is a holistic process of art creation.
- **Usability engineering**. User failure and challenges at difficult interface levels are either frustrating or at least distracting from a narrative experience. This implies that in addition to the creation of art, authoring may require typical tasks of usability engineering, a profession of its own.
- **Appropriate narrative depth and length**. We probably cannot tell every story with every interaction pattern. The range of emotional depth of characters, their arc of change, or embroilments and complication within a storyline, are subject to potential limitations in how they are experienced by the audience in different physical settings. Especially in mobile and public situations, the narrative may need to be rather short.
- **Iterative authoring processes**. It is useful to prototype interactive drafts, test them with end-users, and repeat this process in an iterative cycle. Authoring tools should support the connection between editing mode and play mode, especially when editing occurs at the desk and playing occurs somewhere else in the field. The design cycle between testing and applying ideas for redesign must be as short as possible. The tools should allow creation to begin at any point in the process.

The topics raised illustrate that authoring is more than thinking about the story. Finding the forms of interaction may be another equally important effort in the creation of interactive narrative, turning the setup for interaction into an essential part of the content creation.

References

1. Norman DA (1998) The invisible computer: why good products can fail, the personal computer is so complex, and information appliances are the solution. MIT Press, Cambridge, Mass
2. Mateas M, Stern A (2005) Structuring content in the Façade interactive drama architecture. In: Proceedings of the first artificial intelligence and interactive digital entertainment conference, AIIDE 2005, pp 93–98
3. Mateas M, Stern A (2004) Natural language understanding in Façade: surface-text processing. In: Göbel et al (eds) TIDSE 2004, Proceedings. Lecture notes in computer science, vol 3105. Springer, Heidelberg, pp 3–13
4. Dow S, Mehta M, Lausier A, MacIntyre B, Mateas M (2006) Initial lessons from AR Façade, an interactive augmented reality drama. In: Proceedings of the ACM SIGCHI international conference on ACE'06. ACM, New York, NY, USA. https://doi.org/10.1145/1178823.1178858
5. Aylett R, Vala M, Sequeira P, Paiva A (2007) FearNot!—an emergent narrative approach to virtual dramas for anti-bullying education. In: Virtual storytelling. Proceedings ICVS 2007. Lecture notes in computer science, vol 4871. Springer, Berlin-Heidelberg, pp 202–210
6. Pausch R, Snoddy J, Taylor R, Watson S, Haseltine E (1996) Disney's Aladdin: first steps toward storytelling in virtual reality. In: Proceedings of the SIGGRAPH'96. ACM, pp 193–203
7. Rickel J, Gratch J, Hill RW, Marsella S, Swartout W (2001) Steve goes to Bosnia: towards a new generation of virtual humans for interactive experiences. Aaai.org
8. Traum D, Jones A, Hays K, Maio H, Alexander O, Artstein R, Debevec P, Gainer A, Georgila K, Haase K, Jungblut K, Leuski A, Smith S, Swartout W (2015) New dimensions in testimony: digitally preserving a Holocaust survivor's interactive storytelling. In: Schoenau-Fog H, Bruni L, Louchart S, Baceviciute S (eds) Interactive storytelling. ICIDS 2015. Lecture notes in computer science, vol 9445. Springer, Cham, pp 269–281. https://doi.org/10.1007/978-3-319-27036-4_26
9. Kretschmer U, Coors V, Spierling U, Grasbon D, Schneider K, Rojas I, Malaka R (2001) Meeting the spirit of history. In: Proceedings of the international symposium on virtual reality, archaeology and cultural heritage, VAST 2001, Glyfada, Greece, pp 161–172
10. MacIntyre B, Bolter JD, Gandy M (2004) Presence and the aura of meaningful places. In: Presence: teleoperators and virtual environments, vol 6, no 2, pp 197–206
11. Haahr M, Carrigy T, Naliuka K, Paterson N, Cotton R (2011) Chasing the ghost: reinventing Gothic horror as a location-based mobile game. In: Lucas B (ed) International conference for the fantastic in the arts, Orlando, FL
12. Spierling U, Coors V (2014) SPIRIT—entertaining encounters with ancient history. In: Proceedings of the Eurographics workshop on graphics and cultural heritage. https://doi.org/10.2312/gch.20141322
13. Benford S, Magerkurth C, Ljungstrand P (2005) Bridging the physical and digital in pervasive gaming. Commun ACM 48, 3(March 2005):54–57
14. Misraraj A (2018) Augmented reality UX principles we can learn from Fragments for HoloLens. The future of immersive gaming experiences. https://blog.prototypr.io/augmented-reality-ux-principles-we-can-learn-from-fragments-for-hololens-38ce4c19990b. Accessed 20 May 2022
15. Jin Y, Ma M, Zhu Y (2022) A comparison of natural user interface and graphical user interface for narrative in HMD-based augmented reality. Multimed Tools Appl 81:5795–5826. https://doi.org/10.1007/s11042-021-11723-0
16. Norman D (2010) Natural user interfaces are not natural. Interactions 17(3):6–10. ACM, New York
17. Halatoe S (2015) Beyond Eyes. Independent game, developed by Sherida Halatoe with Tiger & Squid. Team17, NL/UK. https://store.steampowered.com/app/356050/Beyond_Eyes/
18. Dörner R, Kallmann M, Huang Y (2015) Content creation and authoring challenges for virtual environments: from user interfaces to autonomous virtual characters. In: Brunnett et al (eds) Virtual realities. Lecture notes in computer science, vol 8844. Springer, Cham, pp 187–212. https://doi.org/10.1007/978-3-319-17043-5_11

19. Nebeling M, Speicher M (2018) The trouble with augmented reality/virtual reality authoring tools. In: 2018 IEEE international symposium on mixed and augmented reality adjunct (ISMAR-Adjunct), Munich, Germany, pp 333–337
20. Park S, Bokijonov S, Choi Y (2021) Review of Microsoft HoloLens applications over the past five years. Appl Sci 11:7259. https://doi.org/10.3390/app11167259
21. MacIntyre B, Gandy M, Dow S, Bolter JD (2004) DART: a toolkit for rapid design exploration of augmented reality experiences. In: ACM user interface software and technology, Proceedings UIST04. ACM CHI Lett 6(2):197–206
22. Horst R, Dörner R (2019) Virtual reality forge: pattern-oriented authoring of virtual reality nuggets. In: 25th ACM symposium on virtual reality software and technology (VRST'19). ACM, New York, NY, USA, Article 19, pp 1–12
23. Abawi DF, Dörner R, Haller M, Zauner J (2004) Efficient mixed reality application development. In: 1st European conference on visual media production (CVMP), London, England, March 15, pp 289–294
24. Unity website. https://unity.com/
25. Spierling U (2015) Interaction design principles as narrative techniques for interactive digital storytelling. In: Ferri G, Koenitz H, Haahr M, Sezen D, Sezen TI (eds) Interactive digital narrative—history, theory, and practice. ECREA, Routledge, pp 159–173
26. Foley JD, van Dam A, Feiner SK, Hughes JF (1995) Computer graphics, principles and practice. Second edition in C. Reprint with corrections 1997. Addison-Wesley Professional
27. Haller M (2004) Photorealism or/and non-photorealism in augmented reality. In: Proceedings of the ACM international conference on VR continuum and its applications in industry (VRCAI'04). ACM, New York, NY, pp 189–196. https://doi.org/10.1145/1044588.1044627
28. Steptoe W, Julier J, Steed A (2014) Presence and discernability in conventional and non-photorealistic immersive augmented reality. In: International symposium on mixed and augmented reality (ISMAR 2014), Munich, Germany, 10–12 September 2014
29. Spierling U, Winzer P, Massarczyk E (2017) Experiencing the presence of historical stories with location-based augmented reality. In: Nunes N et al (eds) Proceedings of the ICIDS 2017. Lecture notes in computer science, vol 10690. Springer International Publishing, Cham, pp 49–62
30. Bitter JL, Dörner R, Liu Y, Rau L, Spierling U (2022) Follow the blue butterfly—an immersive augmented reality museum guide. In: Proceedings of the HCII 2022 (24th international conference on human-computer interaction), CCIS, vol 1582. Springer
31. Spierling U, Kampa A, Stöbener K (2016) Magic equipment: integrating digital narrative and interaction design in an augmented reality quest. In: Proceedings of international conference on culture and computer science, ICCCS 2016. Windhoek, Namibia, pp 56–61
32. Norman D (1990) The design of everyday things. Doubleday
33. Benyon D (2019) Designing user experience: a guide to HCI, UX and interaction design, 4th edn. Addison-Wesley, Pearson Education Limited
34. Schank R, Abelson R (1977) Scripts, plans, goals, and understanding. Lawrence Erlbaum, Hillsdale, NJ
35. Bayle E (1998) Putting it all together: towards a pattern language for interaction design. SIGCHI Bull 30(1):17–24
36. Borchers JO (2000) A pattern approach to interaction design. In: Proceedings of the 3rd conference on designing interactive systems: processes, practices, methods, and techniques (DIS'00). ACM, New York, NY, pp 69–378. https://doi.org/10.1145/347642.347795
37. Niantic: Pokémon Go. Location-based game, developed for The Pokémon Company, Nintendo, USA (2016)
38. Björk S, Lundgren S, Holopainen J (2003) Game design patterns. In: Copier M, Raessens J (eds) Level up—proceedings of digital games research conference 2003, Utrecht, The Netherlands
39. Fullerton T, Swain C, Hoffman S (2004) Game design workshop: designing, prototyping, and playtesting games. CMP Books, McGraw-Hill Professional
40. Patton S (2019) Brownboxing. The secret to rapid VR prototyping. In: Sherman W (ed) VR developer gems. A K Peters/CRC Press, New York. https://doi.org/10.1201/b21598

41. Kampa A, Spierling U (2017) Smart authoring for location-based augmented reality storytelling applications. In: Eibl M, Gaedke M (eds) Proceedings INFORMATIK 2017. Gesellschaft für Informatik, Bonn, pp 915–922. https://doi.org/10.18420/in2017_93
42. Rau L, Bitter JL, Liu Y, Spierling U, Dörner R (2022) Supporting the creation of non-linear everyday AR experiences in exhibitions and museums: an authoring process based on self-contained building blocks. Frontiers in Virtual Reality, Sec. Technologies for VR. https://doi.org/10.3389/frvir.2022.955437

Writing for Replay: Supporting the Authoring of Kaleidoscopic Interactive Narratives

Alex Mitchell⏺

Abstract The ability for players to go back and replay, either to see the impact of their choices or to experience the story from a different perspective, is one of the fundamental properties of interactive narratives. In this chapter, I focus on replay stories, a form of interactive narrative that is deliberately designed to encourage, or even require, repeat encounters. I begin by providing an overview of what we know about repeat experience of interactive narratives, and the challenges authors face when deliberately designing this type of work. I then explore the question of how authoring tools can provide support for authoring replay stories, suggesting both ways that tools can support this type of authoring, and the possible limitations on tool support for authoring replay stories. The chapter ends with some open questions for future research in this area.

1 Introduction

One of the fundamental properties of interactive narratives is the ability for players to go back and try out different paths or variations, either to see how their choices impact the outcome or to see the story from a different perspective, something Murray [1, 2] refers to as *kaleidoscopic form*. While this notion of interactive narratives as *replay* stories has long been acknowledged as important from the perspective of the player experience [3–6], and as part of the underlying structural patterns of forms such as hypertext fiction [7], little attention has been paid to how an author can attend to and consciously and deliberately design for replay during the writing process, or how this can be supported in the form of authoring tools.

Authoring any type of interactive narrative is inherently challenging, as this potentially requires a wide range of skills, including algorithmic design, programming and artistic design [8]. A key issue is that, as with games, authors of interactive narratives are not able to directly design an experience. Authoring an interactive narrative is akin to what Salen and Zimmerman call "second-order design" [9, 10]: the author

A. Mitchell (✉)
National University of Singapore, Singapore, Singapore
e-mail: alexm@nus.edu.sg

© The Author(s), under exclusive license to Springer Nature Switzerland AG 2022
C. Hargood et al. (eds.), *The Authoring Problem*, Human–Computer Interaction Series,
https://doi.org/10.1007/978-3-031-05214-9_9

creates the computational systems that a player eventually encounters, and through that encounter an experience emerges [11]. This suggests that the author does not directly design the experience, but instead designs the materials that enable that experience. In addition to designing the computational system, the author also needs to consider how the player will interact with this system [12].[1] When the player encounters both the playable system and the units of narrative [13], the resulting experience emerges through the process of interpretation of both the instantiated narrative being encountered, and the player's interaction with and process of making sense of the underlying system [14, 15]. The author's intention is to influence the player's experience, but the author can only do this at one step removed, working at the system level and through the design of the interface to the system.

Much of the work done to develop authoring tools for interactive narratives have focused on the problem of supporting this complex range of skill sets and tasks, as can be seen in recent surveys of authoring tools [16] and discussions of the ways that the authoring problem has been addressed [17]. If, in addition to trying to help authors address the problem of creating an interactive narrative we also want to specifically help authors create interactive narratives that are *meant* to be replayed, we need to consider how this changes the authoring problem.

To create a replay story, "an interactive digital story structure in which the same scenario is offered for replay with significant variations based on parameters that the interactor may control or merely witness in action" [18], the author has to consider not just how the player will experience the story on a single playthrough, but on multiple playthroughs. This involves understanding how to motivate the player to replay and how to reward that replay [5, 19]. It also requires an understanding of how the player's motivations to replay may change over the course of a number of playthroughs [20, 21], how the player's perception of the underlying system may impact replay [22], and whether this creates additional constraints on how much each playthrough can be procedurally varied [23].[2] The author may want to encourage what I have elsewhere described [5, 6] as equivalent to Calinescu's simple or reflective rereading [24], or perhaps something closer to what my co-authors and I call kaleidoscopic play [25]. If the author intends to use a "rewind" mechanic to encourage or perhaps even require replay [26, 27], the author additionally needs to consider how the use of techniques such as cross-sessional memory [28, 29] can impact the experience. I will expand on these various forms of replay in the next section.

These issues are not explicitly addressed in current approaches to designing authoring tools. While current tools tend to focus on the problem of supporting the range of demands that creating an interactive narrative places on authors from a conceptual and technical perspective, as summarised by Szilas [8] and Spierling and Szilas [30], the issues mentioned above arguably require additional support. In

---

[1] For further discussion of the problem of designing how a player will interact with an interactive narrative, see the chapter by Spierling in this volume.

[2] This raises interesting questions regarding replay of emergent narrative, which are arguably by nature designed for replay but can lead to a very different form of repeat experience. While beyond the scope of this chapter, this is certainly worth exploring further. For more on the challenges of authoring emergent narratives, see the chapters by Kreminski et al. and Kybartas in this volume.

this chapter, I reconsider the authoring problem through the lens of repeat experience and explore what it means to provide authors with tools to support authoring of interactive narratives as *replay stories*.

2   What Do We Know About Repeat Experience?

There has been extensive discussion of how people reexperience stories [24, 31–35]. In terms of why people reread non-interactive narratives, Calinescu [24] proposes three forms of rereading. *Partial* rereading involves going back and trying to complete your understanding of a work that you have finished but don't fully comprehend. For example, after watching the film *Memento* [36], with its interweaving of forward and reverse chronology, it is likely that you will need to go back and rewatch the film simply to piece together the chronological order of the events. *Simple* rereading takes the form of returning to a story to recapture the original experience of the story. This could involve, for example, rewatching a romantic film such as *You've Got Mail* [37] to relive the emotions you felt on the first viewing. Finally, *reflective* rereading is an analytical process of returning to a story to look for deeper meanings, investigate the workings of the text, or otherwise critically analyse the work. This is the type of repeat experience that a film with a twist ending such as *The Sixth Sense* [38] encourages, as you are likely to rewatch the film to examine the techniques the filmmaker used to mislead you in your first viewing.

Turning to interactive narratives, early discussions of repeat experience tended to focus on a debate between whether people return to complex hypertext fictions such as *afternoon, a story* [39] to experience variation, or to reach closure [3, 40–42]. More recently, Murray [1] has suggested that although people tend to replay for variation, they are actually looking for some larger meaning and to eventually reach closure, in what she describes as kaleidoscopic storytelling. I build upon this [5, 6], incorporating Calinescu's categories of rereading with the results of empirical studies of player experience to argue that players initially replay interactive stories to pursue particular goals, such as reaching the best ending or seeing variations, something I see as similar to Calinescu's partial rereading. After reaching this goal, I suggest that players shift to something equivalent to simple or reflective rereading. At this point, I argue that players change what they are doing, no longer working towards closure but instead looking for something new in the work.

Taking this further, I have suggested [22] that in order for a work to encourage and reward replay beyond closure, it needs to enable, or even encourage, players to reach both system and narrative closure. One way to do this, I argue, is for the work to manifest Wardrip-Fruin's SimCity effect [43], where the playable system is both appropriately complex, and this complexity becomes apparent to the player through their interaction with the work. I suggest that for this reason, works such as *The Walking Dead* [44] and *Facade* [45], while replayable, do not encourage replay beyond closure, whereas a work such as *Blood and Laurels* [46] does. This position was further refined in my later work [20], reframed in terms of Reed's notion of storygames [13].

More recently, my co-authors and I [20, 21, 25] have argued that my earlier model is too simplistic, failing as it does to capture the more dynamic nature of replay. We claim that rather than moving linearly from partial to simple or reflective replay, a player can instead move back and forth between partial and reflective replay as the player encounters new material which may suggest that they have or have not reached closure. This can be seen in works such as *Bandersnatch* [47] and *Cultist Simulator* [48],[3] where repeat encounters either reveal the system to be less complex than initially thought, or uncover new connections between the story and the playable system [20]. In empirical studies, my co-authors and I observed that players engage in a form of cost–benefit analysis when choosing whether to replay, deciding whether it is worth engaging in a repeat experience based on the likelihood of achieving their goals [21]. Based on these studies, we also suggest that players can engage in reflective replay without coming to a sense of closure, in what we call kaleidoscopic play, after Murray's notion of interactive stories as a kaleidoscopic medium. This can be seen in the player's ability to repeatedly revisit a game such as *Elsinore* [49] without having to replay from the start [25].

Synthesising this work from the perspective of what authors can do to support repeat experience, I propose [19] that there are three ways that an author can encourage and reward repeat experience of interactive stories: by using the (promise of) variation to encourage replay, by requiring replay for the player to work towards closure or by requiring replay for the player to reach a deeper understanding of both the system and the narrative. All these approaches present specific challenges to authors.

3   What Is a *Repeat Experience* of an Interactive Narrative?

Before discussing ways to help authors create an interactive narrative that deliberately supports repeat experience, it is worth considering what exactly we mean by the repeat experience of an interactive story. This may seem trivial: a repeat experience is, by definition, an experience of something *again*, after having *previously* experienced it. For example, you may have read a short story or a novel, and then later in life go back and read the same short story or novel again. While this second reading may possibly involve the same physical text as the first reading, or perhaps a different physical text containing the same words, it is intuitive to say that you are having a repeat experience of that story. You may have changed, if for no other reason than having read the story, but the story itself is the same.

---

[3] As mentioned earlier, it is worth noting that a work such as *Cultist Simulator*, which can be seen as a form of emergent narrative, can lead to a very different form of repeat experience than a hypertext-like interactive narrative such as *Bandersnatch*.

In the context of interactive narratives, this is not so straightforward. If a repeat experience is an experience of something again, after having previously experienced it, we need to know what it means to "experience something again" when, as is the case in an interactive narrative, the thing you are experiencing may be different each time you encounter it, at least at the level of a particular instantiated *process* and resulting *product*, to use Koenitz's SPP model of interactive digital narratives [14, 50]. In addition, we need to know what it means to say that you are doing this "after having previously experienced" the interactive narrative, as this implies some form of *complete* previous experience. What does it mean to have "completed" an interactive narrative such that you can experience it "again"?

Following from my recent work [25], in this chapter I will consider an interactive narrative to have been "completed" in the mechanical sense when the player has run through a *traversal*, which Montfort [51] defines as an encounter a player has with a work from a beginning to an end, where a *beginning* is the point at which the interactive narrative does not differ in any way in terms of stored state from when it was first installed, and an *end* is that point at which the player can no longer take any action without the work being reset to its initial state. It is important to note that this is a purely mechanical definition, without reference to how the player may view their experience of the interactive narrative, or what they feel that they are doing as they experience the story.

This is an important distinction, since as I have argued [5], players tend to only consider themselves to be "rereading" (to use my earlier terminology) when they feel that they "get it", meaning they have reached some form of closure. By "closure", I follow [20] in which my co-authors and I distinguish between *narrative closure* and *system closure*, where narrative closure is "the phenomenological feeling of finality that is generated when all the questions saliently posed by the narrative are answered" [52], and system closure is equivalent to Murray's electronic closure, which "occurs when a work's structure, though not its plot, is understood" [1]. As I have pointed out elsewhere [5], this means that a player can reach the end of a work and not necessarily have reached either narrative or system closure, and conversely could conceivably reach one or both forms of closure without reaching the end of a particular traversal. This suggests that the mechanical and experiential definitions of repeat experience may differ.

In addition, I have proposed [5] that a *replay* represents a complete, new traversal from beginning to end, and following Kleinmann [26, 27], they consider a *rewind* to involve going back to an earlier point within the narrative or gameplay, which may or may not be presented to the player as a restart, such that the player can then progress. As this neither involved reaching an end nor a return to a beginning, it is not a replay in the strict sense I previously defined. Kleinman considers this to be a "rewind mechanic", as it is required to progress play, as distinct from simply reloading a save point. It is also important to note that this is different from a player re-encountering narrative content in the form of what Bernstein [7], after Joyce [4], calls a "cycle", which involves repeat exposure but is not mechanically required for further progression through the work.

This definition of replay necessarily complicates the notion of repeat experience, but in doing so reflects the complexity of this concept in the context of interactive narratives. For example, it raises the question of whether the type of "new game plus" seen in a game such as *Oxenfree* [53], where a player starts a "new game" but the fact that the player has already completed a playthrough is carried over to the subsequent playthrough, can be considered a replay (according to my definition, it would not). It also problematises the repetition seen in games such as *Save the Date* [54] and *Nier: Automata* [55], which as discussed below can be seen more as a "long playthrough" than a sequence of replays.

4   The Challenge of Creating Replay Stories

With a few exceptions, all interactive narratives can potentially be replayed. In this chapter, I am interested specifically in what Murray [18] refers to as replay stories, in which the author deliberately designs the interactive narrative such that players are encouraged, or perhaps even required, to either go back and replay the work, or to revisit particular scenarios or sequences by means of a rewind mechanic or a cycle, so as to reach some form of closure. Examples of this type of work include *Save the Date* [54], *Elsinore* [49], *Overboard!* [56] and *Twelve Minutes* [57].

If replay stories and kaleidoscopic play present particular challenges to authors, what are some of the ways that an author can be supported to tackle these challenges? Is there something that an authoring tool can do to help an author of a replay story, beyond what is required for more general interactive narrative authoring tools? From the above discussion, there are several issues that should be considered when designing a tool for authoring replay stories, including:

1. How can a tool help an author account for how a player's focus on the system and/or the story may change, both within and between play sessions?
2. How can a tool provide abstractions that enable authors to appropriately make visible the relevant details of the underlying computational system for the player without distracting from a focus on the story?
3. What support can tools provide for variation, both within and across play sessions, while maintaining some level of consistency and coherence?
4. How can a tool incorporate support for cross-sessional memory, rewind mechanics and other "meta-game" mechanics such as fast-forward and skip?
5. In addition, how should a tool provide visualisations and abstractions for authors to help them understand and make use of these concepts?
6. Finally, how can a tool support testing and revision of a story that is meant to be played many times?

Exploring solutions to these issues can potentially also help designers of authoring tools to better support all authors, not just those who are interested in creating highly replayable, kaleidoscopic interactive narratives. These explorations can also help us to better understand both the experience of authoring kaleidoscopic interactive narratives, and interactive narratives more generally.

In the next section, I will examine several tools that provide support for authoring specific forms of repetition and replay and consider how this impacts the authoring process.

5   How Can Tools Support Authoring of Replay Stories?

In his seminal discussion of rereading hypertext fiction, Michael Joyce describes a question that he uses to get authors thinking about what it means to reread: "Suppose at this point your reader, before going on, has to reread one part of what comes before, which would it be?" As he says immediately after this, "No one asks why. There are reasons" [4]. This quote, with its suggestion of both the necessity of replay and the challenges of explaining that necessity, highlights the centrality of repeat experience in various forms of interactive narratives, and the difficulty of articulating and expressing the reasons behind and the implications of replay.

This difficulty suggests that any "tool" that we design to help authors create replayable interactive narratives needs to provide some ways for authors to *think* about replay, and by doing so enable them to better make use of replay as part of their process of creating an interactive narrative. Thus, we can broadly think of a "tool" as anything that can help authors with the process of both *thinking* about replay and taking action to *implement* their thoughts about replay concretely in an interactive narrative.

I now explore ways that tools have been designed to help authors both think about and implement repetition and replay within a play session (*Storyspace* [58] and *Stornaway* [59]), across play sessions (*Ren'Py* [60]) and through parameterization (*Timeline* [61]).

5.1   *Supporting Repetition and Replay* **Within** *a Single Playthrough*

As Joyce suggests in the quote above, the simple act of asking a reader to go back and re-encounter a passage of text raises not only conceptual issues but also potentially technical issues in terms of how the author would like the text to respond to that repetition. If, for example, an author has created a hypertext with four nodes, or "spaces" as Joyce refers to them, and after reading the fourth space, the reader is required to go back to the second space, this creates several possibilities for how the author may want to handle this:

> [T]he second space now cries for some way to shape its reading for different readers. We want the reader newly come into this simple story to proceed briskly through its inevitable

narrative, pause at the reentry, and then leap, without orbiting endlessly, unless that is our intention. In any text there are ways to do this, by inference, suggestion, rule, music, or seduction. To these hypertext adds memory and resistance. Storyspace and other complex hypertext systems let a writer set conditions that shape the reading according to simple rules that match the reader's experience of the text against the possibilities it opens to her. In a richly linked hypertext these rules (in Storyspace they are called "guard fields") can compound. [4]

In the context of an interactive narrative, even one that is relatively simple in terms of the computational system such as a hypertext, there is immediately this additional layer of complexity. Authors not only need to think about *what it means* to incorporate some form of explicit, deliberate repetition into a work, but also need to think about *how to implement* this repetition, and what consequences this has for the reader's experience. A tool such as *Storyspace* [58] provides means for an author to procedurally alter both what the reader sees when encountering a portion of a work and what the reader can do from that point in the text. It does not, however, provide any explicit support for how the author should *think* about this, or what it means for the reader to encounter the same text a second time.

Similarly, the interactive video authoring tool *Stornaway* [59] provides a branching view for authors with direct support for revisiting nodes, which it calls "story islands", through the use of multiple "in" tabs, which can be used to vary the node content and the available choices, while retaining the same video. Similar tool-level support for varying content when revisiting a node in a hypertext, although without a clear visual representation, is also provided in tools such as *Twine* [62] and *HypeDyn* [63], all of which allow authors to check if a node is being visited or revisited and change content or behaviour accordingly.[4]

5.2 Supporting Replaying "from the Start"

The tools discussed above help an author to implement repeat experience *within* a specific playthrough of a work, something I refer to as a "micro-rereading" [64]. This is a very particular form of repeat experience. What about a repeat experi-ence that involves going back and replaying "from the start"? How should this be conceptualised, and what issues does this raise for authoring?

One important consideration is whether the repeat experience is extra-diegetic or diegetic—is it only the player who is going back and re-experiencing the events of the story, or is it a "time loop" that also involves the character(s) in the story somehow going back over the same events [65]? If the player character, or other characters within the story, are (within the scope of the narrative) portrayed as being "aware" of the repeated experience, as in a work such as *Save the Date* [54], the process of

---

[4] It is worth noting that what I am describing here, namely the appearance across several tools of similar support for varying the content or behaviour of a node when it is revisited, could perhaps be seen as a "pattern" of the type described by Bernstein [7] in the context of hypertext. For more on the use of patterns for authoring of interactive narrative, see the chapter by Millard in this volume.

replay is likely to shift from one of repeat play to more of a "long playthrough". In this type of replay story, the player needs to make use of information and experiences from previous playthroughs to progress, while at the same time, the system often also needs to track game state across play sessions in the form of cross-sessional memory [28, 29]. This changes both how the author needs to think about the story, and what the author needs to take into consideration when implementing the story.

This is an increasingly common form of replay [26], but it is something that may not even be considered replay by those who are more familiar with these conventions. As Reddit user GreenBallasts explains, in a discussion of replay in visual novels:

> As far as routes, I don't really consider playing a different route in the same VN [visual novel] to be "replaying" it. Admittedly it does depend some on how the route structure is set up, if it's a mostly linear game with only slight deviations then I guess maybe you could get away with calling it that, but as far as games with the standard common route -> branching route structure each "replay" is really just the next stage of what I consider to be a single long playthrough. Almost all of the content you see during each route will be unique, and the common route stuff is usually just skipped over or skimmed on repeat playthroughs, so it's not really the same as playing the same game over and over. [66]

With this type of replay, players often expect that content they have seen in previous playthroughs can be "skipped over or skimmed", with many visual novels providing players with explicit mechanisms for doing this.

Correspondingly, tools that are designed specifically for authoring visual novels, such as *Ren'Py* [60], tend to support this type of structure [67], both at the authoring and playback level. In *Rep'Py*, this takes the form of support for persistent state across sessions or playthroughs [68], and the ability for authors to allow players to "rollback" to replay previous scenes [69] and to skip through text when replaying the work. These features are, in fact, highlighted as reasons for authors to choose *Ren'Py* as a tool, as these are "features players want". Features advertised as supporting player expectations include "[r]ollback, the ability to go back in time to see previously shown screens. The [player] can even make different choices the second time around", and "[t]he ability to skip through text when replaying, including the ability to skip only text that's been read" [70].

In addition to providing support for an author to implement these features into a story, the inclusion of these capabilities also encourages an author to think about interactive narratives in a particular manner. This goes beyond the implementation-level support for micro-rereading found in hypertext authoring tools. In the next section, I will examine a tool that takes this one step further and *requires* a particular way of thinking about replay.

5.3   *Supporting* Parameterised *Replay Stories*

Timeline [61] (and its earlier incarnation, *StoryLines* [71]) is a tool developed by Murray and her students to allow for the authoring of parametric replay stories of the type theorised in Murray's writings. As the developers explain, the tool is based on the idea that these stories are "parameterized", where parameters are settings which can be adjusted by players as they experience the story to see how the story changes as a result. The idea of these parameters is based on Propp's notion of morphemes [72]. In the player's view of the story, choices are "stacked" as tiles representing specific milestones in the story, and the player can slide these tiles up and down to change the currently active parameter. This use of tiles and conditions in "stacks" can be seen as a restricted form of sculptural hypertext [73, 74], where the constraint of tiles to a stack means the ordering of the tiles is always the same, but player choices can change which tiles are available in a given playthrough.

This approach to both the *Timeline* authoring tool and the player's view ensures that all possible paths in the story are always available, allowing the reader to see everything, and never end up in dead-ends. However, as Silva et al. observe, this also requires the author to think this way:

> Maintaining parallelism across all narrative possibilities requires a unique mindset for authors. Choice columns, in particular, require strict design criteria: Choices must be reframed as the narrative permutates and progresses, but must also remain parallel across branches. [61]

As they further explain:

> Emphasizing readable parallels promotes an additional design constraint: ontological consistency across instantiations. Unless motivated by the narrative's causal chain of events, characters should remain consistent between narrative branches. [61]

This idea of constraining variations is similar to the limits imposed on variation during replay that I have discussed elsewhere [23]. In that earlier paper, I suggest that in works that use some form of a reframing or twist ending to encourage replay, there are additional constraints on narrative coherence, selection and ordering that extend across play sessions, rather than simply within play sessions.

The *Timeline* authoring tool provides a visualisation of the story that is similar to the player's view, allowing authors to see the "columns" at the various milestones, and allowing for authoring of conditions determining which video will be played based on the currently selected morphemes. Interestingly, the tool does not seem to support actual authoring of the story structure, simply allowing for the implementation of the tiles and conditions. As Silva et al. explain, "When outlining their narratives, PeNLab members relied on branching diagrams before implementing and tweaking their designs via the authoring tool" [61]. It is worth considering what was missing in the tool such that these authors needed to visualise their stories using branching diagrams external to the tool, rather than working directly in the tool, and how this could be supported in an integrated manner.

6   How Much Support Is Appropriate?

A thread running through the above discussion is that while replay is an essential element of interactive narratives, there are many ways of thinking about and approaching this concept. This raises the question as to how much support for designing repeat experiences is appropriate in an authoring tool. Another way to think about this is to consider whether an authoring tool should embody a specific way of thinking about replay, and if so, whether this will unduly constrain the author. Providing affordances and constraints [75] are an important part of any design process. While it is always possible to work against affordances, and to work around constraints, it is also desirable to choose the tool that best fits what you want to do as an author. This involves being aware of the implications of the affordances and constraints of the tool. Discussions such as [67] highlight the dangers of choosing an authoring tool without fully understanding what it is designed for, leading to a situation where the author is potentially fighting against the tool, rather than being empowered by it.

The approach taken in *Timeline* provides an interesting study of the possibilities, and the challenges, of embodying a particular approach to repeat experience directly into a tool. It is worth comparing how other tools approach this. Rather than simply providing tools to *help* authors think about replay, *Timeline* arguably *requires* a particular way of thinking during authoring, constraining the author to a very specific approach to replay. In fact, the tool's structure seems to require authors to think along the lines of Murray's guidelines for replay stories [18]. In particular, the tool focuses on helping authors create "legible milestones", "parallel choices through icons", and "summary tableaus and jigsaw endings". For example, the use of "icons motivated authors to distil choice options to those most salient to a story's moral physics" [61].

In contrast, hypertext-like branching narrative authoring tools such as *Stornaway* allow authors to directly specify when nodes in the story can be visited, and how the content of those nodes can change on repeat visits. This direct support for variation is like the "choice columns" provided in *Timeline*. However, while *Stornaway* provides visualisation of the choice structure and alternative versions of nodes, unlike *Timeline*, *Stornaway* does not directly embody any theory of what a replay story should support in terms of the player's experience, unlike *Timeline*'s emphasis on "ontological consistency". Instead, *Stornaway* simply provides a mechanism to support and visually represent this variation. It is up to the author how they make use of this mechanism.

For a tool that is designed to support replay, it is important that the tool's designer makes it clear what they mean by replay. In *Timeline*, the tool's designers are clearly following Murray's notion of replay stories. In a replay story of this type, the player is not actually replaying in the sense that was defined earlier in this chapter. The player is also not rewinding in Kleinman's sense, as there is nothing that requires repetition before progression. Instead, the player is repeatedly returning to earlier moments of the story while maintaining an overall view of the story, to tweak parameters and see how this affects the story. The tool directly supports this, encouraging what Kway and I [25] call kaleidoscopic play from the start. To their credit, the designers of *Timeline* are very explicit about the fact that they are embodying Murray's concepts in their tool. If authors who choose to use this tool are aware of this and are trying to create replay stories of this sort, the authoring tool is likely to empower them to do just that.

Similarly, *Ren'Py* is designed for authoring a particular type of story—one that often involves not a repeated return to the same moments so as to tweak the parameters, but instead a replay of entire storylines, often from a different perspective, with less concern about parallelism and more of an interest in moving on to the "next stage of... a single long playthrough" [66]. The tool provides built-in support to help authors enable players to focus on this structure, optimising replay for variation by allowing players to skip over repeated content and focus on what is new. These features are available by default. In fact, as Consalvo and Stains [67] suggest, it can require additional effort for an author to design a story that *does not* make use of these features. Similar mechanisms can be seen in games such as *Elsinore* [49] where, as Kway and I [25] describe, these mechanisms effectively support kaleidoscopic play.

While tools such as *Timeline* and *Ren'Py* provide technical support for *implementing* replay stories, they also tend to embody specific ways of *thinking* about repeat experience. However, even in these tools, few of the challenges mentioned in Sect. 4 have been addressed. In addition, most other authoring tools provide neither direct technical nor conceptual support for authoring replay stories. This is somewhat surprising, given the centrality of replay to the experience of interactive narrative. However, it is also worth noting that other than Murray, my students and I, and perhaps Kleinman, there has been very little work done in the past 10 years to investigate repeat experience of interactive narratives. This suggests that this is an area badly in need of more research, not only in terms of supporting authoring but also in understanding what it means to replay an interactive narrative, and how this impacts how we think about interactive narratives more generally.

7 Conclusion

Authoring an interactive narrative that deliberately both encourages and rewards repeat experience is a challenging process. In this chapter, I have argued that it is important to think about how we, as researchers and technologists, can both help authors to think about the notion of repeat experience and implement these ideas into their interactive narratives. By providing a brief overview of tools that do embody specific approaches to repeat experience, I have tried to suggest that this sort of explicit support can both be helpful and constraining to authors. It is essential that tool designers be clear about what they mean by replay, and how this stance will impact those who use their tools. In addition, I have argued that there are many aspects of repeat experience that have not been explored at the level of tool support. This suggests that there is much room for future work in this area. Better understanding of how to support authors who want to create interactive stories that are meant to be replayed can help us both deepen our understanding of how to support the authoring process, and better understand interactive storytelling more generally.

References

1. Murray JH (1998) Hamlet on the holodeck: the future of narrative in cyberspace. The MIT Press
2. Murray JH (2018) Research into interactive digital narrative: a kaleidoscopic view. In: International conference on interactive digital storytelling, pp 3–17
3. Ciccoricco D (2005) Repetition and recombination: reading network fiction: a thesis submitted in fulfillment of the requirements for the Degree of Doctor of Philosophy in English in the University of Canterbury
4. Joyce M (1997) Nonce upon some times: rereading hypertext fiction. MFS Mod Fict Stud 43:579–597
5. Mitchell A, McGee K (2012) Reading again for the first time: a model of rereading in interactive stories. In: Oyarzun D, Peinado F, Young RM, Elizalde A, Méndez G (eds) Interactive storytelling. Springer, Berlin/Heidelberg, pp 202–213. https://doi.org/10.1007/978-3-642-34851-8-20
6. Mitchell A (2012) Reading again for the first time: rereading for closure in interactive stories
7. Bernstein M (1998) Patterns of hypertext. In: Proceedings of Hypertext '98. ACM Press, pp 21–29. https://doi.org/10.1145/276627.276630.
8. Szilas N (2005) The future of interactive drama. In: IE2005: Proceedings of the second Australasian conference on interactive entertainment. Creativity & Cognition Studios Press, Sydney, pp 193–199
9. Salen K, Zimmerman E (2004) Rules of play: game design fundamentals. MIT Press
10. Mitchell A (2008) Narrative production and interactive storytelling. Refract J Entertain Media 13
11. Wardrip-Fruin N, Mateas M, Dow S, Sali S (2009) Agency reconsidered. In: Barry A, Helen K, Tanya K (eds) Proceedings of the digital games research association conference (DiGRA)
12. Spierling U (2015) Interaction design principles as narrative techniques for interactive digital storytelling. Interact Digit Narrat Hist Theory Pract 159–173
13. Reed A (2017) Changeful tales: design-driven approaches toward more expressive storygames
14. Roth C, van Nuenen T, Koenitz H (2018) Ludonarrative hermeneutics: a way out and the narrative paradox. In: International conference on interactive digital storytelling, pp 93–106
15. Koenitz H (2010) Towards a theoretical framework for interactive digital narrative. In: Aylett R, Lim M, Louchart S, Petta P, Riedl M (eds) Interactive storytelling. Springer, Berlin/Heidelberg, pp 176–185
16. Shibolet Y, Knoller N, Koenitz H (2018) A framework for classifying and describing authoring tools for interactive digital narrative. In: International conference on interactive digital storytelling, pp 523–533
17. Kitromili S, Jordan J, Millard DE (2019) What is hypertext authoring? In: Proceedings of the 30th ACM conference on hypertext and social media. Association for Computing Machinery, New York, NY, pp 55–59. https://doi.org/10.1145/3342220.3343653.
18. Murray JH. Six key design strategies for replay stories. https://inventingthemedium.com/2013/05/15/six-key-design-strategies-for-replay-stories/. Accessed 09 Dec 2021
19. Mitchell A (2020) Encouraging and rewarding repeat play of storygames. In: Dillon R (ed) The digital gaming handbook. CRC Press (Taylor and Francis)
20. Mitchell A, Kway L, Lee BJ (2020) Storygameness: understanding repeat experience and the desire for closure in storygames. In: DiGRA 2020
21. Wang B, Ang ABH, Mitchell A (2021) "I need to play three times before I kind of understand": a preliminary exploration of players' reasons for (and against) replaying a visual novel. Proc ACM Hum-Comput Interact 5:257:1–257:17. https://doi.org/10.1145/3474684.
22. Mitchell A (2015) Reflective rereading and the SimCity effect in interactive stories. In: SchoenauFog H, Bruni LE, Louchart S, Baceviciute S (eds) 8th international conference on interactive digital storytelling, ICIDS 2015. Springer International Publishing AG, Aalborg Univ, Dept Architecture, Design & Media Technol, Copenhagen, pp 27–39. https://doi.org/10.1007/978-3-319-27036-4_3

23. Mitchell A, McGee K (2011) Rereading in interactive stories: constraints on agency and procedural variation. In: Si M, Thue D, Andre E, Lester J, Tanenbaum TJ, Zammitto V (eds) Lecture notes in computer science (including subseries Lecture notes in artificial intelligence and Lecture notes in bioinformatics). Springer, Berlin/Heidelberg, pp 37–42. https://doi.org/10.1007/978-3-642-25289-1_5
24. Calinescu M (1993) Rereading. Yale University Press
25. Mitchell A, Kway L (2020) "How do I restart this thing?" Repeat experience and resistance to closure in rewind storygames. In: Bosser A-G, Millard DE, Hargood C (eds) Interactive storytelling: proceedings of ICIDS 2020. Springer International Publishing, Cham, pp 164–177
26. Kleinman E, Carstensdottir E, El-Nasr MS (2018) Going forward by going back: re-defining rewind mechanics in narrative games. In: Proceedings of the 13th international conference on the foundations of digital games. ACM, New York, NY, pp 32:1–32:6. https://doi.org/10.1145/3235765.3235773
27. Kleinman E, Caro K, Zhu J (2020) From immersion to metagaming: understanding rewind mechanics in interactive storytelling. Entertain Comput 33:100322–100322. https://doi.org/10.1016/j.entcom.2019.100322
28. Koenitz H (2014) Save the date—cross-session memory, metanarrative and a challenge to endings. http://gamesandnarrative.net/save-the-date-cross-session-memory-metanarrative-and-a-challenge-of-endings/
29. Mitchell A (2018) Antimimetic rereading and defamiliarization in save the date. In: DiGRA '18—proceedings of the 2018 DiGRA international conference, Turin, Italy
30. Spierling U, Szilas N (2009) Authoring issues beyond tools. In: Joint international conference on interactive digital storytelling. Springer, pp 50–61
31. Galef D (1998) Second thoughts: a focus on rereading. Wayne State University Press
32. Leitch TM (1987) For (against) a theory of rereading. Mod Fict Stud 33:491–508
33. Brewer WF (1996) The nature of narrative suspense and the problem of rereading. In: Vorderer P, Wulff HJ, Friedrichsen M (eds) Suspense: conceptualizations, theoretical analyses, and empirical explorations. Routledge, pp 107–126
34. Gardner DL (2016) Rereading as a mechanism of defamiliarization in Proust. Poet Today 37:55–105
35. Bentley F, Murray J (2016) Understanding video rewatching experiences. In: Proceedings of the ACM international conference on interactive experiences for TV and online video, pp 69–75
36. Nolan C (2001) Memento. Pathe
37. Ephron N (1998) You've got mail. Warner Bros. Pictures
38. Shyamalan MN (1999) The sixth sense. Hollywood Pictures
39. Joyce M (1990) afternoon, a story. Eastgate Systems, Inc
40. Bernstein M (2009) On hypertext narrative. In: Proceedings of Hypertext '09. ACM Press, pp 5–14
41. Douglas JY (2001) The end of books—or books without end? Reading interactive narratives. University of Michigan Press
42. Harpold T (1994) Links and their vicissitudes: essays on hypertext
43. Wardrip-Fruin N (2007) Three play effects: Eliza, Tale-Spin, and SimCity. Digit Humanit
44. Telltale Games (2012) The walking dead: season 1 [computer game]. Telltale Games
45. Mateas M, Stern A (2005) Facade [interactive drama]. Procedural Arts
46. Short E (2014) Blood and Laurels [iPad app]
47. Netflix (2018) Bandersnatch [interactive film]
48. The Weather Factory (2018) Cultist simulator [PC computer game]. Humble Bundle Inc
49. Golden Glitch Studios (2019) Elsinore [computer game]. Golden Glitch Studios
50. Koenitz H (2015) Towards a specific theory of interactive digital narrative. In: Interactive digital narrative: history, theory and practice. Routledge, pp 91–105
51. Montfort N (2003) Twisty little passages: an approach to interactive fiction. MIT Press
52. Carroll N (2007) Narrative closure. Philos Stud 135:1–15
53. Night School Studios (2016) Oxenfree [PC computer game]
54. Paper Dino Software (2013) Save the date [PC computer game]

55. Taro Y (2017) Nier: Automata [Playstation 4 game]. Square Enix
56. Inkle (2021) Overboard! [computer game]
57. Antonio L (2021) Twelve minutes [computer game]
58. Storyspace [computer software]. Eastgate (1987)
59. Stornaway (2021)
60. Rothamel T (2004) Ren'Py [computer software]
61. Silva P, Gao S, Nayak S, Ramirez M, Stricklin C, Murray J (2021) Timeline: an authoring platform for parameterized stories. In: ACM international conference on interactive media experiences, pp 280–283
62. Klimas C (2009) Twine [computer software]
63. Mitchell A (2009) HypeDyn [computer software]
64. Mitchell A (2013) Rereading as echo: a close (re)reading of Emily short's "A family supper." ISSUE: Art J 2:121–129
65. Lahdenperä L (2018) "Live-die-repeat". The time loop as a narrative and a game mechanic. Int J Transmedia Lit (IJTL) 4:137–159
66. GreenBallasts. Replayability has al…. www.reddit.com/r/visualnovels/comments/6drbm5/rep layability_in_visual_novels/di4unqg/. Accessed 26 Jan 2022
67. Consalvo M, Staines D (2020) Reading Ren'Py: game engine affordances and design possibilities. Games Cult 1555412020973823–1555412020973823
68. Persistent data—Ren'Py documentation. https://www.renpy.org/doc/html/persistent.html. Accessed 27 Jan 2022
69. Saving, loading, and rollback—Ren'Py documentation. https://www.renpy.org/doc/html/save_load_rollback.html. Accessed 27 Jan 2022
70. Why Ren'Py? https://www.renpy.org/why.html. Accessed 27 Jan 2022
71. Murray JH, Goldenberg S, Agarwal K, Doris-Down A, Pokuri P, Ramanujam N, Chakravorty T (2011) StoryLines: an approach to navigating multisequential news and entertainment in a multiscreen framework. In: Proceedings of the 8th international conference on advances in computer entertainment technology, pp 92–92
72. Propp V (1968) Morphology of the folktale. University of Texas Press
73. Bernstein M, Millard DE, Weal MJ (2002) On writing sculptural hypertext. In: Proceedings of Hypertext '02. ACM, pp 65–66
74. Millard DE, Hargood C, Jewell MO, Weal MJ (2013) Canyons, deltas and plains: towards a unified sculptural model of location-based hypertext. In: Proceedings of the 24th ACM conference on hypertext and social media, pp 109–118
75. Norman DA (1999) Affordance, conventions, and design. Interactions 6:38–43

Strange Patterns: Structure and Post-structure in Interactive Digital Narratives

David E. Millard

Abstract Structure is key to interactive narrative authoring. It can be perceived at the micro, meso, and macro levels of navigation, and when presented as common patterns creates a toolbox from which authors can build their stories. This structuralist approach to authoring appeals to the engineer's mindset, but post-structuralists would argue that no patterns are fundamental or universal. As Interactive Digital Narratives become more gamelike they turn into Strange Hypertexts, with playful mechanics deeply aligned with their narrative goals. This ludonarrative aspect of IDNs is exactly the sort of shift in perspective that post-structuralism warned us about and suggests that patterns might limit authors rather than empowering them. This chapter reviews the reported patterns in hypertext and interactive narrative and explores how patterns could continue to be important for authoring in a strange and post-structural world.

1 Introduction

Agency is the defining feature of Interactive Digital Narrative (IDN) and is typically conveyed through player choices that have been arranged into some kind of navigational structure. This structure can be very complex. Patterns are a way of dealing with this complexity by identifying common reoccurring structures or sub-structures. They are therefore a tool for exploring the poetics of IDN.

Although patterns are a part of IDN theory, they are also of direct use in addressing the authoring problem [1]. First, they can be used as a way of informing authors of typical solutions to common problems. Second, they can provide a way for authors to create complex structure quickly within an authoring tool. Third, they can provide a lens by which an author might reflect on an existing structure (this could be directly supported within a tool, but is also possible without software support). In this sense they are therefore a type of Design Pattern and provide a toolbox for IDN authors to create structurally sophisticated interactive experiences.

D. E. Millard (✉)
University of Southampton, Southampton, UK
e-mail: dem@soton.ac.uk

© The Author(s), under exclusive license to Springer Nature Switzerland AG 2022
C. Hargood et al. (eds.), *The Authoring Problem*, Human–Computer Interaction Series,
https://doi.org/10.1007/978-3-031-05214-9_10

147

Over the last few decades a number of people have attempted to identify common patterns, but they are seldom presented in context with one another. The philosophy behind patterns is also rarely interrogated. Patterns are a result of a structuralist analysis of IDN, which inherits its approach directly from the structuralist movement of the twentieth century, but that movement has come under serious criticism, and for decades has been unfashionable in narratology and literary criticism.

In this chapter we will review the different patterns that have been proposed for IDN, by looking at the micro level (the key building blocks of IDN that define its different forms), the meso level (sub-structures that solve certain problems, or create particular effects within an IDN), and the macro level (high level structures that define the whole shape of a story, indicate the number of potential paths and alternative outcomes, and therefore capture a key part of the overall reader experience).

We will also explore the structuralist context of the work on patterns, seeing how IDN patterns fit in to the wider structuralist movement. At the end of the chapter we will consider the post-structuralist criticisms of structuralism and apply them to IDN, shedding light on the shortcomings of patterns and suggesting alternative approaches that might allow patterns to be used in a post-structural way.

The goal is to create both an index of key patterns discussed in the literature, and a theoretical foundation for the use of patterns in the future, which incorporates both their strengths and limitations. We begin with an overview of structuralism, and in particular its manifestation in narratology and IDN.

2   Structuralism, Narratology, and Design Patterns

Structuralism has its foundations in the work of Ferdinand de Saussure who advocated a structural linguistics that focused not on superficial *parole*—actual utterances—but on *langue*, the hidden structures that lie beneath them [2]. Saussure called his approach Semiology, but it was later adopted by the Prague School of linguists who used the term Structuralism and went on to became a popular approach across a range of disciplines. Broadly speaking, structuralist approaches are more interested in relationships or properties rather than objects or values, where "objects are defined by the set of relationships of which they are part and not by the qualities possessed by them taken in isolation" [3]. Structuralism is thus concerned with the underlying rules and patterns of a given phenomena, rather than its actual elements.[1]

The development of Structuralism was heavily influenced by earlier work in literary criticism known as Russian formalism. For example, in *Morphology of the Folktale* Vladimir Propp deconstructed Russian fairy tales into 31 functions which he observed (occurring in order but not exhaustively) throughout all of the 100 stories that he analysed [4]. Later structuralist scholars, like Levi-Strauss, went beyond this syntagmatic analysis of cultural texts, in his case by recognising common compo-

---

[1] As an example, a structuralist does not care that Obi-Wan Kenobi is a Jedi, and Gandalf is a wizard, but does care that they take the same role of a 'supernatural mentor' within their respective stories.

nents of myths, *mythemes*, which appear consistently across multiple cultures [5]. This sort of paradigmatic analysis is key to the structuralist approach. Paradigmatic from the root word Paradigm, itself derived from the Greek word for Pattern.

The structuralist approach to narratology has classical roots in Aristotle's Poetics and observations on the typically elements of Greek Tragedy. These persist to modern dramas, where the three act structure (setup, confrontation, and resolution) have become keystones of script writing technique [6].

Freytag's Pyramid, originally published in 1863 [7], also pre-dates the structuralist movement but nevertheless provides a structuralist analysis of drama: an *introduction* leads to *rising movement* and a *climax* (where the protagonist acts, and the story reaches a reflection point) followed by *falling action* and ultimately *catastrophe* (altered in more recent tellings to *denouement* to reflect the possibility of a happy ending). Later structuralists such as Tzvetan Todorov would undertake an analysis similar to Freytag, describing the shape of a story in five slightly more general parts [8]: an *equilibrium*, a *disruption* to that equilibrium, the *recognition* that all is not well, a struggle to *repair* the disruption, and a *restoration* of a (new) equilibrium.

The Russian formalists noted the distinction between *fabula* (the events of the story in the chronological order they occurred) and *syuzhet* (the order in which they are presented within the story) [9]. Todorov and Freytag's structural analyses of stories can thus be said to be concerned with the events of a narrative, as arranged in the syuzhet, and the way that they convey drama and engage the emotions of the audience over time.

Narratology applies just as much to IDN as it does to traditional storytelling forms, for example Wood uses the fabula/syuzhet distinction [10] to talk about different types of interactive narrative games and experiences; however in IDN the focus is often on the interactive element, so Wood uses her analysis to distinguish between those where players have agency over the fabula (so can dictate the outcome of the narratives) and those where they have agency over the syuzhet (the outcome is fixed, but they have control over how it is revealed). In both cases the player agency is managed by an interactive structure, which can be thought of as a kind of state machine managed by a story engine [11]. A simple example would be a hypertext structure, where the state machine is defined through a set of nodes and links.

Structure in IDN research typically refers to this interactive structure rather than the structures that are embedded in the text (or other media content) itself (as concerned Propp, Freytag, or Todorov). A structuralist approach to IDN thus elevates these structures as the subject of study and looks for common patterns that exist across multiple IDN artefacts.

These common patterns matter when it comes to the IDN authoring process. Using common patterns in design can be traced to the idea of *Design Patterns* first put forward by Christopher Alexander as a way of capturing architectural design ideas [12]. It has become especially popular in software engineering, specifically within Object Oriented Languages like C++ [13] where particular patterns of interacting objects that solve certain common problems can be identified and shared (examples include abstracting object creation to a Factory, restricting object instances via a Singleton, or separating data and behavior through a Model/View/Controller architecture).

Software patterns have been adapted to games. Björk and Holopaine identify a number of areas where patterns can be applied, including player progression, player rewards, game space (virtual worlds), and social patterns [14]. Specific examples include Lewis et al.'s work on motivational patterns in social games [15], and Carstensdottir et al.'s research on Narrative Progression Mechanics (which are effectively Björk and Holopain's player progression patterns)—for example distinguishing between choosing options in an explicit narrative interface, or performing a choice using the game mechanics within the game world [16].

In this chapter we are also concerned with interactions, but in our case it is the patterns within the interactive structure itself (the state machine created by authors that determines how readers can progress). These structures effectively manage both how the fabula expands and how the syuzhet unfolds. Understanding useful patterns is thus critical for informing both IDN authoring education and the design of authoring tools (which may want to explicitly support common patterns).

The next section explores these structural patterns in depth, and then the following section addresses the criticisms of *post-structuralism*, and looks at what shape a post-structuralist approach to IDN patterns might take.

3   Structural Patterns

In the IDN, Hypertext, and Interactive Fiction literature patterns tend to be expressed at three different levels. *Micro patterns* are the building blocks from which stories are constructed, they tend to have low level function, combine easily with each other, and form a kind of grammar, meaning they are often the defining feature of a particular IDN form. Links are micro patterns, and navigational hypertext is the associated form. *Meso patterns* are medium level structures (built from micro patterns) that create particular effects within a portion of a narrative or solve particular problems. A Cycle in a navigational hypertext is a meso pattern. *Macro patterns* are large scale patterns constructed from micro patterns, and which may contain many meso patterns, they describe an entire IDN, and imply a certain interactive experience. The Broomstick is a macro pattern, it is a linear story with a final choice leading to several alternative endings (and thus looks like a witch's besom broom when drawn).

In the following sections we will explore some of the patterns that exist at these different levels.

3.1   Micro Patterns

Micro Patterns are the invisible building blocks of IDN; they are so ubiquitous within certain types of IDN that we do not usually perceive them as patterns at all.

Links may be the **Foundational** structures of navigational hypertext [17] but they are not the only structure. Hypertext often traces its roots back to Vannevar Bush and

(a)   **(b)**

Link Structure in OHP   Trail Structure in FOHM

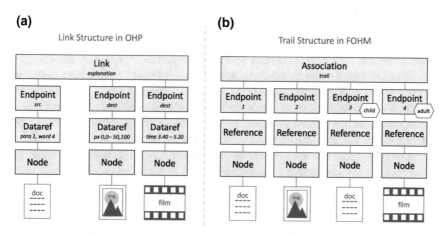

Fig. 1 **a** Left: a link represented in OHP. **b** Right: a trail represented in FOHM

his future gazing paper 'As We May Think', which describes a near instant access knowledge machine (The Memex) based on micro-fiche and *Trails*, sequences of documents that are laid down by readers, and which can be reused by others [18]. In his conceptual Xanadu design, Ted Nelson also describes *Transclusions*, an alternative to navigation between documents where a chunk of text or media is dynamically drawn into a document and presented in-line [19]. This mechanism allowed Nelson to propose a Permascroll, where all writing is stored once, and transcluded when needed rather than copied many times. In the early hypertext systems of the 80s and 90s this idea was adapted to create *Virtual Documents*, structures that transcluded many different sources of information into a single page, and this approach lives on today through content management systems, and data-driven documents [20].

Nevertheless links became the dominant micro-structure in hypertext (leading Frank Halaz to decry the 'Tyranny of the Link' [21]), and were the subject of endless reinvention and deconstruction. One approach is to create **High Level Generalisations**, where the link structures become more complex and expressive. These patterns reached their most sophisticated incarnation within Open Hypertext Systems as these hold links as first class objects. Figure 1a shows an example Open Hypertext Protocol (OHP) Link. The Link itself has a type, describing why the link exists (for example, 'defines'), and contains a set of Endpoints that hold the direction for each end of the link (typically a source or destination). Endpoints have a DataRef that specifies a particular location within a Node, which in turn references a given document or piece of media. With OHP it is thus possible to have semantic links with multiple sources and destinations within arbitrary documents. For example, in Fig. 1a we see an explanatory link with one source on a word in a document, and two destinations, a specific area within an image, and a scene within a video.

My own work on the *Fundamental Open Hypertext Model (FOHM)* is a further generalisation of the OHP Data Model that attempts to break the tyranny. FOHM extends endpoints so that they can have any semantics, meaning that as well as links other structures can be specified [22]. So for example, in FOHM a trail is simply a type of Association (FOHM's general term for link) with enumeration (position in a list) rather than direction specified within its endpoints. FOHM also adds context specifiers to every element that determine in what context those elements are visible, and behaviour specifiers that can modify context. This enables hypertext systems that use FOHM, such as Auld Linky, to drive adaptive hypertext experiences [23]. For example, in Fig. 1b the structure is a trail (of whole documents, images, and videos), where the last item depends on whether the viewer is an adult or a child.

An alternative to this approach is to create **Low Level Generalisations**, where the links are deconstructed into structural atoms that can be combined like Lego blocks to create more complex structure. In the Semantic Web links are re-imagined as RDF triples [24, 25], made up of a subject, object, and predicate, that create a web of knowledge using URIs as symbols in knowledge domains defined by schemas. For example, we might declare that a given 'Document ID' (the subject) was 'Created' (the predicate) by 'Person ID' (the object). Further triples might then add additional metadata, such as the document's version number, by using the same Document ID as the subject; or create relationships to other entities, such as a conference, by using the Document ID as the object.

One issue with RDF is that it is difficult to make statements about statements (as RDF triples do not themselves have an identifier to which you can refer), for example perhaps I want to say that the triple above was created on a particular date. RDF's somewhat clumsy solution to this problem is called Reification (meaning to make the abstract concrete), and involves replacing the original triple with three new triples of the form 'Triple ID' (the subject) has 'Subject' (the predicate) 'Document ID' (the object); this is clumsy as it breaks many of the systems that reason using RDF, although I can now make statements about it by adding new Triples with the Triple ID as subject.

Reification in RDF highlights a core problem with all structural approaches to data, which is that it is always possible that you need to reify relationships in order to make statements about them, and then you might want to reify those relationships, creating a possible infinite recursion.[2] The low level generalisation of links reached its peak in the Elucidate-Analogize-Delete (EAD) model, part of the structural computing movement [26], which has reification built in. In EAD structure is reduced into its simplest form, a structural atom, representing a relationship between two things. The power of EAD is in defining reification as a live recursive operation, called 'elucidate', so that a structure can be modified at run-time to be as granular as required.

The context element of FOHM is a hint that there is a third approach to micro patterns, **Constraint-based** structures, where the structure is not static, but emerges through applying rules and behaviours. *Adaptive links* are the most common, these have conditions that must be met before those links can be seen or followed. Adaptive Links are a key micro structure in IDN (in tools such as Twine, and can be traced

---

[2] For example, a Dataref in OHP is the reification of the relationship between the Node and Link so that there is somewhere to store the anchor information, and the Endpoint is the reification between the Link and the Dataref so there is somewhere to store the semantics of the relationship.

back to early systems such as StorySpace where they were called Guard Fields [27]), but in the last twenty years an alternative structure has emerged: the *Storylet*, which is the basis of sculptural hypertexts [11]. At their most basic storylets are a piece of media with a set of constraints that must be met before that media can be viewed, and a set of behaviours that can set variables to meet those constraints [28]. For example, a paragraph of text that describes a car accident and which sets a variable to remember this fact, coupled with a second paragraph that describes the aftermath but which requires that variable to be set before it can be read. A set of storylets creates a sculptural hypertext [11]. This contrasts with Calligraphic hypertexts built with links. In Sculptural hypertexts everything is initially connected and connections are sculpted away by applying constraints, in Calligraphic hypertext nothing is connected until links are explicitly drawn between them [29].

Despite this distinction storylets are similar to adaptive links (and can be modelled consistently alongside them in a model like FOHM, the difference is simply that adaptive links have a source endpoint in a specific node, whereas storylets have an open source endpoint that can be read from anywhere [30][3]). This consistency means that storylets and links can be combined into hybrid structures. For example, StoryNexus uses *higher level storylets* that combine a storylet with a number of adaptive links: a root event (which has constraints) is thus combined with a set of choices (the alternative links), each of which applies a different behaviour [31].

In this way all manner of micro patterns are possible, Table 1 shows an overview of those discussed here. Any authoring tool needs to choose which of them it will support and how flexibly it might allow them to be combined into hybrid structures. The effect on the authoring experience is significant. For example, combining storylets and links allows StoryNexus authors to create sculptural hypertexts with many choices [11], whereas StorySpace 3 supports both networks of links and storylets, but separates them into different spaces [34]. Storylet support has also recently been added to Twine (which is otherwise based on adaptive links) showing that new micro patterns can also be added to tools over time, expanding their expressive power.

3.2 Meso Patterns

Meso patterns are particular combinations of micro-patterns that can be used to achieve specific but local effects within an IDN. The literature on meso patterns is sporadic, there are a few noted academic papers that perform systemic analyses to identify them, but much is held as craft knowledge and is recorded more informally in the documentation of systems or the blogs of writers and developers. The non-exhaustive list of meso patterns presented here is drawn from five different sources:

Mark Bernstein's classic ACM Hypertext paper 'Patterns of Hypertext' published in 1998 [35], which reports a number of calligraphic patterns (what Bernstein also

---

[3] [30] is a paper that pre-dates the term Storylet, and actually describes them as 'context-source links' containing story fragments, but they are functionally identical to storylets.

Table 1 Micro patterns

Type	Micro pattern	Source	Description
Foundational	Links	[17]	A simple binary navigational connection between two lexia
	Trails	[18]	A sequence of linked lexia
	Virtual Documents	[20]	A set of lexia with rules on how they should be aggregated
	Transclusions	[19]	A connection between two lexia that causes the second to be automatically inserted into the first
High level	Navigational Links (OHP)	[32]	An n-ary link with direction and type
	Associations (FOHM)	[22]	A general association, with semantics on the relationship and each member
Low level	Structural Atoms (EAD)	[26]	A general binary connection that can be recursively reified at runtime
	Triples (RDF)	[24]	A three way semantic relation with subject, predicate, and object
Constraint-based	Adaptive links (Twine)	[33]	A link with contraints based on state
	Storylets (low level)	[29]	A lexia with contraints based on state, and rules that change state
	Storylets (high level)	[28]	A storylet with internal structure so that different rules may be applied depending on player choice

refers to as *complex link structures*) observed in published hypertexts. Bernstein is chief scientist at Eastgate systems, and many of the hypertexts used as a source were written in StorySpace and published by Eastgate.

Emily Short's 2016 blog entry on 'Small Scale Structures in CYOA' also looks at calligraphic patterns [36]. Short is an experienced narrative designer and interactive author who worked extensively with the INFORM 7 project and is Creative Director at Failbetter Games. The article is a description of the patterns that Short finds useful in her own work and is aimed at the Interactive Fiction Community.

Peter Mawhorter et al.'s 2014 paper 'Towards a Theory of Choice Poetics' was presented at the Foundations of Digital Games (FDG) conference and explores a number of *choice idioms*, effectively patterns that look not only at navigational structure, but also the way that the structure is framed, how the options are presented, and what are the outcomes [37]. The paper is written from the perspective of narrative games and is neutral in terms of micro-structure, instead focusing on moments of decision regardless of implementation.

Charlie Hargood and I wrote a 2016 ACM Hypertext paper which explores patterns of sculptural hypertext in the context of location-based narratives [38]. The patterns are extracted from an analysis of 40 different locative stories created by creative writing students. In these stories location is treated as just another constraint, and so the patterns also apply to any storylet based experience.

The final two sources are both material released by Failbetter Games (and therefore the author is obscured). The first is a blog report of a presentation given at the Story conference held in London in 2010 which reflected on the narrative patterns Failbetter had used in its sculptural narrative *Echo Bazaar* [39]. The second is a page on design patterns from the Storychoices wiki which supported authors of the (now defunct) StoryNexus platform [40]. Written in 2012 it reports patterns that have been 'successfully used in storygames'.

Tables 2 and 3 show a summary of the 51 meso patterns in these sources. The names are all taken directly from those sources. Each is given a number so that cross-referencing between the patterns is clear. The descriptions are written using terminology taken from adaptive hypertext, some specific terms are worth defining:

- **Node**—a packaged media item (typically text). In calligraphic systems this would be the source and destinations of links, in sculptural systems it is a storylet
- **Path**—a navigational route through a set of nodes, controlled by either a network of links (calligraphic), constraints/behaviour (sculptural), or both (adaptive)
- **Choice**—an alternative set of nodes presented to the reader as the next potential navigational step (regardless of mechanism)
- **Constraints**—logical rules that must be met before navigation to a particular node can occur (regardless of implementation)
- **Variable**—elements of state that can be checked by a constraint, or modified by behaviours (regardless of implementation).

In almost all cases the meso patterns can be applied regardless of the underlying micro structures. This is because calligraphic and sculptural hypertexts are equally expressive, it is just that some things are easier to do in one form than another. There are three exceptions. A *Simple Chain* is a pattern that allows storylets to function like a chain of calligraphic nodes and links and is therefore superfluous in calligraphic systems. A *Missing Link* requires a hotspot in the text to function and is thus not really applicable in sculptural systems where options typically appear after the content has been presented (and may or may not work in games, where the presentation of onward choices is highly variable). Finally, a *Montage* really requires a link with multiple destinations (to simultaneously open multiple nodes[4]), this is not supported in any existing sculptural systems, although in theory it is possible.

Broadly speaking the reported patterns are either structural, semantic, or presentational or a combination of any two of these. This is shown in the Type column of Tables 2 and 3 using shortened names: Str, Sem, and Pres.

Structural patterns are defined purely by the shape of the navigational paths through the narrative. They are defined as a *sub-graph*. For example, Bernstein defines three types of *Cycle*, all of which are defined purely in terms of nodes and paths. Figure 2 shows his three types of cycles demonstrated with eight nodes.

---

[4] This is how the Montage pattern is defined in Bernstein's original paper: "several distinct writing spaces appear simultaneously, reinforcing each other while retaining their separate identities". However a broader interpretation is possible, what Bernstein refers to as "architectural montage", and this might apply to transcluded content within a node regardless of the micro-structure, as well as the richer environments found in some narrative games.

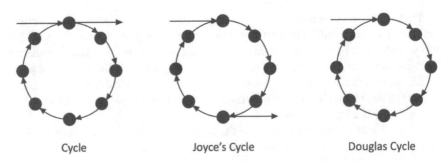

Cycle   Joyce's Cycle   Douglas Cycle

Fig. 2 Bernstein's patterns (like these cycles) are defined purely through navigational structure

Semantic patterns define a *particular way* of using IDN elements for an effect. For example, Mawhorter et al. define a number of choice patterns in this way, such as *Blind Choices* where the narrative has not provided sufficient information to understand the consequences of a choice, or *Delayed Choices* where the consequences are not immediate. In both cases the structure is irrelevant, it is the setup and payoff within the story itself that forms the pattern.

Presentational patterns are the rarest, they define how something should be *presented* to the reader to create an effect. For example, Bernstein defined *Neighbourhoods* as sets of Nodes that have a common presentation to distinguish them from nodes outside of the set—for example, a story interspersed with epistolary nodes (such as diary entries) where those are presented in italics and have different borders to distinguish them from the other nodes in the story.

We also see some patterns that are defined in two of these three ways. The most common is structural combined with semantics. Such as the *Beggar's Banquet* where the structure is a sequence of nodes, and the semantics are that the reader progresses at a known cost, but with the promise of a reward at the end as compensation; or *Counterpoint*, where the structure is two separate chains of nodes with navigational chances to switch between them, and the semantics is that each chain represents a different logical part of the story (for example, switching between different character point of views).

There is only one example of a semantic/presentational pattern, this is the *Interstitial Counterpoint*, the semantics is the same as Counterpoint (two logical parts of the story), but here rather than defining the parts structurally they are separated by presenting one part in the interstitial interface of the system (the example Bernstein gives is by using descriptive file path names).

Similarly there is only one example of a presentational/structural pattern. The *Unchoice* is structural in that it requires a node with only one onward path, but is also presentational as that onward path must be presented specifically as a choice with one option (rather as simply a way of progressing, such as a 'Next' button.

Meso patterns can support authoring by providing them to authors as either inspiration or as part of a toolbox they can use in their creations [1]. But structural patterns could also be identified by the system at runtime allowing them to be presented dif-

Table 2 Purely structural meso patterns

No.	Meso pattern name	Source	Type	Description
1.	Cycle	[35]	Str	A path that starts and ends on the same node
2.	Joyce's cycle	[35]	Str	A *Cycle* (1) but with direct entry and exit nodes
3.	Douglas cycle	[35]	Str	A *Cycle* (1) with no exit points (effectively an end state)
4.	Contour	[35]	Str	A set of *Cycles* (1) with potential navigation between cycles
5.	Sieve	[35]	Str	A tree representing layers of choices that direct readers towards distinct outcomes
6.	Split/join	[35]	Str	Two paths with a shared start node and a different but shared end node (representing a choice that is resolved)
7.	Rashomon	[35]	Str	A *Split/join* (6) within a cycle (1)
8.	Parallel threads	[38]	Str	Two sets of nodes that progress independently producing an effect like *Counterpoint* (26)
9.	Gating	[38]	Str	*Parallel threads* (8), but where progress in one thread is unlocked by progress in the other
10.	Concurrent nodes	[38]	Str	Multiple nodes with the same set of constraints
11.	Alternative nodes	[38]	Str	A set of nodes that cover the entire set of possibilities for a sub-set of variables
12.	Mark of Cain	[39]	Str	A variable that once set excludes a whole sub-set of nodes, the opposite of *Phasing* (30)
13.	Venture	[39, 40]	Str	A sub-set of nodes that all raise a variable, which eventually can be 'spent' (reset) to access a different sub-set of nodes
14.	Simple chain	[40]	Str	A set of nodes controlled by a common variable that changes in value and progresses a player through the set (a meso *Canyon*)
15.	Python	[40]	Str	A start node that unlocks a sub-set of intermediate nodes, a *Phase* (30) that once explored to a certain point exits to a final node
16.	Pyramid	[40]	Str	A *Python* (15), but with multiple sets of intermediate nodes, *Phases* (29), where each is smaller than the last
17.	A Carousel	[40]	Str	A *Python* (15), but with multiple sets of intermediate nodes, *Phases* (29), and multiple potential exit nodes
18.	Midnight buffet	[40]	Str	A *Midnight staircase* (32) but with multiple variables, whose different combinations open different sub-sets of nodes
19.	Grandfather clock	[40]	Str	A subset of nodes that builds a variable, which can be spent (reset) to progress a second variable—works with many other patterns
20.	The road with many faces	[40]	Str	A *Python* (15) or *Carousel* (17) where a second independent variable also builds, occasionally unlocking unique content
21.	False choice	[37]	Str	A choice where all options lead to the same node and have the same behaviour
22.	Re-enterable node	[36]	Str	Several *Cycles* (1) that all return to the same node, similar to *Contour* (4), useful for dialogues or gameplay loops
23.	Limited re-enterable node	[36]	Str	A *Re-enterable Node* (22) but where there is a limit on the number of revisits that is less than the number of *Cycles* (1)
24.	Gated re-enterable node	[36]	Str	A *Re-enterable node* (22) but where certain *Cycles* (1) are protected by constraints

Table 3 Semantic and presentational meso patterns

No.	Meso pattern name	Source	Type	Description
25.	Dead end	[37]	Str/Sem	A choice that prematurely leads to an ending, with no further onward paths
26.	Counterpoint	[35]	Str/Sem	The interleaving of two logically different sets of nodes (e.g. character POV)
27.	Overviews/tours	[35]	Str/Sem	A *Split/Join* (6) where paths are rhetorically similar, but have different levels of detail
28.	Mirror world (structural)	[35]	Str/Sem	*Mirror Worlds* (44), but with identical structure
29.	Tangle	[35]	Str/Sem	A sub-network of navigational options with few clues to guide readers choices, a network of *Blind Choices* (39)
30.	Phasing	[38]	Str/Sem	Grouping a set of nodes together using a common constraint as a way of managing progression or perspective
31.	Unlocking (easter eggs)	[38]	Str/Sem	A subset of main story nodes that together unlock a diversionary node with non-essential content
32.	Midnight staircase	[39] [40]	Str/Sem	A *Venture* (13) but with multiple sub-sets of nodes where the variable might be spent (potentially available at different points)
33.	Beggars' Banquet	[40]	Str/Sem	A *Simple chain* (14) or *Pyramid* (16) where is made clear that progressing has a toll, but the end has a reward
34.	Confirmation choice	[36]	Str/Sem	A sequence of nodes that allow a choice to be made, but which encourage you in stronger and stronger terms not to make it
35.	Track switching choice	[36]	Str/Sem	A dual sequence of interconnected nodes that represent two sides of a choice, and which allow players to change their mind before finalising
36.	Scored choice	[36]	Str/Sem	A *Track switching choice* (35) but the outcome is based on all choices, rather than just the final choice
37.	Chaper One Sorting Hat.	[36]	Str/Sem	Multiple paths with the same start and end node, typically used at the beginning of a story, meso version of *Sorting Hat*, variant of *Split/Join* (6)
38.	Endgame time cave	[36]	Str/Sem	A *Sieve* (5) placed at the end of the story to create alternative endings (especially for cumulative choices)
39.	Blind choice	[37]	Sem	A choice where the outcomes are not well signposted (e.g. because of a lack of information or description)
40.	Dilemma	[37]	Sem	A choice where both options are equally attractive or unattractive
41.	Flavour	[37]	Sem	A choice with minor consequences
42.	Delayed	[37]	Sem	A choice where the difference in outcome is not immediate
43.	Puzzle	[37]	Sem	A choice where the merits of the choices are not obviously apparent (e.g. because of clues)
44.	Mirror world	[35]	Sem	Multiple parallel paths with alternative voices or perspectives
45.	Missing link	[35]	Sem	Content that implies a link, even through there is none
46.	Faust's tea party	[39]	Sem	A node that changes a pair of variables such that you gain with one but lose with the other
47.	Interstitial counterpoint	[35]	Sem/Pres	*Counterpoint* (26) with one set of content presented between writing spaces
48.	Montage	[35]	Pres	Multiple nodes juxtaposed together
49.	Neighborhood	[35]	Pres	Logical sets of nodes that can be identified through proximity, or common ornamentation/landmarks
50.	Navigational Feint	[35]	Pres	Content that reveals structure, without providing exhaustive navigation (e.g. a map)
51.	Unchoice	[37]	Pres/Str	A choice with only one option

ferently from the rest of the structure (similarly to a spatial parser [41]), and can also be baked into authoring tools as templates that allow for the easy creation of common structures. For example, the StoryPlaces authoring tool uses *Phases* as a central way of managing progression [42]. Semantic or presentational patterns could be tagged by authors, also allowing them to be distinguished in the interface (for example, using different colors or symbols for different types of choices).

3.3 Macro Patterns

Macro patterns describe the overall structure of an entire work. Rather than solving specific problems or creating short term effects they instead capture something of the overall feeling of the whole experience, suggesting to authors the sorts of interactive stories that they could be telling. Macro patterns appear in traditional narratology. The Hero's Journey (or Monomyth) from Joseph Campbell's *Hero with a Thousand Faces* is the most famous example, and captures the common events and character archetypes that reoccur in myths [43].

There has also been work on macro patterns in transmedia, although these tend to focus more on how the narrative interacts with the various media channels and instances within the wider transmedia experience. For example, Pratten defines three broad types of transmedia story [44]: a *Transmedia Franchise*, where each element is a self contained story, but comes together to form a broader narrative (e.g. the Matrix trilogy, graphic novels, and films; or the Star Wars Universe), a *Portmanteau Transmedia* where a single story is split across multiple platforms and cannot be experienced properly in any single one of them (e.g. Alternative Reality Games), and *Complex Transmedia Experiences* which combine the two, so that parts can be experienced independently, but full understanding is only possible through the whole (e.g. the TV show Lost with its associated websites and games).

IDN macro patterns are different from both of these approaches in that they tend to capture the agency that a reader has within a story, by mapping out the navigational shape of the work and giving a sense of the number of different paths through it and the potential endings. While Walton and Suckling's notion of modular and fractal choices differentiate generally between structures where choices are constrained and return to a core path (modular) and those that ever expand the story (fractal) [45] there is very little academic work going beyond this and looking at specific IDN macro patterns, although a number are common parlance amongst practitioners. These are neatly presented by Sam Ashwell in his 2015 article *Standard Patterns in Choice-Based Games* published on his personal blog [46]. Ashwell identifies eight IDN macro patterns, shown in Fig. 3, to which I have added a common variation (the Broomstick) [47].

Ashwell presents a number of patterns with a strong directionality, from a start node to one or more end nodes. The *Time Cave* is an unrestrained IDN where every choice leads to a new branch, this creates great variety and high levels of agency, but also causes a *combinatorial explosion* of options [47]. The other directional patterns

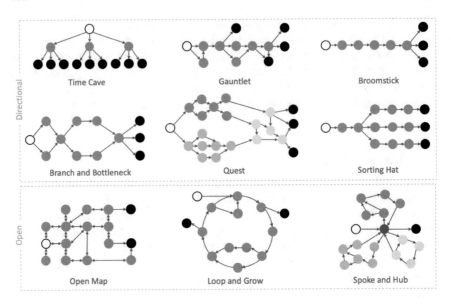

Fig. 3 Ashwell's standard patterns; with white start nodes, black end nodes, and logical sets of intermediate nodes shown in shades of grey

are alternatives that are designed to avoid this problem by constraining choice in different ways: A *Gauntlet* has a central linear path which the reader can stray from but quickly returns, genuine agency is thus left to the end, where a final choice will lead to alternative resolutions (the *Broomstick* is an extreme version of this, where the final choice is the only agency in an otherwise linear story [47]). Gauntlets make it easy to manage agency as any meaningful choices are deferred to the very end of the story, and are popular in games as the otherwise common path makes it easy to create a consistent play experience and to use expensive assets efficiently. A *Sorting Hat* is similar to a Broomstick, but the key choice occurs early rather than late in the story. The reader is thus funnelled into one of several linear stories. *Branch and Bottlenecks* are a compromise pattern, where branches in the story lead to genuine variation, but are quickly resolved back into the main narrative (this structure is essentially a sequence of *Split/Joins*—one of our meso patterns—and is typically referred to in narrative game design as the "string of pearls" approach [48]). The points of convergence also act as bottlenecks, where key narrative information can be conveyed. Finally, *Quests* are more complex structures where modules of the story (networks of nodes exploring a particular scene or event) are connected together in a Gauntlet, or in a Branch and Bottleneck, this scopes most of the variation and agency within the modules and allows the overall narrative to progress towards a common set of conclusions.

In addition to these patterns Ashwell also sets out three more open structures, where the reader is not pushed inexorably towards a conclusion, but instead can wander within the narrative. When presenting these patterns Ashwell assumes end states that readers can eventually choose to take, but it is also possible to use them without end nodes, and instead allow readers to simply exhaust the story, and choose themselves when to stop.

Open Maps are a set of nodes where readers are free to move back and forth, often using constraints and behaviours to modify the content of those nodes between visits. These nodes could represent literal locations, but more abstract waypoints are also possible. An Open Map is the structure assumed by INFORM 7, although that also changes the interaction interface (from selecting options to a parser).

In *Loop and Grow* the reader navigates a repeating cycle of nodes, but on each repetition constraints and behaviours cause the nodes to change and new options to become available. In *Spoke and Hub* a set of these cycles start and end at a single hub, allowing readers to return and relaunch into a different cycle each time. Loop and Grow and Spoke and Hub are patterns that work respectively as macro scale versions of the meso patterns *Cycle* and *Contour*.

Although not depicted in Fig. 3 Ashwell also describes 'Floating Modules', which is a story style where the navigation between nodes (or at least between modules of nodes) is managed purely through constraints and behaviours. This is actually a sculptural hypertext (as described in Sect. 3.1). However, as we have seen, storylets support a wide variety of meso structures, and Short points out that they can also be used to create any of the macro structures as well [49] (the way that Ashwell describes them 'floating modules' is really a type of Quest, where the starting node of each module is a Storylet, which is a good match to the combined storylet and link structures used by Failbetter).

Throughout these descriptions it is clear that many macro patterns are actually meta patterns, which allow for the arrangements of other macro patterns. For example, Spoke and Hub where each spoke could be its own macro pattern, or Quest where each module could be built with its own macro pattern, or Sorting Hat where each branch could lead to a different macro pattern. This high level building block approach is also the one I took in my work with Charlie Hargood when we looked at types of locative experience, resulting in the Canyons, Deltas, Plains (CDP) model which is a broad brush language for describing locative sculptural hypertexts [50].

Canyons are a linear sequence of nodes (often laid out along a real world path), *Plains* are sets of nodes that can be visited in any order (often arranged in open spaces), and *Deltas* are a tree of nodes, where at each point the reader is given a choice (often choices correspond to junctions and branches in real world paths). These correspond to the some of the meso and macro patterns we have already seen. Canyons are Simple Sequences (meso), Plains are Open Maps (macro), and Deltas are Time Caves (macro). The locative experiences did not really include any cyclic structures (Loop and Grow, Spoke and Hub), perhaps because of the reticence of physically located visitors to loop back on themselves [51].

The key insight of the CDP model is that most existing locative experiences can be described as a hybrid of these three structures configured in different ways. For example, Fig. 4 shows how Viking Ghost Hunt can be modelled as a plain where each node leads to a delta [52] (players move to one of several starting points in Dublin to start an interactive AR ghost story), and Riot! can be modelled as a set of

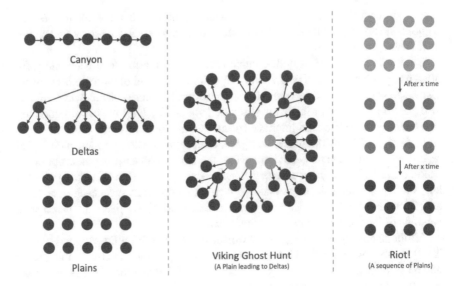

Fig. 4 Canyons, deltas, plains—applied to Viking Ghost Hunt and Riot! Sub-patterns of nodes are shown in shades of grey. (Note, in a Plain all the nodes are connected to all the other nodes, but for visual clarity these connections are omitted here)

overlapping plains where each plain is replaced with the last [53] (players explore a riot occurring in a city square, they are free to wander, and as time progresses the sets of available nodes changes creating a virtual play that unfolds around them). A system that supports all three can thus structurally support the vast majority of locative experiences (this was the starting point for the StoryPlaces system, build around a sculptural IDN engine).

Similarly to meso patterns, macro patterns can be used both educationally for authoring (setting out appropriate high level shapes for IDNs) and as a direct part of authoring tools, as templates, quick ways to sketch out broad designs, or intelligent identification of structures in order to help layout or present otherwise tangled relationships.

We started this chapter by making the case for structure as a tool for understanding complexity, and the micro, meso, and macro patterns described in this section show how this can be done. They are a structuralist approach to IDN poetics, aiding with both analysis and authoring. Patterns provide a way for authors to make sense of complexity, helping them to think about that structure in a more modular and manageable way, which can be indirectly or directly supported by authoring tools. But structuralism as a philosophical movement is not without criticism, so in the next section we will explore what that criticism is, and what it means for how we might use IDN patterns in authoring.

4 Interactive Narratives and Post-structuralism

Structuralism as a movement within the humanities was displaced in the later parts of the twentieth century by post-structuralism, an encompassing approach that is less interested in the structures themselves than it is in why those structures were identified, and what are the consequences of foregrounding them.

4.1 The Post-structural Complaint

In 1967 in an invited lecture titled *Structure, Sign, and Play in the Discourse of the Human Sciences* Jacques Derrida suggested that an 'event' had occurred in the conceptualisation of structures. Derrida argued that while structuralists could play with alternative structural analyses of different phenomena those structures were always centred in some way that was assumed to be fixed. In other words they were always grounded in certain cultural, social, and technological contexts. The event Derrida referred to was the ending of this assumption, and the acceptance that the centre of different structural analyses both could and inevitably would change as those contextual factors evolved. By accepting this chain of substitutions, centre for centre for centre, structuralists could engage in *freeplay* where all of the structural elements are mutable [54].

Post-structuralism therefore embraces structuralism as a partial mode of analysis, but rejects it as revealing universal truths, as these truths might prove to be ephemeral when the centre of that analysis (which might not be clear to the analysers) changes. It is thus part of the more general intellectual movement towards post-modernism, which rejects grand narratives and embraces epistemic instability.

Roland Barthes' *Death of the Author*, published the same year, applies this idea directly to literature, arguing that the meaning of a text is not magically embedded when it is authored, but is instead conjured by the act of reading, and influenced more by the contemporary context of the reader than the historical intentions of the writer. Although Barthes is a touch-stone for IDN scholars, who have long argued over whether the player agency of IDN can be seen as the ultimate realisation of the Death of the Author [55], a post-structural viewpoint raises orthogonal questions about structural patterns in IDN. In particular it questions whether patterns are genuinely universal, implies that common patterns could form artificial constraints on authors, and suggests that any pattern analysis is itself rooted in historical biases, and influenced heavily by contemporary technologies and their affordances, which are destined to change. Obsolescence is built in.

Yet a structuralist approach appeals to an engineering mindset, which is less concerned about *accurately* reflecting reality than it is about modelling that reality *sufficiently* to create working machines. When criticisms are raised about Patterns in the technology sphere they are that patterns are indicative of a failure of expressiveness in underlying representations, such as the 'revenge of the nerds' response from

Paul Graham: "When I see patterns in my programs, I consider it a sign of trouble. The shape of a program should reflect only the problem it needs to solve. Any other regularity in the code is a sign, to me at least, that I'm using abstractions that aren't powerful enough" [56]. This is a cry for more structure, not less.

4.2   A World Without Patterns

If we are concerned about the restrictive view encouraged by patterns there are, of course, alternative ways of capturing craft knowledge and informing design. Exercises in Style is an approach demonstrated in Raymond Queneau's book of the same name [57]. Queneau sets out the same short story in 99 alternative styles, providing a rich set of comparable examples that others are free to draw from as they see fit. The same approach has been taken in IDN, for example, Mason and Bernstein present a similar set of exercises for the use of links [58], developing a set of examples of how links might be used to punctuate a single paragraph of text.

Another approach is to develop classification hierarchies, which map out the design space and provide definitions of categories [59]. While not directed at authoring these help authors contextualise their work, and can provide inspiration. Classifications can be along multiple dimensions, for example Ryan Javanshir and I classify transmedia stories using the narrative relationships between the parts (story), how participants move between parts (navigation), and how they participate in those parts (instance), triangulating the position of any given transmedia story using all three [60]. Classifications are themselves a structural approach (similar to the narratological work of Todorov on Genre [61]) although they do not necessary classify based on interactive structure. A less structural version of this approach is to focus on defining vocabulary, in these cases structure is less important than definitions, although key examples, such as the ongoing INDCOR initiative, still structure that vocabulary around a taxonomy with top-level categories. In the case of INDCOR these are authoring, artefact and critical discourse [62].

Finally, it is possible to create a set of heuristics, sometimes called a toolkit, that provide rules-of-thumb that designers can follow. For example, the principles laid out by Matt Brown in his 2018 GDC talk on lessons drawn from The Sims on fostering emergent storytelling [63], or the toolkit developed by the StoryPlaces project that provides guidance on creating effective locative storytelling experiences [51].

4.3   Post-structural Patterns

Bernstein coined the term *Strange Hypertexts* to refer to hypertext systems that are playful with their mechanics and presentation systems. Narrative games are the ultimate realisation of this [64], in these strangest of hypertexts the game mechanics and presentation choices can themselves convey elements of story. In game design this is called *Ludonarrative*, examples include the inaccessible choices in *Depression Quest* reflecting the mental health of its protagonist [65], or the phantom limb experience of losing a sibling in *Brothers: A Tale of Two Sons* [66].

Perhaps the embracing of ludonarrative is an example of one of Derrida's shifts in the centre, and the consequences for patterns is profound. Firstly, the narrative functions of established patterns are brought into question (as they are affected by the interaction mechanics)—is a cycle still a cycle when it is triggered by Max's power to initiate a restricted rewind in *Life is Strange* [67]? Secondly, ludonarrative reveals that interactive structures are themselves part of how narrative meaning is built, which implies that specific (rather than generic) structures may be needed in every IDN that are tailored to the narrative being told.

In our own work on multiplayer narratives we discovered that our designs often required patterns, but that these patterns were specific to each experience. We called these *Uncommon Patterns* and they offer a post-structural approach to patterns [68]. To support uncommon patterns an authoring tool needs to provide not only a way to create a story using patterns as building blocks, but to assemble new meso patterns from micro patterns such that can be reused again and again. This could be realised through something as simple as structural cut and paste, or more complex approaches such as domain specific languages (DSLs) that support reuse (for example, with functions or macros).

Ludonarrative and the lure of strange hypertexts may well be behind the proliferation of IDN platforms and authoring tools [69]. Uncommon patterns might be a way of mitigating against this proliferation, although I suspect that this mitigation might be limited, as flexibility of form seems baked into the IDN medium, and in resisting it we are like Canute commanding the tide away.

Perhaps the best approach is to see established IDN forms and the common patterns described in this chapter as islands of stability in a swelling sea. They are good to introduce people to IDN, and to act as refuge for those who are still acquiring their technical skills, but ultimately the deep ocean will only be explored by those developing bespoke tools and patterns that tell stories in specialised ways. Uncommon patterns represent a compromise, and their mere existence might encourage exploration around the shore.

5 Conclusions

In this chapter we have set out to understand the different sorts of structural patterns found in IDNs. Although the literature on patterns is sporadic, we have still managed to identify patterns at the micro, meso, and macro levels.

Micro patterns like links and storylets are the building blocks of IDN, we have seen how they really represent two alternative means to represent structure: calligraphic where structure is explicitly drawn (using links), and sculptural where is emerges through the interplay of constraints and behaviour (expressed in storylets). We have also shown how more complex link models can express both forms simultaneously, as well as allowing for lesser known patterns (such as trails).

Meso patterns solve local problems or create particular effects within an IDN. Through a review of five different sources, we have described 51 different meso patterns that broadly fall into three categories: structural (defined purely through navigational relationships), semantic (based on the particular use of interactive narrative elements), and presentational (referring to ways in which those elements can be shown to a reader to create different effects). There are also hybrid patterns, that combine two of these elements (for example, a structure used in a particular way).

Macro patterns describe the broad shape of an entire IDN, revealing the different paths through the work and the different end states. We explored six directional patterns that are defined by alternative paths from a start to an end, three open patterns that describe ways in which IDNs might be structured to allow readers to wander more freely (with or without a final exit), and three patterns from locative narratives that map to how people navigate in physical spaces. We also saw how macro patterns can themselves be combined to create hybrids.

We also explored the assumptions of structuralism and how they apply to patterns, causing us to question the universality of patterns, especially in light of ludonarrative where the interactive structure is itself seen as a way of conveying narrative information – implying that standardising approaches across stories could be harmful. Rather than abandon patterns altogether, we have suggested that they are a starting point for authors, and that a post-structural approach would be to extend their use with uncommon patterns, patterns that can be defined by authors, and which are particular to a given narrative project.

Through this process we have created an index of categorised patterns that is a resource for both educators and authoring tool designers. We have also established a structural theory of patterns that is aware of structural limitations, and provides space for post-structural thought.

This index is of course based on a limited set of work, partly because of a lack of formally published patterns, and could and should be extended. In addition, the impact of ludonarrative on these existing patterns is not clear and remains an open research question. There is also a lack of work on how patterns might be incorporated into authoring tools, for example [1] outlines how patterns might be utilised indirectly through mechanisms such as cookbooks, directly by supporting features such as templates or DSLs, or invisibly by designing the patterns directly into the authoring interface itself, but more work is required to understand the affordances of these approaches and to evaluate their impact. This includes the need to better understand uncommon patterns, and how they might best be expressed and used by authors.

Patterns are a powerful but mostly untapped tool for IDN authors. I hope that by setting out patterns in context, explaining the strengths and weaknesses of the pattern approach, and suggesting possible avenues for post-structural patterns, the information in this chapter will support a new generation of authoring tool designers, and inspire new and stranger IDN works.

References

1. Millard D (2022) Authoring with IDN patterns. In: Proceedings of the narrative and hypertext workshop (NHT22), held in conjunction with ACM hypertext 2022. NHT'22, New York, NY, USA
2. de Saussure F (2011) Course in general linguistics. Columbia University Press
3. de Almeida MWB (2015) Structuralism. In: Wright JD (ed) International encyclopedia of the social and behavioral sciences, 2nd edn. Elsevier, Oxford, pp 626–631
4. Propp V (1971) Morphology of the Folktale, 2nd edn. University of Texas Press, Austin
5. Lévi-Strauss C (1955) The structural study of myth. J Am Folklore 68(270):428–444
6. Field S (1994) Screenplay: the foundations of screenwriting, 3rd edn. Dell Pub. Co, New York
7. Gustav F (1894) Freytag's technique of the drama. Scott, Foresman
8. Todorov T, Weinstein A (1969) Structural analysis of narrative. NOVEL: A Forum Fiction 3(1):70–76
9. Viktor S, Benjamin S, Gerald B (1993) Theory of prose. Dalkey Archive Press, Elmwood Park, Ill
10. Wood H (2017) Dynamic Syuzhets: writing and design methods for playable stories. In: Interactive storytelling, vol 10690. Springer, Cham, Switzerland, pp 24–37. ISSN: 0302-9743
11. Millard DE, Hargood C (2021) Hypertext as a lens into interactive digital narrative. In: Mitchell A, Vosmeer M (eds) Interactive storytelling. Lecture notes in computer science. Springer International Publishing, Cham, pp 509–524
12. Christopher A (1978) A pattern language: towns, buildings, construction: 2. New York, illustrated edition, OUP USA
13. Gamma E, Helm R, Johnson R, Vlissides J (1994) Design patterns: elements of reusable object-oriented software, 1st edn. Addison Wesley, Reading, Mass
14. Bjork S, Holopainen J (2005) Patterns in game design. Charles River Media
15. Lewis C, Wardrip-Fruin N, Whitehead J (2012) Motivational game design patterns of 'ville games. In: Proceedings of the international conference on the foundations of digital games, FDG'12. Association for Computing Machinery, New York, NY, USA, pp 172–179
16. Carstensdottir E, Kleinman E, El-Nasr MS (2019) Player interaction in narrative games: structure and narrative progression mechanics. In: Proceedings of the 14th international conference on the foundations of digital games, FDG'19. Association for Computing Machinery, New York, NY, USA, pp 1–9
17. Conklin J (1987) Hypertext: an introduction and survey. Computer 20:17–41
18. Bush V (1945) As we may think. The Atlantic. Section: Technology
19. Nelson TH (1982) Literary machines 931. Mindful Pr
20. Watters C (1999) Information retrieval and the virtual document. J Am Soc Inf Sci
21. Halasz FG (1991) Seven issues. Revisited, closing Plenary ACM Hypertext'91
22. Millard DE, Moreau L, Davis HC, Reich S (2000) FOHM: a fundamental open hypertext model for investigating interoperability between hypertext domains. In: Proceedings of the eleventh ACM on hypertext and hypermedia, HYPERTEXT '00. Association for Computing Machinery, New York, NY, USA, pp 93–102
23. Michaelides DT, Millard DE, Weal MJ, DeRoure D (2002) Auld leaky: a contextual open hypermedia link server. In: Reich S, Tzagarakis MM, De Bra PME (eds) Hypermedia: openness, structural awareness, and adaptivity. Lecture notes in computer science. Springer, Berlin, Heidelberg, pp 59–70
24. Lassila O, Swick RR (1998) World wide, and web consortium. Resource description framework (RDF) model and syntax specification
25. Tim BL, James H, Ora L (2001) The semantic web. Sci Am 284(5):34–43
26. Nürnberg PJ, Wiil UK, Hicks DL (2004) Rethinking structural computing infrastructures. In: Proceedings of the fifteenth ACM conference on hypertext and hypermedia, HYPERTEXT '04. Association for Computing Machinery, New York, NY, USA, pp 239–246

27. Bernstein M (2002) Storyspace 1. In: Proceedings of the thirteenth ACM conference on hyper-
    text and hypermedia, HYPERTEXT'02. Association for Computing Machinery, New York,
    NY, USA, pp 172–181
28. Kreminski M, Wardrip-Fruin N (2018) Sketching a map of the storylets design space. In:
    Rouse R, Koenitz H, Haahr M (eds) Interactive storytelling. Lecture notes in computer science.
    Springer International Publishing, Cham, pp 160–164
29. Bernstein M (2001) Card shark and thespis: exotic tools for hypertext narrative. In: Proceedings
    of the 12th ACM conference on hypertext and hypermedia, HYPERTEXT'01. Association for
    Computing Machinery, New York, NY, USA, pp 41–50
30. Weal MJ, Millard DE, Michaelides DT, De Roure DC (2001) Building narrative structures
    using context based linking. In: Proceedings of the 12th ACM conference on hypertext and
    hypermedia, HYPERTEXT'01. Association for Computing Machinery, New York, NY, USA,
    pp 37–38
31. Storynexus (2012) Reference guide, version 1.04. Technical report, Failbetter Games
32. Davis H, Reich S, Millard D (1997) A proposal for a common navigational hypertext protocol.
    Technical report, Dept. of Electronics and Computer Science. Presented at 3.5 open hypermedia
    system working group meeting. Aarhus University, Denmark
33. Kaplan G, Wolff G (1990) Adaptive hypertext. In: Proceedings of the intelligent systems
    technical symposium. IBM Endicott, NY
34. Bernstein M (2016) Storyspace 3. In: Proceedings of the 27th ACM conference on hypertext
    and social media, HT'16. Association for Computing Machinery, New York, NY, USA, pp
    201–206
35. Bernstein M (1998) Patterns of hypertext. In: Proceedings of the ninth ACM conference on
    hypertext and hypermedia: links, objects, time and space-structure in hypermedia systems.
    ACM, pp 21–29
36. Author Emily Short (2016) Small-scale structures in CYOA
37. Mawhorter PA, Mateas M, Wardrip-Fruin N, Jhala A (2014) Towards at theory of choice poetics.
    In: FDG
38. Hargood C, Weal M, Millard DE (2016) Patterns of sculptural hypertext in location based
    narratives. In: Proceedings of the 27th ACM conference on hypertext and social media. ACM
39. Echo Bazaar Narrative Structures, part one (2010). Failbetter Games
40. Content Design Patterns—Storychoices (2012)
41. Schedel T, Atzenbeck S (2016) Spatio-temporal parsing in spatial hypermedia. In: Proceedings
    of the 27th ACM conference on hypertext and social media, HT'16. Association for Computing
    Machinery, New York, NY, USA, pp 149–157
42. Millard DE, Hargood C, Howard Y, Packer H (2017) The StoryPlaces authoring tool: pattern
    centric authoring. In: Authoring for interactive storytelling
43. Campbell J (1973) The hero with a thousand faces. Princeton University Press
44. Pratten R (2015) Getting started in transmedia storytelling: a practical guide for beginners, 2nd
    edn. CreateSpace Independent Publishing Platform, North Charleston, South Carolina
45. Suckling M, Walton M (2016) Video game writing: from macro to micro. Mercury Learning
    and Information
46. Ashwell SK (2015) Standard patterns in choice-based games
47. Amy B (1990) The combinatorics of storytelling: mystery train interactive. Interactive Cinema
    Group internal paper, MIT Media Lab
48. Majewski J et al (2003) Theorising video game narrative. Bond University
49. Author Emily Short (2019) Storylets: You Want Them
50. Millard DE, Hargood C, Jewell MO, Weal MJ (2013) Canyons, deltas and plains: towards
    a unified sculptural model of location-based hypertext. In: Proceedings of the 24th ACM
    conference on hypertext and social media, HT'13. Association for Computing Machinery,
    New York, NY, USA, pp 109–118
51. Packer H, Hargood C, Howard Y, Papadopoulos P, Millard D (2017) Developing a writer's
    toolkit for interactive locative storytelling, vol 10690. Springer, pp 63–74

52. Natasa P, Gavin K, Katsiaryna N, Tara C, Mads H, Fionnuala C (2013) Viking ghost hunt: creating engaging sound design for location-aware applications. Int J Arts Technol 6:61–82
53. Reid J, Hull R, Cater K, Clayton B (2004) Riot! 1831: the design of a location based audio drama. In: Proceedings of UK-UbiNet, pp 1–2
54. Derrida J (1967) Structure, sign, and play in the discourse of the human sciences. In: Writing and difference. Éditions du Seuil
55. Sam B (2021) Proposing, disposing, proving: barthes, intentionalism, and hypertext literary fiction. New Rev Hypermedia Multimedia 27(1–2):6–28
56. Graham P (2002) Revenge of the nerds
57. Raymond Q (1947) Exercises in style. Oneworld Classics Ltd, Richmond
58. Stacey M, Mark B (2021) On links: exercises in style. New Rev Hypermedia Multimedia 27(1–2):29–50
59. Elverdam C, Aarseth E (2005) Game classification as game design: construction through critical analysis. In: DiGRA conference
60. Javanshir R, Millard D, Carroll E (2020) Structural patterns for transmedia storytelling. PLoS ONE 15(1)
61. Todorov T (1973) The fantastic: a structural approach to a literary genre. Cornell University Press
62. Koenitz H, Eladhari HP, Louchart S, Nack F (2020) INDCOR white paper 1: a shared vocabulary for IDN (Interactive Digital Narratives). arXiv:2010.10135 [cs]
63. Brown M (2018) Emergent storytelling techniques in the sims. Game Developer Conference
64. Millard D (2020) Games/hypertext. In: ACM conference on hypertext and social media, pp 123–126
65. Chew EC, Mitchell A (2020) Bringing art to life: examining poetic gameplay devices in interactive life stories. Games Cult 15(8):874–901. SAGE Publications
66. Sim YT, Mitchell A (2017) Wordless games: gameplay as narrative technique. In: Nunes N, Oakley I, Nisi V (eds) Interactive storytelling. Lecture notes in computer science. Springer International Publishing, Cham, pp 137–149
67. Kleinman E, Fox V, Zhu J (2016) Rough draft: towards a framework for metagaming mechanics of rewinding in interactive storytelling. In: Nack F, Gordon AS (eds) Interactive storytelling. Lecture notes in computer science. Springer International Publishing, Cham, pp 363–374
68. Spawforth C, Gibbins N, Millard D (2018) Uncommon patterns—authoring with story specific structures. In: Authoring for interactive storytelling workshop—ICIDS 2018
69. Shibolet Y, Knoller N, Koenitz H (2018) A framework for classifying and describing authoring tools for interactive digital narrative. In: Rouse R, Koenitz H, Haahr M (eds) Interactive storytelling. Lecture notes in computer science. Springer International Publishing, Cham, pp 523–533

Mapping the Unmappable: Reimagining Visual Representations of Interactive Narrative

John T. Murray and Anastasia Salter

Abstract The complexity of interactive narratives inspired a variety of visual aids and graphical interfaces that support authoring tasks. This chapter analyzes the visual interface of popular IDN authoring tools that include an explicit visual interface for creating content, including Twine, Storyspace 3, inklewriter, Inform 7, and Adventure Game Studio. We employ a simple proto-IDN consisting of a set of passages that represent locations spatially linked together to compare the interactive and non-interactive visual aids across the five tools. We also identify several organizing metaphors that underly the visual logic, including Spatial Mapping, Scene-driven Structure, Nodal Mapping, and Traversal Mapping. Authors use the graphical interfaces in each of these tools to predict and manage the set of possible traversals that players may take. There identify key features in the interfaces by their function as a visual aid to specific authoring tasks. The interface techniques represented have evolved with these shared features, though they also represent the current limits of a paradigm of interactive narrative authoring where an author has explicit control over the structure and paths of the work.

1 Introduction

Authoring Interactive Digital Narratives (IDNs) requires designing and managing the possibility space of potential paths or traversals [1]. These paths include branches, often choices (see choice poetics [2, 3]) that segment narrative content. Over the years, IDN authoring tools have developed specific techniques and features that support authors in creating IDNs through graphical interfaces that include visual aids for explicit control over the structure of a work. However, generalized game design tools, such as Unity [4] and Unreal [5], do not include support for managing

J. T. Murray (✉) · A. Salter
University of Central Florida, Florida, USA
e-mail: jtm@ucf.edu

A. Salter
e-mail: anastasia@ucf.edu

© The Author(s), under exclusive license to Springer Nature Switzerland AG 2022
C. Hargood et al. (eds.), *The Authoring Problem*, Human–Computer Interaction Series,
https://doi.org/10.1007/978-3-031-05214-9_11

narrative content in their core features, though some extensions do offer support, such as the Unity plugin Fungus [6]. What are the core issues these features address, and how can we compare them? What core design tasks can visualizations support, and what are their limits?

There are numerous IDN authoring tools [7] that range from research prototypes to proprietary tools. Chap. 18 in this volume examines the challenges inherent in evaluating the UX design of authoring tools from a user study perspective. This chapter analyzes and compares the visual aids of five popular and widely studied IDN tools to identify core trends and challenges their designs address. We selected these tools based on several criteria: Each has a strong user community, has a history of active development and current maintenance, and is used by entries to competitions and festivals outside of research studies. Our approach in this chapter draws from platform studies [8], which examine the intertwined technical and cultural factors, rather than a human–computer interaction and experimental approach. These authoring tools represent interfaces adopted by communities and actively developed for at least ten years. We begin with a brief overview of the history of mapping in interactive fiction and broader contexts, then examine the selected tools: Inform 7 (2006) [9], Adventure Game Studio (1997) [10], Twine (2009) [11], Storyspace 3 (Storyspace 1: 1987 [12, 13], StorySpace 3: 2016 [14, 15]) and inklewriter (2012) [16, 17]/freeinklewriter (2021) [18]. We identify and describe four metaphors that characterize the organizing principles for the selected tools: Spatial mapping, scene mapping, traversal mapping, and nodal mapping. Finally, we describe a path toward future visual interfaces for authoring IDN.

Traditional interactive fictions and their graphic-driven descendants, such as adventure games and role-playing games, frequently rely upon strong mapping structures that keep the player anchored in their environments: From the incredibly complex maps of *World of Warcraft*'s regions, which reveal their full geographies as the player explores, to the simple block-based room maps of Inform 7's interactive fictions, such player-facing maps suit games that rely upon versions of environmental storytelling. Game maps are so compelling as objects that they are frequently among the paratexts of classic games [19]. This approach in classic narrative games proved particularly valuable for providing players with an effective second screen, often with greater visual fidelity than was possible for older graphic cards to render. Indeed, such physical maps, and the spatial dimensions of their narrative, have reshaped our expectations of maps as navigation broadly [20]. The most fully realized "infinite canvas" (to quote Scott McCloud's term for his envisioned future of narrative imagetexts beyond the page [21]) is arguably Google Maps itself, with its expansive locative features promising a true sense of spatial here-ness.

Yet despite this compelling history of mapping, we observe that core elements of interactive narrative "content," especially relationships and actions, are inherently unmappable. Some exemplars of these narratives are those that have no sense of "location" or presence in a physical sense, but instead bring you as the player through an internal or emotional journey. For you as the player, such texts might not require you to have a sense of precise presence: Works of hypertext, for instance, often forgo any visible map or markers of position, relying upon the player to track their own sense of narrative progression.

For these narratives, the map *flattens* play rather than expands upon it; play, therefore, cannot be meaningfully represented through traversals of physical geography alone (if at all). The "mental mapping" of an interactive narrative from a player's perspective is unlikely to be grounded in geography, as one study analyzing a player's own video game mapping suggests [22]. Furthermore, the making of a map may be crucial to the building of a world, but it is even further from the designer's experience of charting, or the structural design, an interactive narrative.

It is this authorial perspective on interactive narrative visualization that we take up here, while acknowledging that the making visible of pathways through a work often involves a layer of communication with the player. Historically, different authors have solved the problems of mapping choices through different mechanisms: Deena Larsen's shower curtain, which used printouts of the main pages of her hypertext *Marble Springs*, is a particularly telling early example in which links are represented by multicolored threads, connected words and options across the screens [23]. The spatial components of Larsen's shower curtain return us to Scott McCloud's vision of the "infinite canvas," a vision for extensible panels using the computer screen as a portal to entry that has proven more useful for thinking about mapping and visualization than it has for its original use case, comics [21]. Spatial thinking around non-spatial relationships is particularly telling of how interactive narrative visualization problems have historically been addressed and frames the fundamental challenges we address here: How might we map the unmappable of interactive narrative in a way that enables more complex design through visualization tools? Is there a visual metaphor outside the map, with its embedded bias towards the locative, that offers a more compelling path forward for interactive narrative tools? We revisit this after first addressing the attractiveness of the map as a tool and a metaphor.

2 Mapping the Unmappable Through Visualization

This idea of mapping physical locations and transcribing them onto the experience of reading and writing interactive stories, as we've examined in this short history, is both compelling and deceptive. Any traversal is a linear sequence, yet given the possible changes that result from choices, the collection of possible traversals does not form a map with connected locations. In the domain of hypertext, for instance, a common practice is to reuse content by allowing a reader to revisit it through a loop. While the loop itself is easily imagined by depicting the node connecting to itself, the number of times the loop may be traversed is less easy to represent. This drives home that even though IDN authoring tools have embraced the node-link representation due to its accessibility and its expressive power, the author of an IDN is not a mapmaker but rather a time-traveler and a logician. They must both determine and predict how different selections of choices can result in a satisfying story without succumbing to unnecessarily burdening the author with content creation. Here, we see the interactive narrative mapping problem come into view from the authorial perspective: Existing metaphors of visualization capture some, but not all, of these narrative relationships.

This "authorial burden" has been a topic of intense study in the community (and the subject of Chap. 3 in this volume), with works addressing it through specific systems [24–26], generative methods [27, 28], modeling [29] and external visualizations [30–32]. This complexity can take different forms since not every story has the same constraint of diegetic consistency [33]. Indeed, many hypertext works depend on the encounter of the text and the potential effects of re-reading to achieve the literary effects [34]. This chapter will closely analyze the visualizations present in current tools and their evolution, noting the implicit and explicit goals they aspire toward and connecting these to ongoing efforts to understand the authoring process.

As discussed elsewhere in this book and defined by Shibolet et al. [28], Authoring tools provide technical solutions to the range of challenges for IDNs, from design and development to testing and publishing. Each tool differs in its interface design but shares the concerns of managing story content and showing authors possible traversals of a work. Each tool also supports the goal of assessing the emerging narrative in a more linear or traditional fashion that players will experience through their own traversals. A central task of an IDN authoring tool is assisting authors in managing (and assessing) the complexity of writing non-linear stories. The degree to which a tool can provide "authorial leverage [35]" depends on how well the tool's editing interface matches the problem domain and the author's conception of that domain. The development of such tools can be understood from the intersecting domains of user experience [36] and narratology [37].

Authoring tool visual aids support specific authoring tasks, including content organization, traversal planning, assessing ombinatorics variation (for procedural or generative implementations), and testing. These tasks are often interwoven with one another, as adding a branch in a story may have implications for both structural features (which sections are accessible) and the semantic level (what consequences there are for the story events themselves).

We focus our attention on the problem that these aids attempt to solve and use comparisons of the five exemplar tools to explore the visualization problem through different degrees of mapping and narrative agency. Most tools we survey here in our analysis focus on structural features of interactive stories—namely choices, lexia (a unit of text that resembles a paragraph, often presented on a screen all at once) and ordering of content. We conclude with a discussion of the unsolved problems that future IDN visualization tools might address.

2.1 Contextualizing Approaches to Visual Language

For another approach to visualization, we turn to existing approaches to visual languages. These act as 2-dimensional analogs to traditional languages and are used across disciplines to represent structures and relationships between entities. They build on the theoretical framework of distributed representations, where the cognitive load is lessened by representing relationships and processes in external representations [38]. There are many examples of visual languages outside of computing, with the visual notation developed for music being a prominent example. The traditional definition of a *visual language* is one where information is encoded in more than one dimension [39], and which can be divided into visual programming languages (which are executable) and the more broad term visual languages (including Universal Modeling Language (UML) diagrams among others). These contrast with *textual languages,* which can be parsed as a stream of characters. Visual programming languages (VPLs) are attractive partly because programming using a textual language is perceived as difficult due to the abstractions involved and the memorization required to be fluent. These barriers to entry led to the design of visual programming languages for beginners, with a focus on the benefits to "end users" [40] and "student engagement" [41]. Indeed, several visual programming languages have become standard methods of introducing computer programming, and many use simple interactive stories as first programs. The visualizations we discuss are all non-executable, as they are diagrams of content rather than operators. Flowcharts used in Fungus [6] can be considered executable.

VPLs offer attractive features for beginners in programming. They eliminate syntax errors by giving feedback on possible connections and configurations and will present a user with the current configuration without the need for mental tracing, as is the case with variable declarations and function calls. Scratch [42], for instance, and Blockly [43] are both used in schools around the world and enjoy thriving communities of developers and users. Some VPLs have proven successful outside of education: Unreal Engine offers a VPL for its engine called Blueprints, while Unity recently acquired visual scripting product Bolt [44]. Both offer alternative views on manipulating game assets and engine APIs than the traditional programming languages, C# or C++ . In IoT, visual programming has addressed the need of configuration of actions and a controller for embedded devices through Node-RED [45]. These languages have proven promising in a variety of studies, especially when focusing on broadening participation in computing [46].

Integrated Development Environments or IDEs employ a number of visual aids (also called "source code editor augmentations" in the context of text editors) that do not rely on visual languages, such as syntax highlighting, annotations (including highlighting syntax errors through squiggly lines and other methods), and hover effects that describe type and related documentation [47]. Many of the scripting features in the tools described in this chapter that otherwise connect to visualizations employ these source code editor augmentations, with the most prominent one being auto-complete. Spelling errors or typos can prevent identifiers from linking with the corresponding term and without some level of augmentation support, these can be easily missed. Inklewriter, Adventure Game Studio and Twine all include some level of textual support in this fashion.

2.2   Visualizations and Content Type

Throughout our assessment of these tools, we rely on a framework for two broad classes of interactive narrative content types identified by Spierling [48]: Explicit and Implicit. Other scholars have used various terms to describe how content is structured, including Michael Mateas calling them "content selection architectures" [49]. The nature of a unit of content is also a term that has various proposals from the community, with lexia being the most persistent term, though it emphasizes text-based passages, which may not easily apply to screens as presented by Adventure Game Studio.

Explicit content is where an author specifies the ordering and the output, and tools that support explicit content authoring provide the ability to make changes directly to output text, links, or ordering instructions that determine the sequence of content in any given traversal. Random elements may be present in the surface text or in the logic, but they do not take a primary role in the organization and structure. This fact makes explicit visual representations of the structure useful, either in authoring the work itself or in previewing the structure from another source format. Twine is the classic example, but Novella [50, 51] and StudyCrafter [52] are two other examples.

Implicit content is created using definitions of behavior which may not be as easily represented. This would include Versu [24], and Scenejo Authoring Tool (which runs on the Scenejo engine) [53]. Implicit structures include transitions between content segments, but these transitions and relationships do not map cleanly onto a node-link visualization. Often, these will include states that gate progression from one stage of a work to the next. This also encompasses work where content is organized into a database, and where content is chosen by an algorithm to be included by some criteria. Examples of this include Façade [25], Prom Week [26], and Bad News [54].

3   Visualization in Popular IDN Authoring Platforms

This section uses a sample story to compare approaches to IDN visualization in five popular and actively updated tools. As discussed earlier, these tools were selected as active, popular, well-maintained platforms with both a design and educational following: Inform 7 [9], Adventure Game Studio [10], Twine [11], Storyspace 3 [14], and freeinklewriter [18]. Other platforms with similar visualization methods are noted in the discussions of each tool: However, taken together, they represent the state of the field in popular IDN visualization features, and thus reflect the vocabulary of visualization that new authors are frequently trained in and familiarized through. Through this overview, we contextualize the use cases and affordances of each tool.

3.1 Inform 7

One subgenre of interactive digital narratives is parser-based fiction. In parser play, each turn is taken by entering a command that is parsed by the engine and which results in a reply. Although the general description of parser-based interactive digital narratives suggests a wide range of possible conversations, such as chatbots, in practice, the type of work is shaped mainly by convention and by the tools available to support those conventions. Inform 7 [9] is one of the most popular tools for authoring parser-based fiction, and though its capabilities in terms of representing characters, events and objects are immense, we focus our attention on the fundamental unit of its simulation space: Room.

Unlike other parts of content that an author might create, such as rules, actors, and objects, rooms are organized in relation to one another through connections. These links are drawn from a set of relations, including cardinal directions and inside and outside, above and below. The links can either be two-way links or one-way links. The constraint on how rooms are connected and how they are represented allows for the tool to generate a map of the work based on these relationships. This graph is a rendering of those relationships as they are understood by the compiled version of a work and cannot be clicked on by the user.

To show off the relative similarities and affordances of the different tools we discuss, we have created a configuration of nodes that are connected with either two-way connections or one-way connections. Figure 1 shows these lexia (each in Inform 7 is called a room) with specified relationships. Because the Forest (labeled Fr in the generated graph) is to the west of the Clearing (Cr), the graph can be laid out without additional input or positioning by the author. The choice of the tool to represent the two words (Fortress and Forest) using Fr is interesting, though unfortunate: there is no built-in capacity to distinguish them. Two spaces cannot reside in the "west" link. The Fortress (Fr) is inside the Meadow (Md), and so this relationship is represented through a colored annotation which frees the Fortress to have other rooms in each direction. These maps can be helpful in orienting not just authors as to the layout of their creation, but also players, and there are now extensions that provide this in Inform 7, the Automap by Mark Tilford being the most well-known. Games that use this feature are said to be in the style of "Beyond Zork," which included one of the first examples. The extension supports the generation of maps for the player view that show which room they are in during the running of the compiled work.

3.2 Adventure Game Studio

Adventure Game Studio [10] is a tool for making graphical adventure games initially developed by Chris Jones for release in 1997, and still actively in development with a last release in September 2021, a notable longevity for a tool associated with a genre that has fluctuated in popularity [55]. Adventure games structurally have

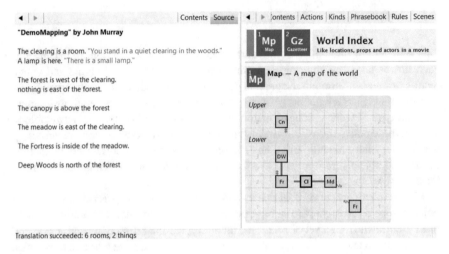

Fig. 1 Inform 7 interface

many similarities to interactive fiction, and particularly share a tendency towards environmental storytelling with that genre [56]. It also here acts as an entry point for understanding the environment-driven design representation trends in current graphical game engines, including popular platforms such as Unity [4], Construct 3 [57], Godot [58], and GameMaker [59]. However, Adventure Game Studio's strongly narrative focus makes it more of interest for the problem of IDN visualization.

Notably, Adventure Game Studio has a strong visual vocabulary available but employs that visualization within a fundamentally database-driven approach to project organization, as shown in Fig. 2. An author working in Adventure Game Studio will use the room editor, as shown in the figure below, to craft a detailed visual map of walkable spaces on any displayed screen. Objects and possible verb interactions within the room are handled through scripted code, but ultimately, everything that can be manipulated must be in some way made visible to the player.

This distinction is crucial for understanding the difference between text-driven IDN visualization challenges and graphical ones. While Adventure Game Studio has similar underlying metaphors and conceptual tendencies as interactive fiction, we see here how its authoring tool is fundamentally driven by making the same world logics visible to the player as they are to the author. For more on the connections between representations and logics in games, see Wardrip-Fruin's *How Pac Man Eats* [60]. However, one interesting consequence of the single-screen model of authoring (which hearkens back to LucasArts and Sierra adventure games [56]) is that spatial cohesion is only important within a room view: Outside of the room view, rooms exist as named and numbered locations, but are not charted with any visual relationship to one another beyond the convenience of edge-based navigation (with a top, bottom, left and right edge having convenient hooks to be associated with both logic and room changing functions). Changing rooms is not limited to these edges, as hotspots and other mechanics can also call the changeroom script, but they do offer a default

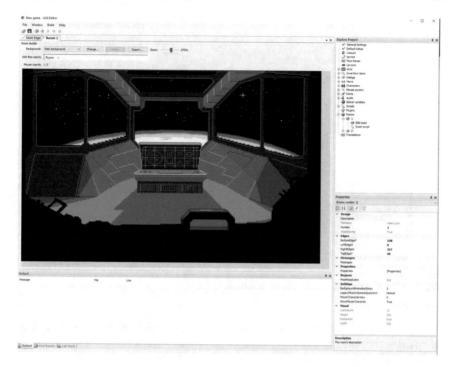

Fig. 2 The adventure game studio room editor

cardinal navigation scheme. Navigation between rooms is in many ways as arbitrary
as the linked threads of Deena Larsen's shower curtain [23]: There is no requirement
for rooms to physically map, beyond the desire to meet the expectations of the player,
as long as the graphical representation of each stage provides internal cohesion and
continuity. The requirement to both include and rely on graphical features further
distinguishes Adventure Game Studio from the other four text-centric tools.

3.3 Twine

Our next tool, Twine [11], is highly recognizable in the traditions of hypertext:
Through its multiple versions, story formats, and iterations, it has become one of
the most popular and accessible tools for making hypertextual narratives [61]. This
can be attributed in part to its card-driven, intuitive visual display for passages and
linking, shown in Fig. 3. Notably, this system allows the designer to manipulate
their view of the story visually without any consequence to the player experience:
It can become a mindmap as much as it is a storymap, and authors can see the
density of their narrative linking and structures in the flow of the lines to passages.

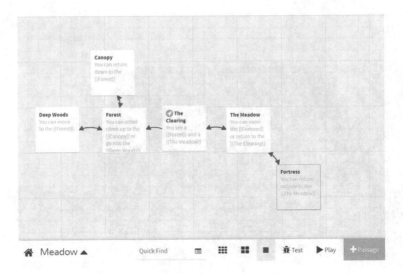

Fig. 3 A Twine storymap, with arrows indicating links

Arrows indicate directional relationships between passages and thus provide a sense of possible traversals.

This does defy an expectation of sequencing—the home for the "first" passage is indicated by a green rocket, and items that are spatially juxtaposed do not necessarily have meaningful connections. This can make a storymap in Twine difficult on a newcomer, as linearity is completely abandoned. However, to return to McCloud, there is also an enticing potential in the Twine map's use of a scrolling canvas, which allows the author to expand in any direction and move freely and conceptually in creating the story.

However, the "map" that results from Twine's approach to visualization is misleading, as Kolb's discussion of the complexity of representing hypertext notes: "the landscape created in the richer hypertext exceeds the dual categories and it refuses to be confined on a single level" [62]. Complex coded jumps are not visualized as easily as links, and apparent dead ends and disconnected passages might in fact be accessible through routes in the story that are not recognized by Twine's engine. Current experiments in Twine, such as Harlowe's storylets, expand this potential for this type of non-linearity, also explored as sculptural hypertext [63], with card-deck style, disconnected fragments: The challenges of visualizing them meaningfully are now underway.

3.4 Storyspace 3

Eastgate Systems Storyspace 3 [15] represents one of the more complex systems for authoring hypertext. Unlike Twine, the software allows for resizing and editing

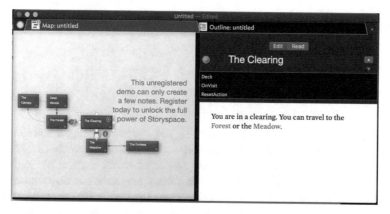

Fig. 4 Storyspace 3 interface

every aspect of a lexia, in addition to providing several types of links. The core unit in Storyspace 3 is the note. Notes can contain textual links or basic links. In the implementation shown in Fig. 4 of the same set of lexia, the same topography was achieved through selecting links and then dragging the "text link" icon at the top of the interface to a destination passage. The actual selection and modification of links is handled through annotations in the visualization, including removing links and adding features such as guard fields, which can contain predicates that prevent the display or navigation of certain links. Finally, a "shark link" is one that is automatically followed (or added to the current lexia) if its preconditions are met. For instance, if the player were to be immediately sent to the dungeon, a shark link could be created between The Fortress and The Dungeon with no pre-requisites. All links are displayed through annotations when the associated passage is selected, making Storyspace 3's visual editor dependent on the layout of both the elements and the currently selected note to make changes to links or the size and layout of the rectangle representing a note or writing space.

The type of the link is represented by whether the arrow is solid or dashed, with solid being a "Basic link" navigated upon clicking on the lexia, and individual dashed links representing potentially multiple links from one passage to another. Shark links are rendered as a red dashed line. Like Inform 7 and the others here, one-way links are easy to implement. Inform 7's textual interface included implicit two-way connections between rooms. The player, for instance, could move freely between the Canopy and the Forest, but could not return from the Forest to the Clearing. In Inform 7, a one-way link is the exception and requires an additional instruction: "nothing is east of the forest." In Storyspace 3, authors have several auto-layout features if they do not wish to specify the position of the lexia in the space.

One of the features in Storyspace but not Twine is the notion of multiple spaces for the visual nodes. This can represent a set of nodes inside the Fortress, for instance, without placing them in the same plane as the other locations outside of the Fortress.

In Inform 7, this same relationship is handled through the "inside" and "outside" relations.

3.5 inklewriter

inklewriter (specifically, freeinklewriter [18]) is a web application and authoring interface developed by Inkle, inc. It provides a point and click authoring interface for interactive fiction features that focus on choice-based stories. While the tool shares philosophical commonalities with the ink language, the two do not completely overlap in capabilities, nor can the output of one be used in the other. Inky [64] is the editor for the ink language that includes a runtime player that resembles some of the reader views of inklewriter. Unlike the other tools discussed, the primary authoring mode for inklewriter (Fig. 5) is through a more readerly perspective. Authors create each lexia in the order they are encountered, while the interface helps by notifying them of any "loose ends." Authors create new links by adding "options" as inklewriter's primary unit is a passage with a set of choices. Those choices can lead to new passages.

In the web interface, two-way links were implemented by connecting the passage to a previous passage, which warns the user of a potentially unintended loop. This is particularly interesting given the lack of similar warnings in any of the other tools. This is in part due to ink's prioritization of choices and progression over spaces and simulations, though the engine can easily be used to represent locations and state. Unlike other tools, inklewriter's editor also allows the depictions of traversals as the work is being played or edited (Fig. 5), which shows the history of lexia visited as well as the current lexia. Unlike Twine or Storyspace 3, though, inklewriter's visualization is laid out automatically in a standard tree format.

Inklewriter supports other features such as variables or data structures in the same way that Twine does. However, the domain-specific language, ink, is a distinct language with different features from inklewriter. The lack of a user-managed interactive visualization is partly by design—in the view of ink's creators, the language is designed to support the type of writing they prefer. Certain concepts are much harder to implement in inklewriter, such as cycles, which are concise to represent in ink as self-references.

As Jon Ingold describes his perspective, "we don't bother mapping the cause/effect and consequence graphs of scenes… Instead of making a graph, we index all the 'major events' by creating boolean VARs for them, and then make sure scenes are robust against that index" [65]. However, this approach demands the author pay significant attention to the underlying code, rather than mapping a visualization to scene structures and possibility spaces.

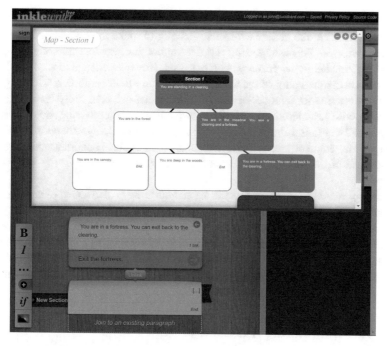

Fig. 5 inklewriter authoring interface (top: static, bottom: primary)

4 Common Visualization Features

All visualizations depict elements in the story, though some function more as editor features and others operate more as analytical tools. For the latter, snapshots of the structure or statistics of an interactive story can be valuable in making changes, especially in the case of procedurally generated story content. For the former, the node-link diagram has become the standard editing visual interface for the content in choice-based tools. In this section, we discuss different ways to break down these constituent tasks and how they affect the overall authoring process. These subtasks can be combined together with different choices around how the visuals aid in creating, deleting, or organizing content. For instance, Bernstein notes that authors using the Storyspace tool prefer the map view of the tool, and describes several possible applications of spatial layout beyond simple navigation [66]. An automated layout engine may erase these important distinctions. It's also the case that most visualizations that allow direct manipulation are for stories with an explicit structure, as the author is determining the ordering and relative proximity of content and so directly changing the position of lexia allows for that, as we demonstrate in the sample stories presented in Sect. 4.

While writing, both ink and Twine prioritized a playable rendering of the output that is available to the author while also striving to make the text content the main interface with templates supporting variables rather than a more traditional programming language being the primary source format. However, they take vastly different positions on the metaphor of the underlying structure being authored. The language ink considers a work as a collection of threads that are constantly branching and collecting with parameterized variation a frequent occurrence and the choice a central figure. The Twine authoring interface, on the other hand, displays a network of written passages that connect through directed links, with choices becoming one possible implicit use of the link figure that connects passages and changes the state of the work.

Both approaches recognize that the act of authoring is also an act of reading, that to understand what any potential reader should feel or think about a character or how that character should act, the author must alternate between reader and writer. Newer approaches, discussed later in this chapter, attempt to supplement authorial imagination of these facts and constraints on the storyworld through adding labels to the entities and using algorithms to constrain their inclusion or combination.

4.1   Visual Authoring Aid Classification

The tools assessed in this chapter enable authors to perform a variety of tasks to navigate and edit the content, structure, and conditions of IDNs either directly manipulating or consulting visual diagrams or maps. These include *selecting content* to be edited (accomplished by overviews or indices of content segments or lexia), *understanding sequence* of content presentation (often through directed graphs), *assessing distribution* of generated content, and *identify gaps or inconsistencies* in a story using the results of automated analysis as well as *identifying and applying patterns*, such as episodes or chapters, or bottlenecks.

- **Selecting and Adding Content**—When making changes to an interactive story, authoring tools typically group content into some sort of node or lexia. This allows for an overview where the label for the content can be displayed without all of the details. Such visualizations often most resemble maps.
- **Understanding Sequence**—At its simplest, this is the question of "what order" does content occur in? Some stories allow a set of nodes to be visited in any order, but from the visualization, it would be clear that they must be viewed either before or after other nodes. This grouping may not be explicit in a simple node-line graph, as the interconnections between these nodes may obscure the availability or logic behind their presentation. In ink, this common pattern of visiting content in any order is built into the implicit behavior of the asterisk, which allows a choice to be displayed repeatedly if the same content is shown again.
- **Assessing Distribution**—For selection-based interactive narratives, a common question is "Where should I add content?" This question drove the authors to create

an interactive visualization tool for Ice-Bound which visualizes the distribution of content by tags [31].

- **Identifying Gaps and Loose Ends**—Stories require certain elements to make sense. This is best captured by the efforts in planning, where a story tool can identify a missing precondition for an action.
- **Identifying and Applying Patterns**—There is a wealth of knowledge about structure in traditional branching narratives, which can be summarized and depicted through graph patterns. Where in a story are choices located, and what type of structure does the placement and timing of the structure give rise to? These are represented through structures in a twine context through the distribution of nodes and edges in a graph and are visually apparent despite potential variations in number or connections. Emily Short reviews several of these in her blog post, "small scale patterns in CYOA" [67].

4.2 Types of Mapping

Creating compelling interactive narratives does not inherently depend on the tool or approach, as the variety of tools, philosophies and methodologies have successfully combined the elements of story, puzzles, and exploration [55]. But the essential challenges that face authors remain relatively consistent: How to evaluate the story being created while managing the content that ultimately forms it. While there have long been discussions about the importance of guard fields and the value of incorporating variation and stretch text, there are few instances where these features are directly incorporated into either a visual interface or a visual authoring tool.

Graph visualizations are an authoring aid that allows authors to trace structural form while supporting the core editing and testing cycle. Authors can group content by nodes and see where nodes occur during a traversal through the display of directed edges. Given these discrepancies, it can be challenging to compare structures across works meaningfully: Important distinctions exist in content modeling, organization, production, editing, and presentation, all or some of which might incorporate visual metaphors for authorial or user manipulation. However, previous work suggests these prevalent metaphors, each with its reductive consequences, summarized in Table 1 and expanded upon in the following sections.

Table 1 Tools and their Primary Metaphors and Emphasis

Tool	Primary metaphor	Emphasis
Inform 7	Spatial mapping	Actions and navigation
Adventure Game Studio	Scene-driven structure	Place and actions
Storyspace 3	Spatial mapping	Traversals and lexia
Inklewriter	Traversal mapping	choices
Twine	Nodal mapping	Sequences and paths

Spatial mapping

Familiar to users of Inform 7, spatial mapping presumes an environmental design metaphor (though one is not required, and "rooms" in Inform 7 can contain multitudes.) Perhaps the most game-like, spatial mapping frequently visually breaks when the "rules" of physical space are violated by authorial possibility spaces. Adventure Game Studio uses the four screen edges as offsets for triggering player navigation scripts in addition to sub-regions of a room to suggest possible connections to other rooms, though without a map of the rooms themselves.

Scene-driven structure

Common to visual novel tools such as Adventure Game Studio and Ren'Py Visual Novel Engine [68], scene-driven structures often flatten their contents, suggesting a fundamental linearity to the actions within a "scene" and placing the emphasis on the paths possible between scenes. AGS, however, allows authoring affordances for describing different paths through a scene, based on interactions with objects for instance.

Nodal mapping

Prevalent in Twine and Storyspace 3, nodal mapping structures flatten the content of passages, emphasizing the links between them. However, such maps only track simple linking mechanisms: Generative, scripted movement and techniques such as storylets [49] and stretchtext [15] are erased from the visual structure, and guard fields (though available) cannot be visualized outside of a textual representation. Nodal mapping is attractive to visual programming languages in the dataflow category, in part because of the simplicity of representing units and connections. One aspect that is not used in IDN tools is the labeling of "ports" in diagrams. There is also the distinction between static visualizations, such as present in Inform 7 and inklewriter, and the authoring UI featured in Twine and Storyspace 3, where the user describes relationships directly through the diagram.

Traversal Mapping

This metaphor is best described as focusing on a path taken through a network rather than the network structure itself. The authoring interface of inklewriter and even the ink language itself emphasizes the importance of a choice and previously made choices, but less the exact configuration of choices in a static arrangement. One example of a common structure in a traversal mapping approach is the cycle: In ink, it is common for a choice set to be presented multiple times and to remove a previously taken choice. This path is easier to trace using the tool, and such loops are hard to visualize in a more traditional nodal mapping visualization, and even inklewriter's interface makes it difficult to author these even though the effects are displayed through a specific traversal.

5 Conclusions

The visual aids we described in this chapter represent the varied efforts by authoring tools to lower barriers for entry for creators to create interactive stories and to alleviate some of the authorial burden of tracing complex networks of possible traversals. This may be a result of the increased control an author feels through seeing a story structure that resembles a storyboard, and one where tracing a playthrough involves following links. As we noted, this trend is present in the popularity of novice-friendly visual programming languages, such as Unity's Visual Scripting system [69], Unreal Engine's Blueprints [70], and Rec Room's Circuits [71]. These systems share many concerns with interactive narrative systems and may eventually be capable of including narrative-oriented features in the future. A major challenge is how to represent visually the semantics of events, characters and values into authoring tools, as the tools described in this chapter rely heavily on the author's understanding of the content contained in lexia, passages and screens in order to chart dependencies and meaning. Work on modeling story itself and not just structures include several efforts, including Story Intention Graphs [72], Interactive Cinematic Experience [73] and Progression Maps [29]. Of these, only Progression Maps have been incorporated into an authoring tool.

To return to the player experience from our opening, expectations of interactive narrative complexity have increased alongside the potential of authoring tools. Responsiveness to choices has become a subject for reviews, and interest in emerging methods of IDN personalization is on the rise. The demands of increasingly complex methods of narrative design, from procedural content generation to storylet systems, is likely to continue to defy easy visual representation. Each new level of complexity offers the temptation to layer further complexity on the various structures documented in the case studies here.

From an authorial perspective, however, addressing the authorial burden is not necessarily a matter of more information: It is the emphasis on different information and making important relationships easy to identify and prioritizing different types of connections, that makes these authoring tools (and their corresponding output) so interestingly distinct from one another. Thus, it is in the possibilities of multilayered and expansive, author-customizable views that we see the most potential for moving forward: The more ways of seeing we build into the canvases of authoring tools, the more we will likely see their potential realized in the future of playable and experimental interactive narratives.

References

1. Montfort N (2003) Twisty little passages: an approach to interactive fiction. http://www.ama zon.ca/exec/obidos/redirect?tag=citeulike09-20&path=ASIN/0262134365
2. Mawhorter P, Mateas M, Wardrip-Fruin N, Jhala A (2014) Towards a theory of choice poetics. In: Proceedings of foundations of digital games

3. Mawhorter P, Zegura C, Gray A, Jhala A, Mateas M, Wardrip-Fruin N (2018) Choice poet example. Arts 7:47. https://doi.org/10.3390/arts7030047
4. Unity (2020) https://unity.com
5. Unreal Engine (2020) https://unrealengine.com/
6. Gregan C, Halliwell S (2022) Fungus. https://fungusgames.com/
7. Shibolet Y, Knoller N, Koenitz H (2018) A framework for classifying and describing authoring tools for interactive digital narrative. In: Rouse R, Koenitz H, Haahr M (eds). In: Interactive storytelling. Springer International Publishing, Cham, pp 523–533. https://doi.org/10.1007/978-3-030-04028-4_61
8. Bogost I, Montfort N Platform studies: frequently questioned answers. 7
9. Graham N (2015) Inform 7. http://inform7.com/about/
10. Chris J (2022) Adventure game studio
11. Klimas C (2009) Twine
12. Bolter JD, Joyce M (1987) Hypertext and creative writing. In: Proceedings of the ACM conference on hypertext. Association for Computing Machinery, New York, NY, USA, pp 41–50. https://doi.org/10.1145/317426.317431
13. Jay DB, John BS (1987) Storyspace 1
14. Mark B: Story space 3
15. Bernstein M (2016) Storyspace 3. In: Proceedings of the 27th ACM conference on hypertext and social media. Association for Computing Machinery, New York, NY, USA, pp 201–206. https://doi.org/10.1145/2914586.2914624
16. Inklewriter beta (2012)
17. Write 'Choose Your Own Adventure' books through this clever HTML5 App. https://www.fastcompany.com/1670294/write-choose-your-own-adventure-books-through-this-clever-html5-app. Accessed 26 April 2022
18. Maxence, Alban, Inkle Studios (2021) Freeinklewriter. https://github.com/inklewriter/freeinklewriter
19. Consalvo M (2019) Hot dates and Fairy-tale romances: studying sexuality in video games. https://www.taylorfrancis.com/, https://doi.org/10.4324/9780203700457-15. Accessed 31 May 2019
20. Edler D, Dickmann F (2017) The impact of 1980s and 1990s video games on multimedia cartography. Cartographica 52:168–177. https://doi.org/10.3138/cart.52.2.3823
21. McCloud S (2000) Reinventing comics: how imagination and technology are revolutionizing an art form. Harper Collins
22. Minassian HT (2018) Drawing video game mental maps: from emotional games to emotions of play. Cartogr Perspect 47–62. https://doi.org/10.14714/CP91.1435
23. Larsen D. Marble springs shower curtain. https://archive.mith.umd.edu/larsen/items/show/42.html, Accessed 2 February 2022
24. Evans RP, Short E. The AI architecture of versu, 1–37
25. Mateas M, Stern A (2003) Façade: an experiment in building a fully-realized interactive drama. In: Game developers conference, p 24
26. McCoy J, Treanor M, Samuel B, Reed AA, Wardrip-Fruin N, Mateas M (2012) Prom week. In: Proceedings of the international conference on the foundations of digital games—FDG '12. ACM Press, New York, USA, p 235. https://doi.org/10.1145/2282338.2282384
27. Compton K, Filstrup B, Mateas M (2014) Tracery: approachable story grammar authoring for casual users. In: seventh intelligent narrative technologies, pp 64–67
28. Garbe J, Kreminski M, Samuel B, Wardrip-Fruin N, Mateas M (2019) StoryAssembler: an engine for generating dynamic choice-driven narratives. In: Proceedings of the 14th international conference on the foundations of digital games. ACM, San Luis Obispo California, pp 1–10. https://doi.org/10.1145/3337722.3337732
29. Carstensdottir E, Partlan N, Sutherland S, Duke T, Ferris E, Richter RM, Valladares M, Seif El-Nasr M (2020) Progression maps: conceptualizing narrative structure for interaction design support. In: Proceedings of the 2020 CHI conference on human factors in computing systems. Association for Computing Machinery, Honolulu, HI, USA , pp 1–13 https://doi.org/10.1145/3313831.3376527

30. Sali S, Mateas M (2011) Using information visualization to understand interactive narrative: A case study on Façade. In: lecture notes in computer science (including subseries lecture notes in artificial intelligence and lecture notes in bioinformatics), pp 284–289. https://doi.org/10.1007/978-3-642-25289-1_31.

31. Garbe J, Reed AA, Dickinson M, Wardrip-Fruin N, Mateas M (2014) Author assistance visualizations for Ice-Bound, A combinatorial narrative. In: Foundations of digital games

32. Swinehart C One book, many readings. https://samizdat.co/cyoa/. Accessed 31 Jan 2022

33. Ryan M-L (2002) Beyond myth and metaphor: narrative in digital media. Poetics Today 23:581–609. https://doi.org/10.1215/03335372-23-4-581

34. Moulthrop S, Grigar D (2017) Traversals: the use of preservation for early electronic writing. MIT Press

35. Chen S, Nelson M, Sullivan A, Mateas M (2009) Evaluating the authorial leverage of drama management. In: Proceedings of the AAAI 2009 spring symposium on interactive narrative technologies II, pp 20–23

36. Revi AT, Millard D, Middleton SE, A systematic analysis of user experience dimensions for interactive digital narratives, p 17

37. Harmon S, Jhala A (2015) Imaginative recall with story intention graphs. In: Computational models of narrative, pp 71–81. https://doi.org/10.4230/OASIcs.CMN.2015.71

38. Zhang J, Norman DA representations in distributed cognitive tasks. p 34

39. Erwig M, Smeltzer K, Wang X (2017) What is a visual language? J Vis Lang Comput 38:9–17. https://doi.org/10.1016/j.jvlc.2016.10.005

40. Myers BA (1990) Taxonomies of visual programming and program visualization. J Vis Lang Comput 1:97–123. https://doi.org/10.1016/S1045-926X(05)80036-9

41. Kuh GD (2009) What student affairs professionals need to know about student engagement. J Coll Stud Dev 50:683–706. https://doi.org/10.1353/csd.0.0099

42. Maloney J, Resnick M, Rusk N, Silverman B, Eastmond E (2010) The scratch programming language and environment. ACM Trans Comput Educ 10:1–15. https://doi.org/10.1145/1868358.1868363

43. Fraser N (2015) Ten things we've learned from Blockly. In: 2015 IEEE blocks and beyond workshop (Blocks and Beyond). IEEE, Atlanta, GA, USA, pp 49–50. https://doi.org/10.1109/BLOCKS.2015.7369000

44. Bolt visual scripting is now included in all Unity plans. https://blogs.unity3d.com/2020/07/22/bolt-visual-scripting-is-now-included-in-all-unity-plans/. Accessed 14 December 2020

45. NodeRED (2021)

46. Andujar M, Jimenez L, Shah J, Morreale P (2013) Evaluating visual programming environments to teach computing to minority high school students. J Comput Sci Coll 29:140–148

47. Sulír M, Bačíková M, Chodarev S, Porubän J (2018) Visual augmentation of source code editors: A systematic mapping study. J Vis Lang Comput 49:46–59. https://doi.org/10.1016/j.jvlc.2018.10.001

48. Spierling U (2007) Adding aspects of "implicit creation" to the authoring process in interactive storytelling. In: Virtual storytelling using virtual reality technologies for storytelling, pp 13–25. https://doi.org/10.1007/978-3-540-77039-8_2

49. Kreminski M, Wardrip-Fruin N (2018) Sketching a map of the storylets design space. In: Rouse R, Koenitz H, Haahr M (eds) Interactive storytelling. Springer International Publishing, Cham, pp 160–164. https://doi.org/10.1007/978-3-030-04028-4_14

50. Green D, Hargood C, Charles F, Jones A (2018) Novella: a proposition for Game-based storytelling, p 6

51. Green D, Hargood C, Charles F (2019) Novella 2.0: a hypertextual architecture for interactive narrative in games. In: Proceedings of the 30th ACM conference on hypertext and social media. ACM, Hof Germany, pp 77–86. https://doi.org/10.1145/3342220.3343655

52. Harteveld C, Manning N, Abu-Arja F, Menasce R, Thurston D, Smith G, Sutherland SC (2017) Design of playful authoring tools for social and behavioral science. In: Proceedings of the 22nd international conference on intelligent user interfaces companion. ACM, Limassol Cyprus, pp 157–160. https://doi.org/10.1145/3030024.3040981

53. Spierling U, Weiß SA, Müller W (2006) Towards accessible authoring tools for interactive storytelling. In: Proceedings of the Third international conference on technologies for interactive digital storytelling and entertainment. Springer-Verlag, Berlin, Heidelberg, pp 169–180. https://doi.org/10.1007/11944577_17

54. Samuel B, Ryan J, Summerville AJ, Mateas M, Wardrip-Fruin N (2016) Bad news: an experiment in computationally assisted performance. In: Nack F, Gordon AS (eds) Interactive storytelling. Springer International Publishing, Cham, pp 108–120. https://doi.org/10.1007/978-3-319-48279-8_10

55. Reed AA, Murray J, Salter A (2019) Adventure games: playing the outsider. Bloom Acad. https://doi.org/10.5040/9781501346576

56. Salter A (2014) What is your quest?: from adventure games to interactive books. University of Lowa Press

57. Construct (2022) https://www.construct.net/en

58. Juan Linietsky Ariel Manzur (2022) Godot engine. https://godotengine.org/

59. GameMaker (2022) https://gamemaker.io/en/gamemaker

60. Wardrip-Fruin N (2020) How Pac-Man eats. The MIT Press, Cambridge, Massachusetts

61. Salter A, Moulthrop S. Twining: critical and creative approaches to the twine platform. Amherst Press (Pending)

62. Kolb D (2013) Narrative hypertext, on the level. In: Proceedings of the 3rd narrative and hypertext workshop on—NHT'13. ACM Press, Paris, France, pp 1–4. https://doi.org/10.1145/2462216.2462219

63. Bernstein M, Millard DE, Weal MJ On writing sculptural hypertext. p 2

64. Inky (2022)

65. Ingold J Visual documentation of stories Issue #22 inkle/ink. https://github.com/inkle/ink/issues/22. Accessed 26 April 2022

66. Bernstein M (2002) Storyspace 1. In: Proceedings of the thirteenth ACM conference on hypertext and hypermedia. Association for Computing Machinery, New York, NY, USA, pp 172–181. https://doi.org/10.1145/513338.513383

67. Short AE Small-scale structures in CYOA. https://emshort.blog/2016/11/05/small-scale-structures-in-cyoa/. Accessed 31 Jan 2022

68. Ren'Py visual novel engine

69. Unity visual scripting | unity. https://unity.com/features/unity-visual-scripting. Accessed 26 April 2022

70. Blueprints visual scripting. https://docs.unrealengine.com/5.0/en-US/blueprints-visual-scripting-in-unreal-engine/. Accessed 26 April 2022

71. The circuits handbook. https://blog.recroom.com/posts/2021/5/03/the-circuits-handbook. Accessed 26 April 2022

72. Elson DK, McKeown KR (2009) A tool for deep semantic encoding of narrative texts. In: Proceedings of the 47th annual meeting of the association for computational linguistics and the 4th international joint conference on natural language processing of the AFNLP, Software demonstrations, pp 9–12. https://doi.org/10.3115/1667872.1667875

73. Murray JT (2018) Telltale hearts: encoding cinematic choice-based adventure games. https://escholarship.org/uc/item/1n02n02z

On Story

Mark Bernstein (ID)

Abstract Category fiction—mystery, science fiction, fantasy, and horror among others—arose as a way to sell magazines and books to an audience that was eager to explore specific serious, storyable questions about the nature of the world and its woes. Understanding the frameworks on which these categories rest can inform the craft of interactive fiction while reminding us (and our readers) of the questions these stories address.

1 The Uses of Writing

Stories have many uses.

In 1802, an American ship captain named Nathaniel Bowditch arranged to publish *The New American Practical Navigator.* For centuries, the craft of guiding a sailing ship had been handed down from one generation of officers and gentlemen to the next; a mere seaman or an outsider could not aspire to command. Bowditch thought this un-American, and his book covered everything one needed to know to guide a sailing ship to port. It had worked examples, and at its heart is an exemplary narrative—a detailed log of an oceanic voyage. The title page boasted that the volume would be "sold by every book-seller, ship-chandler, and mathematical-instrument-maker in the United States and West Indies", and it was not wrong. Bowditch, much revised, remains in print today. You will find a copy aboard every American ship, merchant or naval [40]. Bowditch implicitly argues that anyone, regardless of birth or education, may through diligent study learn what a captain needs to know: all that you need is a diligent study and the cost of a single volume.

My second text was found in the grave of an eleven-year-old Mashantucket Pequot girl, who was buried in the late seventeenth century [2]. Beside her, archaeologists found the remains of a medicine bundle, converted by happenstance to iron salts leached from a ladle in which the bundle had been placed. The bundle included a

M. Bernstein (✉)
Eastgate Systems, Inc., 134 Main Street, Watertown, MA 02472, USA
e-mail: bernstein@eastgate.com

bear's paw and a strip of finely-woven wool cloth which had been carefully inter-folded with a page torn from a printed book, on which a few letters could (with difficulty) be distinguished. These few letters were sufficient not only to identify the Biblical psalm from which they were taken, but even the specific edition, a single copy of which survives in the library of Penn State University. The girl (or her parents) likely obtained both the psalm and the fabric in which they wrapped it in an attack on a clerical residence during King Philip's War, 1675–1678. They could not read the verse, but they believed it had power.

Each of these texts is interactive by design. Each demands the reader's intention and reflection, and the merely passive reader is unlikely to realize the benefits each text offers. Both must be read and reread, and their components must be examined not just in isolation but also in many combinations. They are, in the jargon of interactive narrative, *ergodic* texts [1]. If your Captain were to ask you, "at this moment, how far are we from Brown University?", you would know that Bowditch lists the positions of such coastal landmarks as the dome of Brown's observatory, provided you had considered what the dreary tables of *Appendix IV: Maritime Positions* might allow. A strip of Psalm 98, torn from a clergyman's pocket Bible, could help protect a spirit on her long journey to Cautantowwit, ruler of the underworld, but only if that spirit was prepared for the arduous trek. These texts can do a lot, but they ask a lot, too.

2   Twice-Told Tales

We tell many stories. We always have: to say that "of making many books there is no end" (Ecclesiastes 12:12) was already proverbial in the Hellenistic era, and by 938 CE a Baghdad bookseller, Ibn al-Nad, had compiled a catalog of the Arabic works of more than 3500 authors [9]. We may revisit the same story many times, and we frequently find that we want to revisit topics addressed in tales we have enjoyed. This is not new: for example, Euripides wrote (at least) *The Trojan Women, Hecuba,* and *Andromache*—all stories of the aftermath of the Trojan war and its impact on the same surviving, defeated civilians.

We might classify stories in many ways: tales told in winter, fish stories, stories in which a dog appears, stories that conclude in weddings, and stories popular in 1862. We can readily imagine that some enthusiast might eagerly seek out and collect any of these. Yet these are not the taxonomic lines that direct the attention of the majority of avid readers. Nor are readers completely at the mercy of advertising and fashion [49].

Very often, readers choose to revisit narratives that address a core concern that interests them or that gives rise to anxieties they wish to quiet. Thus, a long chain of stories beginning (roughly speaking) with Jane Austen explores the tenuous economic status of women in the modern world. If you like *Pride and Prejudice,* you might well like *Mansfield Park, Tess of the d'Urbervilles,* and perhaps *The Hunger Games.* Readers are typically drawn to these stories not because they have crinolines and pinafores (though some people are interested in costumes), but because they explore the desire for, and dangers of, independence. It may sometimes be tempting to suppose that readers chiefly want period costumes, or dark and handsome suitors, but these are not really the point [22].

Two story frameworks clearly lend themselves to game-like interactive digital narratives because computer games literally enact them. First, we have Comedy, the story of a hero who, despite disadvantages and difficulties, prevails through skill and persistence. The second framework is the super-heroic melodrama, in which the reader-enactor faces innumerable opponents which, like the enemy soldiers in *Call Of Duty*, are no match for the hero's abilities. There may be setbacks and blunders as we master the mechanics, but we surely triumph in the end [39].

This chapter explores the relationship between interactive narrative and several other story frameworks of particular interest in contemporary publishing, among which we may number mystery, science fiction, horror, and fantasy. It is important to distinguish the framework and underlying concern of the narrative from its trappings: a superhero need not wear tights. A story may feature scientists and laboratories and yet not be science fiction [26], nor must a story with monsters be fantasy[1]. We can tell one story in many ways. Sometimes, we may tell a familiar story in a new mode or an unexpected setting, moving "Heart Of Darkness" to Vietnam, "The Hidden Fortress" to a galaxy far, far away, or "Little Red Riding Hood" to high society [5]. Though the setting changes, the underlying framework of the story remains.

Some frameworks pose notable difficulties for interactive narrative, while others appear to embrace interactivity naturally. This is only to be expected: all media embrace some things readily while other ambitions are more difficult. It's hard to sustain a narrative in music, and it's not easy to explore the third law of thermodynamics in painting. In passing, I will note story frameworks that seem notably receptive or resistant to interactivity.

3   Money and Media

Not everyone wants to command a ship, or has an immediate need to seek out a distant god. What else do we want from our interactive digital narratives? Robert Coover's essay on "The End Of The Golden Age" of literary hypertext envisions a coming, web-borne Silver Age, exulting in the imminent era of "this magical fusion of image, sound, and text, and perhaps of aroma and tactility as well." [16] The millennium clamored for sensually immersive media, for Hamlet on the Holodeck [43]. This

---

[1] Beowulf, for example, is not fantasy. Beowulf has a job to do, a place in the world. In the world of the Beowulf-poet, everyone does. Beowulf's job sometimes involves fearsome beasts, but this is no great surprise to Beowulf and his men. [47] Fantasy concerns our suspicion that the world we know is an illusion, a veil that conceals the world as it really is; elves and faeries are sometimes a convenient shorthand, but they are not the point. Just as it can be rewarding to stage a familiar story—*Hamlet*, say—in modern dress, writers may borrow the trappings associated with a popular framework without attempting to explore that framework's story.

posed aesthetic as well as engineering problems because sensorily-immersive narrative experiences require lots of information. If you're writing about postwar Paris, you need to know the places and the people, and you need the skill to sketch them. If you want to be immersive, you also need to know—and reproduce—how the Metro smelled and what the porters at Les Halles ate [12, 32]. A book requires a writer, but immersive media takes a team—and a lot of money.

There's nothing wrong with media that require capital. Drama needs a theater, and that's not cheap: at one point, Shakespeare and his company stole the timber from the theater they had been leasing to build a new one elsewhere [50]. Opera needs a theater (though a beer hall may serve in a pinch), a composer, a librettist, an orchestra, singers, dancers, concessionaires, and ushers. The bigger the investment, the greater the number of investors and managers who must be convinced that the production will be profitable, and the greater the temptation to endlessly tinker with the work in order to please the patron or the crowd [34].

At some moments (and for some art forms), the taste and interests of artists and financiers have coincided well enough. Fifth-Century Athens hosted dramatic competitions, and we generally think they awarded their prizes sensibly. Shakespeare's audience may sometimes have annoyed him by favoring the eyrie of children who were competing down the street, but on the whole, they seem to have liked what he liked [46, 50]. These were good times, fondly remembered; but our era is not such a time.

When the audience is not coherent—when some people want Braque and Brancusi and others prefer Norman Rockwell or Vargas girls—consensus breaks down [28]. This is precisely the situation in which digital stories now find themselves. Symbols that made sense to Tolkien and C. S. Lewis mean something else now [48]. One response to the failure of verities is to interrogate closely what everyone can in fact see: the immediately material properties of the work itself [23]. This is the definition of avant-garde, which digital narrative calls *ergodic* [1] and everyone else calls "difficult": the subject of the work becomes the medium itself [51]. Difficulty is neither arbitrary nor perverse: if Le Corbusier's church is arguing with van der Rohe's pavilion and both are in debate with Gropius's factory for learning, you need to know quite a lot before you can enjoy the discussion [41].

One alternative is *kitsch*: industrialized, mass-produced art designed to be apprehended by everyone, and to tell them precisely what they already know. Kitsch is art created by pollsters and focus groups. By design, kitsch says nothing beyond assuring its audience that the audience is wise and virtuous. Through kitsch, the audience elects itself superior to reason [28, 36].

Like all corporate art, AAA games incline toward kitsch: industrial products devised and approved by committees to please a mass audience. Often, a game measures what players do and changes itself to increase player engagement or to provoke player purchases. Game studios are drawn to popular but uncontroversial intellectual property, especially to characters that have been tested as kitsch through comic books and film, but studios also recycle characters and situations from previous incarnations of the game franchise or from conventionally sentimental situations [10]. Game studios go to great lengths to meet or anticipate player desires. For example, it is now common for role-playing games to offer the player-protagonist opportunities to choose skin color and appearance and to regard that choice as inconsequential to game mechanics [45], thus propounding a theory of race in which race simultaneously matters and does not matter [4].

In the book world, trade publishers can resist kitsch because each book represents a modest investment [27] and because there are lots of books [53]. In contrast, cinematic budgets of immersive digital experiences demand cinematic strategies and staffing. Because theatrically-released movies require movie theaters—dedicated facilities that occupy real-estate and must pay their mortgage—the number of theatrical releases that can appear at any one time is limited, and extra investment in production can return improved revenue from many places at once. Nonetheless, the cinema—while notoriously kitschy—has in some times and places managed to resist the allure of kitsch. Might digital narratives adopt those strategies to free itself from its endless repetition of imperial power fantasies?

The central fact that has (sometimes) facilitated film's escape from kitsch is that movies employ actors, and actors are ephemeral. In the end, the film records what some specific person said and did in front of a camera. What shows up in the film, and how audiences will understand it, is often hard to predict or to explain. Actors may have something to say—something that might not be entirely in accord with the production company's drive toward kitsch.

> An actor's scowl, a small subversive gesture, a dirty remark that someone tosses off with a mock-innocent face, and the world makes a little bit of sense. [30]

A director, a cinematographer, an editor: these too may sometimes find a way to make the world make sense. It's difficult to contradict the financiers and pollsters, but in the film, they're not always entirely in control.

Whatever the original intention of the writers and director, it is usually supplanted, as the production gets under way, by the intention to make money—and the industry will judge the film by how well it fulfills that intention [30]. Financiers are always in a hurry because interest is always accruing. Once actual production has begun, moreover, the film offers strong incentives to finish quickly. Sets deteriorate. Actors have contractual commitments, and actors age. They sometimes suffer injury or illness. Risks abound: the only scenes you know you've got are those you have already shot. Even if polls or focus groups indicate that shooting some scenes differently might yield additional sales, reshooting is difficult: the April sun that was streaming through the apartment window when you shot it the first time will be in a different place when you try to reshoot part of the scene in July.

In any case, film audiences, like book readers, are famously hard to predict. Frances Ford Coppola was sure that *Apocalypse Now!* was a lousy movie. Twentieth Century Fox had thought *Cleopatra* was terrific and that *Doctor Dolittle* was the answer to *Easy Rider, The Graduate, Bonnie and Clyde, In The Heat Of The Night, and Guess Who's Coming To Dinner* [31]. Financiers want reliable kitsch, but they want the production to wrap up. Sometimes, you tolerate flaws, and so, sometimes, you tolerate art.

The game industry, at least in our era, isn't like that. If a game is held back a month for an additional round of focus groups, the loss is simply the cost of deferring revenue. If focus groups indicate that people would like the game more if the bad guys were darker and more reptilian, or if they spoke with Chinese rather than Russian accents, game assets can be swapped. If a voice actor's work doesn't align with the corporate vision of a game, the corporation will find a different take or a different actor. If a programmer has an idea that turns a game franchise on its head, management isn't going to risk everything on her whim—not without a ton of testing and a slew of focus groups to ensure that the new idea is even kitschier than the original[2]. In book publishing, the stakes are small. In movies, the risks often outweigh the temptation to reshoot. Games are different: in the game industry, the simulated sun is forever in the same place and the Church clock always stands at ten to three.

4   Category Fiction

Category fiction—often called genre fiction[3]—is an important segment of publishing that has cast a long shadow over interactive digital narratives. Category fiction is often poorly understood, its popularity attributed to an immature or unserious audience. Many attempts in interactive narrative to enter category of fiction have been disappointing. I would suggest that the difficulty lies both in misunderstanding the utility of category fiction and the nature of the stories that each category tells.

4.1   Why Categories Are Useful

Retail bookstores may stock 40,000 different books, but most of them are of scant interest to any one customer. Prominent placement in windows or on tables may be accorded to a few titles of particular importance at the moment, but how may a bookseller increase the likelihood of a customer finding a book they wish to purchase? Even better, once the customer has located the book they want, can the seller increase the probability that a customer will purchase additional books?

One way to increase sales, of course, is simply to know your customers, to know one's stock, and to recommend books to people who are likely to enjoy them [21]. This sort of hand-selling is easiest to do for a clientele that has intense and specialized

---

[2] Kitsch can have its own pleasures, and is comparatively harmless when seen for what it is. Occasionally, even corporate investors may take modest risks, as when a troubled publisher tried to revive a moribund franchise with *Spec Ops: The Line*—a costly AAA war game that adopted a moderate anti-war stance. It remains a beloved IDN, though this 2012 title failed to save its publisher's balance sheet or its creative team.

[3] I use "category fiction" here in preference to "genre fiction", because "genre" has a different meaning in literary criticism.

interests. Paris bookseller Sylvia Beach built Shakespeare & Co. by catering to the Anglophone avant-garde of the Lost Generation [25]. Expatriate writers and their fans read a lot, they were eager to read more, and their tastes were distinctive and poorly-served by the general run of booksellers. After the War, Chicago bookseller Stuart Brent built a clientele of Chicago psychoanalysts eager to obtain the latest psychoanalytic treatises; not only was this specialized audience a reliable market, but they proved willing to refinance his store when banks would not [10].

Even if a bookseller has no great expertise in a specific domain, it makes good sense to shelve related titles together. A customer who buys one cookbook might be tempted to buy two. A customer looking for a history of ancient Greece might be persuaded to buy a book about Greek art, or a history of the Persian Empire. Organizing non-fiction titles by subject or field makes good business sense. How might a store apply similar principles to fiction?

Between the wars, a number of editors discovered (or created) magazine audiences that possessed an insatiable appetite for stories of a specific kind. Fifty-six stories and four novels about Sherlock Holmes led the way, and inspired waves of emulation and response [14, 20]. American magazine publishers discovered niche markets for science fiction [29], horror, tales of the American frontier, superhero comics, lurid descriptions of crime, and for stories of romance. Magazine distributors created a mechanism for selling paperback books in stores that sold magazines, and these mass-market paperbacks built an audience for the sort of story that the specialized magazines carried. Because these books were intended for the magazine distribution channel, readers were accustomed to find this sort of literature shelved together. As bookstores gradually embraced paperbacks, it made sense to retain the custom.

The audience for category fiction is attractive to publishers and booksellers alike. First, these readers are voracious; where many people read a handful of books a year, some fans of category fiction read several each week [52]. Second, category fiction, because it was long held in low esteem by journalists and critics, created an active amateur press to exchange reviews and news. In the late twentieth century, as book titles multiplied while the number of published reviews plummeted, these amateur magazines became a powerful engine for spreading the word about new titles and new movements. At the same time, rapid publication and intense community discussion gave rise to the expectation that books in a category existed in discourse with other books, giving rise to a virtuous circle of literary consumption.

4.2   What Categories Are About

Digital narrative has frequently adopted the trapping of a category, hoping to exploit the popularity of a category by borrowing its trappings or licensing characters. For example, we periodically see "mystery games" in which the reader is meant to puzzle out who committed a crime, much as Sherlock Holmes was wont to do. Any number of digital narratives feature zombies, ravening monsters, or Nazi soldiers who must be fought (and whom can be vanquished without moral hazard). Having monsters, these digital narratives seem to be horror. Others feature elves, princesses, and magic spells; these seem to be fantasy.

However, these surface attributes are not the central concern of their categories.

Consider mystery, the most popular book category. Mystery is not, in fact, particularly concerned with deduction. Rather, the mystery story recounts the repair of a damaged world: something has gone wrong, and the protagonist's task is to learn what is wrong and to restore the world to the extent that restoration is possible.

> But down these mean streets, a man must go who is not himself mean, who is neither tarnished nor afraid. The detective in this kind of story must be such a man. He is the hero, he is everything. He must be a complete man and a common man and yet an unusual man. He must be, to use a rather weathered phrase, a man of honor, by instinct, by inevitability, without thought of it, and certainly without saying it. He must be the best man in his world and a good enough man for any world…. He will take no man's money dishonestly and no man's insolence without due and dispassionate revenge. He is a lonely man and his pride is that you will treat him as a proud man or be very sorry you ever saw him. He talks as the man of his age talks, that is, with rude wit, a lively sense of the grotesque, a disgust for sham, and a contempt for pettiness. The story is his adventure in search of a hidden truth [13].

Since the late 20th Century, the mystery has focused on telling this story of the world's cure at the hands of physicians of dazzling variety: priests, rabbis, women, gay people, bipolar people, enslaved people, and supernatural people. The internal grammar of the mystery has proven a potent engine for exploring character, while its narrative framework has closely examined how a damaged world might be cured.

Attempts to create interactive investigations have seldom been interpretable as mysteries. The mystery is, in fact, resistant to first-person interactivity because its very premise alienates us. The fictive world is damaged and requires repair, but we ourselves inhabit another world, and we are at best pretending to cure an imagined world. The most successful interactive mysteries have neither criminals nor investigators nor even explicit narratives: they are the complex skill trees of complex open-world adventure games. The player begins by learning a few simple skills and gradually learns how different actions support later actions, and how buffs and debuffs interact in different circumstances and environments. With time and experience, the player learns to understand the system, which is to say, to comprehend the logic of the world.

Fantasy. Fantastic trappings pervade videogames: elves, orcs, and princesses seem to be everywhere. Once more, though, our interactive artifacts seldom address fantasy itself [15]. Fantasy argues that the world we experience is wrong, and that we have been charmed or deluded into accepting it. We live peacefully in our little Shire, oblivious to the storms that beset the world beyond. In the fantasy story, the mundane world dims and we come to see the real world as it is, and so become our true selves [42]. Having remade ourselves, we can return home once more, no longer the thrall of illusion. Fantasy needs neither unicorns nor antique weapons [11, 18]. Fantasy's central premise, the falsity of the world, was underlined by the horror of the First World War and all that followed. The Somme and Auschwitz are always what lies beyond the fields we know.

One difficulty that fantasy poses for interactive narrative is our tendency to identify the protagonist with the interactor. The core of fantasy is the thinning of the illusory world. Whose illusion is this? It is the protagonist that is deceived—the protagonist, but not the reader. Frodo believes that the Shire is real and that its pastoral life will unfold forever. Pullman's Lyra believes that hiding in wardrobes is good fun and that the worst outcome is that she will be scolded by one of the schoolmasters [48]. The reader knows better. But, if we are asked to make diegetic choices on behalf of the protagonist, our knowledge gets mixed up with the protagonist's . This difficulty is not intractable, but it is ever-present in interactive fantasy.

Science Fiction. If a best-selling videogame has no elves or wizards, it very likely features spaceships. Yet again, digital narratives sometimes borrow the decor of a genre without adopting the corresponding story. Science fiction, like fantasy and mystery, posits that there is something wrong with the world, and it describes the development of a solution. For example, civilization itself is threatened with collapse: can it be saved? [3, 17, 33] Indeed, the protagonist in science fiction is often the world, a world that struggles to make itself known—a *horta* striving to get Captain Kirk's attention, a lovable *eloi* girl who explains to a time traveller the ills that ensue from late capitalism. Science fiction dates from the late eighteenth century and Kipling wrote SF, but it became popular in the U.S. between the wars as an assertion that the world might be fixed, and that skill, knowledge, and a can-do attitude would carry the day [15].

Science fiction imagines a cure for the World Storm, an antidote discovered by people who live (as they must) beneath an empty sky. If an interactive fiction reduces the cure to a puzzle—a singular solution the protagonist must unpuzzle—this tells a different story entirely. We no longer have science fiction: we have the cult myth of a new Eleusis in which the initiate learns the correct gestures and appropriate ritual words to propitiate the deity.

Horror. Just as Fantasy need not concern elves, horror need not concern gore. Horror is Fantasy's weird twin, and like Fantasy it begins with a realization that the world is wrong. Where Fantasy reveals the world as it truly is and makes us whole again, horror instead shows the world as the face of God which blinds us [16]. The world thickens and impedes us as we approach its true nature, and eventually, we see the awful truth, after which we must find a way to live in the world we now understand. The denouement may be bloody, but need not be. *Heart Of Darkness* is horror, as is "It's A Wonderful Life". The internal logic of the horror story may be, in fact, uniquely suited to interactive fiction [8]; if we move through the fiction with halting steps and slow, and if the story sometimes resists and sometimes traps us, the faults of interaction coincide with horror.

Romance. The term "romance" means different things in literary criticism and in the category of fiction. The romance *genre* pertains to a story framework in which the protagonist wins through (in some sense) because of who they are—because of their intrinsic excellence. This stands in contrast to "comedy," in which the protagonist succeeds (in some sense) through hard work. The romance *category* describes stories about the course of love, typically complicated by obstacles and misunderstandings. That is what we consider here.

Two problems of craft confront authors of interactive romance fiction. The first problem is the description and delineation of the beloved. In prose, we can establish the beloved by making the inner life of the object of our affection opaque, and describing only their effect on the protagonist. This trick is difficult to apply if the reader makes choices for the protagonist. We know what we are thinking. Lots of description of ourselves is a distraction, and the more we identify with the protagonist, the more intrusive such description becomes.

The second craft problem is that I know of no interactive sex scene that is entirely convincing. At Readercon 2017, Naomi Novik remarked that, after having been employed to write vivid pornography, describing dragons in aerial combat was easy. In both cases, the writer needs to communicate lots of geometry without actually focusing on that geometry. If the reader is to have agency, they will make choices to which the system must be prepared to respond [37]. Moreover, while manipulating a fictive construct through diegetical choice may generally be a game, we might question whether seducing a fictive construct is entirely right: if Ophelia is on the Holodeck, could she possibly consent to Hamlet's proposal of marriage? [7]

These problems can likely be overcome, but each poses real difficulties that demand careful attention.

Western. Although it is at present a category in decline, the Western story lends itself particularly well to interactive narrative. The surface trappings of the Western—Stetson hats and palomino ponies, cowboys and deserts—are incidental. The framework beneath the Western story is the tension between the hero's duty to what is right, to family, to the town, and to the world. It is not a coincidence that a core audience for the Western story has long been German. Like horror, the Western seems to incline toward interactivity; the Western is a story about responsibility, a question that interaction always raises.

5 Limits of Interactivity

Janet Murray [43] anticipated that interactive stories would have four distinctive characteristics: that they would be procedural, participatory, encyclopedic, and spatial. This prediction provided a useful analytical frame, though many interactive stories in the succeeding decades have lacked some or all of these properties. The inclination toward encyclopedism in interactive stories was likely influenced by "The Database As Symbolic Form", Lev Manovich's contemporary essay, which posited a vision of computation, specifically the separation of data from procedure, that computer science was already putting behind it [4]. Artifactual stories like *Uncle Buddy's Phantom Funhouse* and *Gone Home* have been successful, but remain exceptional in current practice. MMORPGs do tend to tell stories across space, but Em Short's *Galatea, Prom Night*, and a considerable body of Twine fiction are not notably spatial.

What has become clear over the years is that some kinds of stories are more difficult to tell in a medium in which the reader is able to assert agency and expects the story to respond [37]. Consider, for example, the "Southern Story", a narrative built around the storyable premise that "there is a terrible secret." Our characters know the secret, but do not speak of it. They never think about it, but nevertheless, it warps everything they do. The drama erodes the fog that surrounds that secret, and ultimately we glimpse the suppressed violence, racial hatred, miscegenation, or female sexuality that underpins the secret. Examples are plentiful: *The Glass Menagerie, To Kill A Mockingbird, The Light In The Piazza,* and much else. The secret is the spring that turns the story, and we must not know it. Indeed, Southern stories interrogate the limits of agency: the situation is only storyable because an exceptional situation has occurred. If Scout Finch was not precisely who she is, and were her father not precisely who he is, there would be no story—just a report of another sad injustice in another sad Southern town. The difference between witness and interrogator is the difference between *Who's Afraid Of Virginia Woolf* and its interactive adaptation, *Façade* [38].

Other common story frameworks are also hostile to interactive agency. Farce, for example, is precipitated by a character who makes an impulsive but bad decision. Instead of making the miscreant suffer the consequences, however, others proceed to make bad decisions as well. Soon, everything is topsy-turvy. This is often hilarious— *The Menaechmi, Duck Soup, Fargo*—but is not always funny. If you let a sensible person into the world of *Romeo and Juliet*, nothing happens: the story occurs because everybody makes bad choices that reinforce each other while also postponing the inevitable return to normalcy. Some stories, like Job, are better to witness than to experience.

This is not to argue that interactive digital narrative is impossible or inferior, but rather that we should recognize its distinctive challenges and address them.

6 Discontent

The field has thus far been unwilling to think clearly about immersivity, sexuality, and art. Here, the forces of kitsch and the avant-garde [28] have worked at cross purposes, as have the proponents of the ergodic [1] and the seamlessly immersive [44].

One remedy to these problems is confidence, the conviction that the work you have done was the right work to do [24]. This may not be the sole answer, but it seems a necessary precondition: an audience is seldom persuaded by lukewarm enthusiasm. Disciplinary fragmentation has frequently led new media enthusiasts to contrast their group's excellence to the risible failures of some adjacent practice; typically, this teaches the audience to ignore the entire business until the dust has settled. Fragmentation has also led to a literary world in which too few writers read outside their narrow circle, and fewer new media critics read widely. The result is often incomprehension and write-only research literature.

Bowditch's ambition was not merely to write a book so successful that it would be sold by every bookseller and ship-chandler. By insisting that any sailor—through diligence and a single volume—could learn to command a ship, Bowditch argued for and demonstrated a new idea of society. Instructional interactive narratives are not unknown, but their ambitions have been slight. They let you practice a skill; they seldom offer to teach you a profession [31].

That eleven-year-old Mashantucket Pequot girl of whom we were speaking at the start of this chapter was buried with a powerful text in the confident belief that it, like the bear paw, would help her spirit reach Cautantowwit. No interactive digital narrative to date is in a position to make such a promise. "The cake is a lie," is widely remembered, but it is not "O sing unto the Lord a new song, for he hath done marvelous things." It is not even "yes I said yes I will Yes," nor yet "Arise, ye prisoners of starvation!".

Acknowledgements I am grateful for advice from numerous colleagues, of whom I would particularly like to thank John Clute, Kathryn Cramer, Andy van Dam, Sarah Smith, Sally Starrels, and Adam Zehner for their patient assistance.

References

1. Aarseth EJ (1997) Cybertext: perspectives on ergodic literature. Johns Hopkins University Press, Baltimore
2. Amory H (1986) The trout and the milk: an ethno-bibliographical talk. Harv Libr Bull 7:50–65
3. Asimov I (1953) Second foundation. Gnome Press, New York
4. Bernstein M (2020) In spite of ourselves: our duty to our slaves of steel. In: Proceedings of the 3rd international conference on web studies, pp 4–8
5. Bernstein M (2009) On hypertext narrative. In: ACM Hypertext 2009
6. Bernstein M (2019) Ophelia in my pocket. In: Intertwingled. Eastgate Systems, Watertown MA
7. Bernstein M, McMorris S (2022) Links of darkness: hypertext and horror. In: Hypertext '22
8. Blair A (2010) Too much to know: managing scholarly information before the modern age. Yale University Press, New Haven
9. Bogost I (2009) Persuasive games: video game kitsch. Gamasutra
10. Brent S (1962) The seven stairs. Houghton, Mifflin, Boston
11. Buchan J (1916) Greenmantle. Hodder and Stoughton. London, New York [etc.]
12. Bywater M (2006) Big babies: or: why can't we just grow up. Granta, London
13. Chandler R (1950) The simple art of murder. Houghton, Boston
14. Clute J (2011) Pardon this intrusion: Fantastika in the world storm. Beccon Publications, Essex
15. Clute J (2014) Stay. Beccon Publications, Essex
16. Coover R (2000) Literary hypertext: passing of the golden age. Feed Mag
17. De Camp LS (1941) Lest darkness fall, with decorations. H. Holt and company, New York
18. Dean P (1991) Tam Lin. Tom Doherty Associates, New York
19. Dirda M (2012) On Conan Doyle, or, the whole art of storytelling. Princeton University Press, Princeton, N.J.
20. Dunne JG (1969) The studio. Farrar, Straus & Giroux, New York
21. Fitzgerald P (1997) The bookshop. Houghton Mifflin, Boston
22. Fowler KJ (2004) The Jane Austen book club. Putnam, New York
23. Gaggi S (1997) From text to hypertext: decentering the subject in fiction, film, the visual arts. The University of Pennsylvania Press, Philadelphia and Electronic Media
24. Ginna P (2017) What editors do: the art, craft. The University of Chicago Press, Chicago and Business of Book Editing

25. Glass C (2009) Americans in Paris: life and death under Nazi occupation, 1940–1944. Harper Press, London
26. Goodman A (2006) Intuition: a novel. Dial Press, New York
27. Gottlieb R (2016) Avid reader: a life. Farrar, Straus and Giroux, New York
28. Greenberg C (1939) Avant-garde and kitsch. Partis Rev 34–49
29. Hartwell DG (1996) Age of wonders: exploring the world of science fiction. Tor, New York
30. Kael P (1969) Trash, art, and the movies. Harpers
31. Knutov E, De Bra P, Pechenizkiy M (2009) AH 12 years later: a comprehensive survey of adaptive hypermedia methods and techniques. New Rev Hypermed Multimed 15:5–38
32. Laurain A (2018) Millésime 54: Roman. Flammarion [Paris]
33. Le Guin U (1973) The ones who walk away from Omelas. New Dimensions 3
34. Mamet D (2007) Bambi vs. Godzilla: on the nature, purpose, and practice of the movie business. Pantheon Books, New York
35. Mamet D (1998) Three uses of the knife: on the nature and purpose of drama. Columbia University Press, New York
36. Manovich L (2001) The language of new media. MIT Press, Cambridge, Mass
37. Mason S (2021) Responsiveness in narrative systems
38. Mateas M, Stern A (2001) Towards building a fully-realized interactive drama. Digit Arts Cult
39. Mccloud S (2000) Reinventing comics. Paradox Press, New York, N.Y.
40. Mcphee J (1990) Looking for a ship. Farrar Straus Giroux, New York
41. Menand L (2021) The free world: art and thought in the cold war. Farrar, Straus and Giroux, New York
42. Miéville C (2009) The city & the city. Del Rey Ballantine Books, New York
43. Murray J (1997) Hamlet on the holodeck: the future of narrative in cyberspace. The Free Press, New York
44. Murray JH (2012) Inventing the medium: principles of interaction design as a cultural practice. MIT Press, Cambridge, Mass
45. Nakamura L (2008) Digitizing race: visual cultures of the internet. University of Minnesota Press, Minneapolis
46. Nicholl C (2008) The lodger shakespeare: his life on silver street. Viking, New York
47. Price N (2019) The Viking way: magic and mind in late iron age Scandinavia. Oxbow, Philadelphia, PA
48. Pullman P (2011) His dark materials: the golden compass, the subtle knife, the amber spyglass. Everymans Library, New York
49. Rose J (2001) The intellectual life of the British working classes. Yale University Press, New Haven [Conn.]
50. Shapiro J (2005) A year in the life of William Shakespeare, 1599. HarperCollins Publishers, New York
51. Sontag S (1964) Against interpretation. Evergreen Rev 34
52. Walton J (2011) Among others. Tor, New York
53. Zaid G (2003) So many books: reading and publishing in an age of abundance. Paul Dry Books, Philadelphia

Form

Authoring for Story Sifters

Max Kreminski, Noah Wardrip-Fruin, and Michael Mateas

Abstract We discuss the issues of authoring for *story sifters*: systems that search for compelling emergent narrative content within the vast chronicles of events generated by interactive emergent narrative simulations. We describe several different approaches to the authoring of *sifting patterns* that specify how to locate particular kinds of narratively potent situations; address the relationship between sifters and the simulations they operate over from an authoring perspective; and sketch several possible approaches to the authoring of *sifting heuristics*, or high-level encodings of what makes for a compelling story that could be used to guide a sifter's behavior.

1 Introduction

Interactive emergent narrative (IEN) [15, 21, 31, 38] is an approach to interactive narrative design in which narrative is allowed to emerge organically from open-ended interactions between autonomous simulated characters, as well as the actions of the human player. Like many other approaches to interactive narrative design, IEN attempts to solve the *narrative paradox* of reconciling open-ended interactivity with the communication of a coherent story [19].

Most existing approaches to interactive narrative design take a *top-down* approach to the narrative paradox: they attempt to ensure narrative quality by allowing only events that follow a preordained high-level plot structure to occur. For example, in linear interactive storytelling (often employed in many commercial story games), the player is able to interact within and between story scenes (plot points) but with no influence on their linear order. In branching interactive storytelling, the space

M. Kreminski (✉) · N. Wardrip-Fruin · M. Mateas
University of California, Santa Cruz, 1156 High St, Santa Cruz, CA, USA
e-mail: mkremins@ucsc.edu

N. Wardrip-Fruin
e-mail: nwardrip@ucsc.edu

M. Mateas
e-mail: mmateas@ucsc.edu

C. Hargood et al. (eds.), *The Authoring Problem*, Human–Computer Interaction Series,
https://doi.org/10.1007/978-3-031-05214-9_13

of all possible story traces is pre-authored as a graph structure, often with choice points explicitly presented to the player. And in *strong story* generative narrative approaches [22, 27] such as story planning [26, 39], the system reasons about story structure to generate linear or branching stories with a focus on story-centric characteristics such as causality.

IEN, in contrast, takes a *bottom-up* approach to the resolution of the narrative paradox, sacrificing fine-grained authorial control over plot structure in exchange for a greater degree of novelty and responsiveness to player action. In IEN, because the player and the simulated characters are free to take actions that don't line up with a preordained plot structure, the actions they take can vary significantly from one playthrough to the next, and the player-perceived narrative outcomes of this open-ended interaction can often surprise even the people who created the simulation.

Canonical works of IEN (such as *Dwarf Fortress* [1], *The Sims* [2, 6, 24], and *Stellaris* [17]) are known not only for their propensity to generate compelling and unexpected stories but also for their tendency to overwhelm players with the sheer volume of narrative content that they produce. Many of these works present players with complicated user interfaces that allow them to access a great deal of detailed information about the simulated storyworld, but at the cost of requiring users to spend a great deal of time learning to use this interface before they can reliably get compelling stories to emerge [16]. From a narrative design perspective, the central problem with IEN is one of unpredictability: because there is no central plot thread in relation to which the importance of individual events can be gauged, the system has no way to reliably determine which of the many events that take place within the storyworld are likely to hold particular narrative significance for the player. As a result, the most common failure condition for IEN play experiences involves the dissolution of the player-perceived story into a structureless mess, breaking the perception of narrativity [32] and causing players to understand the events of play not as a story but as "just one damn thing after another" [29, p. 4].

Story sifting [29, 31] attempts to address the problems of overwhelm and structurelessness in works of IEN by augmenting the underlying simulation (which is responsible for generating narrative events) with an additional technical system: the *story sifter*, which aims to detect narrative events or event sequences that make for compelling *narrative material*. Sifting thus allows the adoption of an 'overgenerate and test' approach to storyworld simulation, in which simulations are allowed to generate a wide variety of surprising juxtapositions; sifters are tuned to detect and surface the most interesting narrative situations that emerge from the simulation; and the overwhelmingly vast amounts of uninteresting or nonsensical material *also* generated by the simulation along the way can be downplayed or dismissed, allowing for a coherent story to solidify. James Ryan (who introduced the term 'story sifting') refers to this IEN design strategy as the *curationist* approach [29, p. 6].

However, beyond the known issues of authoring for IEN [20], story sifting introduces new authoring challenges of its own. In particular, current approaches to story sifting are heavily reliant on human-authored *story sifting patterns*: short blocks of code that a sifter can execute to detect instances of a particular type of narratively potent situation that have emerged within the storyworld. Additionally, sifting also has implications for simulation authoring, particularly around the need to keep track of causality relationships between events at the simulation level and the possibility of integrating sifting into simulation design. And finally, although there has been little concrete research in this direction to date, sifting could also be augmented by *sifting heuristics*. These are higher level, more generic descriptions of what makes emergent narrative content potentially compelling. Such heuristics could be used to prioritize some sifting pattern matches over others when deciding what narrative material to highlight, though identifying these heuristics is still an open research problem.

In this chapter, we discuss these three key authoring issues. First, we discuss the challenge of sifting pattern authoring and present a brief history of attempts to improve the ergonomics of writing sifting patterns. Second, we consider the issues of simulation design for curationist IEN experiences and the need to construct simulations in sifting-compatible ways. And third, we briefly discuss the possibility of developing higher level sifting heuristics that could further improve the authorial leverage [5] of story sifting as an approach.

2 Authoring Sifting Patterns

Modern story sifters make extensive use of *story sifting patterns* to detect emergent narrative content that might be worth incorporating into a story. A sifting pattern is a block of code that specifies how to find instances of a particular kind of narratively potent situation that might emerge within a storyworld, for instance, an escalating cycle of revenge between two characters; a character who is consistently unable to hold down a job; or a sequence of events in which a social contract (such as the expectation that hosts do not harm their guests) is betrayed. These 'nuggets' of potentially interesting narrative content can then be woven—either by a human interactor, a computational system, or both working together—into a coherent story.

The more sifting patterns a sifter has at its disposal, the wider the range of emergent microstories that it can detect and reason about, and the better its ability to respond to the unexpected consequences of player interaction. Consequently, a number of efforts have recently been made to improve the efficiency of sifting pattern authoring. In this section, we briefly recount the history of these efforts.

2.1 Procedural Sifting Patterns

The term 'story sifting' was first employed to describe the role of the *wizard* (performed by a member of the design team) in the simulation-driven interactive theater experience *Bad News* [33]. The wizard is responsible for manually searching for interesting narrative material in a Talk of the Town [30] simulation. To perform this search, they make use of the *wizard console*, a Python REPL equipped with a number of predefined functions for conveniently executing specific types of queries against the full simulation state. Attempts to automate *Bad News*'s wizard role resulted in the Sheldon sifter [29, p. 657], which executes sifting patterns specified as chunks of procedural Python code against a Talk of the Town-like simulation state to identify sets of interrelated storyworld entities (such as events and characters) that meet certain criteria. Below is an example of a Sheldon sifting pattern, which is executed against many possible candidate events to find those representing the enactment of an *arson revenge scheme* (in which a character who has been harmed by another character burns down a building belonging to that character as a means of getting revenge) and bundle them with some relevant context for narration:

```
self.match = (
  candidate.name == "set-fire" and candidate.find_ancestor(
    name="hatch-revenge-scheme",
    initiator=candidate.initiator
  )
)
if self.match:
  self.set_fire = candidate
  self.hatch_scheme = (
    candidate.find_ancestor(
      name="hatch-revenge-scheme",
      initiator=self.set_fire.initiator
    )
  )
  self.arsonist = self.hatch_scheme.binding("arsonist")
  self.target = self.hatch_scheme.binding("target")
```

Though this example is relatively readable for an experienced programmer, it also highlights some of the weaknesses of the procedural (as opposed to declarative) approach to specifying sifting patterns. In particular, it makes heavy use of chained object graph traversal to access event sequences and properties of matched events, limiting the ability of sifting patterns to flexibly traverse the graph 'in reverse'. The find_ancestor method on event data structures represents a particularly thorny part of the Sheldon API, since it forces all event sequence access to begin at the last event in sequence unless the simulation authors also define a mirrored find_descendant function (thereby increasing the authoring burden on the simulation side). In general, this example illustrates how the procedural (non-declarative) approach to writing sifting patterns ties the pattern strongly to the implementation details of the simulation. Ideally, we would like to be able to specify sifting patterns independently of these implementation details. Additionally, because Sheldon patterns are expressed in plain Python code, potential authors of Sheldon patterns must learn the syntax and semantics of general-purpose Python language constructs (such as method calls, boolean operators, and if statements) before they can write patterns effectively. This reduces the approachability of pattern authoring to those with limited programming experience.

2.2 Declarative Sifting Patterns

Felt [14] attempts to alleviate the difficulty of writing procedural sifting patterns by instead applying a *declarative* approach to sifting pattern specification. Felt patterns specify what to find instead of how to find it, and are expressed in a small domain-specific query language that compiles down to a subset of Datalog instead of a Turing-complete programming language. Consequently, they are often more concise than equivalent Sheldon sifting patterns; can perform bidirectional traversal of the entity graph without any extra authoring effort on the simulation side; and can be authored by people with less programming experience, since the surface area of Felt as a language is much smaller than that of Python or a similar scripting language.

Felt sifting patterns look like the following:

```
(eventSequence ?e1 ?e2)
[?e1 eventType hatchRevengeScheme] [?e2 eventType setFire]
(contributingCause ?e1 ?e2)
[?e1 actor ?arsonist] [?e2 actor ?arsonist] [?e2 target ?target]
```

Like the example Sheldon sifting pattern listed above, this pattern locates instances of an arson revenge event sequence in which an ?arsonist character burns down a building belonging to another character as part of a revenge scheme against them. Identifiers preceded by a ? character represent *logic variables*, which are bound to concrete values when an instance of the pattern is successfully found. Square-bracketed clauses (such as [?e1 actor ?arsonist]) represent assertions that the entity on the left-hand side (here, ?e1, or the first event in the matched sequence) has an attribute with the name in the middle (actor) whose value is the entity or constant on the right (?arsonist, or the character responsible for the arson scheme). Equality checks are often handled by *unification*: here, we specify that the actor for the first and second events in the sequence must be the same character by assigning both of them to the same logic variable, ?arsonist, so that only matches in which both events have the same actor will succeed. Meanwhile, clauses surrounded by parentheses (such as (contributingCause ?e1 ?e2)) invoke simulation-specific inference rules that can be used to make judgments about the relationships between entities—here, to judge whether the first event in sequence (?e1) is causally related to the second (?e2).

A small authoring study of Felt [14] found that relatively programming-inexperienced users (four high school-aged research interns) were successfully able to use Felt to write working sifting patterns after one day of training. However, they used only a minimal subset of the Felt language constructs available to them and did not make full use of the available simulation domain constructs, suggesting that further guidance in exploring the space of possible sifting patterns would be necessary to assist novice programmers in making full use of story sifting affordances.

In addition to the approach taken by Felt, inspiration for future declarative approaches to story sifting may be found in the approaches taken by Playspecs [25], which apply regular expressions to the recognition of patterns (sometimes narrative) in gameplay traces but are limited in expressiveness by their inability to capture variable bindings; by prior work on plan recognition in narrative domains [3], some approaches to which closely resemble story sifting from a technical perspective; and by the use of story intention graphs for analogy search between plot structures [7], which could be leveraged for sifting via the analogical comparison of simulation outputs against structural patterns extracted from known-good stories.

2.3   Sifting Pattern Authoring Tools

A small ecosystem of authoring tools and higher level domain-specific languages based on Felt have emerged, with each presenting a slightly different form of assistance to users in the definition of Felt sifting patterns.

Synthesifter [18] (Fig. 1) aims to support the authoring of Felt sifting patterns by presenting users with an example-based interface for pattern specification. Once users provide a small number of concrete example event sequences matching their intended sifting pattern, Synthesifter uses inductive logic programming [23] to automatically synthesize a sifting pattern capable of matching these sequences, and presents the user with further possible matches of this pattern against a corpus of test events. Users can then refine the synthesized sifting pattern by marking these additional matches as positive or negative examples, or modify the synthesized pattern directly to get live feedback on which event sequences are matched by their modified pattern. By obviating the initial need to create new sifting patterns by writing code from scratch and using program synthesis to introduce new syntactic and semantic concepts in the sifting pattern language to the user, Synthesifter provides the user with well-formed concrete examples of how to use potentially unfamiliar parts of the Felt language and/or simulation domain, and thereby aims to mitigate the tendency of novice Felt users to use only a limited subset of the available constructs.

Centrifuge [9] (Fig. 2) is a visual editor for Felt sifting patterns that uses a node-graph model to make the Felt syntax more approachable. Elements of the Felt syntax and the simulation domain are represented as nodes, and connections between these nodes indicate the relationships between pattern-relevant simulation domain entities. This approach helps users avoid low-level syntax errors and view the pattern as a whole graphically, with the goal of making the connections between entities clearer—especially in complex patterns containing many interrelated entities. It also provides a palette of constructs that can be added to a pattern, allowing users to more readily explore the space of possible patterns.

And finally, **Winnow** [11] is a higher level domain-specific query language for story sifting that aims to save authoring effort by asking users to write a smaller number of explicitly staged sifting patterns, which can be executed *incrementally* to identify partial instances of desired microstories (e.g. the first few events of an arson revenge event sequence) before the sequence has run to completion and without

6	rejectSuperiority	Emin	Sarah
7	askOut_accepted	Zach	Vincent
8	begForFavor	Emin	Mira
9	getCoffeeWith	Sarah	Mira
10	collab:goAboveAndBeyond	Zach	Sarah
11	getCoffeeWith	Vincent	Mira
12	askOut_rejected	Emin	Sarah
13	propose_rejected	Mira	Emin
14	askOut_rejected	Mira	Zach
15	flirtWith_accepted	Emin	Vincent
16	apologizeTo	Emin	Sarah
17	apologizeTo	Mira	Vincent
18	askForHelp	Vincent	Mira
19	disparagePublicly	Zach	Emin
20	deliberatelySabotage	Emin	Vincent
21	apologizeTo	Zach	Emin
22	collab:phoneItIn	Emin	Sarah
23	flirtWith_accepted	Mira	Zach
24	apologizeTo	Sarah	Mira
25	disparagePublicly	Emin	Vincent
26	buyLunchFor	Sarah	Vincent
27	propose_rejected	Emin	Mira
28	physicallyAttack	Mira	Sarah
29	callInFavor	Sarah	Mira
30	extortFavor	Emin	Zach
31	physicallyAttack	Sarah	Mira
32	collab:goAboveAndBeyond	Sarah	Mira
33	inviteIntoGroup	Vincent	Mira
34	deferToExpertise	Mira	Sarah
35	callInExtortionateFavor	Mira	Vincent
36	getCoffeeWith	Emin	Vincent
37	collab:goAboveAndBeyond	Emin	Vincent

Sifting Pattern

```
(eventSequence ?e1 ?e2 ?e3)
[?e1 actor ?elactor]
[?e2 actor ?e2actor]
[?e3 actor ?e3actor]
[?e1 tag negative] [?e1 tag romantic]
[?e2 tag negative] [?e2 tag romantic]
[?e3 tag positive] [?e3 tag romantic]
[(= ?elactor ?e2actor ?e3actor)]
```

Positive Examples (add current)

78	flirtWith_rejected	Sarah Mira
85	askOut_rejected	Sarah Mira
103	askOut_accepted	Sarah Emin

Remove

105	askOut_rejected	Zach Emin
107	rekindle_rejected	Zach Sarah
141	flirtWith_accepted	Zach Mira

Remove

Negative Examples (add current)

...

Possible Matches

67	flirtWith_rejected	Emin Vincent
81	flirtWith_rejected	Emin Sarah
103	flirtWith_accepted	Emin Mira

Add Positive | Add Negative

13	propose_rejected	Mira Emin
14	askOut_rejected	Mira Zach
23	flirtWith_accepted	Mira Zach

Add Positive | Add Negative

Fig. 1 Screenshot of the Synthesifter user interface (taken from [18]). On the left sits a scrolling, filterable log of all events that have occurred in the storyworld so far, allowing the user to select event sequences to use as examples. On the right sits an editable view of the current synthesized sifting pattern; the sets of positive and negative examples the user has provided; and the set of additional matches for the current candidate sifting pattern, which the user can add as positive or negative examples

any extra authoring effort. Consider the following Winnow translation of a slightly expanded `arsonRevenge` sifting pattern:

```
(pattern arsonRevenge
  (event ?harm where
    tag: harm, actor: ?victim, target: ?arsonist)
  (event ?scheme where
    eventType: hatch-revenge-scheme,
    actor: ?arsonist, target: ?victim,
    (ancestor ?harm ?scheme)),
  (event ?arson where
    eventType: set-fire, actor: ?arsonist, target: ?victim,
    (ancestor ?scheme ?arson)))
```

By explicitly incorporating the initial `?harm` event that leads to the revenge scheme into the sifting pattern and dividing the pattern into three explicit stages (one per matched event), we enable Winnow to automatically detect instances in which

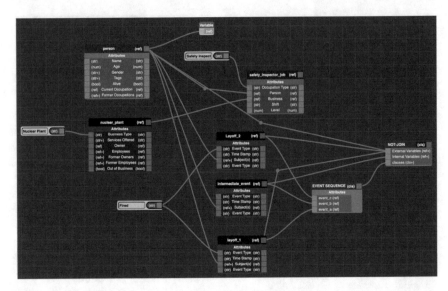

Fig. 2 Partial screenshot of the Centrifuge user interface, showing the graphical specification of a moderately complex sifting pattern. The depicted pattern is used to find instances of a nuclear plant safety inspector who has been fired twice in a short time period, without any other interceding life events

the first two events of the sequence (or any other prefix) have taken place, but the remaining events have not yet transpired. This allows for the procedural generation of foreshadowing for later events in the sequence; the suggestion or promotion of simulation actions that would advance this partially-formed microstory; and the capacity for avoidance of actions that would cut this microstory off before it has the chance to run to completion. To perform similar partial matching with Felt patterns alone would require pattern authors to maintain several partial variants of each pattern in parallel with the complete version; this increases the likelihood that errors will be introduced in the copying process, as well as the burden of synchronizing changes between the full pattern and its variants.

Though the tools and languages discussed in this section have introduced substantial subjective improvements to sifting pattern authoring processes from the authors' perspective, little evaluation of pattern authoring tools has been done, and none of these tools have been put through a formal user study at the time of this writing. Consequently, one potentially beneficial direction for future work in this area would be to perform a more thorough evaluation of the strengths and weaknesses of these authoring tools, particularly for less programming-experienced users.

3   Authoring Siftable Simulations

Beyond the authorship effort that is put into the construction of story sifting patterns appropriate for a particular emergent narrative domain, creators of IEN systems also have the option of crafting simulations with sifting in mind. This entails additional authoring effort at the simulation level, but can make it substantially easier to write sifting patterns that match relevant narrative situations. In this section, we describe three major levels of engagement with sifting at the level of simulation authoring.

3.1   Authoring Sifters for Existing Simulations

One advantage of story sifting as an approach is that it can be applied to the output of a simulation that was created without story sifting in mind. However, this often requires the construction of an adaptation layer that transforms the output of the simulation engine into a form that is more amenable to sifting—typically including what Ryan calls a *chronicler*, or a system that extracts a list (i.e. a 'chronicle') of all the potentially narratively significant events that have transpired in a storyworld's history [29, p. 236].

A number of chroniclers have been authored for existing IEN systems, including several distinct chroniclers (with slightly different aims) created to extract event sequences from the *Blaseball* simulation[1] and the Legends Viewer chronicler for *Dwarf Fortress*[2]. Legends Viewer is notable because it also provides some lightweight interactive sifting affordances on top of the extracted data, and because it has been used as a base for autonomous sifter development—for instance, by the Dwarf Grandpa project [8]. The creators of these chroniclers often need to exercise editorial judgment as to how the continuous output of an IEN system can best be quantized into discrete events: there is a balance to be struck in chronicler authoring between capturing enough data that a wide variety of expressive sifting patterns can be written over the data, and providing a sufficiently summarized view of the data that sifters do not get bogged down in considering many narrative-irrelevant events (e.g. movement events with little narrative content) when executing sifting patterns.

3.2   Co-designing a Simulation and Its Sifter

One difficulty of sifting the output of a simulation that was not designed for story sifting is that information about the causality relationships between events (which plays an important role in narrative) is not preserved or made retroactively available by most simulations. Consequently, Ryan argues that simulation authors who

---

[1] https://sibr.dev/apis.

[2] http://www.bay12forums.com/smf/index.php?topic=154617.0.

intend their simulations to be amenable to curation should ensure that the simulation performs *causal keeping* in its recording of events [29, p. 162], taking note of which events led to other events and making these causality relationships available alongside the records of the events themselves.

More broadly, in authoring simulation actions, it can be beneficial to include extra information alongside the events themselves that are useful in writing more abstract story sifting patterns. Rather than specifying only a single string to identify a simulation event's type, for instance, we have found that it can make authoring sifting patterns much easier if you also attach a variable-length list of string tags to each event. For example, an event representing asking someone out on a date and being turned down can be tagged with `romantic` and `failure`. This allows different sifting patterns (for example, some that are looking for looking for 'any romantic event', and some that are looking for 'any failure') to consider the same event for inclusion in matches. This *event polymorphism* increases the potential for narratively interesting emergent behavior to be captured by sifting.

When authoring both a simulation and the sifter meant to operate over that simulation in parallel, it is important not to create *only* the simulation actions that lead to satisfaction of your existing sifting patterns—this misses the point of IEN (increased novelty and emergence) and falls back into what Louchart and Aylett call 'plot-based authoring' [20]. Consequently, it may be advantageous to follow an iterative three-step process: first, author a number of simulation actions without considering the sifting patterns that they might be matched by; second, test the simulation to see what surprising new emergent microstories appear; and third, author sifting patterns to capture these new microstories. Alternating between simulation-focused authoring and sifting-focused authoring creates mental distance between the action sequences that you expect to occur and the action sequences that you are attempting to recognize, allowing emergent behavior to appear independent of attempts to recognize that behavior.

3.3 Designing Simulations That Incorporate Sifting

Beyond authoring a simulation and its sifter in parallel, it is also possible to incorporate sifting directly into the simulation—for instance, by enabling certain character actions within the simulation if and only if certain sifting patterns have been matched. Felt and Kismet [37] both play double duty as sifters and simulation engines by allowing incorporation of sifting patterns into the preconditions of simulation actions.

The co-creative IEN writing game *Why Are We Like This?* [12, 13], which uses Felt as its underlying simulation engine, employs this feature to implement character subjectivity. In addition to taking simulation actions that update the state of the outside world, individual simulated characters can also perform *introspection actions* in which they apply one of their own preferred sifting patterns to a sequence of past events and formulate a narrative *perception* of those events. This mechanism can be used to craft characters with distinct reactive procedural personalities [36] by giving them access to different sifting patterns: for instance, a melancholy character might be assigned a pool of sifting patterns that allow most social interactions to be interpreted as indicative of hostility, causing the character's interpretations of the world to be biased systematically toward the negative.

Though it has not yet been attempted to the best of the authors' current knowledge, it is also possible to construct a sifting-based *drama manager* [28] that uses sifting to gather information about the current state of the storyworld, then makes targeted interventions at the simulation level to influence the development of emergent storylines based on the sifted information. This would likely represent a relatively light-handed approach to drama management, attempting to gently nudge emergent storylines toward completion (in much the manner of the 'narrative promotion' techniques employed in *The Sims 2* [2, 24]) rather than to impose a single overarching plot structure on the entirety of a storyworld's history.

4 Toward Sifting Heuristics

The sifting patterns that are used in existing story sifters tend to be fairly low-level, concrete specifications of emergent story patterns that make for good narrative material. Patterns at this level, however, do not necessarily capture more generic notions of what makes for a good story, for instance, those that have been set out in cognitive narratology research. This raises the question of how a more generic sense of narrativity could be encoded into the machine, such that sifters can leverage this information to better understand the player-perceived story—for instance, by using abstract narrativity to gauge which of many viable sifting pattern matches are most likely to be important to the player-perceived narrative. In the story sifting literature, encodings of abstract narrativity are called *sifting heuristics* [29, p. 237].

Sifting heuristics may attempt to operationalize constructs from cognitive narratology, including story *interestingness* as defined by Schank [35] and *event salience* [10] (a proxy for story *memorability*) as operationalized in Indexter [4]. An operationalization of *surprise*—which is often treated as a key component of interestingness, and which may be detectable via statistical approaches such as anomaly detection—could also prove useful in sifting heuristics. Since surprise tends to trade off against narrative coherence, striking an appropriate balance between these dimensions is likely to be a central challenge in pursuing this approach.

Sifting heuristics might also be learned from data on how users interact with existing interactive story sifters, for instance, the *Bad News* 'wizard console' or the Legends Viewer interface for exploring *Dwarf Fortress* worlds. Samuel et al. have recently conducted an analysis of interaction trace data with the *Bad News* wizard console [34], revealing that certain sets of wizard console commands are often executed together. Recurring patterns of interaction with these lower-level sifting interfaces could potentially be abstracted into high-level sifting heuristics, since a human user's sense of what information is needed to identify a compelling narrative throughline for a whole *Bad News* play session (for instance) could be expected to serve as a good proxy for the information that a computational system would need to make similar determinations.

5 Conclusion

Story sifting presents a potential solution to one of the key difficulties of interactive emergent narrative: that of mitigating overwhelm and perceived narrative structurelessness while preserving responsiveness and the potential for surprising but compelling emergent narrative developments. However, sifting also introduces new authoring difficulties, particularly around the authoring of story sifting patterns; the construction of simulations that are amenable to sifting; and the definition of highly general sifting heuristics. Several technical and design problems remain to be solved if sifting is to become a more widely deployed solution to the difficulties of IEN.

References

1. Adams T (2019) Emergent narrative in Dwarf Fortress. In: Procedural storytelling in game design. AK Peters/CRC Press, pp 149–158
2. Brown M (2006) The power of projection and mass hallucination: practical AI in The Sims 2 and beyond. Invited talk at AIIDE 2006
3. Cardona-Rivera R, Young R (2015) Symbolic plan recognition in interactive narrative environments. In: Proceedings of the AAAI conference on artificial intelligence and interactive digital entertainment, vol 11
4. Cardona-Rivera RE, Cassell KB, Ware SG, Young RM (2012) Indexter: a computational model of the event-indexing situation model for characterizing narratives. In: Proceedings of the 3rd workshop on computational models of narrative, pp 34–43
5. Chen S, Nelson M, Mateas M (2009) Evaluating the authorial leverage of drama management. In: Proceedings of the AAAI conference on artificial intelligence and interactive digital entertainment, vol 4
6. Eladhari MP (2018) Re-tellings: the fourth layer of narrative as an instrument for critique. In: International conference on interactive digital storytelling. Springer, pp 65–78
7. Elson DK (2012) Detecting story analogies from annotations of time, action and agency. In: Proceedings of the LREC 2012 workshop on computational models of narrative, Istanbul, Turkey, pp 91–99
8. Garbe J (2018) Simulation of history and recursive narrative scaffolding. http://project.jacobgarbe.com/simulation-of-history-and-recursive-narrative-scaffolding
9. Johnson-Bey S, Mateas M (2021) Centrifuge: a visual tool for authoring sifting patterns for character-based simulationist story worlds. In: Proceedings of the AIIDE workshop on programming languages and interactive entertainment (PLIE)
10. Kives C, Ware S, Baker L (2015) Evaluating the pairwise event salience hypothesis in Indexter. In: Proceedings of the AAAI conference on artificial intelligence and interactive digital entertainment, vol 11, pp 30–36
11. Kreminski M, Dickinson M, Mateas M (2021) Winnow: a domain-specific language for incremental story sifting. In: Proceedings of the AAAI conference on artificial intelligence and interactive digital entertainment, vol 17, pp 156–163
12. Kreminski M, Dickinson M, Mateas M, Wardrip-Fruin N (2020) Why are we like this?: exploring writing mechanics for an AI-augmented storytelling game. In: Proceedings of the electronic literature organization conference
13. Kreminski M, Dickinson M, Mateas M, Wardrip-Fruin N (2020) Why are we like this?: the AI architecture of a co-creative storytelling game. In: Proceedings of the fifteenth international conference on the foundations of digital games (2020)

14. Kreminski M, Dickinson M, Wardrip-Fruin N (2019) Felt: a simple story sifter. In: International conference on interactive digital storytelling. Springer, pp 267–281
15. Kreminski M, Mateas M (2021) A coauthorship-centric history of interactive emergent narrative. In: International conference on interactive digital storytelling. Springer, pp 222–235
16. Kreminski M, Mateas M (2021) Toward narrative instruments. In: International conference on interactive digital storytelling. Springer, pp 499–508
17. Kreminski M, Samuel B, Melcer E, Wardrip-Fruin N (2019) Evaluating AI-based games through retellings. In: Proceedings of the AAAI conference on artificial intelligence and interactive digital entertainment, vol 15, pp 45–51
18. Kreminski M, Wardrip-Fruin N, Mateas M (2020) Toward example-driven program synthesis of story sifting patterns. In: Joint proceedings of the AIIDE 2020 workshops
19. Louchart S, Aylett R (2004) The emergent narrative theoretical investigation. In: Narrative and interactive learning environments conference, pp 21–28
20. Louchart S, Swartjes I, Kriegel M, Aylett R (2008) Purposeful authoring for emergent narrative. In: Joint international conference on interactive digital storytelling. Springer, pp 273–284
21. Louchart S, Truesdale J, Suttie N, Aylett R (2015) Emergent narrative, past, present and future of an interactive storytelling approach. In: Interactive digital narrative: history, theory and practice. Routledge, pp 185–199
22. Mateas M, Stern A (2000) Towards integrating plot and character for interactive drama. In: Working notes of the social intelligent agents: the human in the loop symposium. AAAI, pp 113–118
23. Muggleton S, De Raedt L (1994) Inductive logic programming: theory and methods. J Logic Program 19:629–679
24. Nelson MJ (2006) Emergent narrative in the sims 2 (2006). https://www.kmjn.org/notes/sims2_ai.html. Accessed 20 Aug 2021
25. Osborn J, Samuel B, Mateas M, Wardrip-Fruin N (2015) Playspecs: regular expressions for game play traces. In: Proceedings of the AAAI conference on artificial intelligence and interactive digital entertainment, vol 11
26. Porteous J (2016) Planning technologies for interactive storytelling. In: Handbook of digital games and entertainment technologies. Springer
27. Riedl MO, Bulitko V (2013) Interactive narrative: an intelligent systems approach. AI Mag 34(1)
28. Roberts DL, Isbell CL (2008) A survey and qualitative analysis of recent advances in drama management. Int Trans Syst Sci Appl, Spec Issue Agent Based Syst Hum Learn 4(2):61–75
29. Ryan J (2018) Curating simulated storyworlds. PhD thesis, University of California, Santa Cruz
30. Ryan J, Mateas M (2019) Simulating character knowledge phenomena in talk of the town. In: Game AI Pro 360. CRC Press, pp 135–150
31. Ryan JO, Mateas M, Wardrip-Fruin N (2015) Open design challenges for interactive emergent narrative. In: International conference on interactive digital storytelling. Springer, pp 14–26
32. Ryan ML (1992) The modes of narrativity and their visual metaphors. Style 368–387
33. Samuel B, Ryan J, Summerville AJ, Mateas M, Wardrip-Fruin N (2016) Bad news: an experiment in computationally assisted performance. In: International conference on interactive digital storytelling. Springer, pp 108–120
34. Samuel B, Summerville A, Ryan J, England L (2021) A quantified analysis of Bad News for story sifting interfaces. In: International conference on interactive digital storytelling. Springer, pp 142–156
35. Schank RC (1979) Interestingness: controlling inferences. Artif Intell 12(3):273–297
36. Short T (2017) Designing stronger AI personalities. In: Proceedings of the AAAI conference on artificial intelligence and interactive digital entertainment, vol 13, pp 111–117
37. Summerville A, Samuel B (2020) Kismet: a small social simulation language. In: Joint workshops of the international conference on computational creativity
38. Walsh, R.: Emergent narrative in interactive media. Narrative 19(1):72–85 (2011).

39. Young RM, Ware SG, Cassell KB, Robertson J (2013) Plans and planning in narrative generation: a review of plan-based approaches to the generation of story, discourse and interactivity in narratives. Sprache Und Datenverarb, Spec Issue Form Comput Model Narrat 37(1–2):41–64

Authoring Locative Narratives–Lessons Learned and Future Visions

Valentina Nisi

Abstract New narrative technologies build on previous languages and aesthetics until they reach their own maturity and disappear from the foreground, leaving us totally immersed in the emotional journey that a story proposes. Locative technologies are no different. Space and place, as location, started to fascinate philosophers and content creators, even before digital technologies came around, but with the advent of GPS in the '90s, locative media exploded. Academic investigations match artistic explorations within the locative media umbrella. Visual artists, writers, animators, filmmakers, and locative technologies inspire each other in the pursuit of the unique language and aesthetics of this new genre. In this chapter, we will reflect on the role of locative narrative authors through seminal and cutting-edge locative narrative authored works, with special attention to examine the challenges and lessons learned from these projects. With this chapter, we envisage benefiting creatives and technologists with a repertoire of examples, insights, and wisdom for locative narrative authors.

1 Introduction

As Janet Murray explains in her seminal book on interactive digital narrative, *Hamlet on the Holodeck* [1] technologies continuously influence and challenge the ancient craft of storytelling. New technologies build on previous ones; as they mature, developing their languages and aesthetics, they recede from the foreground and become seamless conduits for engaging experiences. Similarly, Interactive Digital Narrative (IDN) technologies have evolved and become transparent, leaving the audiences to enjoy the narrative journeys that authors crafted for them. This chapter looks at the authors' challenges when engaging with interactive locative narratives. Since the times when people gathered around a fire to tell and listen to stories, audiences have challenged authors to adapt their recounts on the spot. In the last fifty years, fascinated by the potential of digital technologies, authors embraced new narrative modalities

V. Nisi (✉)
Lisbon University, IST, ITI/LARSyS, Lisbon, Portugal
e-mail: Valentina.nisi@tecnico.ulisboa.pt

© The Author(s), under exclusive license to Springer Nature Switzerland AG 2022
C. Hargood et al. (eds.), *The Authoring Problem*, Human–Computer Interaction Series,
https://doi.org/10.1007/978-3-031-05214-9_14

and created new ways for the audience to interact with the story material. Today, from Hypertext to Artificial Intelligence, technology is pushing the boundaries of storytelling, authoring, and participation. Recently, with the democratization of location-aware mobile and networked personal devices, locative media exploded. While several definitions of locative media co-exist [2–4], in this chapter, we refer to it as digital content and media designed to trigger narrative interactions in real spaces. Mobile technologies enable many types of locative media narratives and challenge authors to push its aesthetic potential and creative appropriations.

2 Place and Space and as a Narrative Palimpsest

Stories and places have always had an inspiring and fractious relationship. Storytelling, space, and place fascinated philosophers and content creators, way before digital technologies came around. In geography, a *place* is a space endowed with context and meaning [5]. *A place* is a space that is perceived through individuals' experiences, but because of its subjective perception it is difficult to quantify and describe in empirical terms [6]. The processes involved in forming a sense of place, the connection between a space and the individual, are complex and it has been said that we can "sense" places in many subtle and subjective ways. The *sense of place* is focused on the singularity of a particular view of a geographical area. In other words, the place is the unique experiences and perceptions that a human being might encounter within a specific surrounding [7]. Because of this richness of values and its emotional power, space, and place have been the palimpsest for narratives of different kinds, for millennia.

The Method of Loci, by which memories are referenced directly onto spatial maps, is a technique dating back to the ancient Greeks, adopted by the Romans, and described by Frances Yates in her book "The Art of Memory" [8]. In debt to the pioneering explorations of artists, such as Sophie Calle [9], documenting strangers' movements through space, Janett Cardiff's entrancing audio walks [10], storytelling continues to intertwine with space and place, and recently, with digital and location-aware technologies.

Technologies can support locative narrative authoring in many ways; they can help authors in capturing and communicating place-based knowledge, memories, emotions, and drama [11]; they can augment the space by merging virtual and physical realities [12] fostering a sense of *place* [13]. This chapter focuses on the combination of storytelling and locative technologies, where the technology comes in support of the authoring task, in crafting place-based narratives.

3 Location-Aware Narratives and the Role of the Author

As locative technologies evolve, artists and authors explore the relationship between narrative and physical and geographical spaces. The human experiences and interactions with technology are extensively studied and reported in academic conferences and journals. But what challenges do authors encounter when combining narrative skills with the possibilities offered by technology? What new roles do authors forge for themselves when narrating through new tools? From the author's point of view, the potential is vast. Supported by locative forms of media and location-aware technologies authors have experimented with several narrative formats and authoring roles. Authors have widely engaged with and expressed themselves in locative media and gaming. They have created, used, and assessed authoring tools for interactive narrative and gaming, experimenting with live and broadcasted dramas and performances, and used locative narratives and technologies to facilitate encounters with culture and heritage indoors and outdoors. In this chapter, we look at which roles and challenges authors pick up in crafting emotional journeys and transformational experiences for wandering audiences.

As the interactive narrative panorama keeps evolving, old challenges are solved, and new ones come forward. Aware of the existence of many nuances, combinations of roles, genres, and subgenres, in the rest of this section, we look at the author's roles through three main lenses that can be described as follows—(i) The author as an enabler, facilitating and collecting story material from non-professional storytellers and arranging the content in expressive collections of location-specific stories; (ii) the author as a 3D artist, plotting dramas distributed in space, and in time, designing emotional journeys that take advantage of the physical exploration of space; (iii) and finally, authors as a new breed of game designers, designing physical treasure hunts that combine game design skills with the storytelling craft, exploiting the affordances of location-aware, portable and networked technologies.

While it is impossible to silo the authorial craft into clearly defined boxes, these roles intertwine and overlap with each other. For example, the authors embracing the role of the enabler are never free of the subjectivity of their point of view on the matters they collect, and the way they are recounted; moreover, in this role the authors still choose which style to use, if journalistic, documentarist or dramaturgic, using plot and drama to forge the message they want to convey. Similarly, the 3D artist/narrator borrows techniques and tools from the spatially distributed materiality of the theater (playwriting), as well as from the textual novel and writing for the screen (screenwriting); the author approaching locative narrative as a game, designs treasure hunts where the audience can be cast as subjects or a third-person characters, as protagonist or helpers. The author/gamer can play with the drama versus game relationship, building games that rely on drama, using the skills of a novelist to motivate their audiences to progress through the game, leveraging players' participation, crowdsourcing comments, and stories directly from their audiences. Moreover, authors across all three roles share the architects' skills in conceiving 3-dimensional experiential spaces, that are co-created together with their clients (or public), that change over time, as well as across space. The roles outlined in this chapter are more of an opportunity to think about rather than to rigidly classify the location-aware authoring practice. The reader should take what is needed to extend their understanding and awareness of the complex role of the locative media author and use this chapter to further unpack the intricate craft of location-aware story-making, as it evolves into a successful art form.

Finally, while witnessing a renaissance of Virtual, Augmented, Mixed, and Hybrid realities (also known as eXtended Realities- XR), avenues for new kinds of narratives continue to open. This chapter leaves the readers at the door of a new set of challenges, the ones brought about by the emerging XR technologies. Extensions of this chapter, examining the new emerging narrative languages, aesthetics, and challenges, will be written in the following years.

4   The Author as an Enabler: Crowdsourcing Site-Specific Stories from Storyteller's Participants

The democratization of personal and mobile devices in the early 2000 opens to new ways of embodying the readerly and writerly characteristics of a text [14]. Authors experiment with collections of place-based stories provided directly from the communities inhabiting the place. This form of narrative challenges the notion of the author as the one in charge of the narrative journey. The structure of the narrative and its plot open to modular and democratic collections of people's memories, personal stories, and points of view. These collections often document and record memories about specific geographic locations recounted from the point of view of those who once inhabited those premises. This genre combines crowdsourcing with storytelling and documentary making, merging oral history with locative media, creating opportunities for unusual, often excluded voices to be heard (Fig. 1—Building rapport with the local community while collecting and filming stories).

In 2002, the pioneering Canadian project, *[murmur]*,[1] presented community collected oral histories involving mobile phones and visual tags placed in strategic sites in the city of Toronto. People's personal histories and anecdotes were collected and audio recorded by the authors of the project. A [murmur] sign with a telephone number was placed at each location. Calling the number, the audience can listen to a story while standing in that exact spot that the story relates to, engaging in the physical experience of being right where the story took place. The story is recounted directly from the voice of the protagonist. Similarly, across the world, several initiatives fascinate audiences by exploiting the power of location-aware technologies and the community storytelling [15]. Some experiences suggest to the listener to walk around, following a certain path through a place, while others allow a person to wander with their gaze while standing still. What these experiences have in common is that the authors situate their audiences simultaneously at the site of the referent

---

[1] Created by James Roussel, Shawn Micallef and Gabe Sawhney.

Fig. 1 Collage of moments from Ha Vita and Fragment of Laura transmedia locative narrative. The authors spend time building rapport and collecting testimonials with and from the local community

and within an imaginary (aural) space of representation, inviting them to reconcile the two fields [16].

In early 2000, Dublin-based MIT Media Lab Europe research group, Storynetworks, investigates the potential of technologies in connecting local communities' stories and memories with places. With projects such as the *Hopstory* and the *Media Portrait of the Liberties* (MPL), the lore of the rapidly gentrifying inner-city neighborhood of the Liberties is rendered through the eyes of its community of inhabitants [13]. The strong Gaelic tradition of its residents is captured by the MPL project collection and made available through GPS-equipped mobile phones. Following up on this project, some years later Fattoria Mediale engaged the inhabitants of two challenged Amsterdam neighborhoods, in sharing their stories conveying the neighborhood's history, and counteracting the bad reputations of their areas [17]. When engaging with stories in this way, the authors act as enablers for the voices of those who might be excluded or unheard. Setting aside their plotting skills, the authors embrace a more objective and journalistic stance, tasked with building rapport with the locals, deciding a point of view of the collection, and facilitating the community members in sharing their stories. The authors will then design paths through the content and the physical space, guiding the audiences in exploring the geographical spaces imbued with the local memories and pride.

Recently, the EU-funded *MEMEX* project[2] complements these efforts by reaching out to migrants and communities at risk of exclusion, to capture their stories, memories, tangible, and intangible heritage [18]. Despite the potential of locative media, combining location with Augmented Reality and Artificial Intelligence, the project faces authoring challenges in involving communities at risk in sharing their memories

---

[2] https://memexproject.eu/en/.

and anecdotes. From the storytelling point of view, the challenges are not technological, as much as social. How do the MEMEX story facilitators build a fair rapport, based on mutual trust and balanced exchange, engage in a non-exploitative way with the community of non-professional storytellers that provide the content and lend their voices to the locative narrative project? How to collect, select, and curate the content inclusively and transparently. How to make the content available to a wide audience to generate awareness about the stories of the communities that engaged with the process.

Protecting the storyteller's privacy as well as ownership of the content, being their life material, storytelling facilitation is a complex and delicate task. It requires time and commitment, but mostly empathy with the generous story providers. The responsibility for curating other people's content raises multiple questions in the author's mind, ranging from: is this what the storytellers would want to say and share? Am I going to do them justice through my curation of their content? Am I respecting privacy, authorship, and copyrights? Are their vulnerabilities taken care of and how do reward or pay back the efforts? Are digital tools the best ones to be used for the inclusion and participation of these people? Is technology facilitating their voices to be heard, or is it a further obstacle to it? Far from being able to answer all these questions at once, or once and for all, authors embarking on this challenge will have to face and solve these problems case by case, time and time again, building up expertise and sensibility toward their generous collaborators. It is the author's responsibility to share the knowledge acquired through this process and to help create a shared vocabulary, set of guidelines, and aesthetic for this kind of narrative project, where everyone and every role is respected and celebrated.

5   The Author as a 3D Artist: Distributing the Story in Time and Space

Another strand of locative narrative explorations sees the authors seize the combination of narrative drama and physical spaces. The authors investigate the potential of spaces as the canvasses of carefully crafted dramatic plots; as 3D artists, they build their storytelling artifacts in real physical spaces. Besides dramatic devices such as the inciting incident, point of no return, climax, character transformation, etc., their palette includes the latest location-aware and multimedia technologies. The real physical space becomes the backdrop of the unfolding drama, the intrigue is distributed in space as well as in time [19]. By merging physical spaces with fictional (or historically) inspired content, the authors remain in charge of the story structure and plotting of the events, enabling the design of complex emotional journeys. Authors distribute the plot points which can be experienced linearly, one after the other. While they can suggest the best path through the real space, they cannot control the sequence order of the audiences' explorations. The challenge is twofold. While on one side the authors must craft the story in three dimensions, time, and space of the story world, as well as a real physical space where the audience is immersed, on the other one they must let go of controlling the way the audience will ultimately decide to browse it. The second challenge regards the space layout, the light, the smells, and the noises of the real space which play a role in the narrative experience of the audience. These elements need to be considered, studied, integrated into the story, exploited for maximum effect of the audience's experience, and always in favor of progressing the storytelling. Research is opening up to investigate further the authoring challenges of creating location-aware drama [20], but its business models are still lagging. The blockbuster locative narrative has still a long way to go, and so authors have plenty of space for experimentation and knowledge sharing in this domain. As long as the business does not seize locative drama, authoring will remain appanage or research rather than a product for a mass audience.

In 2002 Knowlton et al. pioneered what they called "narrative archeology", connecting drama and poems to satellite navigation technologies [21]. Their pioneering project "*34 North 118 West*" reconstructs the atmosphere of a rundown Los Angeles area through a GPS-equipped laptop that detects where the poem is located and plays it to the audience, embodying the warehouses and train station workers' voices. The authors orchestrate content discovery with the physicality of the surroundings. Walking around the area thus becomes a treasure hunt for ghostly local voices and their points of view.

The authors as 3D artists are inspired by the place, by its genius loci, what was once there, and is now gone. Authors orchestrate drama like a ghost symphony. Thanks to location-aware (and other) technologies, the audience tunes in and experiences the past, present, and possibly the future of those premises. Different technologies can support different experiences and grant the effects of different types of storytelling devices. Technology can be used as a design material, the same as an artist choosing to use wood to represent their idea, rather than cement or steel. For example, the coarse-grained accuracy of the GPS technology allows for a loose tagging of the space while the more precise Bluetooth can grant alerts at a few meters distance from the exact locations that the authors have in mind. Finally, the precise accuracy of NFC or Visual Markers can bring the audience's attention to the fine-grained physical details of the space [11]. Self-reporting can also be considered an option when it adds to the telling of the story or gameplay of the narrative game [22]. Technology is to the 3D artist authors similarly to a painter's palette or a sculpture set of materials; each technology can support a different experience in the drama orchestration [23].

Aware of the aesthetics of locative drama, authors can bring history alive through audio-only and/or Augmented Reality. Projects such as *Riots! 1831* [24], *Spirit* [25], *Bram Stoker the Vampire* [26], and *Walk1916* [27] are prominent examples of explorations of the nuanced aesthetics of combining historically inspired dramas with narrative and place. Projects such as *Hopstory* [28], and *Yasmine's Adventures* [29] on the other hand, do not rely on history but portray the spirit of places through character transformation and a plot orchestration that involves carefully distributing the drama in space and time. Authors make use of traditional narrative devices such as character evolution, and inciting incidents, combined with location-aware technologies. Transmedia storytelling utilizes multiple channels of communication as further spaces were to develop drama and progress the story. Projects such as *TravelPlot Porto* [30], and *Fragments of Laura* [31] exploit the transmedia potential through locative media, adding extra channels for the storytelling, such as combinations of mobile and web platforms to deliver story content and capture the audience participation, enabling some agency through content sharing, commenting, and gaming (see Fig. 1 Fragments of Laura project).

When authors tackle locative narratives as 3D artists, the choice of technology is always at the service of storytelling. Authors mastering traditional narrative techniques paused before embracing the potential of digital locative technologies, keeping their storytelling crafts sharp for writing for more traditional media, such as books, films and radio and television. Today, younger generations of writers and storytellers combine the use of narrative devices with the most recent technologies, striving to discover their aesthetic potential. The use of technology as a tool for crafting dramatic narrative journeys is combined with the challenge of creating meaningful plots, believable and rounded characters that transform across the narrative and inspire the mobile audiences to walk with them. While the challenges of crafting powerful and meaningful stories are always the same, the skills of delivering a powerful experience through novel technologies are still in experimentation. Despite business models lagging, some locative dramas are starting to find their own grounds and aesthetic pleasures.

6   The Author as a Game Designer: Locative Storytelling in Story-Driven Games

As large portions of the western population live with their mobile devices at hand, opportunities for stories, games, and entertainment at large keep merging and emerging. Another role and set of challenges for the locative author comes with the combination of narrative with gaming. This combination is often based on the gaming aesthetics of the treasure hunt. Authors seized the opportunity of using gaming aesthetics and mechanics to trigger the interests of the wider public in stories. Stories have cohabited with games for a long time. Games are often supported by a back story, where the player ends up motivated to help a character accomplish his/her goals, find someone or something, return home, change his status, and transform into a different and better being. Many stories have been conceived to boost players' motivation to progress through digital video games.

The world as a game board was the catchy title of a seminal paper that set the academic beginning of location-aware gaming, in the early 2000 [32]. Researchers, gamers, and creative communities, quickly appropriated the technology and started to experiment with its aesthetics. Blast Theory and Mixed Reality Labs pioneered the pervasive games genres with projects such as *Can you See Me Now* and *Uncle Roy All Around You* [22], mixing theater and storytelling with gaming and locative

Fig. 2 Elements form the locative AR narrative Memories of Carvalhal-The collage presents shots of the interface of the mobile application and users in action inside and outside the museum of Natural History of Funchal, premises, where the narrative is set

technologies. Alternate Reality Games [33] such as *Majestic* or *I Love Bees* open the way to a new challenge for authors: the puppet master role, an uber director who orchestrates the story game from behind the curtains, while a wide variety of audiences engage with it in real-time. Shortly after, many kinds of culturally rich sites inspire story-driven games and explorations [25, 34]. Pioneering work such as the SPIRIT project and the work of the Haunted Planet studios[3] are based upon a strong storytelling metaphor while exploiting locative game mechanics. Using mobile devices (smartphones, tablets) as "magic equipment", users can meet the restless spirits of historical characters. Expanding on this research, the *Memories of Carvalhal Palace* project (see Fig. 2) compares a game-driven story and a story-driven game based on similar content [35]. Authors in this role, move between story-driven games, where the gameplay is contextualized by a background story and a game-driven story in which narrative advances through players engaging in game-like actions (such as treasure hunting or solving riddles and puzzles).

In game-driven stories, the authors use game mechanics to motivate and drive the audience to move through the story plot. The story is supported by the game mechanics, but unfolding plots and character transformations are still the driving force for the audience engagement. While *ludologists* and *narratologists* engaged in articulating the qualities of games and narrative as separate fields of studies[4]—in

---

[3] https://hauntedplanet.com/.

[4] The narratological view is that games should be understood as novel forms of narrative while the ludological claim is that games should be understood on their own terms. Aarseth, early participant of the debate clarifies: *In reality this is not one, but two debates conflated: one is the design-oriented discussion of the potential and failings of game-based narratives, and another is the discussion of whether games can be said to be stories.* Aarseth points the finger at Henry Jenkins' *Game Design as Narrative Architecture*, for setting up the two sides of Ludologists and Narratologists.

this role, the authors exploit locative narratives games as a self-standing genre. The experience of the audience is connected to the character's transformation and the sequence of plot points designed by the author. The author designs the game to invite the audience to playfully explore the real space and in doing so uncovers dramatic content. The game mechanics pace the story fruition and provide playful challenges and a sense of achievement along the way. But it is through the story that the authors develop and deliver messages and emotional involvement. If the two components are not balanced, the audience can get lost. The audience should not rush the story to win the game, but similarly, if the narrative is not well crafted, or the pace is too slow, the player can abandon the quest and exit the experience.

Gaming and storytelling skills are also combined in the transmedia genre. While transmedia storytelling, as defined by Jenkins [36], has been around for some years, recently, audience participation has been designed as a physical space treasure hunt. Nisi refers to it as Locative Transmedia [37]. Often connected to tourism services, locative transmedia is exemplified in projects such as the *Roosevelt Experience,*[5] *TravelPlot Porto, Fragments of Laura* [31, 38]. Besides combining gameplay and locative narrative, in these projects, the authors progress the same story through several different media channels. Transmedia digital artifacts can be quite complex. The authors engaging with this emerging genre need many skills. While spatial thinking and architectural skills are in common with many of the locative narrative authoring roles, locative transmedia authors need to be able to work with large teams of collaborators. If they need to design a forum for the players to express themselves, they will need some facilitator skills; if they add a printed or digital book, they need to be skilled narrators or illustrators. If they plan to add a TV board cast or podcast to it, then theater and directing skills will be useful. Besides orchestrating narrative in real space, they need to master game mechanics and gameplay interactions. They need to mold good storytelling, plotting, story worlding, and character-building, with game design and locative technologies. The complexity of this role calls for a team of interdisciplinary-minded experts, to work closely with the author and support them in their creative vision, making this possibly more than the others, a role suited to team-oriented artists and group efforts.

7 Reconciling the Trade's Challenges

As a Human–Computer Interaction (HCI) academic as well as author and researcher of Location-Aware Multimedia Stories (LAMS) I find myself reflecting on authoring Location-Aware Narratives from multiple perspectives and thinking about how to reconcile these roles with the open challenges that locative narrative still poses to its authors.

As an author, I strive to find good stories and grapple with my narrative skills to plot them into engaging emotional journeys for readers, players, and audiences at

---

[5] https://blog.conducttr.com/small-town-tourism-and-transmedia-storytelling.

large. The narrative craft has many devices for the author to master to deliver the best story experience to its audience. Understanding how to use these devices for locative narrative artifacts and audience is important but often neglected. Defining the plot, inciting incidents, climax, and conclusions; exposition and subtext; selecting the point of view, first, second, or third person. Designing rounded characters, that undergo deep and meaningful transformations, and communicating messages that touch the audiences' hearts, is paramount for any storyteller. This is the core competency of the author, who should then use technology and interactions to deliver a well-crafted story to the audience. As an interaction designer and HCI academic, I am fascinated by technologies and the experiences that they can support. For a storyteller and interaction designer, technology is the design material that brings locative narrative artifacts to life. Which devices to use, which proximity technology? As they all bear different aesthetic potential in the story delivery, the author as an interaction designer needs to design interactions as meaningful actions inside the story experience.

8 Conclusions

Technologies push the boundaries of our experience. Through them we can experiment with new ways of authoring, delivering, and experiencing stories. Anyhow, what is "good storytelling" has been evolving for thousands of years. For a good story to manifest, in the end, the technology should disappear and leave space for emotions, reflection, and transformations of both characters and audiences alike. The locative narrative authors, regardless of the lenses we use to disentangle their craft, are similar across all their roles. Designing for transformational experiences is what a storyteller does, and transformational experiences are also what technology strives to deliver. The challenge for authoring interactive narratives is the continuous evolution and innovation of technologies that can support the ancient craft of storytelling. Keeping up with them, mastering them, and finally being ready to say goodbye as they disappear into the background is indeed one of the challenges for IDN practitioners and researchers. On the other hand, the narrative is a millennia-old craft, but new aesthetics come into play with each new incoming technology. How do we appropriate its quality and evolve the sense of beauty and pleasure that we get from reading a story, through a new technological proposition? These are questions that continuous practice and experimentation will tackle and continuously answer for us, as we keep an eye on the human creativity that fuels both storytelling and technological advancements.

Acknowledgements I'd like to acknowledge the Fundação Ciencia e Tecnologia ITI-LARSyS Pluriannual funding, 2020–2023 (UIDB/50009/2020); the EU funding for the Future Fabulators project Culture/Culture program, Cooperation action. EACEA, 536237; 536237-CU-1-2013-1-AT-CULTURE-VOL.121, and MEMEX European Union's Horizon 2020 grant agreement No. 870743. I wish to thank all my colleagues and researchers, students, and artists who over the years accompanied me through 20 years of locative media studies and productions. It is impossible to name all but I am very grateful to each one of you. Thanks to Ana Bettencourt for putting together the images for this chapter on very short notice.

References

1. Murray JH (1998) Hamlet on the holodeck: the future of narrative in cyberspace. MIT Press, Cambridge, MA
2. Galloway A, Ward M (2006) Locative media as socialising and spatialising practices: learning from archaeology. Leonardo Electron Alm 14(03)
3. Zeffiro A (2012) A location of one's own: a genealogy of locative media. Converg Int J Res New Media Technol 18(3):249–266. https://doi.org/10.1177/1354856512441148
4. Pope S (2009) The shape of locative media. Mute 1(29)
5. Tuan Y-F (1991) Language and the making of place: a narrative-descriptive approach. Ann Assoc Am Geogr 81(4):684–696
6. Cross J (2001) What is sense of place?
7. Steele F (1981) The sense of place. CBI Pub. Co., Boston, MA
8. Yates FA (2001) The art of memory. University of Chicago Press, Chicago, IL. https://press. uchicago.edu/ucp/books/book/chicago/A/bo91674300.html. Accessed 4 Feb 2022
9. Calle S, Baudrillard J (1983) Suite vénitienne. Editions de l'Etoile, Paris
10. Janett Cardiff—the walk book. Buch. König, Walther, Köln (2005)
11. Nisi V, Costanza E, Dionisio M (2016) Placing location-based narratives in context through a narrator and visual markers. Interact Comput 29. https://doi.org/10.1093/iwc/iww020
12. de Souza e Silva A (2006) From cyber to hybrid: mobile technologies as interfaces of hybrid spaces. Space Cult 9(3):261–278. https://doi.org/10.1177/1206331206289022
13. Nisi V (2006) Media portrait of the liberties: design and experience of a location based non linear narrative, presented at the ISEA, San Jose, USA
14. Newton KM (1997) Roland Barthes: 'the death of the author'. In: Newton KM (ed) Twentieth-century literary theory. Macmillan Education, UK, London, pp 120–123. https://doi.org/10. 1007/978-1-349-25934-2_25
15. Rieser M (ed) (2011) The mobile audience: media art and mobile technologies. Rodopi, Amsterdam
16. Eaket C (2008) Project [Murmur] and the performativity of space. Theatre Res Can 29(1):29–50. https://doi.org/10.3138/tric.29.1.29
17. Nisi V, Oakley I, de Boer M (2010) Locative narratives as experience: a new perspective on location aware multimedia stories, presented at the ArTech, Porto, Portugal
18. MEMEX H2020 project, MEMEX project. Memories and experiences for inclusive story-telling. https://memexproject.eu/en/home. Accessed 27 Apr 2021
19. Crow D, Pan P, Kam L, Davenport G (2003) M-views: a system for location-based storytelling
20. Millard DE, Hargood C (2017) Tiree tales: a co-operative Inquiry into the poetics of location-based narrative. In: Proceedings of the 28th ACM conference on hypertext and social media. Prague Czech Republic, pp 15–24. https://doi.org/10.1145/3078714.3078716
21. Knowlton J, Spellman N, Hight J (2002) 34 North 118 West [Locative media]. http://34n118w. net/
22. Benford S et al (2004) Uncle Roy all around you: implicating the city in a location-based performance
23. Benford S, Giannachi G, Koleva B, Rodden T (2009) From interaction to trajectories: designing coherent journeys through user experiences. In: Proceedings of the SIGCHI conference on human factors in computing systems. Boston, MA, USA, pp 709–718. https://doi.org/10.1145/ 1518701.1518812

24. Reid J, Hull R, Cater K, Fleuriot C (2005) Magic moments in situated mediascapes, p 293. https://doi.org/10.1145/1178477.1178529

25. Spierling U, Coors V (2014) SPIRIT—entertaining encounters with ancient history. Eurographics Workshop Graph Cult Herit—Short Pap Posters 4 pp. https://doi.org/10.2312/GCH. 20141322

26. Haahr M (2015) Literary play: locative game mechanics and narrative techniques for cultural heritage. In: Göbel S, Ma M, Hauge JB, Oliveira MF, Wiemeyer J, Wendel V (eds) Serious games, vol 9090. Springer International Publishing, Cham, pp 114–119. https://doi.org/10. 1007/978-3-319-19126-3_10

27. Cushing AL, Cowan BR (2017) Walk1916: exploring non-research user access to and use of digital surrogates via a mobile walking tour app. J Doc 73(5):917–933. https://doi.org/10.1108/ JD-03-2017-0031

28. Nisi V, Wood A, Davenport G, Oakley I (2004) Hopstory: an interactive, location-based narrative distributed in space and time. In: Technologies for interactive digital storytelling and entertainment. Berlin, Heidelberg, pp 132–141

29. Nisi V, Dionisio M, Hanna J, Ferreira L, Nunes N (2015) Yasmine's adventures: an interactive urban experience exploring the sociocultural potential of digital entertainment. In: Chorianopoulos K, Divitini M, Hauge JB, Jaccheri L, Malaka R (eds) Entertainment computing—ICEC 2015, vol 9353. Springer International Publishing, Cham, pp 343–356. https://doi.org/ 10.1007/978-3-319-24589-8_26

30. Ferreira S, Alves AP, Quico C (2015) Transmedia storytelling meets tourism: the TravelPlot porto case study. In: Not ever absent: storytelling in arts, culture and identity formation, BRILL, pp 219–229. https://doi.org/10.1163/9781848883376

31. Dionisio M, Nisi V (2021) Leveraging Transmedia storytelling to engage tourists in the understanding of the destination's local heritage. Multimed Tools Appl 80(26–27):34813–34841. https://doi.org/10.1007/s11042-021-10949-2

32. Falk J, Ljungstrand P, Björk S, Hansson R (2001) Pirates: proximity-triggered interaction in a multi-player game. In: CHI'01 extended abstracts on human factors in computing systems—CHI'01, Seattle, Washington, p 119. https://doi.org/10.1145/634067.634140

33. Salen K, Zimmerman E (2003) This is not a game: play in cultural environments. Digra 03—Proc 2003 DiGRA Int Conf Level Up 2. http://www.digra.org/wp-content/uploads/digital-library/05164.10000.pdf

34. Ballagas R et al (2007) REXplorer: a mobile, pervasive spell-casting game for tourists, p 1934. https://doi.org/10.1145/1240866.1240927

35. Cesário V, Petrelli D, Nisi V (2020) Teenage visitor experience: classification of behavioral dynamics in museums. In: Proceedings of the 2020 CHI conference on human factors in computing systems. Honolulu, HI, USA, pp 1–13. https://doi.org/10.1145/3313831.3376334

36. Jenkins H (1958) Convergence culture: where old and new media collide. New York University Press, New York (2006) ©2006, 2006. https://search.library.wisc.edu/catalog/9910021660902121

37. Nisi V (2017) The changing panorama of interactive storytelling: a review from locative to transmedia. DOC Online—Rev Digit Cine Doc no 2017S:43–68. https://doi.org/10.20287/ doc.esp17.dt02

38. Ferreira S, Alves AP, Quico C, Location based transmedia storytelling: the travelplot Porto experience design. Revista Turismo e desenvolvimento 17/18(4):95–99

Shower Curtains of the Mind

Stuart Moulthrop

Abstract Among certain veteran hypertext experimentalists, the words shower curtain stand as shorthand for what may be the most profound problem in multi-cursal authoring: visualizing and mapping the work. The reference is to Deena Larsen's Marble Springs, a sprawling, densely intertwined labyrinth of poems and stories originally developed on Apple's HyperCard platform. To keep track of the project's burgeoning complexity, Larsen built a physical network with notecards and string, taped to the most capacious household surface she could find. (The object now resides in the Larsen Collection at the Maryland Institute for Technology in the Humanities.) Larsen's famous curtain calls to mind the evidence boards endemic to police procedural fiction, and perhaps also the densely inscribed dens of the mad criminals in those stories. These associations remind us that "non-linear writing," as Ted Nelson famously defined hypertext, breaks the existing laws of discourse, bringing unique problems for authors and designers of authoring systems. This chapter will review some of the solutions the writer has encountered in three and a half decades, including the directed graphs of early hypertext systems such as Intermedia, Note-Cards, and Storyspace, the revolutionary but unrealized 3D innovation of Apple's HotSauce experiment, and the current vernacular of Twine. The chapter will draw on work in information science from Halasz, Horn, Marshall, Bernstein, and others, as well as discussions with hypertext authors and Chris Klimas, the main developer of Twine.

All art constantly aspires towards the condition of music. For while in all other kinds of art it is possible to distinguish the matter from the form, and the understanding can always make this distinction, yet it is the constant effort of art to obliterate it.

—Walter Pater, "The School of Giorgione" (1873) [1]

S. Moulthrop (✉)
University of Wisconsin-Milwaukee, Milwaukee, USA
e-mail: moulthro@uwm.edu

© The Author(s), under exclusive license to Springer Nature Switzerland AG 2022
C. Hargood et al. (eds.), *The Authoring Problem*, Human–Computer Interaction Series,
https://doi.org/10.1007/978-3-031-05214-9_15

In a way, the present essay is also concerned with a tension between "matter" and "form" in a certain kind of art—not painting but what I will call *deep-form narrative*,[1] the sort of text-making that reaches full expression with digital computing. Examples include text adventures, hypertext fictions, and story-intensive video games, for which Espen Aarseth's descriptor *cybertext* still seems useful [6]. Works like this are not the only places to look for insight into "the authoring problem," but doing so may shed light on questions of broader relevance. Deep-form fictions intensify what may be a general problem for narratives, captured in the Formalist distinction between *fabula* and *syuzhet* (thematic and discursive aspects of story—see [7]). Arguably this distinction becomes even more essential—and perhaps fraught—as writers begin to work with computational tools. Proceeding from Aarseth's dualism of *scripton* (what a reader/player/user sees at runtime) and *texton* (the data and logic underpinning any presentation), we know that though the authoring problem spans both domains, its most immediate challenges appear to be textonic—though that appearance may be deceptive. I will argue in this chapter that a purely textonic (or at least schematic) understanding of digital texts cannot capture the complexity of operation that is implicit in computational storytelling.

"Matter" and "form" become complex in the domain of digital authorship. There is the *matter* of the fiction—some story, experience, or fictional world that invites various unfoldings—but this conceptual structure depends on an assemblage of possible elements deployed as organized data. We might think of this textonic material as the *underlying matter* of the cybertext. Likewise, *form* may have more than one dimension. In play or reading, this term could refer to operational rules, play mechanics, or aspects of user interface. Before anything reaches a user, however, someone—most often a team—must have designed and built a framework that represents and enables multiple relations among elements. In one way or another, this effort involves an underlying form, often but not always dependent on graphical schemata and visualizing tools.

These days, there is no need to "obliterate" these formalities at the point of presentation. In almost all cases, cybertexts withhold or conceal their data infrastructure as a matter of operation. If data structures and directed graphs are like brush strokes, they are invisible, at least by convention or expectation.[2] Assuming the "condition of music" can be (however dubiously) reduced to playback or performance, then there is no aspiration involved here. The effect is wired in.

---

[1] "Deep-form narrative" is offered here as my own coinage, though of course no term is ever new. I am indebted to N. K. Hayles' thinking on "deep and hyper" cognitive styles [2] and to Jason Mittell's notion of "complex television" [3] and Richard Grusin's ideas about "radical mediation" [4]. Readers should also see more recent work on "deep narrative," e.g., Phoebe Tickell's recent *Medium* post in this line [5]. There are many ways to talk about a supposed increase in narrative complexity; this is my name for the phenomenon.

[2] All rules are proved by exception, and there are many here, perhaps the most common being URLs visible in a Web browser. Storyspace, to which we are coming, included a reader mode that showed its graph, a feature used by numerous authors, including Shelley Jackson in *Patchwork Girl* (1995) [8]. This mode remains accessible in Eastgate's Tinderbox authoring system. With the emphasis on user-generated content in the second Web era, these exceptions arguably became rare.

While we're at it, we may want to set aside Pater's debatable claim about visual art and music. Deep-form cybertexts imply a different pairing, less aesthetic than disciplinary. We might say that as fiction sprawls and deepens, its impulses increasingly align with anthropology. In many ways, narrative of this sort aspires to the condition of ethnography. There has always been a wild, carnivalesque side of prose fiction given to what Gilbert Ryle called "thick description" [9], from *Gargantua and Pantagruel* to *Tristram Shandy* to *House of Leaves* and *Against the Day*. Likewise, the main or "great" tradition of the novel (see Leavis) has often favored elaborately hierarchical structures for which Forster's dictum "only connect" was in every sense made to order. As we will see, operationalizing this dictum is the heart of the problem: connect what, how, and according to what mechanism or schema?

Arguably cybertexts represent at least a fork off this older creative history, if not a direct continuation. If it takes a novel to explain a village or city, as in *Middlemarch*, *Ulysses*, or *Howards End*, we need something more like a dynamic simulation to evoke a culture—see just about any narratively ambitious video game, such as the *BioShock*, *Mass Effect*, or *Witcher* series. (Also see again Tickell [5], who makes a similar observation.) Culture is concerned not just with epic struggles, grand events, heroes, and tragedies, but with non-player characters, side quests, and details that are often far from trivial. In the words of one deeply superficial example, *Katamari Damacy*, "Earth really is full of things" [10].

More often than not, this scattered or buried evidence can be revealing. In the second of the *Portal* games, for example, it is possible to discover documents describing the early days of Aperture Laboratories, the sinister research outfit that entraps our player character in murderous experiments [11]. These traces tell us the company was originally Aperture Fixtures, a manufacturer of military-grade shower curtains during the Second World War [12]. This bit of history confirms our sense that Aperture is a lunatic enterprise—literally so, as its founder has been driven mad by exposure to Apollo-era moondust. It underscores Aperture's parodic relationship to Black Mesa, the pan-dimensional research lab from the *Half-Life* series, whose fictional universe *Portal* shares.

Suggesting possible alternative employment for the player character at the end of the first game, the dungeon mistress sings: "Maybe Black Mesa/That was a joke, ha ha, fat chance" [11]. Indeed, the *Portal* series is itself a dark joke at the expense of video games, comics, tentpole films, and other fantasies about serially saving the world. It is, after all, a game in which we spend a lot of time shooting holes in the architecture to enable bizarre, non-Euclidean connections between points A and Q. None of this is to be taken too seriously, no matter how many times we suffer ruthless in-game extinction. Taken as a whole, the game is darkly funny: *Military-grade shower curtains*, for pity's sake. The likelihood of such things having existed (and existing) only makes it funnier.

And yet, for a certain small group of people, the shower curtain reference opens, portal-wise, onto something more than a joke. The *Portal* game has been usefully described as an artistic response to the "algorithmic experience" of a software-saturated culture [13]. We can tell another story about a shower curtain, not really a joke, that also speaks to this experience. The story involves an object that now

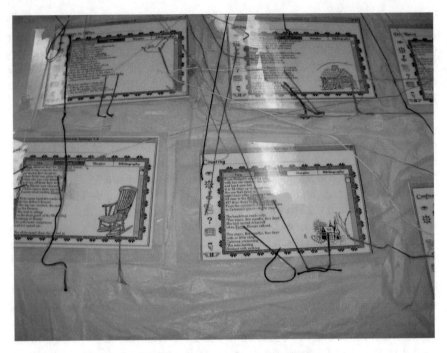

Fig. 1 Deena Larsen's improvised map of *Marble Springs*, 2007 [14]

resides in the Deena Larsen Collection of the Maryland Institute for Technology in the Humanities (MITH). Here is an image (Fig. 1):

At a first glance, this might look like a prop from a film or TV show, some thriller or police procedural—which is not such a bad guess, as it happens. The distressed condition of the object may suggest a villain's lair more than a detective's murder room, but as fans of crime drama know, those are versions of the same thing. In a way this object is indeed a prop—a "property" used in the telling of a story—though it is entirely non-cinematic.

This artifact is what we might call a literary-grade shower curtain. It consists of a series of screenshots printed from a personal computer, glued to a large sheet of transparent vinyl originally intended as a bathroom fixture. Strands of variously colored yarn run from words and images to counterparts on other printouts. The object was created by the writer and artist Deena Larsen as a visual schematic for *Marble Springs*, a multimedia poem cycle she originally created in HyperCard, the authoring tool for linked documents popularized by Apple Computer between 1987 and 2006 [14].[3] There are several of these curtain maps, part of a continuing series whose most

---

[3] *Marble Springs* is a hypertextually linked collection of poems that capture the experience of women, from various social strata, races, and nationalities, in a Colorado town during the nineteenth century. As a work of what was called "new media," it consists, as Lev Manovich has said, of "one or more interfaces to a database" [15] p. 37. Larsen's various shower-curtain assemblages might be seen as authorial interfaces to her literary database.

recent instalment was added in 2018. According to the author, the MITH version was created in 2007, part of an effort to move *Marble Springs* out of HyperCard, which by that point would no longer run on contemporary machines [14].

If there is something humorously funny about the curtain reference in *Portal 2*, Larsen's artifact suggests another sense of "funny:" odd, unexpected, or revealingly weird. This is the way the word is used in automotive circles to refer to drag racers ("funny cars") engineered to probe extremes of performance. By analogy, Larsen was operating beyond the standard affordances of the available software. With its organizing metaphor of file cards oriented in serial stacks, HyperCard offered no convenient visual guide to articulated structure. Larsen's improvised network map provides an entrée into one of the most important aspects of the authoring problem: how to graphically represent complex, contingent relations among elements of a digital text.

Larsen's map brings to light several key features of this task. Her use of a bathroom fixture addresses questions of scope and scale. The shower curtain was the largest convenient surface she could find, offering sufficient area to deploy full-sized printouts of her HyperCard screens so their text and graphics remain legible and thus linkable. This decision is interesting, as it bypasses the option of icons or symbols. The choice likewise finesses another basic problem, the ontology of nodes and links. Nodes or *lexias* (to use the vernacular of electronic literature) are represented by the cards of her stack, captured in a given state by the printer. Links are threads of connection, in at least some instances (though perhaps not all) indicating hyperlinks on words and images. Larsen's runs of yarn imply some further thinking about the meaning of links, evocative of Jim Rosenberg's enduringly fascinating query about *what's inside a hyperlink* [16].[4] Larsen's links are typed by color, either to indicate types or categories, or possibly differences in function.

Larsen's visualization is an elegant improvisation for a crucial task, a definitive bit of creative DIY. For all its virtues, though, its limitations are also instructive. The curtain map is confined to two axes—no interdimensional portals here. It thus allows the author to express relationships either through adjacency and contiguity, or yarn-spanned linkage. Beyond these arrangements, there are no clear affordances for dividing the work into segments or regions. Likewise, there is no support for the kind of hierarchy or embedding possible in a chart or outline view. To those who know this artist and her work, these preferences are understandable. Like many of her fellow digital creators, she has been committed to complicating and undermining hierarchies—our way, perhaps, of "obliterating" form.

However, there is always something paradoxical about artists setting out to obliterate form—especially if our work doesn't so much aspire to be music as need to be software. No artist can ever eliminate form or technique. Musicians have instruments—even vocalists, who make music in the most intimate way, refer to their bodies as such—and cybertextualists are a very long way from singers. For software artists

---

[4] Rosenberg's remark led to an important exchange with the hypertext author and editor Kathryn Cramer, on the Usenet forum Ht-lit in 1994. Rosenberg has shared the transcript with me. Unfortunately, the forum has not been otherwise archived.

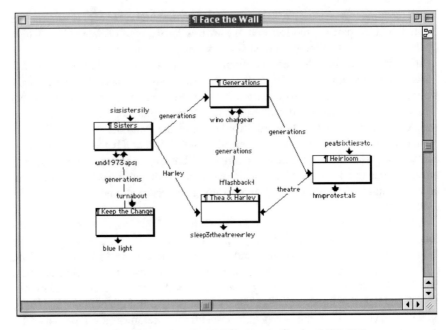

Fig. 2 Structure map of the lexia "Face the Wall" in *Victory Garden* (1991) [17]

like us, the instrument will always be a complex, densely interdependent, external contrivance. That externality implies an element of risk, making obliteration less object of desire than cause for anxiety. Many of us who became active in the 1980s also worked in the heyday of the multimedia tool Adobe Flash, and now find some of our projects inaccessible after the end of browser support for that software. Yet this large-scale failure of form (or platform) may not be the only cause for uneasiness among makers of cybertexts. Failures or breakdowns of form may affect us long before our works are finished, even at the stage of composition. To understand this effect, we need to consider some other examples of visualized structure. Here is one (Fig. 2).

This example crosses from the physical world entirely into the domain of software; though as we'll see, there may yet be a lingering suggestion of detective work, if not the traditional evidence board. The project from which this image comes, the hypertext fiction *Victory Garden*, is roughly coeval with *Marble Springs*, written in 1991 using pre-release versions of the authoring tool Storyspace [18].[5] With the help of the Electronic Literature Laboratory at the University of Washington Vancouver, I have made a new version of the work using Hypertext Markup Language, Cascading

---

[5] Like *Marble Springs*, *Victory Garden* is a network of stories involving people in or attached to a particular place, the imaginary American college town of Tara. Its occasion is the outbreak and prosecution of the first Gulf War in 1990–91. The work includes approximately 1,000 lexias 2,800 explicit hyperlinks, and (as we'll see) a quantity of implicit or emergent links that is difficult to calculate.

Stylesheets, and JavaScript.[6] (The new version can be found at www.victory-gar den2022.com [19].) This effort has required considerable attention to the structural representation of the original, using vintage computers to run an early release version of Storyspace.[7] Returning to an authoring tool I first used more than 30 years ago has yielded many insights—about hypertext fiction, the affordances of Storyspace, and its interpretation of the directed-graph concept, and perhaps some larger aspects of the Authoring Problem.

There are certain clear resemblances between this map and Larsen's vinyl visu- alizations: division of the work into discrete display states or reading units (lexias, called *spaces* in Storyspace), which are connected by link lines. As in Larsen's multicolored strands of yarn, the links here are differentiated. The first versions of Storyspace did not support color but allowed links to be tagged with words or phrases, some of which are visible in Fig. 2: "theatre," "generations," and "Harley." These markers could be used on multiple links. The "generations" tag occurs three times here. When used in this way, named links constitute a *path*. Links in Storyspace are reversible in reading (there is a go-back function), but essentially monodirectional in the authoring mode, connecting two lexias in succession. Link lines thus end in a directional arrowhead. Note, however, that four of the spaces in Fig. 2 feature arrowheads with only the stubs of link lines ("Sisters," "Keep the Change," Thea & Harley", and "Heirloom"). These details reveal an important advantage of virtuality. The truncated arrows indicate links coming from spaces not visible in the current view because they are mapped elsewhere in the hypertext. In Storyspace, it is possible to embed a compartmentalized directed graph within a parent lexia, as in this case (Fig. 3).

Here, four of the spaces, "Name That Fear," "Bird Fiver-Two," "Talkin' bout the Horror," and "P.C.," have spaces embedded within them. The embedded material in the last of these is itself a fairly complex graph (Fig. 4).

The semiotics of embedding is up to the author. A graph tucked inside a lexia might contain subordinate or specialized material, a fork off the main path. In a narrative, levels of embedding might represent successive advances along a particular line, which is essentially the case in Fig. 4, where the embedded spaces further elaborate an elliptical digression that begins in the parent space "P.C." Like any gain in complexity, however, the embedding feature brings cognitive challenges. Working on the new version of *Victory Garden* has made this apparent. A certain digression at this point is unavoidable—a diversion into what may at first appear to be the second sort of problem not necessarily confined to authoring.

The vernacular of hypertext linking has gone through several important changes. In the first era of the World Wide Web, the point-and-click grammar became estab- lished, based on graphic and typographic link anchors. That style remains important, though in recent decades it has been undermined, if not displaced, by pushed content,

---

[6] An Addendum addressing the design differences between the 1991 and 2022 versions of *Victory Garden* appears at the end of this chapter.

[7] The images in this paper were produced on an iBook G4 that left the factory in 2004—as the poet says, *long may you run.*

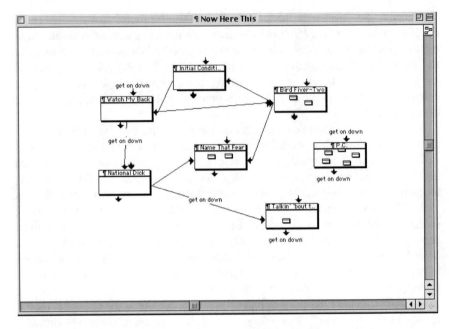

Fig. 3 Structure map of the lexia "Now Here This" in *Victory Garden*

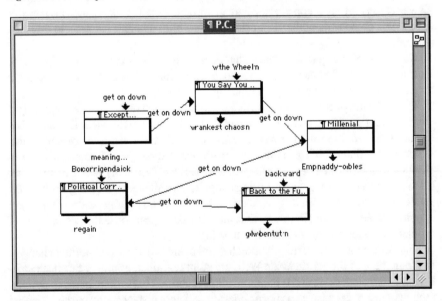

Fig. 4 Map of structure embedded within the lexia "P.C." in *Victory Garden*

tracking algorithms, and gestural interfaces on portable devices. It is worth remembering, though, that for a few early moments the point-click paradigm was not the dominant option. In *afternoon* [20], where a lot of things first began, Michael Joyce offers readers the option to "march through on a wave of returns," highlighting the operation of *default links* in that work which could be activated by pressing the Enter or Return key, without selecting anything on the screen.

Though *Victory Garden* goes in another direction from *afternoon*'s enigmatic elegance, it retains that work's investment in default or non-selective linking. On entry, readers are offered two ways to proceed. One presents a stylized map offering a selective table of contents. This feature was added shortly before publication, essentially as afterthought.[8] The original conception was and remains an introductory sequence called the Labyinth, a series of spaces offering a choice between two words, one of which may be added to an unfinished sentence. There are 52 ways to exit the Labyrinth, most of them tied to completed sentences. Each of these release points places the reader at the beginning of a defined sequence of links, the structure that Storyspace recognizes as a path. The paths were meant to represent custom traversals of *Victory Garden*'s nearly 1000 lexias.

Another literary vector for *Victory Garden* leads from the late, great Joan Didion's "White Album" essay (1979), with its angst-ridden evocation of late-stage modernity:

> I was supposed to have a script, and had mislaid it. I was supposed to hear cues, and no longer did. I was meant to know the plot, but all I knew was what I saw: flash pictures in variable sequence, images with no 'meaning' beyond their temporary arrangement, not a movie but a cutting-room experience [22].

Didion's *cri de coeur* deserves respect. It was a definitive (and still relatable) expression of American anxiety, motivated not just by general chaos but also by the possible onset of multiple sclerosis in the writer. With flagrant disregard for this seriousness, *Victory Garden* makes a home in that metaphorical cutting room. By intention at least, some of its paths seem a bit like cinematic trailers, excerpts from various sequences intended to impart an impression of the work. Others cross-edit narrative arcs involving related characters. Some appear to operate mainly through word association or dream logic. One jumps immediately to a series of final moments ("Praecox"), while another loops back to the start ("One Way Street"). Perhaps the strangest of all, "ABW," promises an anti-chronological tour—ABW seems to be shorthand for "ass backwards."

In discussing paths in the original *Victory Garden*, I have been careful to use expressions like "were meant to" and "by intention." This is necessary because of that second authoring problem hinted at earlier. This problem is associated less with schematization—arranging the frames in Didion's cutting room, to extend the metaphor—than the workings of an apparatus, or as Aarseth calls it, a "traversal function" that converts texton to scripton [6]. This is the Storyspace Page Reader application. In the cutting-room analogy, we might think of this device as moviola

---

[8] At least one authoritative reader of the original *Victory Garden*, Alice Bell, seems understandably to have chosen the map. See her *Possible Worlds of Hypertext Fiction* (2010) [21].

or projector, but the workings of *Victory Garden*'s paths suggest something more complex and vexing.

At this point I need to make a crucial confession about the original *Victory Garden*: following a given path has always been much harder than I wanted it to be. Recall that paths are supposed to be nearly automatic, a "wave of returns" in Joyce's phrase. Well, not exactly.

Consider the lexia "P.C." discussed above. It belongs to a path called "workout." This path comprises 24 lexias, dipping in and out of several riffs and episodes, beginning with a lexia called "Our Work." Using Storyspace 1.3 on vintage equipment, I call up that lexia and start a reading within the authoring system. The resulting traversal follows the designed path for only two steps. On the lexia "Cyborg Politics," pressing Enter/Return to follow the default path takes me—with acute but unintended irony—to a lexia called "Drama of Return," rather than to "Observer," which is the next stop on the "workout" path as listed in the authoring system. If I continue relying on default links from "Drama of Return" I will not find my way back to "workout," but will skip unbeknownst along a variety of paths. The experience is, to say the least, chaotic.

There are two reasons for this bewilderment. First, any lexia in Storyspace may be the start and endpoint of multiple links. Have another look at Fig. 4, paying particular attention to the rightmost space, the interestingly spelled "Millenial."[9] The non-local link stub at the bottom of the rectangle appears to be tagged "Empnaddy-oibles," a bit of nonsense reminiscent of a CAPTCHA challenge. In fact, this phrase results from superimposition of two link names, "Empire crumbles" and "naddy-o." Clicking on the arrowhead resolves the reading to one link or the other. In cases involving more than two links, multiple clicks are required to cycle through the set. The complexity of this design is obvious.

The lexias in *Victory Garden* are heavily linked, with nearly three per space on average, though the distribution is not uniform. "Millenial" has two incoming and two outgoing links. "Cyborg Politics" is the destination for 14 links and the starting point for six. Links come in three forms: the familiar word-anchored sort (text links), non-selection default links associated with paths, and in some cases, a localized default that is not on any path. Any or all these types may be present. Notably, "Cyborg Politics" contains multiple non-selection or default links. On the authoring side, Storyspace allows sorting of links into a hierarchy or stack. This arrangement has no consequences for text links, which always operate when their anchors are selected. In the case of non-selection links, order in the stack is dispositive. When the Return/Enter key is pressed, the topmost link is followed. (Authors can re-order the link stack using the *Change links* tool, but the order remains fixed thereafter.) In the case of "Cyborg Politics," the topmost link in the stack is not the one that follows the "workout" path, but a localized default which produces the drama of (no) return.

---

[9] Unsure if the spelling error should be attributed to the implied speaker of the passage or my younger self, I have corrected it in the new version.

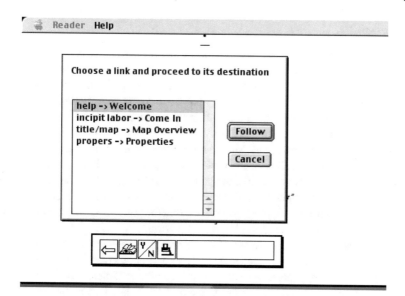

Fig. 5 Storyspace "Page Reader" interface with "Follow Link" activated

The "workout" path is not definitively lost, however. Readers of the original *Victory Garden* can follow the desired path by using an interface feature called *Show Links* depicted in the reader interface by a stylized open book (Fig. 5).

Clicking this operator produces a pop-up window with a list of outgoing links. The list for each link consists of two elements divided by a stylized arrow (->). The term to the right of the arrow is the destination space. The term on the left is the tag assigned to the link by its author, which as we have indicated, may also be the name of a path. Theoretically, this mechanism allows readers to pursue a path—assuming they know or have deduced the path name, which seems unlikely. Even allowing for this tenuous possibility, the affordances of the Page Reader in this case are far from the Joycean ideal of fluid, headlong traversal.[10] They also distort my idea of discrete storylines radiating from a labyrinthine sorting hub. The paths may be present, but the effort required to follow them is, I confess, excessively non-trivial. I have removed this mechanism from *Victory Garden 2022* in favor of what I believe to be a less disruptive strategy (see the Addendum).

At this point, readers of this chapter may be experiencing their own pathfinding troubles, hoping perhaps for an undramatic return to first principles. We set out, after all, to discuss the challenge of representing the complexities of hypertext fiction in one or more graphical planes. Where has this digression into vagaries of a reader interface gotten us? Does any of this shed light on authoring? Could we please follow the link that gets us back to shower curtains?

---

[10] Though both *afternoon* and *Victory Garden* use the Page Reader, explicit paths are not as heavily emphasized in the earlier work, so the "wave of returns" is better realized there.

Link selected.

Though it may be disorienting, a visit to the cutting room can also be enlightening. In the case of *Victory Garden*, intercutting between delivery interface and creative tool reveals a serious authoring problem indeed, which we might call the seduction of the map. I should concede, before taking this assertion further, that maps and other visualizations are desirable both for authors and for those ingenious researchers who explain (sometimes to authors) how complex texts work. The efforts of Jeremy Douglass, Jessica Pressman, and Mark Marino deserve mention in this regard [23]. Maps are fine for scholarship. In the writer's room, however, they can be trouble.

For at least some writers, there can a tendency to become obsessed with textonic manipulations to the neglect of the scriptonic, or reader experience. It has taken a scandalously long time—31 years—to realize that the paths in *Victory Garden* do not work as I desired and to set about building something better. I could suggest many reasons for this. For starters, *Victory Garden* was the second of its kind, following *afternoon*. It was in many respects an early experiment given up to contingency. That it worked even imperfectly was for a long time sufficient. During that time, I turned in other technical directions, to the non-schematic idioms of the Web and Flash, though the latter-day hypertext tool Twine [24] has lately brought me back to directed graphs. It is also worth noting that *Victory Garden* has been inaccessible for many years, and this lapse has proved tempting. Some writers may prefer to let old work go unexamined—an authoring problem that decidedly does not belong to software studies.

The seduction of the map arguably does, however. There is something to be said in the end for the obvious yet charming limits of Deena Larsen's glued and threaded curtains. What's so bad about two dimensions? Aperture Fixtures never killed any test subjects that we know of. Maybe non-Euclidean wormholes, or the intricate linking schemes that mimic them, have limited utility. We might be better off keeping things simple.

And yet, makers of deep-form poems and fictions live by disruption and complication. We can no more "obliterate" our more baroque impulses than we can free ourselves from the systemic dependencies on which all mediated works inevitably rely. Still, we can remember that complexity runs both ways. Texton must become scripton. Marvelous to say, somebody somewhere may actually want to read, or play, or play with, what we are building, and from this follows the most important of authoring problems.

In this regard, the move to Web technologies becomes paradoxically crucial. The World Wide Web is infamously blind to structure. Web browsers do not generally include the maps furnished to readers in texts like *Patchwork Girl* [12], David Kolb's *Socrates in the Labyrinth* (1994) [25], Bill Bly's *We Descend* (1997) [26], or Richard Holeton's *Figurski at Findhorn on Acid* (2001) [27]. Though applications like Storyspace, Tinderbox, and Twine can be used to produce Web hypertexts, it is a great challenge to bridge from those elegantly detailed environments to the brutal simplicity of the Web. (For many Twine writers, the overt procedurality of adventure games is often a saving grace.) Yet that challenge is precisely what the seduction of the map entails—finding ways to mediate between very high levels of complexity and a system whose basic grammar is not far from Neil Postman's *now, this* [28].[11] The work is difficult but arguably important, as it also makes connections between current practices and more sophisticated conceptions of digital textuality—connections that may span generations.

It has been edifying to work on the new version of *Victory Garden* with designers in the Electronic Literature Laboratory, much younger colleagues born into a world I once struggled to imagine. Their names, for the record, are Austin Gohl, Arlo Ptolemy, Holly Slocum, and Andrew Thompson. It goes without saying they are much more finely attuned to the ecology of design and use, informed not just by the Web and social media, but perhaps crucially, by digital games, where interactivity finds its most vivid expression. It is hard to imagine any of these designers falling into my three-decade sleep. They are considerably more attuned to user experience, and to the life cycle of software and platforms as well. While the existence and tenuous accessibility of early Storyspace maps have been indispensable to our project, the heart of the effort lies in the work I share with my co-designers—telling, explaining, questioning, interpreting, making, testing, and making again. Critical, skeptical readers are indispensable (and it doesn't hurt when they sometimes find bits of the work worth reading). It is strange to think about storytelling without the social context of sharing. The shower curtain collage or murder board is always just an indication of a much deeper mystery—a word that can mean discipline, procedure, and community, as well as enigma. The shower curtain of the mind is a prop, and as such necessary—but never sufficient—to the drama of return.

Addendum—A Note on Victory Garden 2022

The project is available on the Web at www.victory-garden2022.com.

There are two reasons for rebuilding *Victory Garden* using Web formats. The most obvious is accessibility and durability, the desire to keep the text available to future writers and researchers. Aside from some editorial corrections and updates to the graphics, I am not changing the contents of spaces (now pages). The writing is largely what it was in 1991. Likewise, virtually all original text links remain unchanged. Non-text links, however, have been significantly revised. In addition to *paths*, there is a new text link alternative called *streams*.

In the case of paths, a primary assignment is made on the landing page of the site. This path is called "Garden," and it comprises a 580-page traversal through the major parts of the work. If the reader chooses to go through the Labyrinth, the path assignment will be (in all but a few cases) reset on exit. Either way, the reader can move along their designated path from any page by pressing an assigned key, activating a feature of the visual interface, or performing a swipe on a haptic device. Progress along the path is tracked by a persistent variable. Unlike in the original, readers may return to the path at any point in the work, even if they have departed

---

[11] Postman offered that phrase as a formula for broadcast television—compare the famous Monty Python catchphrase, "and now for something completely different." It seems suggestive for Web hypertext as well.

from its sequence by following a text link or some other digressive possibility such as a *stream* (see below). The name of the current path is visible in a header at the top of every page in the main reading sequence. A list of all paths is also available through the reader interface. I hypothesize that paths will mainly come into play when readers find themselves on pages without text links, or revisit pages they have already seen, or if they prefer variety to consistency. Many path sequences are closely based on those in the 1991 version, and though I have expanded some others, they retain their elliptical quality.

For the new version, I have added a second non-text-link category called *streams*. Stream transitions are activated in the same way as in paths (keypress, interface click, or swipe). Streams are series of pages making up coherent narrative episodes or following unified themes. *Victory Garden* has always had these structures, and I want to make them more accessible. A stream link may be activated from any page, though not all pages in the work belong to streams. If a page is not on a stream when stream access is requested, the reader is shown a list of available streams and may either choose one or go back to the previous page to try another strategy. Stream names are also shown in the header and there is an interface option to see the complete list of streams at any point. I expect the default "Garden" path (which unifies the streams) and the individual streams to be the most popular ways of approaching the work. However, these structures are not definitive. Because there are some pages in the work not accessible on streams, there may be some reason for readers to use all the affordances: paths, streams, and text links—though what readers actually make of *Victory Garden 2022* of course remains to be seen.

Acknowledgements The author wishes to thank the editors of this book for their cross-disciplinary generosity. Much credit is also due to Dene Grigar and her colleagues at the Electronic Literature and The Next. Appreciation to Matthew Kirschenbaum of the University of Maryland for the crucial photograph.

References

1. Pater W (1901) Collected works. Macmillan, London
2. Katherine Hayles N (2007) Hyper and deep attention: the generational divide in cognitive modes. Profession 2007:187–199
3. Mittell J (2015) Complex TV: the poetics of contemporary television storytelling. New York University Press, New York, NY
4. Grusin R (2015) Radical mediation. Crit Inq 42(1):124–148
5. Tickell P (2021) New deep narratives: we need stories of what it means to be human. Medium
6. Aarseth E (1997) Cybertext: perspectives on ergodic literature. Johns Hopkins Press, Baltimore, MD
7. Shklovsky V (1965) Sterne's Tristram Shandy: stylistic commentary. In: Lemon LT, Reis MJ (eds) Russian formalist criticism: four essays. University of Nebraska Press, Lincoln, ND, pp 27–57
8. Portal Wiki (2011) Aperture science
9. Ryle G (1968) The thinking of thoughts: what is "Le Penseur" doing? Stud Anthropol 11:11

10. Takahashi K (2004) Katamari damacy. Namco, Tokyo
11. Valve Software (2011) Portal 2. Valve, Seattle, WA
12. Jackson S (1995) Patchwork girl. Eastgate Systems, Watertown, MA
13. Burden M, Gouglas S (2012) The algorithmic experience: portal as art. Game Stud 12(2)
14. Larsen D (1993) Marble springs. Eastgate Systems, Watertown, MA
15. Manovich L (2000) The language of new media. MIT Press, Cambridge, MA
16. Rosenberg J (2021) Personal correspondence, 15 June 2021
17. Moulthrop S (1991) Victory garden. Eastgate Systems, Watertown, MA
18. Bolter J, Joyce M, Smith JB (1990) Storyspace. Eastgate Systems, Watertown, MA
19. Moulthrop S (2022) Victory garden 2022. The Next, Vancouver, WA
20. Joyce M (1990) afternoon: a story. Eastgate Systems, Watertown, MA
21. Bell A (2010) The possible worlds of hypertext fiction. Palgrave Macmillan, London
22. Didion J (1979) The white album. Washington Square Press, New York, NY
23. Douglass J, Pressman J, Marino M (2015) Reading project: a collaborative analysis of William Poundstone's project for Tachistoscope {Bottomless Pit}. MIT Press, Cambridge, MA
24. Klimas C (2009) Twine [Open-source software]. https://twinery.org/
25. Kolb D (1994) Socrates in the labyrinth. Eastgate Systems, Watertown, MA
26. Bly W (1997) We descend. Eastgate Systems, Watertown, MA
27. Holeton R (2001) Figurski at Findhorn on acid. Eastgate Systems, Watertown, MA
28. Postman N (1985) Amusing ourselves to death. Macmillan, New York, NY
29. Leavis FR (1948) The great tradition. Chatto and Windus, London
30. Larsen D (2022) Personal correspondence, 11 January 2022

Game Mechanics as Narrative Mode

Alex Mitchell⬤

Abstract Focusing on game mechanics as a narrative mode, rather than considering story and game as two separate but related experiences, allows narrative designers to take a more integrated approach to authoring interactive digital narratives. In this chapter, I explore two ways of doing this: by making use of game mechanics as an experiential metaphor and by using poetic gameplay. I provide a survey of work that has explored each of these approaches and then suggest ways of making use of both techniques together. I then argue that both the metaphoric possibilities of game mechanics for storytelling and careful undermining of players' expectations for gameplay, provide powerful tools for authors to create compelling interactive digital narratives.

1 Introduction

As a player interacts with a story-focused game, the moment-by-moment actions the player is taking, based on the game mechanics, potentially work together with the other modalities (visual, auditory, and verbal) to create a story experience. By focusing on the game mechanics as a narrative mode, rather than considering story and game as two separate but related experiences, a narrative designer can more strongly integrate the gameplay and the story.

One way to do this is to make use of the game mechanics as an *experiential metaphor*, in which the player's experience of the game mechanics provides a means of understanding something else within the narrative. For example, in the game *Gravitation* [1], one of the core game mechanics involves throwing a ball back and forth with a child, an action that comes to represent the playable character's relationship with their son [2].

Another approach is using *poetic gameplay*, where the details of the game mechanics deliberately undermine player expectations to foreground certain aspects of the game experience and connect these elements to the unfolding narrative. This

A. Mitchell (✉)
National University of Singapore, Singapore, Singapore
e-mail: alexm@nus.edu.sg

can be seen in *Gravitation*, in the tension between the above-mentioned ball-throwing mechanic and the other core game mechanic, which involves exploring the game world and collecting "stars". The game is designed such that it is impossible to succeed at both mechanics, and therefore, at the goals these mechanics support, foregrounding this tension and encouraging the player to reflect on what this means [2, 3].

This chapter explores the ways that the design of the game mechanics, both in terms of the use of game mechanics as metaphor and through poetic gameplay, can form an integral part of the toolkit available for authoring an interactive story. Based on a survey of work that has explored these two approaches to using game mechanics as a narrative mode, I argue that authors who want to make use of game mechanics as part of storytelling should carefully consider the use of both approaches together. As can be seen in the examples presented above, these two approaches are closely related. When used in a complementary fashion, they can help an author of an interactive narrative to create a more cohesive integration between the game mechanics and the narrative.

2 Defining Game Mechanics and Narrative

Before talking about the role of game mechanics in creating an interactive narrative, it is important to clearly define what I mean by "game mechanics" and "(interactive) narrative".

2.1 Game Mechanics

As with many concepts in game design and game studies, the idea of game mechanics is at once immediately obvious and endlessly debated and redefined [4]. For the purposes of this chapter, I draw on Sicart's [5] definition of game mechanics as the "methods invoked by agents, designed for interaction with the game state". For Sicart, the notion of an "agent" is not limited to the human player, but also includes "artificial agents" that are "part of the computer system" [5]. In the context of an interactive narrative, this could include, for example, a drama manager and/or agents controlling characters in a multi-agent system [6]. Sicart's definition of game mechanics is consistent with Nealen et al.'s [7] definition of rules as "all state changes/transitions in the game", and mechanics as "a subset of these rules that might be dependent on the game state, and can be (directly or indirectly) invoked by the player/agent through the controls." Nealen et al. go on to also consider controls to be "the direct manipulation (hardware) actions provided to the player", and interface to be "the entirety of the input/output feedback loop", of which the controls are a component. Thus, the player manipulates the controls to invoke the game mechanics, which, in turn, changes the game state, which is reflected in the interface, and perceived by the player. This is similar to Aarseth's [8] notion of the Game Object, which consists of a semiotic and a mechanical layer. Aarseth's semiotic layer "informs the player about the game world and the game state", whereas the mechanical layer affords game actions by means of the game mechanics.

2.2 Narrative

As with "game mechanics", the terms "narrative", and perhaps more problematically "interactive narrative" (whether or not it is coupled with "digital"), are equally contested. For this chapter, I follow other scholars such as Dubbelman [9], Koenitz [10], and Roth et al. [11] and adopt a cognitive narratological perspective on narrative [12, 13]. From this viewpoint, as Ryan argues, "narrative is a mental image—a cognitive construct—built by the interpreter as a response to the text" [14]. As Dubbelman suggests, this cognitive narratological perspective enables us to look beyond the traditional devices used for narrative expression when considering how to tell a story in a game, and also to consider "the procedural devices that are responsible for creating events real time, like game mechanics and rules, since the player's engagement with these devices can trigger the construction of stories in the embodied mind of the player" [9].

Similarly, Larsen and Schoenau-Fog [15] take the position that there is a "narrative quality" to game mechanics, which contributes to the player's experience of the narrative in a game. They argue that a game consists of the mechanics and the context. By mechanics, they follow Frasca's [16] categorization of mechanics into manipulation rules, goal rules, and meta rules, adding in an additional layer of "system rules" to represent any rules the player does not directly interact with. By context, they mean the various ways in which the game is presented to the player, including the graphics, audio, and so forth. As they explain, these elements are essential as "mechanics by themselves are often hidden from the player". At the same time, the context is more than simply a way of making the mechanics visible—the two elements "combine when the player begins to play", from which the meaning of the game emerges. Larsen and Schoenau-Fog see this process as paralleling the Mechanics-Dynamics-Aesthetics (MDA) model [17], with the dynamics combined with the context to create meaning, which then leads to the experience of the narrative. This narrative can be viewed as consisting of a resulting "aesthetic" experience, similar to the MDA model, plus an "after story", or the recollection of the narrative as experienced by the player during play. It is important to note that under the MDA model, "[a]esthetics describes the desirable emotional responses evoked in the player, when she interacts with the game system" [17], rather than audio-visual elements. In fact, Larsen and Schoenau-Fog highlight that "these aesthetics are understood purely as the aesthetic qualities of the ludic elements (the mechanics), and disbarring any of the context" [15]. This is consistent with Roth et al.'s [11] use of Koentiz's [10] System-Process–Product (SPP) model of interactive digital narratives to explain how the player engages in a process of interpretation that forms a double-hermeneutic circle, or hermeneutic strip. In this model, the player is simultaneously engaged in interpretation of their interaction with the system and interpretation of the currently instantiated narrative.

Chew's [18] work on the role of interactivity in storytelling has strong similarities with the above discussion, although Chew focuses on the idea of interactivity more generally as a narrative "mode". Drawing on Page's [19] definition of mode as "[a] system of choices used to communicate meaning", and Kress's [20] consideration of mode as "a socially shaped and culturally given semiotic resource for making meaning", Chew argues that "interactivity can contribute to meaning-making and can be considered a mode [but] does not function alone… It needs to work with narrative content and other perceptual and semiotic modes". Here Chew is focusing on interactivity rather than game mechanics, but she later extends this argument to include game mechanics [2, 21]. This later notion of game mechanics as a narrative mode, which I follow in this chapter, is consistent with Larsen and Schoenau-Fog's model of the narrative quality of game mechanics, and Roth et al.'s double-hermeneutic circles.

3   The Role of Game Mechanics in Meaning-Making

There has been increasing interest in the question, not of whether games can tell stories, but *how* games can tell stories [15, 22–32]. There are several strategies that authors can take to create meaning within their interactive stories. One way is to make use of traditional storytelling techniques at the level of context or the semiotic layer, while at the same time avoiding what is often referred to as ludonarrative dissonance [33], or a disconnect between embedded narrative and the game mechanics. Although potentially effective, this is a very traditional approach to game storytelling, one that fails to see game mechanics as an active, integral part of the process of forming the cognitive construct that is the narrative in the player's mind. It also ignores the possibility that some forms of dissonance, and the effort required to overcome or make sense of that dissonance, as Roth et al. [11] have argued, can itself form part of the process of meaning-making.

An alternative approach is to focus specifically on the design of the game mechanics to convey the desired narrative and create the intended meaning. Given the above discussion, e.g., that game mechanics work together with the other modes (context in Larsen and Schoenau-Fog's model, or the semiotic layer to use Aarseth's terminology) to create narrative meaning, it is important to consider, in the context of this volume, what can be done to help authors to make use of game mechanics as an integral part of their efforts to tell interactive stories. One way to do this is to harness the ability of game mechanics to encourage meaning-making through the use of *game mechanics as metaphor* [30, 34, 35]. The other possibility that I will discuss in this chapter is to undermine a player's expectations regarding the game mechanics, making use of my notion of *poetic gameplay* [3, 36, 37].

I will begin by discussing the idea of game mechanics as metaphor in the following subsection, then shift to a focus on poetic gameplay.

3.1 Game Mechanics as Metaphor

There has been considerable attention paid to the idea of using game mechanics as metaphors in games that attempt to create some meaning through play [34, 35, 38–50]. Here, I will focus largely on the work by Rusch [41–46], Begy [34, 47], and Möring [35, 48–50]. I begin by considering how narrative meaning is created in a game and the role of game mechanics in this process. This leads to the potential of using metaphor to create meaning.

According to Rusch and Weise:

> For a game to successfully convey its message it needs to be implemented within the rule system. It has to become tangible to the player in the moment-to-moment game-play. It must make use of the medium-specific possibilities to get the experience across, and strategies that worked well in traditional media may not work the same way in games. [42]

One way to do this, they argue, is through the use of metaphor, as "the essence of metaphor is understanding and experiencing one kind of thing in terms of another" [51] (quoted in [42]).

3.1.1 Interface Metaphors and Experiential Metaphors

As Rusch and Weise argue, games are always a mediated experience [42]. The player can't reach into the screen and touch the game world. Everything is mediated through the game interface. As a result, there is a need to represent the game world in the interface. This involves providing the player with *interface metaphors* through a systematic process of abstraction [52], deciding what is implemented into the rule system and what is purely fictional (in Juul's [53] sense of the terms). An important point here is that there is a strong connection between metaphor and meaning-making. As Rusch and Weise explain, "[w]e classify our experiences in terms of complex concepts, so called *multidimensional gestalts*... consist[ing] of a variety of structural elements (dimensions) that have a fairly obvious experiential basis" [42]. This builds from Lakoff and Johnson's position that:

> It is by means of conceptualising our experiences in this manner that we pick out the "impor-tant" aspects of an experience. And by picking out what is "important" in the experience, we can categorize the experience, understand it, and remember it. [51] (quoted in [42])

This suggests that metaphors, when embodied in game mechanics, don't just enable the player to successfully interact with the game or interactive narrative, but also to *make sense* of the experience, focus on the "important" aspects, and internalize these meanings. It also suggests that game designers can make use of the various elements of the game experience, its participants, parts, stages, linear sequence, and purpose [51], when designing a metaphor for use in a game.

However, games traditionally use interface metaphors to provide abstractions of concrete, physical concepts, such as shooting a gun or running. These concrete experiences are then abstracted into interface metaphors, such as pressing a button on a controller to shoot or pushing an analogue stick forward to run. There is a clear mapping [54] between the interface action and the game action. The challenge when trying to represent more abstract concepts, such as LOVE,[1] is figuring out the *experiential* dimension, and how this can be abstracted and translated into the game world, in terms of goals and obstacles. Essentially, the abstract concept needs to first be made concrete before it is again abstracted as a metaphor.

Rusch and Weise suggest that this can be done by recognizing that complex abstract concepts can be considered *experiential gestalts*, and then using these experiential gestalts to structure the concrete goals and obstacles in the game world that correspond to the abstract concept. They provide two examples of games that they claim do this effectively: *Passage* [55], which represents the abstract concept of LOVE and *Ico* [56], which represents COMPANIONSHIP. These games use straightforward interface metaphors to represent an abstract concept. For example, the game *Passage* involves walking through a maze together with your "spouse", and *Ico* gives the player's character a companion whom you need to always be with.

Rusch and Weise argue that it is possible to use more complex, what they call "more visible", multi-modal interface metaphors to expand the range of experiences that can be represented metaphorically. However, this suggests a possible danger in terms of the use of abstraction:

> To avoid breaking the "immersive spell" with interface metaphors that draw attention to themselves, the physical concepts employed tend to be either very simple to begin with or, if they are very complex, they are often so abstracted that they can be conveyed in a simple manner. This strategy may foster immersion, but the drawback is that a lot of meaning potential is lost. [42]

To go beyond this, they argue that using a more complex *experiential metaphor* that draws the connections to the surface and makes them visible, while possibly disrupting immersion, can actually be a powerful way to encourage meaning-making:

> These sense-making processes are largely unconscious. To make games that successfully tackle abstract ideas, it is crucial to make these sense-making processes conscious again, to abstract from the abstract and to make it concrete by finding suitable metaphors that can be enacted by the player. [42]

This can be seen in their discussion of the games *Vanguard* [57], which provides a complex interface for parleying, and *Mr. Mosquito* [58], with its highly sexualized depiction of a mosquito's process of feeding. As the authors suggest, "[h]aving to identify metaphors for everyday experiences to bridge this gap can make the player see the usual from an unusual perspective" [42].

---

[1] Following Rusch and Weise [42], I adopt Lakoff and Johnson's [51] convention of writing concepts represented by a metaphor in capital letters.

The emphasis here, on the use of an unusual perspective and potentially deliberately breaking immersion, is very similar to the process of foregrounding and defamiliarization that I will discuss below, in the context of my notion of poetic gameplay. I will return to this when discussing ways of combining these two approaches in interactive narratives.

3.1.2 Simulation and/versus Metaphor

At this point, it is worth considering the relationship, if any, between other approaches to meaning-making in games and the use of metaphor. Rusch [41] suggests that there are three different "design devices" that can be used to express deeper meanings in games: fictional alignment, procedurality, and experiential metaphors. Device I, *fictional alignment*, is very much the same as the avoidance of ludonarrative dissonance mentioned above. Rusch's device II, *procedurality*, is the notion that a game can "foster reflection and understanding about *how things work*" [41]. This draws on Bogost's procedural rhetoric [59], which involves "enhanc[ing] our understanding of the human condition… by representing the processes inherent in it" [41]. However, as Rusch argues in her analysis of *The Marriage* [60], this approach only works if the player is already aware of what the game is about. In this case, there is a fictional metaphor at work, in the form of the representation of the partners in the marriage as coloured squares, but the metaphor does not extend to the gameplay. This, Rusch suggests, can be compensated for by using an *experiential metaphor* of the type described earlier by Rusch and Weise [42], which Rusch proposes as device III.

Rusch is careful to point out that there is not a clear distinction between devices II and III—in fact, they simply focus on different aspects of the meaning-making process. Device II appeals more to the cognitive understanding of the concepts being represented, whereas device III works at an immediate, emotional level. Rusch suggests that designing for both levels can enhance game comprehension.

The relationship between simulation and metaphor is further explored by Begy [34]. He makes use of Bogost's concept of the "simulation gap" [59, 61], or the "gap between the rule-based representation of a source system and a user's subjectivity" [61] (quoted in [34]) to explain how, in the case of a simulation, the player is given a source system, whereas, in an experiential metaphor, interpretation tends to take place either during play or in later analysis, *without* the nature of the source system being provided ahead of time.[2] This aligns with Rusch's comments regarding her difficulty understanding *The Marriage*, where Rusch struggled to make sense of the game due to her lack of understanding of the details of the source system, other than what was provided by the title of the game.

However, the notion of metaphor as used in game studies has been criticized by Möring [35, 48–50] as being somewhat problematic, particularly in terms of the

---

[2] Note that here the term "source" does not refer to the underlying computer source code of a given simulation. Instead, the "source" system refers to the simulation as experienced by the player, which is intended to represent a given "target" system, e.g., the thing being simulated.

(lack of) distinction between the concepts of simulation and metaphor. He considers this to be what he calls the "simulation/metaphor paradox", referring to how the two concepts seem to come to mean the same thing in many discussions, but that the two terms continue to be used separately. In particular, he uses an analysis of the game *The Marriage* to show how the game is simultaneously a simulation and a metaphor. He contends that Juul [52], Rusch [41], and Bogost [62] see *The Marriage* as a metaphor, whereas Begy [47] sees it as a simulation, and uses his analysis of the game to attempt to clarify the distinction between the two concepts.

Looking back over the use of the term "simulation" in game studies, Möring observes that Frasca sees simulation as high-fidelity and detailed, by which one is able "to model a (source) system through a different system that maintains to someone some of the behaviours of the original system" [63] (in [50]), whereas a metaphor is viewed as abstract and low fidelity. Thus, the difference between simulation and metaphor is one of high versus low fidelity. Möring disputes this, arguing that simulations can be either high or low fidelity, detailed or abstract. Instead, Möring highlights Begy's distinction between games as simulations, where the source system is communicated directly to the player, and games as metaphors, where the player figures out the outside system during play. Möring suggests this makes *The Marriage* a simulation—but of what?

Drawing on the same definition of metaphor as Rusch and Weise [42], Möring contends that most of our understanding of the world is structured through conceptual metaphors, in which "one conceptual domain is understood 'in terms of another conceptual domain'" [51] (quoted in [48]). Conceptual metaphors provide us with a cognitive model for understanding the world. Following from this, Möring argues that conceptual metaphors of love form the basis for the simulation in *The Marriage*. In addition, *The Marriage* realizes the conceptual metaphor at the semiotic (Aarseth) layer, but also at the mechanical and dynamics level. Thus, the game is a *simulation of a metaphor*, and can only be interpreted by drawing on our conceptual model of that concept. However, Möring [35] emphasizes that "the game does not simulate love, and the player does not experience love when playing the game". Instead, the game simulates "the spatial precondition of our metaphorically structured understanding of love".

This discussion seems to imply that, as Rusch suggested, there is an important distinction here, possibly regarding the relationship between experiential metaphors and non-experiential metaphors. Perhaps the important distinction is not in terms of whether a metaphor is a simulation, but rather a question of *what* is being simulated?

When trying to resolve this, Möring suggests that "the notion of simulation should be taken for granted for all computer games, due to their procedural character". Further, he proposes a distinction "between a first-order simulation and a second-order simulation, of which the latter can be considered metaphoric" [48]. He argues that a "self-contained game" refers to itself, e.g., *Space Invaders* [64] is about an alien invasion, represented by the pixels on the screen and the game mechanics of moving the player's turret and shooting at the aliens. If the community interpreting the game has always seen it this way, then it is considered a first-order simulation. However, if the simulation, in this case, *Space Invaders*, instead "associates the conventional object of a symbol with a seemingly unconventional object through a change of context" [48] (such as associating the alien invasion with societal frustration), then it can be seen as a metaphoric simulation, what he refers to as a *second-order simulation.*

Implicit here seems to be a claim that for the player to create new meaning from the experience, there is a need to structure the game mechanics (or the broader game experience) such that the player looks beyond the accepted interpretation of the first-order simulation and instead makes an unconventional association, resulting in a metaphoric (or second order) simulation. Although the game mechanics clearly simulate some source system (the pixels simulate an alien invasion), something about the mechanics or the game experience encourages the player to further interpret this source system as representing something else (the alien invasion represents societal frustration). This is reminiscent of Rusch and Weise's [42] argument that using experiential metaphors in unexpected ways forces the player to work to make sense of the connection between the representation and represented, therefore, encouraging meaning-making and reflection. It also sounds similar to the process of foregrounding and defamiliarization that forms the core of my [36] notion of poetic gameplay.

3.1.3 Other Perspectives on Metaphor and Meaning in Games

At this point, it is worth noting that in psychology there are several competing theories about how people process metaphors that may or may not align with the above discussion, which draws exclusively on Lakoff and Johnson's conceptual metaphor theory (CMT). As summarized by Karzmark [65], deliberate metaphor theory (DMT) distinguishes between a *deliberate* metaphor, where the receiver is made aware that a metaphor is being used, and a *non-deliberate* metaphor, where the receiver is unaware of the use of metaphor [66, 67]. A weaker version of this theory argues that a deliberate metaphor arises in the context of communicative purpose, contested metaphors, and humour [68]. Through an empirical study of player response to the game *Loneliness* [69], Karzmark [65] found that players who were aware of the metaphorical nature of the game showed a significant change in feelings of both loneliness and acceptedness after playing the game, whereas those who were unaware showed little or no change. This suggests that conscious awareness of metaphor may have a role in whether there is an emotional impact on the player. As Karzmark observes, *Loneliness* is an abstract game and can be considered an "artgame", one where the use of metaphor is used to prompt reflection. In this case, it is possible that this reflection may be necessary for the game to have an emotional impact. He suggests that on repeat experience, players may be more likely to view the game mechanics metaphorically. The same may be true for players who are more experienced with this type of game.

Wardrip-Fruin [70] provides another perspective on meaning-making through game mechanics, building from his earlier concept of operational logics [71, 72] and his and Mateas's notion of playable models (first mentioned in [73]). Wardrip-Fruin defines an operational logic as consisting of an abstract process and a communicative role, where "an abstract process is a specification for how a process operates", and "a communicative role describes how the logic is being employed by an author, as part of the larger game system, to communicate something to players" [70]. Playable models "encompass the abstract processes and structuring information that allow the model to operate as well as the types of domains the model is designed to represent and enable play in terms of" [74]. While Wardrip-Fruin suggests that most games make use of conventional operational logics and playable models, there are three approaches that game designers can use to create new meanings from games: alternative approaches, expansive approaches, and inventive approaches. I will briefly discuss expansive and inventive approaches here, as they parallel the approaches to metaphor I have covered above. I will return to alternative approaches in the discussion of poetic gameplay in Sect. 3.2 below.

According to Wardrip-Fruin, expansive approaches "start with an existing logic or model, then seek to add an additional communicative role, one that moves beyond the activities games conventionally make playable through this logic or model" [70]. An example of this approach can be seen in *Papers, Please* [75], where the use of a pattern-matching logic functions in two roles: that of the player's need to engage in informational pattern matching, and the playable character's need to satisfy bureaucratic requirements as a border guard. The deciphering required of the player due to this doubling of meaning is very similar to the sense-making required by an experiential metaphor. In addition, Wardrip-Fruin describes inventive approaches as the use of "one or more operational logics and/or playable models that aren't in the common vocabulary of video games" [70]. An example of this approach can be seen in games that use social models, such as *Prom Week* [76] and *Blood and Laurels* [77]. Again, there is a similarity here with experiential metaphors.

3.1.4 Applying Experiential Metaphors to Interactive Stories

In the context of this chapter, it is important to acknowledge that most of the previous work discussed above, particularly that of Möring and Karzmark, is in the context of abstract games, without an explicit narrative framing. What happens if there is a consistent narrative presented as part of the experience, together with the use of metaphor in the game mechanics? To phrase this differently, what if there was more to the context, in Larsen and Schoenau-Fog's sense of the term, rather than simply abstract shapes as in *The Marriage* and *Loneliness*? Would this narrative context work together with the game mechanics to create meaning? Interestingly, Larsen and Schoenau-Fog do not make any explicit reference to metaphor, although their description of the game *Papers, Please* seems to be drawing both on procedural rhetoric and experiential metaphors. Similarly, Sim [29] analyses several "wordless" games to explore the role of gameplay in conveying the narrative, without direct reference to metaphor. Finally, Dubbelman [9] also presents an analysis of several narrative games, exploring how the game mechanics directly influence the type of story being told, but without any direct use of concepts related to metaphor. However, all these discussions seem to imply that the game mechanics are enabling the player to understand one thing (the narrative) in terms of another (the game mechanics). This suggests that it would be productive to consider how game mechanics as metaphor fits with these various discussions of narrative game mechanics.

Before doing this, I will consider another approach that has been taken to understand the use of game mechanics to create meaning: poetic gameplay.

3.2 Poetic Gameplay

The second approach to making use of game mechanics as a narrative mode that I will discuss draws on my concept of poetic gameplay [3]. This involves undermining the player's expectations for gameplay, to draw attention to the game mechanics and thereby encourage reflection. Whereas looking at game mechanics as metaphors focuses on *what* the mechanics mean, poetic gameplay instead focuses on *how* the mechanics mean.

3.2.1 Defamiliarization and Meaning-Making

When people repeatedly encounter a phenomenon, such as a game mechanic, they tend to become desensitized to that phenomenon, in a process known as automatization. This automatization can be disrupted through a deviation from expectations, what is referred to as foregrounding [78]. In the context of literature, Balint et al. [79] argue that this foregrounding can take the form of deviations, or specific textual features; perceptions, when a recipient perceives these deviations; and experiences, which is the way that a recipient senses the perceived deviation. This process of foregrounding is what Shklovsky [80] describes as defamiliarization, or the undermining of expectations so as to slow down perception and "impart the sensation of things as they are perceived, and not as they are known." From the perspective of cognitive poetics, Tsur describes this delay in perception as resulting from "[s]ystematic disturbance of the categorization process [which] makes low-categorized information, as well as rich pre-categorial sensory information, available to consciousness" [81].

This process of defamiliarization or de-automatization has been connected to meaning-making. Leech and Short [82] argue that it can lead to new awareness and insights. Empirical studies by Fialho [83] and Miall and Kuiken [84] explore the role of defamiliarization in meaning-making. Miall and Kuiken assert that "during an encounter with foregrounded text, the reader may engage in what we have called 'refamiliarization': the reader may review the textual context in order to discern, delimit, or develop the novel meanings suggested by the foregrounded passage". While these studies have focused on literature, there has been work to explore similar experiences in games. My co-authors and I [85] explored player responses to defamiliarization, finding that players did begin to "reflect upon issues beyond their immediate game experience... when the gameplay was made unfamiliar in ways that directly supported the emerging meaning of the game".

3.2.2 Poetic Gameplay Devices

This suggests that, in an interactive narrative, one way to encourage meaning-making and to convey something of the experience of the story through the game mechanics is to make use of defamiliarization, to engage players in the process of refamiliarization and connect this to the context or semiotic layer of the interactive story. Here, I will focus specifically on my notion of poetic gameplay, which I have elsewhere defined as:

> the structuring of the actions the player takes within a game, and the responses the game provides to those actions, in a way that draws attention to the form of the game, and by doing so encourages the player to reflect upon and see that structure in a new way. [36]

I see poetic gameplay as a way to encourage the player to reflect on the structure of the work, and from there see those structures in a new way. While I only hint at the meaning-making potential of this approach, and I do so in the context of artgames [62, 86], rather than interactive narratives, this work was extended by Chew [21, 87] in the context of interactive life stories. Chew argues that in some cases, poetic gameplay doesn't just promote critical appreciation of the form of the work, but also draws the player back into the work, much like the refamiliarization process described by Miall and Kuiken.

My development of poetic gameplay parallels work by Pötzsch [88–90] on the application of Shklovsky's concepts to games. Pötzsch identifies a form of defamiliarization particular to games, which he labels "procedural *ostranenie*". This involves the use of "formal devices to slow down and complicate the acquisition of play skills thereby bringing otherwise internalized frames for interaction with game-worlds to the sudden awareness of players" [88]. There have been numerous uses of defamiliarization and poetic gameplay to critically analyse games. For example, Pötzsch [88] examines *This War of Mine* [91], and drawing from Pötzsch, Gerrish explores the use of defamiliarization in *Nier: Automata* [92]. My co-authors and I [36, 37, 85, 93, 94] have analysed several games and artworks, including *Kentucky Route Zero* [95], *Thirty Flights of Loving* [96], *Save the Date* [97], and *Project December* [98]. Finally, as mentioned above, Chew [21, 87] has explored the use of poetic gameplay in interactive life stories.

The most comprehensive discussion of the various poetic gameplay devices is by my co-authors and I [3], which combines and expands upon my earlier work, and draws from Chew's application of poetic gameplay to interactive life stories, to present a set of 26 poetic gameplay devices, grouped into 5 categories: interaction, gameplay, agency, time, and boundaries. While many of these devices, such as "unfamiliar interface controls" and "game objective is not what it seems", are not specific to games with a strong narrative component, others, such as "non-chronological game sequences" and "repeated refusal of closure", while not requiring that a game have a narrative component, suggest an application to interactive narrative.

As with the discussion of experiential metaphors, there is an interesting parallel here with Wardrip-Fruin's approaches to the use of operational logics and playable models to create meaning in games. I briefly described Wardrip-Fruin's expansive and inventive approaches in Sect. 3.1.3 above. In the third approach described by Wardrip-Fruin, alternative approaches, "models and logics employ the same abstract processes and communicative roles as mainstream uses. However, they employ them in a domain that is novel or unusual and may remove them from common groupings with other logic or models" [70]. An example of this approach can be seen in *Gone Home* [99], with its use of first-person shooter spatial logics and removal of any combat, combined with its initial framing as a horror game and eventual exploration of the playable character's "high school sister's discovery of her queer identity and of the fateful choices made by her and her partner" [70]. This clearly involves defamiliarization of the game mechanics, but also of the genre and type of story players expected of this type of game at the time of its release.

3.2.3 Defamiliarization Beyond Gameplay

It is important to note that undermining a player's expectations for gameplay is not the only way to trigger the process of defamiliarization and refamiliarization. As mentioned earlier, game mechanics work together with other narrative modes as part of the process of meaning-making. As van Vught [100] has suggested, while the poetic gameplay devices described by my co-authors and I [3] are very much ludically focused, other conventions within a game can also be thwarted. Drawing on Thomashevsky's [101] concept of motivations, van Vught proposes that a broader range of devices can be categorized in terms of compositional, realistic, transtextual, artistic, and ludic motivations. The poetic gameplay devices discussed in this chapter fall under the category of ludic motivations. It is worth considering, in future work, the ways in which devices with other motivations can work together with poetic gameplay devices to create meaning in interactive stories.

In the next section, I will discuss ways that both poetic gameplay and game mechanics as metaphors can be harnessed by authors of interactive stories.

4 Telling Interactive Stories Through Game Mechanics

So far, I have laid out two approaches to understanding how game mechanics create meaning: game mechanics as metaphor, and poetic gameplay. Chew [18] argues that although interactivity in general, and gameplay more specifically, cannot create meaning on its own, gameplay works together with other narrative modes to support the overall meaning-making process. This aligns with Larsen and Schoenau-Fog's [15] description of the contribution of game mechanics, together with context, to the creation of narrative meaning, and with Roth et al.'s [11] notion of the double-hermeneutic circles which work at the System and Process layer of an interactive digital narrative. In all these descriptions of narrative meaning-making in interactive narratives, there is a role for the game mechanics, not simply to allow access to additional elements of the narrative, but to themselves be an integral part of that meaning-making process.

To design an interactive narrative in which the game mechanics are actively contributing to the overall narrative meaning, there needs to be some reason for the player to pay attention to the game mechanics while building their mental model of the storyworld. Recalling Rusch and Weise's discussion of complex, experiential metaphors, they suggest that using these types of metaphors can "make these sense-making processes conscious again [and] make the player see the usual from an unusual perspective" [42]. This parallels my definition of poetic gameplay as something that "draws attention to the form of the game, and by doing so encourages the player to reflect upon and see that structure in a new way" [36]. This is also reminiscent of Möring's argument that game objects "become second-order simulations, and therefore, metaphors, when they are associated with an additional referent through a change of context" [48]. Interestingly, this emphasis on the need for there to be something that draws the player's attention either to the relationship between the source and target domain in the case of metaphor, or to the structure of the game mechanics in the case of poetic gameplay, also echoes Karzmark's [65] finding that players of an abstract game were more impacted by the use of metaphor when they were aware of the metaphoric nature of the game.

This suggests that authors of interactive narratives who want to make use of the game mechanics as a narrative mode can make use of two strategies for meaning-making:

1. Think about unusual associations between what they want to describe in the narrative and the way they embody this metaphorically in the game mechanics. This will encourage players to actively engage in a meaning-making process to make sense of the connections suggested by their gameplay experience.
2. Think of ways that they can break the player's expectations for the way that the game mechanics work, to create a sense of defamiliarization. This will trigger the process of foregrounding and refamiliarization, drawing the player's conscious attention to the work and forcing them to put in the effort to connect the poetic gameplay device to the context.

The parallels between these two approaches suggest that they can, and perhaps should, be used in combination such that the unusual nature of the metaphor underlying the game mechanics and the unexpected structure of the game mechanics can work together to help the player attend to both hermeneutic circles (system interaction and narrative), integrating them into a coherent model of the storyworld.

An example of the use of both a complex experiential metaphor and poetic gameplay can be seen in the game *Brothers: a Tale of Two Sons* [102]. The game tells the story of two brothers going on a quest to save their dying father. As described in [29], the player "simultaneously controls both brothers on the same controller, the elder brother [is] controlled using the left joystick and triggers and the younger brother using the right joystick and triggers." Each brother has slightly different strengths and abilities. While games often involve the player controlling more than one character, this is rarely something that happens simultaneously. This simultaneous control comes to represent the interdependence and at the same time the difference between the two brothers, in the form of an interface metaphor. The complex control scheme creates the sort of visible, multi-modal interface metaphor that Rusch and Weise suggest makes visible the relationships being represented. Arguably, this creates what Möring sees as a second-order simulation. At the same time, the use of two joysticks to simultaneously control two slightly different characters violates the player's expectations for a control scheme, creating what my co-authors and I [3] refer to as *unfamiliar interface controls*.

Later in the game, further use is made of the experiential metaphor by first breaking what has by then likely started to become familiar, when the elder brother dies. At this point, the player first discovers that they only need to use one joystick, with the sudden loss of the use of the second joystick mirroring the younger brother's loss of his elder sibling [29, 103]. This can be seen as what my co-authors and I call an *unexpected change of controls*. Later, the player encounters challenges that seem to require both brothers to work together. By asking the player to make use of both joysticks in these moments, the game makes use of the experiential metaphor to mirror the younger brother's ability to draw on his dead brother's strength in his moments of need. In this example, the use of poetic gameplay draws the player's attention to the structure of the interaction. This, coupled with the complex experiential metaphor embodied in the dual controls, encourages the player to focus both on the system interaction and the emerging narrative, drawing together both hermeneutic circles and forming a unified narrative from the gameplay.

From this example, and based on the discussion above, I suggest that authors who intend to make use of game mechanics as an integral part of the narrative meaning-making process in an interactive narrative should consider both the metaphor that connects the game mechanic to the narrative and the ways in which this game mechanic can be structured to create some sense of defamiliarization. This will, in turn, begin the process of foregrounding and refamiliarization, which encourages a deeper narrative meaning-making that draws on both the game mechanics and the narrative context of the interactive narrative.

5   Conclusion

In this chapter, I have explored ways that game mechanics can be used as a narrative mode. Drawing on two different but related approaches to this, game mechanics as metaphor and poetic gameplay, I have argued that authors should consider the game mechanics not as something that simply needs to be carefully designed so as not to conflict with the narrative, but instead as something that actively supports and forms an integral part of the narrative meaning-making process. To do this, I encourage authors to think of suitably complex, multi-modal experiential metaphors that will engage players in meaning-making and signal the metaphorical nature of the game mechanics, and at the same time to consider how the game mechanics themselves can be structured so as to defamiliarize the gameplay and de-automatize the process of narrative meaning-making, so as to help players experience the evolving game narrative in a new way.

References

1. Rohrer J (2008) Gravitation [PC computer game]
2. Chew E, Mitchell A (2016) "As Only a Game Can": re-creating subjective lived experiences through interactivity in non-fictional video games. In: Reinerth MS, Thon JN (eds) Subjectivity across media: interdisciplinary and transmedial perspectives. Routledge, pp 214–232. https://doi.org/10.4324/9781315643625
3. Mitchell A, Kway L, Neo T, Sim YT (2020) A preliminary categorization of techniques for creating poetic gameplay. Game Stud 20
4. Lo P, Thue D, Carstensdottir E (2021) What is a game mechanic? In: International conference on entertainment computing. Springer, pp 336–347
5. Sicart M (2008) Defining game mechanics. Game Stud 8:1–14
6. Mateas M, Stern A (2000) Towards integrating plot and character for interactive drama. In: Socially intelligent agents: the human in the loop, AAAI symposium
7. Nealen A, Saltsman A, Boxerman E (2011) Towards minimalist game design. In: Proceedings of the 6th international conference on foundations of digital games, pp 38–45
8. Aarseth E (2011) Define real, Moron! DIGAREC Series, pp 50–69
9. Dubbelman T (2016) Narrative game mechanics. In: Interactive storytelling. Springer, Cham, pp 39–50. https://doi.org/10.1007/978-3-319-48279-8_4
10. Koenitz H (2015) Towards a specific theory of interactive digital narrative. In: Interactive digital narrative: history, theory and practice. Routledge, pp 91–105
11. Roth C, van Nuenen T, Koenitz H (2018) Ludonarrative hermeneutics: a way out and the narrative paradox. In: International conference on interactive digital storytelling, pp 93–106
12. Herman D (2002) Story logic: problems and possibilities of narrative. University of Nebraska Press
13. Ryan ML (2006) Avatars of story. University of Minnesota Press
14. Ryan M-L (2004) Narrative across media: the languages of storytelling. University of Nebraska Press
15. Larsen BA, Schoenau-Fog H (2016) The narrative quality of game mechanics. In: Interactive storytelling. Springer, Cham, pp 61–72. https://doi.org/10.1007/978-3-319-48279-8_6
16. Frasca G (2003) Simulation versus narrative. In: Wolf MJP, Perron B (eds) The video game theory reader. Routledge, New York, pp 221–235
17. Hunicke R, LeBlanc M, Zubek R (2004) MDA: a formal approach to game design and game research. In: Proceedings of the challenges in game AI workshop, nineteenth national conference on artificial intelligence
18. Chew E, Mitchell A (2016) How is empathy evoked in interactive multimodal life stories? Concentric: Literary Cult Stud 42:125–149. https://doi.org/10.6240/concentric.lit.2016.42.2.08
19. Page R (2009) New perspectives on narrative and multimodality. Routledge
20. Kress G (2009) Multimodality: a social semiotic approach to contemporary communication. Routledge
21. Chew EC, Mitchell A (2020) Bringing art to life: examining poetic gameplay devices in interactive life stories. Games Cult 15:874–901. https://doi.org/10.1177/1555412019853372
22. Dubbelman T (2021) Teaching narrative design. Narrative mechanics: strategies and meanings in games and real life. 82:79
23. Elson M, Breuer J, Ivory JD, Quandt T (2014) More than stories with buttons: narrative, mechanics, and context as determinants of player experience in digital games. J Commun

24. Haahr M (20187) Playing with vision: sight and seeing as narrative and game mechanics in survival horror. In: International conference on interactive digital storytelling. Springer, pp 193–205
25. McGill KM (2018) Narrative game mechanics and interactive fiction. In: International conference on interactive digital storytelling. Springer, pp 289–292
26. Mitchell A, McGee K (2009) Designing storytelling games that encourage narrative play. In: Iurgel I, Zagalo N, Petta P (eds) Interactive storytelling. Springer-Verlag Berlin, Guimaraes, Portugal, pp 98–108. https://doi.org/10.1007/978-3-642-10643-9_14
27. Suter B, Bauer R, Kocher M (2021) Narrative mechanics: strategies and meanings in games and real life. Transcript Verlag
28. Aarseth E (2021) A narrative theory of games. In: Proceedings of the international conference on the foundations of digital Games, pp 129–133
29. Sim YT, Mitchell A (2017) Wordless games: gameplay as narrative technique. In: Nunes N, Oakley I, Nisi V (eds) Interactive storytelling, ICIDS. Springer, Madeira Interact Technologies Inst, Funchal, Portugal, pp 137–149. https://doi.org/10.1007/978-3-319-71027-3_12
30. Magnuson J (2019) Playing and making poetic videogames. eScholarship, University of California
31. Fernández-Vara C (2010) Innovation methods in story-driven games: genre variation
32. Logas H (2011) Meta-rules and complicity in Brenda Brathwaite's train. In: DiGRA conference. Citeseer
33. Toh W (2018) A multimodal approach to video games and the player experience. Routledge
34. Begy J (2013) Experiential metaphors in abstract games. Trans Digital Games Res Assoc 1
35. Möring S (2015) 16 what is a metaphoric artgame? A critical analysis of metaphor in the artgame discourse and in artgames. In: Embodied metaphors in film, television, and video games: cognitive approaches
36. Mitchell A (2016) Making the familiar unfamiliar: techniques for creating poetic gameplay. In: Proceedings of DiGRA/FDG 2016
37. Mitchell A (2014) Defamiliarization and poetic interaction in Kentucky route zero. Well Played: J Video Games, Value Meaning 3:161–178
38. Brathwaite B, Sharp J (2010) The mechanic is the message: a post mortem in progress. In: Ethics and game design: teaching values through play. IGI Global, pp 311–329
39. Extra Credits (2012) Mechanics as metaphor—I: how gameplay itself tells a story—extra credits
40. Extra Credits (2012) Mechanics as metaphor—II: creating narrative depth—extra credits
41. Rusch DC (2009) Mechanisms of the soul-tackling the human condition in videogames
42. Rusch DC, Weise MJ (2008) Games about love and trust? Harnessing the power of metaphors for experience design. In: Proceedings of the 2008 ACM SIGGRAPH symposium on video games, pp 89–97
43. Phelps AM, Rusch DC (2020) Navigating existential, transformative game design. Proceedings of DiGRA 2020
44. Rusch DC, Phelps AM (2020) Existential transformational game design: harnessing the "Psychomagic" of symbolic enactment. Front Psychol 11:3021
45. Rusch DC (2020) Existential, transformative game design. JGSS 2:1–39
46. Rusch DC (2017) Making deep games: designing games with meaning and purpose. Routledge
47. Begy JS (2010) Interpreting abstract games: the metaphorical potential of formal game elements
48. Möring S (2013) The metaphor-simulation paradox in the study of computer games. Int J Gaming Comput Mediated Simul (IJGCMS) 5:48–74
49. Möring S (2013) Games and metaphor–a critical analysis of the metaphor discourse in game studies. IT University of Copenhagen
50. Möring S (2015) Simulated metaphors of love: how the marriage applies metaphors to simulate a love relationship. In: Game love: essays on play and affection, pp 196–215
51. Lakoff G, Johnson M (2008) Metaphors we live by. University of Chicago Press

52. Juul J (2007) A certain level of abstraction. In: Situated play: DiGRA 2007 conference proceedings, pp 510–515
53. Juul J (2005) Half-real: video games between real rules and fictional worlds. MIT press
54. Norman D (2013) The design of everyday things: revised and expanded edition. Basic books
55. Rohrer J (2007) Passage
56. Team Ico (2001) Ico [playstation game]. Sony
57. Sigil Games Online (2007) Vanguard: saga of heroes [PC game]. Sony Online Entertainment
58. Eidos Interactive (2002) Mr. Mosquito [playstation 2 game]. Sony Computer Entertainment
59. Bogost I (2007) Persuasive games. MIT Press, Cambridge, MA
60. Humble R (2007) The marriage [computer game]
61. Bogost I (2006) Unit operations: an approach to videogame criticism. The MIT Press
62. Bogost I (2011) How to do things with videogames. U of Minnesota Press
63. Frasca G (2003) Simulation versus narrative. The video game theory reader, pp 221–235
64. Nishikado T (1978) Space invaders. Taito
65. Karzmark CR (2020) Lonely or just distant? The role of interpretation in the emotional impact of a metaphorical game. https://escholarship.org/uc/item/90b42276
66. Steen G (2008) The paradox of metaphor: why we need a three-dimensional model of metaphor. Metaphor Symb 23:213–241
67. Steen GJ (2008) When is metaphor deliberate. Selected papers from the, pp 43–63
68. Steen G (2017) Deliberate metaphor theory: basic assumptions, main tenets, urgent issues. Intercult Pragmat 14:1–24
69. Magnuson J (2007) Loneliness [computer game]
70. Wardrip-Fruin N (2020) How Pac-Man eats. MIT Press
71. Mateas M, Wardrip-Fruin N (2009) Defining operational logics. In: Conference of the digital games research association-DIGRA
72. Osborn JC, Wardrip-Fruin N, Mateas M (2017) Refining operational logics. In: Proceedings of the 12th international conference on the foundations of digital games. ACM, New York, NY, USA, pp 27:1–27:10. https://doi.org/10.1145/3102071.3102107
73. Scacchi W (2012) The future of research in computer games and virtual world environments. University of California, Irvine, Institute for Software Research
74. Wardrip-Fruin N (2018) Beyond shooting and eating: passage, Dys4ia, and the meanings of collision. Crit Inq 45:137–167. https://doi.org/10.1086/699587
75. Pope L (2013) Papers, please [computer game]
76. The Prom Week Team (2012) Prom week [computer game]. UCSC
77. Short E (2014) Blood and laurels [iPad app]
78. Mukařovský J (2014) Standard language and poetic language. Chapters from the history of Czech functional linguistics
79. Bálint K, Hakemulder F, Kuijpers MM, Doicaru MM, Tan ES (2016) Reconceptualizing foregrounding. Sci Study Liter 6:176–207. https://doi.org/10.1075/ssol.6.2.02bal
80. Shklovsky V (1965) Art as technique. In: Russian formalist criticism: four essays. University of Nebraska Press, Lincoln/London, pp 3–24
81. Tsur R (1992) Towards a theory of cognitive poetics. North Holland Publishing Co
82. Leech GN, Short M (2007) Style in fiction: a linguistic introduction to English fictional prose. Pearson Education
83. da Fialho OC (2007) Foregrounding and refamiliarization: understanding readers' response to literary texts. Lang Lit 105–123. https://doi.org/10.1177/0963947007075979
84. Miall DS, Kuiken D (1994) Foregrounding, defamiliarization, and affect: response to literary stories. Poetics 22:389–407. https://doi.org/10.1016/0304-422X(94)00011-5
85. Mitchell A, Sim YT, Kway L (2017) Making it unfamiliar in the "Right" way: an empirical study of poetic gameplay. In: DiGRA 2017. Melbourne, Australia
86. Sharp J (2015) Works of game: on the aesthetics of games and art. MIT Press
87. Chew E (2018) How can I tell you what I felt? Conveying subjective experience in computer-mediated interactive life stories

88. Pötzsch H (2019) From a new seeing to a new acting: Viktor Shklovsky's ostranenie and analyses of games and play. In: Viktor Shklovsky's heritage in literature, arts, and philosophy. Lexington Books, pp 235–251
89. Pötzsch H (2017) Playing games with Shklovsky, Brecht, and Boal: Ostranenie, v-effect, and spect-actors as analytical tools for game studies. Game Stud 17
90. Pötzsch H (2016) Constraining play: steps toward a neo-formalist game analysis. In: WAR/GAME: extending perspectives. Charles University, Prague, 1 June 2016. Available at: http://wargameuit.wikidot.com/constraining-play-neo-formalist-game-analysis. Accessed 18 Dec 2017
91. 11 Bit Studios (2014) This war of mine [computer game]. 11 Bit Studios
92. Taro Y (2017) Nier: automata [playstation 4 game]. Square Enix
93. Mitchell A (2018) Antimimetic rereading and defamiliarization in save the date. In: DiGRA '18—proceedings of the 2018 DiGRA international conference. Turin, Italy
94. Mitchell A (2022) Repetition and defamiliarization in AI dungeon and project December. EBR
95. Cardboard Computer (2013) Kentucky Route Zero [PC computer game]
96. Blendo Games (2012) Thirty flights of loving [PC computer game]
97. Paper Dino Software (2013) Save the date [PC computer game]
98. Rohrer J (2020) Project December [conversational AI]
99. Gaynor S (2013) Gone home [computer game]. Fullbright
100. Van Vught J (2021) What is videogame formalism? Exploring the pillars of Russian formalism for the study of videogames. Games Cult. https://doi.org/10.1177/15554120211027475
101. Tomashevsky B (1965) Thematics. In: Russian formalist criticism: four essays. University of Nebraska Press, Lincoln/London, pp 61–95
102. Starbreeze Studios (2013) Brothers—a tale of two sons [Xbox 360 Game]
103. May A, Bizzocchi J, Antle AN, Choo A (2014) Fraternal feelings: how brothers: a tale of two sons affects players through gameplay. In: 2014 IEEE games media entertainment, pp 1–4. https://doi.org/10.1109/GEM.2014.7048074

Working with Intelligent Narrative Technologies

David Thue

Abstract Artificial Intelligence systems have been used to generate narrative structures and simulate virtual story characters at a variety of different scales, across both academia and industry. Such systems are often built from specialized components known as intelligent narrative technologies. The goal of this chapter is to highlight some of the challenges that can arise when such technologies are used as part of authoring or executing an interactive story. Authoring in a way that works with these technologies often requires a host of technical skills, such as writing computer code, building mathematical models, or predicting the effect of a simple change on a large, complex system. In addition to explaining why these skills are needed and the problems that they help to solve, this chapter will highlight recent and ongoing efforts to make authoring for intelligent narrative technologies more accessible to those with fewer technical skills.

1 Intelligent Narrative Technologies

The phrase "intelligent narrative technologies" can have (at least) three meanings. One is that it describes a field of research, which studies how the techniques used by Artificial Intelligence (AI) systems can be applied in the context of narrative. While there are examples of such research from the early 1960s [1], it became more widespread in the 1990s [2–6] and continues actively to this day. Mateas and Sengers offer a detailed account of the early years of this research field in the first chapter of their book [7].

The second meaning of "intelligent narrative technologies" is that it is the name of a series of academic events, which began in 2007 [8] and was held most recently in 2020 [9]. In total, these events included two research symposia [8, 10], several workshops co-located with three academic research conferences [9, 11–18], and a special track at the International Conference on Interactive Digital Storytelling [19].

D. Thue (✉)
RISE Research Group, School of Information Technology, Carleton University, Ottawa, Canada
e-mail: david.thue@carleton.ca

Department of Computer Science, Reykjavik University, Reykjavik, Iceland

C. Hargood et al. (eds.), *The Authoring Problem*, Human–Computer Interaction Series,
https://doi.org/10.1007/978-3-031-05214-9_17

For the past 15 years, these events have been a common home for early-stage research done in the field of intelligent narrative technologies. A related series of events featured a recurring workshop on Computational Models of Narrative [20–26].

The third meaning of the phrase is more pragmatic, and it is the one that we focus on in this chapter: *intelligent narrative technologies* (INTs) are technologies that apply AI techniques in the context of narrative. They are the focus and products of the research done in the field of INT, and the primary topic of the papers that are published via the INT series of events.

What does it mean, then, to apply AI techniques in the context of narrative? Fundamentally, AI techniques can be applied to make decisions in an automated way, and working in narrative means making decisions in that context. In Interactive Digital Narrative (IDN), many decisions have been made using AI techniques, and these decisions have centered primarily on the potential *products* of an IDN system [27]. They answer questions that include (but are not limited to):

- *What characters and objects should exist in the narrative world?*
- *What should happen next in the story?*
- *What should this character do next?*
- *How should this character perform its next action or line of dialogue?*
- *How should the system respond to the player's last action?*

The methods that have been used to answer these questions are many and varied, and citations to works that explain some of them will appear throughout this chapter. The focus of this chapter, however, is different: rather than explain how a collection of INTs work, it aims to equip IDN authors with general strategies that might help them work more effectively with intelligent narrative technologies.

1.1 Authoring with a Narrative AI System

For the purposes of this chapter, we consider *authoring* to be a process of making and acting upon decisions about how some elements of a narrative (or perhaps many possible narratives) should be. This could involve creating characters, locales, key props, storyboards, and more. Furthermore, we consider a *narrative AI system* as a structured collection of one or more intelligent narrative technologies, each of which might apply different AI techniques; the system accepts one or more inputs (some provided by authors in advance, others provided by players at run-time) and produces one or more outputs using the technology therein. For example, the AI-driven "drama manager" in *Façade* [28] accepts inputs including (i) a collection of dramatic beats (bundles of narrative content), (ii) an estimate of the story's current level of dramatic tension, and (iii) an authored trajectory of dramatic tension over time [29]. Given these inputs, it uses an optimization technique to identify a particular dramatic beat from the collection as its output: the one that best matches the next author-desired level of tension in the story.

It is common to say that an AI system "decides" which output(s) it should produce as it operates. Since authoring is about making and acting upon decisions, we say that an authoring process can *include* a narrative AI system; in such cases, the decisions that are made during authoring will be shared between the author(s) and the system. From an author's perspective, it can thus be useful to understand what drives a narrative AI system's decisions, along with how those decisions can be influenced. To build such an understanding, an author can pursue answers to the following key questions. We discuss strategies for tackling these questions as the core content of this chapter.

- How does the AI system behave?
- How can I influence the AI system's behaviour?

  - How can I determine the AI system's inputs?
  - What of the AI system itself can I change?
  - How can I refine or repurpose the AI system's outputs?

2   Understanding the Behaviour of a Narrative AI System

What can an author do to understand how a narrative AI system behaves? Following some suggestions for initial preparation, we discuss two types of strategy: experimentation and examination.

2.1   Preparation: Understand the IDN System

Fundamentally, every IDN system requires a *protostory* [27], which represents what exists in the narrative world, the properties of those objects, and how they can change during a player's experience—either in response to player input or due to the passage of time. Narrative AI systems act upon this protostory, either by helping to define its elements before any player's experience begins or by steering how the narrative world changes as each experience unfolds. When attempting to understand a narrative AI system, it can therefore help to first learn about the IDN system's protostory. Given this knowledge, the author can approach the AI system by first assessing which parts of the protostory the AI system is used to determine or change, and then applying the strategies in Sects. 2.2 and 2.3 to learn about each part. An example that explains *Façade*'s protostory and how *Façade*'s drama manager changes it can be found in prior work [27], and we will revisit it before the end of this section.

In addition to understanding how a narrative AI system might affect an IDN system's protostory, it can be helpful to know how a player's actions might affect the AI

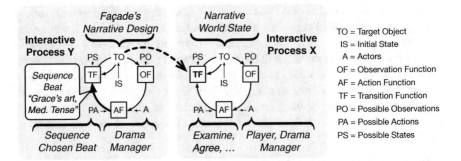

Fig. 1 A partial interactive process model [30] for *Façade* [28], where both the player and *Façade*'s drama manager are modelled as agents. Each interactive process models how a particular Target Object (TO) can be changed by the Actors (A) that participate in that process. Actors execute the Action Functions (AF) to perform specific actions, and the IDN system executes the Transition Functions (TF) and the Observation Functions (OF) to produce, respectively, new states of each Target Object and new specific observations for each actor to observe. For a complete presentation of Interactive Process Modelling, see Chap. 'Getting Creative with Actions'

system. A method for understanding player actions in IDN systems (Interactive Process Modelling) is presented in Chap. 'Getting Creative with Actions'. By building an interactive process model for the IDN system that treats both players and narrative AI systems as agents, an author can visualize and reason about how a player's actions might influence the behaviour of a narrative AI system. Figure 1 shows an example of such a visualization for *Façade*.

The player performs actions via the action function (AF) in Interactive Process (IP) X, such as examining an object or agreeing or disagreeing with characters Grace or Trip. As they do so, the state of the narrative world changes and the result can be observed by both themselves and the drama manager (via the observation function, OF, in IP X). Meanwhile in IP Y, the drama manager is able to use what it previously observed in IP X to inform how it chooses which dramatic beat should occur next. By executing IP Y's action function (AF) to make this choice, it alters *Façade*'s narrative design, which is the part of the protostory that represents how the world changes during player experiences. *Façade*'s narrative design is both the target object (TO) of IP Y and the transition function (TF) of IP X, as shown by the figure's *target object link* (dashed arrow). This link models how the manager's action to sequence a subsequent dramatic beat (which happens in IP Y) ultimately affects what beat occurs next in IP X, as the player's experience in IP X proceeds.

By understanding a player's ability to influence a narrative AI system, authors can be better equipped to anticipate the effects that player interaction might have on their uses of that system.

2.2 Experimenting with a Narrative AI System

The first method for system-learning that we consider is experimentation. This method of learning requires having access to the narrative AI system in a way that lets the author trigger and observe the results of system decisions under a variety of different circumstances. This might involve using support tools created by the system's developers. For example, *Sentient Sketchbook* allowed authors to see examples of the maps that it could generate and tune parameters that affected how they were generated [31], while *Mimisbrunnur* allowed authors to view potential sequences of narrative action that could occur during gameplay, given the content and constraints that the author had created [32]. Experimentation might also involve playtesting an IDN process that the narrative AI system influences, to bring the narrative world state into particular situations and observe how the AI system reacts. For example, much can be learned about *Façade*'s drama manager [33] by playing *Façade* and observing how the AI system behaves [28].

In general, an author can produce different circumstances for a narrative AI system by modifying the system's inputs. Depending on what INTs the system uses, these inputs might include collections of various kinds of content, or parameters or utilities. We consider some examples of each.

2.2.1 Collections of Content as System Inputs

It is quite common for a narrative AI system to require one or more collections of content among its inputs, and the types of required content can vary widely across different systems.

As one example, several narrative AI systems that produce natural language text (*e.g.*, for character dialogue) require large collections of text to be provided as inputs; such collections might include film scripts, blog posts, news articles, and more. At a high level, such systems contain one or more INTs that perform natural language generation—they use the provided collections of text to build a general model of how people tend to write sentences and paragraphs in a given context (*e.g.*, in Science Fiction movie scripts), and then use the model to predict the words of new sentences and paragraphs. A compelling IDN system that uses this sort of technology is *AI Dungeon* [34].

Collections of images or 3D models are common inputs to narrative AI systems—particularly for those that are embedded in video games and generate some of their game's content. Procedural Content Generation (PCG) describes a process of automatically creating content (typically to be used in a game). When applied to narrative contexts, PCG methods become INTs, as they are used to make decisions about how narratively-important content should be. Examples include the generation of non-player characters (including their appearance and attributes) [35], towns [36], and more. Two compelling IDN systems that use PCG to create narrative content are *Dwarf Fortress* [37] and *RimWorld* [38].

A frequently studied subtopic of INT research is Narrative Planning [39], which uses automatic, logical reasoning to find plans of action for story characters that satisfy goals given by an author. To form such plans, the narrative planner (which is a narrative AI system) requires a collection of potential actions for characters to perform, plus a collection of characters and other entities (*e.g.*, props and locations) whose attributes can be changed by the given actions. For example, the authoring tool *Mimisbrunnur* allowed authors to create collections of actions and entities, and then preview examples of how a narrative planner might use those actions to achieve different story goals [32].

By adjusting the collections that a narrative AI system receives in its inputs, an author can put the system in different circumstances and observe how it behaves therein.

2.2.2 Parameters and Utilities as System Inputs

Many narrative AI systems have *parameters*—variables that are meant to be adjusted (sometimes by players, sometimes by designers) to alter its behaviour. For example, at the beginning of a game of *RimWorld*, players are able to set a variety of parameters that control how the game's narrative AI system will behave [38]. The system generates notable events from a library of templates (*e.g.*, attacks by hostile creatures or extreme weather), and the parameters affect various aspects of how those events get generated (*e.g.*, their frequency or severity).

One weakness of parameters is that they each remain fixed at their given value, regardless of what might happen while the system is operating. When it is important for a variable's value to change in response to changing circumstances, a narrative AI system might require an input that helps it compute new values for that variable. This sort of input can be well thought of as a *utility*—something that allows new values of a variable to be calculated given other values (*e.g.*, of other variables, or of attributes of entities in the narrative world). For example, the drama manager in *Façade* [28] required a designer-provided utility that does the following: It starts by considering the history of the story's events thus far, and retrieves estimates of how each event should have contributed to the story's dramatic tension. Then, by adding these contributions together, the utility produces an estimate of the *current* state of dramatic tension in the story. This utility is used regularly during gameplay to estimate the story's current tension level [29].

In *RimWorld*, players can choose between three "AI storytellers" [38], each of which activates a separate collection of parameter values and utilities that were specified by the game's designers. In particular, each collection has a utility to measure the player's level of success (*e.g.*, based on their accumulated wealth in-game) as well as a utility to determine how soon the next dangerous event should occur, given the player's current level of success.

2.2.3 Understanding versus Complexity

The goal of experimenting with a narrative AI system is for the author to build a useful understanding of how that system behaves. The degree to which such experimentation is effective, however, depends on the complexity of the INTs that are used in the AI system and the amount of precision the author needs. For example, the INTs used by *AI Dungeon* [34] are *transformer neural networks*, which are models of English language usage that come from an enormous corpus of written text [40]. These models are capable of generating coherent English prose, but their internal workings are so complex (with millions to billions of parameters) that understanding them perfectly is all but impossible. Nevertheless, a large community of users has gained a sufficient understanding of *AI Dungeon* to author their own narrative scenarios [41]. Given the generative nature of *AI Dungeon* experiences, even an imprecise understanding of its models can allow authors to set up interesting player experiences.

2.3 Examining a Narrative AI System

Beyond observing a narrative AI system to gain an impression of how it behaves, authors who are more technically inclined may be able to examine the system itself, toward learning how its internal mechanisms lead it to behave in different ways. Such an examination might involve reading publications or other technical documents, or reading the program code that executes while the system operates.

When a narrative AI system is described across multiple publications of different types and lengths, it can be challenging to know where to start. Research papers published at academic workshops or conferences, as well as white papers and blog posts written by developers, typically contain high level explanations in a relatively compact presentation. These works can be useful for identifying the required inputs of a given system, but many also contain a concise description of how the system works, either through figures, pseudocode, or both. Writing in pseudocode allows a system developer to express the key steps of the system's program code in a way that is more readable than the program code itself, and pseudocode should ideally be understandable even with only a limited knowledge of computer programming.

As an example, Algorithm 1 shows pseudocode that explains the operation of a kind of narrative AI system called a *player-specific experience manager*[1] [43]. The inputs and expected output are stated at the top. On Line 1, a current model of the player (*e.g.*, representing their preferences) is updated based on the current narrative world state and the player's most recent action. On Lines 2 to 7, the set of possible adaptations is searched, element by element, while estimating how well each possible adaptation matches with the current player model (Line 4). Each time a better match is found, it is set as the next adaptation that should be performed to adapt the current

---

[1] The term *experience manager* is due to Riedl et al. [42], and refers to an AI system that attempts to modify the course of a player's experience as it proceeds.

Algorithm 1: Pseudocode showing the high-level operation of a narrative AI system that adapts a story using a learned player model. Italics show variables and upright text shows utilities that compute useful values. The notation '$x \leftarrow y$' means 'x gets set to the value of y'.

Inputs : *narrativeWorldState*: the current state of the narrative world
playerAction: the most recent action that the player performed
currentPlayerModel: prior information learned about the player
possibleAdaptations: a collection of ways to adapt the current story
Outputs: *nextAdaptation*: the adaptation that best matches with the player model

1 *currentPlayerModel* ←
  GetUpdatedPlayerModel(*currentPlayerModel*, *narrativeWorldState*, *playerAction*)
2 *bestMatchQuality* ← 0
3 **for** each *adaptation* in *possibleAdaptations* **do**
4 | *matchQuality* ← EstimateMatchQuality(*adaptation*, *currentPlayerModel*)
5 | **if** *matchQuality* > *bestMatchQuality* **then**
6 | | *bestMatchQuality* ← *matchQuality*
7 | | *nextAdaptation* ← *adaptation*
8 |
9 **return** *nextAdaptation*

---

story (Line 7). The result is that the adaptation that matches the player model the best is the one that will be output. Although this example has been simplified for the sake of introducing the concept (notably by avoiding most mathematical notation), it nonetheless demonstrates the rough character of how pseudocode is presented in technical writing about narrative AI systems.

For authors who have the needed technical background to understand program code directly, some narrative AI systems can be understood in depth by requesting the code from its authors or by finding it in a public repository online. A recent example is *Imaginarium* [44], a casual tool for generating narrative content (*e.g.*, characters or objects) whose source code was made available online [45].

Given the ability to read its pseudocode or program code, an author can directly examine the operation of a narrative AI system, and use what they discover to understand the system's general behaviour.

3 Ways to Influence a Narrative AI System

Once an author has come to understand how a narrative AI system might behave, their attention might turn to the question of how they can make it behave *differently*. In this section, we consider the remainder of the questions that we asked in Sect. 1.1, including how an author might determine the inputs of a narrative AI system, how they might alter the system itself, and how they might refine or repurpose what the system produces as output.

3.1 Determining the System's Inputs

As we discussed in Sect. 2.2, it is often possible for an author to change various inputs of a narrative AI system. Indeed, the majority of the inputs of many narrative AI systems are expected to be authored by one or more people. For example, *RimWorld*'s world generator (another narrative AI system) can generate an entire unique planet, including terrain, biomes, creatures, settlements, and inhabitants. From a player's perspective, it seems to generate all of this from very little: a single starting seed (a random string of characters) and a handful of generation parameters. In reality, the world generator works by cleverly combining many collections of pre-authored content, including trees, boulders, creatures, building materials, props, character attributes, character appearances, and more. The starting seed and generation parameters matter, but the pre-authored content provides the bulk of the resources that are used while the generator works. As a result, one way to influence how *RimWorld*'s world generator behaves could be to modify one or more of these collections of content, all of which the generator uses as inputs. Other ways include changing either the starting seed or the generation parameters.

An important difference can be seen between these methods of exerting influence: some are more *controllable* than others, in that the outcome of any change is easier to predict and thus easier to use in intentional ways. While the effects of replacing a boulder in the pre-authored content seems relatively easy to predict and thus more straightforward to control, the effects of changing a starting seed are nearly impossible to predict. This makes the seed value more challenging to use when pursuing particular authorial aims.

Beyond parameters and collections of content, it is also often expected that the utilities that are required by a narrative AI system will be authored by one or more people. For example, the trajectory of dramatic tension over time that *Façade*'s drama manager requires is explained as being provided by an author [28, 33]. Utilities offer a way to influence the way that a narrative AI system will behave, because they are often used by such systems to (i) differentiate between potential alternatives and (ii) infer useful meaning from the narrative world state. *Façade*'s desired tension trajectory is an example of the former, while its method for estimating the story's *current* level of dramatic tension is an example of the latter.

In player-specific experience management (recall Algorithm 1), one or more utilities are used to estimate a player model [43, 46–48]. A *player model* is a mathematical representation of some aspect of a player; this might represent their personality, their knowledge of the story, their preferences over different types of content, their expected emotional reactions, or more. By defining the dimensions of a player model and creating a utility to estimate each of them, an author can influence how the experience manager makes its decisions.

3.2   Altering the System

If an author can gain access to the program code that defines how a narrative AI system works, they might be able to change it to make it work in a different way. In one example, Riedl & Stern took the *ABL* behaviour specification language that was created for *Façade* [28, 49] and combined it with an experience manager based on Narrative Planning called the *Automated Story Director* [50]. Later, Ramirez and Bulitko obtained the source code to the *Automated Story Director* and adapted it to add a player model based on Thue et al.'s *PaSSAGE* [46], creating a player-specific experience manager called *PAST* [51, 52].

Notably, all of the prior works are examples of technically-savvy people acting both as the developers of narrative AI systems *and* as the authors of the IDNs that included those systems. While positive examples exist of diversely skilled teams creating compelling IDNs that rely on narrative AI systems (including *Prom Week* [35, 53], *The Ice-Bound Concordance* [54, 55], *Blood & Laurels* [56, 57], *Nothing for Dinner* [58, 59], and more), finding a way to make system modification more widely accessible to authors remains an open research problem.

With *Mimisbrunnur*, authors were able to preview outputs of its narrative planner and, if desired, mark any outputted plan of action as an unacceptable solution [32][2]. From that point forward, the system would remember and abide by that decision, never showing the marked solution again. While simple in this application, adding a similar capacity for incremental modification to future narrative AI systems might allow authors to alter their operation in a more accessible way.

3.3   Refining or Repurposing a System's Outputs

Throughout this chapter, we have considered authoring as a process of making and acting upon decisions in a narrative context. While narrative AI systems have been used to make a variety of authoring decisions, the task of acting upon those decisions (*e.g.*, making the next dramatic beat actually happen in *Façade*) it is typically left to other parts of the IDN system. This interface that exists between the narrative AI system's output and the remainder of the IDN system presents the last opportunity for an author to influence the decisions that the narrative AI system makes: if each decision can be intercepted and revised or repurposed as desired, the author can gain the benefit of the AI system's operation while still influencing its results. The mode in which an author can do this sort of refinement or repurposing depends on the timing of the narrative AI system's decisions, relative to any player's experience of the larger IDN system's product.

For AI system decisions that are made *before* any player's experience (*e.g.*, to generate a backstory for a character that every player will encounter), choosing

---

[2] Both *PaSSAGE* [46] and *Mimisbrunnur* [32] are the result of collaborations between this chapter's author and others.

among several of the system's outputs by hand can be a viable option—provided that the system can generate outputs quickly enough to be useful. In this mode of refinement, the system's output serves a starting point for the author's subsequent creative process. When the size of the set of possible outputs is very large, a degree of automation can help. *Story sifting* [60, 61] is a process of searching through a generated sequence of events and identifying subsequences that are salient in some way, and this is typically done on the basis of flexible patterns that one or more authors specify to guide the search.

When AI system decisions are made *during* any player's experience, a more nimble approach is required. For example, given an interactive narrative AI system that simulated the social interactions of several story characters, an author might create one or more utilities that attempt to recognize certain patterns of happenings (*e.g.*, those that involve one character betraying another) and bring the matches to the player's attention. This process is called *incremental story sifting* [62], and it represents some of the newest work in this direction. More about story sifting can be learned in Chap. 'Authoring for Story Sifters'.

4 Summary

From an author's perspective, intelligent narrative technologies are the elements of narrative AI systems, and these systems can share in the task of authoring IDN systems and products. When working with a narrative AI system, it can benefit an author to understand both how the system behaves and what they might do to influence its behaviour. This behaviour can be understood by either experimenting with the system to observe it under different circumstances, or examining its pseudocode or program code to learn about how it works. Meanwhile, an author's opportunities to influence a narrative AI system's decisions come in three forms. First, they can determine its inputs, either by building the collections of content that it uses, setting its parameters, or defining the utilities that it uses as a part of its operation. Second, they can modify how the system itself works by altering its program code, though this avenue presently lacks accessibility for non-technical authors. Third, they can refine or repurpose the output that the AI system produces, potentially by specifying patterns that identify outputs that are of particularly high value. By understanding how a narrative AI system behaves and what they can do to make it better, authors can benefit from the generative capabilities of AI systems while still pursuing the stories they wish to tell.

Acknowledgements The author acknowledges the support of the Natural Sciences and Engineering Research Council of Canada (NSERC), Grant #2020-06502.

References

1. Ryan J (2017) Grimes' fairy tales: a 1960s story generator. In: Nunes N, Oakley I, Nisi V (eds) Interactive storytelling. Springer International Publishing, Cham, pp 89–103
2. Bates J (1992) Virtual reality, art, and entertainment. Presence: J Teleoper Virtual Environ 1(1):133–138
3. Kelso MT, Weyhrauch P, Bates J (1993) Dramatic presence. Presence: J Teleoper Virtual Environ 2(1):1–16
4. Weyhrauch P (1997) Guiding interactive drama. PhD thesis, School of Computer Science, Carnegie Mellon University, Pittsburgh, PA
5. Mateas M (1997) An OZ-centric review of interactive drama and believable agents. Carnegie Mellon University
6. Mateas M, Sengers P (eds) (1999) Narrative intelligence—papers from the 1999 fall symposium, vol FS-99-01. AAAI Press
7. Mateas M, Sengers P (eds) (2003) Narrative intelligence. John Benjamins. https://www.jbe-platform.com/content/books/9789027297068
8. Magerko BS, Riedl MO (eds) (2007) Intelligent narrative technologies—papers from the 2007 AAAI fall symposium. AAAI Press
9. Osborn JC (ed) (2020) Joint proceedings of the AIIDE 2020 workshops, co-located. In: CEUR workshop proceedings on 16th AAAI conference on artificial intelligence and interactive digital entertainment (AIIDE 2020), vol 2862. http://ceur-ws.org/Vol-2862/
10. Louchart S, Mehta M, Roberts DL (eds) (2009) Intelligent narrative technologies II—papers from the 2009 AAAI spring symposium, vol SS-09-06. AAAI Press
11. Bahamón J, Fassone R, Mawhorter P, Poulakos S, Robertson J, Ryan J (eds) (2017) Intelligent narrative technologies—papers from the 2017 AIIDE workshop, vol WS-17-20. AAAI Press
12. Barot C, Li B, Rowe J, Tomai E (eds) (2015) Intelligent narrative technologies and social believability in games: papers from the 2015 AIIDE workshop, vol WS-15-22. AAAI Press
13. Cavazza M, Si M, Zook A (eds) (2013) Intelligent narrative technologies: papers from the 2013 AIIDE workshop, vol WS-13-21. AAAI Press
14. Jhala A, Riedl M, Roberts DL (eds) (2010) INT3'10: proceedings of the intelligent narrative technologies III workshop. Association for Computing Machinery, New York, NY, USA
15. Tomai E, Elson D, Rowe J (eds) (2011) Intelligent narrative technologies IV—papers from the 2011 AIIDE workshop, vol WS-11-18. AAAI Press
16. Ware SG, Zhu J, Hodhod R (eds) (2012) Intelligent narrative technologies—papers from the 2012 AIIDE workshop, vol WS-12-14. AAAI Press
17. Wu HY, Si M, Jhala A (eds) (2018) Proceedings of the joint workshop on intelligent narrative technologies and workshop on intelligent cinematography and editing co-located. In: CEUR workshop proceedings on 14th AAAI conference on artificial intelligence and interactive digital entertainment (AIIDE 2018), vol 2321
18. Zhu J, Horswill I, Wardrip-Fruin N (eds) (2014) intelligent narrative technologies 7—papers from the 2014 workshop, vol WS-14-21. AAAI Press
19. Nack F, Gordon AS (eds) (2016) Interactive storytelling. In: 9th international conference on interactive digital storytelling (ICIDS 2016), LNCS, vol 10045. Springer, Cham
20. Finlayson MA, Richards W, Winston PH (2010) Computational models of narrative: review of a workshop. AI Mag 31(2):97. http://orcid.org/10.1609/aimag.v31i2.2295, https://ojs.aaai.org/index.php/aimagazine/article/view/2295
21. Finlayson MA (ed) (2010) Computational models of narrative—papers from the 2010 AAAI fall symposium, vol FS-10-04. AAAI Press
22. Finlayson MA (ed) (2012) The third workshop on computational models of narrative (CMN'12). http://narrative.csail.mit.edu
23. Finlayson MA, Fisseni B, Löwe B, Meister JC (eds) (2013) 2013 workshop on computational models of narrative (CMN 2013), vol 32. OASICS
24. Finlayson MA, Meister JC, Bruneau EG (eds) (2014) 2014 workshop on computational models of narrative (CMN 2014), vol 41. OASICS

25. Finlayson MA, Miller B, Lieto A, Ronfard R (eds) (2015) 6th workshop on computational models of narrative (CMN 2015), vol 45. OASICS
26. Miller B, Lieto A, Ronfard R, Ware SG, Finlayson MA (eds) (2016) 7th workshop on computational models of narrative (CMN 2016), vol 53. OASICS
27. Koenitz H (2010) Towards a theoretical framework for interactive digital narrative. In: Aylett R, Lim MY, Louchart S, Petta P, Riedl M (eds) Interactive storytelling. Springer, Berlin, Heidelberg, pp 176–185
28. Mateas M, Stern A (2007) Façade. http://www.interactivestory.net/
29. Mateas M (2002) Interactive drama, art, and artificial intelligence. PhD thesis, Carnegie Mellon University
30. Thue D (2020) What might an action do? toward a grounded view of actions in interactive storytelling. In: Proceedings of the 13th international conference on interactive digital storytelling (ICIDS'20), LNCS, vol 12497. Springer, Cham, pp 212–220. https://rise.csit.carleton.ca/pubs/Thue_ICIDS_2020.pdf
31. Liapis A, Yannakakis GN, Togelius J (2013) Sentient sketchbook: computer-aided game level authoring. In: Proceedings of the 8th international conference on foundations of digital games, society for the advancement of the science of digital games, pp 213–220
32. Stefnisson I, Thue D (2018) Mimisbrunnur: AI-assisted authoring for interactive storytelling. In: Proceedings of the 14th AAAI conference on artificial intelligence and interactive digital entertainment, AAAI Press, pp 236–242. https://aaai.org/ocs/index.php/AIIDE/AIIDE18/paper/view/18116/17248
33. Mateas M, Stern A (2005) Structuring content in the Façade interactive drama architecture. In: Proceedings of the AAAI conference on artificial intelligence and interactive digital entertainment, AAAI Press, pp 93–98, https://ojs.aaai.org/index.php/AIIDE/article/view/18722
34. Latitude (2019) AI dungeon. https://play.aidungeon.io/
35. McCoy J, Treanor M, Samuel B, Reed AA, Mateas M, Fruin NW (2012) Prom week. https://promweek.soe.ucsc.edu/
36. Salge C, Green MC, Canaan R, Togelius J (2018) Generative design in minecraft (GDMC): settlement generation competition. In: Proceedings of the 13th international conference on the foundations of digital games, FDG'18. Association for Computing Machinery, New York, NY, USA. https://doi.org/10.1145/3235765.3235814, https://doi.org/10.1145/3235765.3235814
37. Bay 12 Games (2006–2021) Dwarf fortress. http://www.bay12games.com/dwarves/
38. Ludeon Studios (2013) Rimworld. https://rimworldgame.com
39. Riedl MO, Young RM (2010) Narrative planning: balancing plot and character. J Artif Intell Res 39:217–268
40. Brown T, Mann B, Ryder N, Subbiah M, Kaplan JD, Dhariwal P, Neelakantan A, Shyam P, Sastry G, Askell A, Agarwal S, Herbert-Voss A, Krueger G, Henighan T, Child R, Ramesh A, Ziegler D, Wu J, Winter C, Hesse C, Chen M, Sigler E, Litwin M, Gray S, Chess B, Clark J, Berner C, McCandlish S, Radford A, Sutskever I, Amodei D (2020) Language models are few-shot learners. In: Larochelle H, Ranzato M, Hadsell R, Balcan MF, Lin H (eds) Advances in neural information processing systems. Curran Associates, Inc., vol 33, pp 1877–1901
41. Author Unknown (2020). https://prompts.aidg.club/
42. Riedl MO, Stern A, Dini D, Alderman J (2008) Dynamic experience management in virtual worlds for entertainment, education, and training. Int Trans Syst Sci Appl Spec Issue Agent Based Syst Hum Learn 4(2):23–42
43. Thue D (2015) Generalized experience management. PhD thesis, University of Alberta, Canada
44. Horswill I (2020) A declarative PCG tool for casual users. In: Proceedings of the AAAI conference on artificial intelligence and interactive digital entertainment, vol 16. AAAI Press, pp 81–87
45. Horswill ID, Robison E (2022) Imaginarium—January 2022 release. https://github.com/ianhorswill/Imaginarium
46. Thue D, Bulitko V, Spetch M, Wasylishen E (2007) Interactive storytelling: a player modelling approach. In: 3rd AI and interactive digital entertainment conference (AIIDE 2007). AAAI Press, Palo Alto, California, pp 43–48

47. Sharma M, Mehta M, Ontañón S, Ram A (2007) Player modeling evaluation for interactive fiction. In: Technical report on AIIDE 2007 workshop on optimizing player satisfaction. AAAI Press, Palo Alto, California
48. Thue D, Bulitko V, Spetch M (2008) Making stories player-specific: delayed authoring in interactive storytelling. The first joint international conference on interactive digital storytelling. Springer, Berlin/Heidelberg, Erfurt, Germany, pp 230–241
49. Mateas M, Stern A (2004) A behavior language: joint action and behavioral idioms. In: Prendinger H, Ishizuka M (eds) Life-like characters: tools, affective functions, and applications. Springer, Berlin, Heidelberg, pp 135–161
50. Riedl MO, Stern A (2006) Believable agents and intelligent story adaptation for interactive storytelling. In: 3rd international conference on technologies for interactive digital storytelling and entertainment. Springer, Darmstad, DE, pp 1–12
51. Ramirez AJ, Bulitko V (2012) Telling interactive player-specific stories and planning for it: ASD + PaSSAGE = PAST. In: The eighth artificial intelligence and interactive digital entertainment conference (AIIDE 2012). AAAI Press, Palo Alto, California, pp 173–178
52. Ramirez A, Bulitko V (2015) Automated planning and player modelling for interactive storytelling. IEEE Trans Comput Intell AI Games 7(4):375–386
53. McCoy J, Treanor M, Samuel B, Reed A, Mateas M, Wardrip-Fruin N (2013) Prom week: designing past the game/story dilemma. In: Proceedings of the 8th international conference on the foundations of digital games (FDG 2013), Chania, Crete, Greece
54. Reed A, Garbe J, Apostol N (2013) The ice-bound concordance. www.ice-bound.com
55. Reed A (2017) Changeful tales: design-driven approaches toward more expressive story games. PhD thesis, UC Santa Cruz
56. Evans R, Short E, Nelson G (2014) Blood and laurels. https://versu.com/2014/05/28/blood-laurels/
57. Evans R, Short E (2014) Versu—a simulationist storytelling system. IEEE Trans Comput Intell AI Games 6(2):113–130. https://doi.org/10.1109/TCIAIG.2013.2287297
58. Szilas N, Dumas J, Richle U, Boggini T, Habonneau N (2015) Nothing for dinner. http://nothingfordinner.org/
59. Szilas N (2015) Reconsidering the role of AI in interactive digital narrative. In: Ferri G, Haahr M, Sezen D, Sezen TI, Koenitz H (eds) Interactive digital narrative. Routledge
60. Ryan J (2018) Curating simulated storyworlds. PhD thesis, University of California, Santa Cruz
61. Kreminski M, Dickinson M, Wardrip-Fruin N (2019) Felt: a simple story sifter. In: Proceedings of the 12th international conference on interactive digital storytelling (ICIDS 2019). Springer, Berlin, Heidelberg, pp 267–281
62. Kreminski M, Dickinson M, Mateas M (2021) Winnow: a domain-specific language for incremental story sifting. In: Proceedings of the AAAI conference on artificial intelligence and interactive digital entertainment, AAAI Press, pp 156–163. https://ojs.aaai.org/index.php/AIIDE/article/view/18903

Research Issues

Authoring Issues in Interdisciplinary Research Teams

Nicolas Szilas and Ulrike Spierling

Abstract The field of Interactive Digital Narration (IDN) is inherently interdisciplinary—since its inception, it has struggled to unite artistic and technical expertise. In this chapter, therefore, we reflect on the extent to which the interdisciplinarity at play in IDN is specific to the field and the implications this has for authoring research. To this end, we consider several issues related to the collaboration of tool engineers with storytellers and designers on a team. We group these challenges into four main categories and suggest recommendations to address them: dealing with change, sharing a vision, dealing with a range of data representations, and fighting opacity.

1 Introduction

Claiming that the field of Interactive Digital Narrative (IDN) is fundamentally inter-disciplinary is by no means an original viewpoint today, since it has been struggling with combining artistic and technical expertise since its creation [1–3]. Furthermore, which domain is not claiming to be interdisciplinary nowadays? The concerns of this chapter are therefore more precisely: to which extent is the interdisciplinarity at work in IDN specific to the field, and what are the implications regarding authoring? We look at various challenges that come along with the collaboration of tool engineers with storytelling artists and designers in one team, and we document the scope of these issues in our field of research in authoring and in the development of IDN solutions and applications.

At first, let us delimit the scope of the works covered by this review. IDN emerged in the late 1990s as an academic field that is strongly grounded in technical innovations [4]. Often led by researchers in computing (but not exclusively), it has

N. Szilas (✉)
TECFA, FPSE, University of Geneva, Geneva, Switzerland
e-mail: nicolas.szilas@unige.ch

U. Spierling
Hochschule RheinMain, Wiesbaden, Germany
e-mail: ulrike.spierling@hs-rm.de

© The Author(s), under exclusive license to Springer Nature Switzerland AG 2022
C. Hargood et al. (eds.), *The Authoring Problem*, Human–Computer Interaction Series,
https://doi.org/10.1007/978-3-031-05214-9_18

always included a strong focus on technological innovation, such as Artificial Intelligence techniques or novel interfaces (e.g., Augmented Reality). These technological components make the interactive work procedural [5], which implies that authors need to gain some understanding of the story engine that runs these procedures. Next to purely narrative content, variables, conditions, and rules need to be defined that drive the resulting experience according to authors' intentions. In that sense, we are concerned with IDN works that are fundamentally different from hypertext and hypermedia [6]. Corresponding works are experimental, in the sense that, in many cases, the development of the underlying technology is still in progress when authoring starts. In this chapter, we zoom in on these experimental works, conducted mostly within academic research labs, as we draw our own experience from such contexts. Nevertheless, it certainly can apply to most IDN projects based on dynamic systems (simulations, rules, behavior trees, etc.), once their complexity reaches a point where it makes the creation processes difficult to grasp for non-programming authors in a development team.

Historically, as mentioned above, IDN started with technical innovations: algorithmic engines generating narratives. However, even for these engines, authoring was necessary, not only to create works from a practical perspective, but also simply to validate the technical approaches [2, 7, 8]. In fact, it is impossible to demonstrate novel IDN systems without any narrative content. This is one reason why authoring and creative writing with these prototype systems make up an inherent part of the research. In addition, collaboration at this point is also important to enable researchers to understand authors, the authoring tasks, and to incorporate this knowledge into system design. This has led to a series of workshops on IDN authoring, starting in 2006 [9]. In 2009, we, the two authors of this chapter, wrote an article entitled "Authoring Issues Beyond Tools" [10], in which a series of repeating problems in IDN research projects were listed. Our reflections were based on several concrete design experiences and focused on the insight that these problems would not be automatically solved by just creating better authoring tools.

In this chapter, we want to revisit some of these issues. After all, 12 years later, we now indeed have more general authoring tools, which are getting much more attention in the IDN community.[1] We also have more examples of IDN artifacts than back then [11, 12],[2] and can assume more experience in management of such projects. Our question in this chapter is to what extent the issues still occur—in other words, are they indeed issues beyond tools? To anticipate the answer, from our point of view, not much has improved, despite the fact that researchers are now more aware of these issues. More precisely, we find that the discussed issues shift more toward issues related to interdisciplinary collaboration, which had been rather overlooked in earlier considerations. "The Authoring Problem" cannot be reduced to insufficient authoring tools. Nor can it be attributed exclusively to the individual technical and artistic skills of the various experts involved in a project. Moreover,

---

[1] For more on authoring communities, see Cox's chapter in this volume.

[2] See Brooker's chapter for an overview of IDN works.

collaboration between team members in an interdisciplinary context appears to be a crucial dimension for authoring.

Here, we describe experiences with these collaborative issues and seek to understand to what extent they are specific to the field of IDN, and how they compare to other domains such as software development, game design or filmmaking. Although not the central contribution of this chapter, some suggestions for solutions are also proposed and discussed. The chapter shall be food for thought for young researchers who must collaborate with other disciplines in a research endeavor that engages in building authoring tools or novel IDN systems.

2 IDN-Specific Features

Like multimedia or game projects, IDN projects involve managing interdisciplinary teams with members coming from two radically different domains: arts (storytelling, graphical, and audio design) and computing (general programming, AI, graphical programming, interfaces, databases, networking). Acknowledging this difficulty in IDN, with reference to the concept of the "two-culture divide" from Snow [13], Crawford [14] calls for people who would merge the two cultures in one person. In addition, Andrew Stern claimed "artists must program" [15]. However, it appears that multimedia and games have faced that challenge and have solved it in a different way, at least to a certain extent, by using project management approaches. In these fields, the solution consists of

- Clarifying the tasks of each team member and formalizing the workflow between them.
- Training a project manager to be able to dialogue with people from both technical and artistic background.
- Progressively creating new interdisciplinary specialized job profiles, such as graphical designers, user experience designers for games, and narrative designers.

This is certainly a relevant model to follow, especially in well-established production workflows. However, the experimental nature of IDN makes the situation more complex. One striking characteristic of IDN projects is a blurry line between the content—written and designed by artists—and the runtime engine or interactive narrative system (as well as the user interface or graphics/media level) that processes that content—written by computing persons [16]. In research projects, both are often created in parallel [17]. For example, suggestions by artists motivate the creation of new features, while technical features inspire artists to create specific content. In such a context, in which several team members have to work with moving targets, authoring tools are difficult to create and, at best, are created during the project, when some stability has been reached. Consequently, project methods (workflows, pipelines, task division) also need to be created on the fly. Also related to the experimental and innovative nature of IDN, project members do not know in advance what the final user experience will be like, unlike most games or media products that fit into known genres with established conventions.

From previous work, we can extract other important IDN features that may influence the authoring process:

- Complexity: Generally speaking, IDN products are complex systems [10], showing behavior that is sometimes difficult to predict during authoring, a characteristic that they share with some games.
- Abstraction: Authoring occurs at an abstract level, due to the partly generative nature of the underlying technology [10]. This abstraction creates difficulties for creative authors trained in traditional media. Programmers also face obstacles, as they need to handle more complex types of knowledge representation.
- Formatted writing: Content is no longer a meaningful artistic element to be directly experienced (full sentences, images, film clips). Rather, it tends to be scattered into several fragments (e.g., short text chunks), with parameters that drive the assembling of these fragments into perceivable content. In the extreme case, content is to be coded using a programming language syntax, as in *Façade* [18].

In addition, funding options may influence how the authoring expertise in a team is represented. Frequently, academic IDN projects are based on research grants that need to justify their expenses with their technical novelty, while authoring tasks and content creation are not considered research. As a result, these projects are limited in budget and involve only few people, compared to big productions in the game industry. While it can be argued that small teams—if not individuals—have produced great games, academic projects often have limited or no budget to hire dedicated staff for artistic creation. In most cases, they must make do with existing academic staff, or with novice academic personnel such as PhD students.

Although project management methods coming from other creative domains are relevant, our experience shows that they may not be sufficient in the context of IDN due to the greater interdependence of the different tasks. Collaboration issues in IDN deserve specific analysis, which we will develop in the following sections.

3   Approach

The ambition of this chapter is to collect a number of collaboration issues that we assume are induced by specific structures within our creative research topic.

For our 2009 paper, we analyzed and compared experience reports and feedback from authors in our own research projects. In fact, these were only a subset of all possible IDN forms at a time, with less general tools available than today. Collaboration issues can have many causes, including coincidental or individual reasons, such as the qualifications and idiosyncrasy of personnel, individual or project-specific resources, or constraints on management, which would reduce any experience reports to arbitrary insight. Especially in small teams, elusive factors like these have more influence than in bigger productions. However, only if reports and feedback from different sources showed that similar problems occurred in several projects did we regard these as interesting enough to be considered.

For the current chapter, we first reflected on the authoring issues that were mentioned in our previous article, and then asked fellow researchers in the field to share their points of view with us, addressing each of these issues individually. Based on this, we hypothesize how these issues can be explained by the collaboration of different disciplines involved.

4 Reflections on Interdisciplinary Authoring Issues Beyond Tools

We revisited the "authoring issues beyond tools" that we summarized in 2009, first by comparing them with our own experiences from recent IDN projects and many discussions in authoring workshops since then (in 2010 [19], 2014 [20], 2016 [21], 2017 [22], 2018 [23], and 2020 [24]), and second, by having dedicated conversations with fellow colleagues about each issue. We have found that some of these issues, while better understood today, are still relevant overall—some of them for certain types of projects. Novel developments in IDN with their combination of cutting-edge technology and artistic creation naturally require the involvement of different disciplines. However, it is precisely the greater interdependency of the various tasks—compared to traditional media projects—that are also reasons for interdisciplinary friction.

4.1 Issues in Authoring Research

When we start a new research project in IDN, we first have to acknowledge that the field is still young and in flux. There are different IDN communities (as different as Hypertext, Interactive Fiction, Games, or Intelligent Narrative Technologies) with diverse historical roots that have only recently started to talk to each other. In addition, standard levels of knowledge and available talent in authoring IDN depend on external, societal developments beyond our control, such as education and computer literacy in general and more specifically in the humanistic fields. This influences the extent to which traditional authors, media designers, or storytellers can give appropriate feedback to innovative technological approaches. There is no common ground (yet) on how the target group for the tools, prospective interactive narrative designers, actually "want" to author with procedural tools. This is also considered research for storytellers, not only for the computer scientists who need to evaluate their tool approaches with storytellers. Linear project plans based on waterfall models probably fail in this chicken-and-egg situation. In order to understand the problem, solutions need to be built beforehand, resulting in a "wicked problem" [25].

Nevertheless, in the last decade, progress has been made. We now have tools such as Twine[3] and Unity[4] with big user groups. We also have choice-based films like *Bandersnatch* [26] and narrative games with a massive increase in worldwide audience attention. This helps to communicate at least the concepts of interaction in terms of branching and choices within a storyworld that lead to individual progress for each user. While this supports the education of interactive storytellers, the main problems are still prevalent: either having to put up with the combinatorial explosion of content or to manage the complexity of structures that support automated—and therefore unpredictable—behavior.[5]

Thus, with regard to research projects, we assume an exploratory design-science approach, in which the building of a system and its evaluation is central to the research results. There is no ideal division of labor, and the borderline between authoring and narrative system design is blurry. A diagram shown in our 2009 paper assumed a distinction between a storyworld created as the result of authoring versus a runtime engine created as the result of engineering development, with both together forming part of the artifact delivered to end-users. In many discussions since then, a preferred way to revise this could be to see the whole unit as an interactive narrative system, with several modules and different authors for these modules. Still, for the following discussion between the disciplines, it is useful to distinguish between some tasks leaning more toward the creative writing and design world, and other tasks leaning more toward computation. The IDN community dreams of an ideal profession of creatives who are experts in both cultures [14]. However, realistically speaking, when we try to hire personnel for research, we often find only a subset of talents in one person (such as storyteller, literary researcher, interactive designer, programmer for graphics or for AI or databases, etc.), and need to decide who to hire within these constraints. Moreover, if the merits of academic research lie in a higher degree, such as a PhD, this requires projects to fit within single faculty regulations and work cultures, which are mostly discipline oriented.

4.2 Authoring Stories and Algorithms

In 2009 [10], we called one determined category of authoring issues "Story ideas that do not fit into an engine's approach". This circumscribes a group of issues that has been an effect of the interdisciplinary nature of our research projects. For programmers, a compiler can be kind of an authoring tool they are happy with. One can—theoretically—create every idea for an IDN with it, but hardly anybody would be able to enter artistically meaningful content for an IDN piece into such a tool. Even if a talented artist is also a skilled programmer, it would at the very least be cumbersome. At the other end of the spectrum, we may consider very domain-specific

---

[3] https://twinery.org/.

[4] https://unity.com/.

[5] For a discussion of the authoring burden concerning complexity, see Jones' chapter in this volume.

tools with simply arranged options or even templates tailored to a task. These tools would be easier to use, but they can be too constraining and many creative authors' ideas would not fit. When developers invent a new interactive narrative system, it mostly means introducing constraints and domain structures. These constraints imply that the artists involved in the project are no longer free in their creations. In our recent work, we experienced many different kinds of interdisciplinary complications, of which two examples shall be mentioned here.

In one of our location-based storytelling systems [27], a programmer included possibilities to use a time-out for user choices in order to create running challenges in an adventure-like interaction, coupled with image recognition. The feature could have been demonstrated with a story including a scavenger hunt. However, the hired artist thought differently and came up with a great story idea that made this feature obsolete. Instead, it required more algorithmic precision in positioning, which the system eventually could not offer. In this case, both involved project members had to cope with frustration and disappointments, caused both by parallel diverging development and by communication issues.

In another recent project, we offered authors the new possibility to create their own narrative acts [28], which was a novel feature with regard to the previous narrative engine (IDtension [29]). However, authors had difficulty entering corresponding data, with recurrent confusion between narrative acts and simple tasks. Also, some free-form text was frequently added by authors in places where simple conditions were expected, which shows that the structure did not match the authors' reasoning.

Both examples illustrate different forms of a typical problem in interdisciplinary projects involving authors. On the one hand, there is the issue of the necessary skillset of authors, who must be able to adapt content to given algorithms. Authors must understand limitations of the technology and adopt new conceptual models for creation. On the other hand, algorithmic structures must be designed to approximate authors' existing conceptual models. By listening to authors' ideas as part of a collaborative project, tool developers must ensure that authors' creative potential is not lost.

In 2009, we found several reasons why there often have been problems with matching great story ideas to engines: (1) finding and hiring creative authors who were willing and skilled enough to use novel technology was difficult in the first place, (2) often, they had problems with the necessary abstraction, and (3) they experienced antipathy toward the demand for formatted and constrained writing (see Sect. 2). Revisiting these issues, we reflect that today this very much depends on the kind of IDN that is at the center of interest. After 12 years, we observe more general opportunities for education in writing for interactivity and semi-automatic structured content. For example, in journalism, online text formats that require the filling of forms or the use of formulas and hyperlinks are becoming more commonplace. Well-known interactive stories such as *Bandersnatch* motivate more storytellers to step into this field. The field of interactive media design, including time-based media such as film, is increasingly using content structures made of components and chunks, instead of giving birth to one holistic piece. We also believe that there is a trend toward teaching more procedural literacy. However, this is not a given for a digital native. Instead, it indeed requires education.

Not only artists, but also experienced computer scientists have problems understanding how to tune more dynamic behavior, if certain goals shall be reached: how to optimize the structure of a state machine, how to find reasonable defaults for every variable, or how to obtain control of the outcome only by configuring a set of rules.[6] In phases of exploratory research, there may even be no clear division of work between authoring content and programming an engine. Authoring and programming intersect, and possible issues could be that either the potential of engines is underused, or story design is purely algorithm centered.

4.3 Pain and Frustration

For many people, being creative is associated with something positive, as we can assume that there is a link between feelings of happiness and creativity. At the same time, there is the notion of a suffering and struggling artist, and not only in public perception [30]. There are several opportunities for suffering in IDN research projects. Another group of issues from our 2009 paper dealt with the "painful process of storyworld implementation" through the time-consuming task of entering content and, after that, the difficulty in understanding what is going on "under the hood"— meaning, how the engine processes that content. The first part of the problem has a great similarity to all media creation tasks that can occasionally get tedious; however, artists more than computer scientists have also fed back that it can be fun to do somewhat repetitive work. After entering the content, however, things may turn out differently than expected, especially with non-linear storytelling. Here begins the second issue, which is a classic case of what programmers call "debugging", but which is new to most traditional artists and designers. In IDN, it is often the case that entering content may take a long time, leading to a lengthy delay before designers themselves, as testers, understand for the first time what shape the whole story will take. Then, they might not be immediately satisfied and start the iterative process of re-editing, repairing, and testing. In IDN, "debugging" does not only mean fixing programming mistakes. Any unexpected result can lead to a long search for the reason, to frustration, and—naturally—to requests for changes that affect teammates. Discussing in a team whether an undesired result is an engine bug, an authoring error, a misconception of end-user behavior, or a conceptual discrepancy between interactive storyworld ideas and intended system capabilities may take up extra time for communication.

Furthermore, it is not only the extra time that causes stress. The necessary task of determining reasons for malfunctioning in the work of team members entails a huge potential for personal misunderstandings, which finally may result in hurt feelings. It

---

[6] See Thue's chapter in this volume on working with intelligent narrative technologies for more on these challenges.

is too easy to fall into the trap of blaming others and feeling attacked. When working with team members from different disciplines, it is crucial to not only perceive their lack of skills, but also one's own.

These repair loops are normal procedures; therefore, the following section discusses management techniques such as agile development and the need for iterative design in small cycles of prototypes. The main point here is that based on much feedback, we argue that interdisciplinary communication as such has the potential to stress people and can be the cause for negative emotions and conflicts. Within narrow professional cultures, there are often implicit rules at work that seem confusing and not at all matters of course, particularly when viewed from the outside. Frustration occurs, for example, if expectations of a lean process are violated—therefore, teams are better off being prepared for this necessary but time-consuming exchange.

5 Key Collaboration Issues Regarding Research on Authoring

In this section, we classify reported collaboration issues into groups of typical issues at a more abstract level.

5.1 Dealing with Change (Agility)

Being engaged in an experimental endeavor, collaborators involved within an IDN research project cannot clearly envision the future product from the start. This is the case regarding necessary technical features, the possibility spaces for storytelling, and the user experience it will propose for the audience. From a project management perspective, this requires agile methods, to allow the team to design iteratively and deal with change efficiently. Nevertheless, the best methodological principles, even when adopted from the beginning of the project, sometimes seem insufficient to prevent issues regarding collaboration.

Creatives need a kind of sandbox to prototype and test their ideas with new technical features in small cycles [31]. As long as technology is under development, it is not yet ready for testing (see Sect. 5.4 regarding opacity), and too much has to be envisioned blindly. The more it gets ready to use, step by step, the better the creative designers are able to identify what they do *not* want, which also inspires novel ideas that lead to changes in their concepts. However, software developers do not like sudden changes during development phases, even in projects using agile methods. In practice, when artists and developers collaborate, having to deal with changes is a common source of conflicts.

The main issue that can be encountered regarding agility is a confusion between what is seen by the designers as an attempt to test a technical possibility and what is considered by the developer as a module in the final solution. In such a situation, what is implemented by the developer is quite difficult to change, because he or she sees it as final, while other participants would tend to modify it, if not discard it, if it finally does not meet expectations. Moving backward is of course not quite satisfying, but it must be accepted as part of the process in such projects.

Another case of lack of agility concerns the writing. At the beginning of the project, a certain way to enter content may be found by the team, mostly pushed by the creative people, since the technical part may not be formalized yet. When the technical components are implemented, it may constrain the writing differently, and the creative writers must adapt to the new way of entering content.

The ability for each member of the team to deal with change is therefore critical in an IDN project. It is both an individual attitude and the project culture that must emerge quickly during the project. At the same time, as with any agile project, it is necessary to specify at certain points that some elements will no longer change. If this is clearly stated during the project after phases of iterations, discussions, and negotiations, then this must be accepted by all members, and the project can move forward.

5.2 Sharing a Vision

At the beginning of a project, its goals are rather clear. They are even usually written in a document, the project proposal used for funding. Everybody has read the document, and kickoff meetings enable the team to discuss these goals together. Everybody seems to agree on these goals, but in reality, individual motivations may be different, without these differences being made explicit. For example, we noticed several times that the goal of the developer is to produce high-quality code, built in such a way that it can be easily modifiable, meeting requirements of modern good practices in programming. However, this legitimate aspiration may appear counter-productive if it does not meet other goals in the project in terms of which features should be developed in priority, within a certain period. This may even appear as a hidden agenda that may be discovered late in project development.

The designer/writer would reason differently. Starting from the project's narrative domain, he or she gathers documentation, starts creating storytelling content, and progressively sharpens his or her vision. This vision shapes the produced content, but it is not necessarily easily shared with other members of the project. With time, there is a risk that visions diverge, because other team members have not fully embraced the artistic vision, the latter potentially requiring changes in the technical specification.

A specific extreme case occurs when each member considers himself or herself as an independent "consultant" or "provider", meeting the requirements of others, as a "supplier" to a "customer". While this approach may appear structured and appropriate, it is detrimental in an IDN research project, because it does not allow a vision to emerge, to be shared and to evolve within all the project's team members.

Experience reports showed that often we cannot rely on our colleagues being mature experts in IDN authoring. In an academic research environment, in which young people may be starting their PhD, we often have the hiring problem mentioned above. So, if we treat team members as customers, we more often experience the frustration that they change their mind about what they want (see the section above on dealing with change), because they still have to learn about their own requirements as their research progresses.

5.3 Dealing with a Range of Data Representations

A specific characteristic of IDN is that in terms of content creation, what you see is not what you get. The author may create a series of text snippets that will effectively create a dialog in a story only when running the program. Or the designer may create a graphic element for the user interface that will make sense only during interaction. Nevertheless, these non-trivial data representations are a necessary material to be created for the project. Because of their abstraction and formalness (see "Abstraction" and "Formatted and Constrained Writing" in our earlier paper [10]), these materials are not created in a straightforward manner by creative authors. A range of intermediate documents is usually created, varying from informal text descriptions to more structured documents or spreadsheets. These different data representations are usually interconnected. For example, a character action with a gesture involves the writing of the causes and consequences of the action, the corresponding animation, and the corresponding text. They are different types of data representations, stored in various places, written by different persons, but interconnected. These intermediate data serve two goals: first, progressively changing the design elements from an informal description to formal content that can be entered into the system, and second, selecting what part of it is implemented, if necessary, with priorities.

A part of the project's life consists of defining and agreeing on these various schemes of data representation, and on the pipeline of content creation through the corresponding documents. During this process, the team may meet several issues.

First, at the very beginning of the project, we have a chicken-and-egg problem: the developers need some content to create data structures for the program, but the creative authors need guidance, that is structures, to write that content. As a result, creative authors need to start with their own data representation, which probably needs to change later in the project.

Second, there is a tendency for each project member to create their own data format, fitted to their ways of understanding the content. Typically, members would add a column to a shared spreadsheet, or create a new sheet. As a result, the conversion from these data to the effective data for the program (to be either read automatically or entered manually by the technical author) may become painful.

Third, even if developers and authors do work together, some data formats may appear obscure to the non-technical members. Making sure that data representation schemes are well understood by everybody in the project is critical and far from easy. This requires some negotiations and iterations.

Fourth, as these intermediate representations are fault tolerant, for example, text in a spreadsheet, creatives can easily fail to strictly comply to engine-dependent rules for entering content (rules that are not necessarily clearly stated). This may lead technical members to interpret and change the content, leading them inadvertently to possibly radically alter some of its subtleties.

The views of project members on these various formats for entering content are diverse, and of course are related to their respective disciplinary background. Some data will be considered as too fuzzy, and not structured enough, leaving too much room for interpretation, while conversely, other data (or even the same data!) will be regarded as too structured, preventing expression of the desired effect. From a global perspective, it is reasonable to think that the multitude of formats and the pipeline between them allows for diversity in structuring, until the final data is entered into the system. But from the inside of the project, managing this heterogeneity of vision regarding data is a tedious task (see "The Time-Consuming Task of Entering Content" [10]).

5.4 Fighting Opacity

As it has been observed before, authors in IDN projects do not easily anticipate the result of their creation (see "Foreseeing the End Result of the Storyworld Possibilities" [10]). In particular, the design cycle between an idea and its concretization tends to be long, compared to that of a novel writer, for example. Other media, such as film, also face this issue, but have developed other intermediate products for authors to work on, such as scripts or storyboards. Such intermediate forms are often still unclear in the IDN domain, under development and mostly system dependent [31, 32]. IDN authors are like blind painters: they cannot see the result of their creative activity while they are using their tools.

This problem of opacity seems closely linked to the tools that are available to enter content, but as mentioned in the introduction, these tools are, by definition, not available. What emerges in various IDN research projects is the necessity for quick and dirty ways to enter the content, and quick and dirty tools to experience this content. However, this is in conflict with computing philosophy, based, to a large extent, on the idea of clear specifications and clean programming. The evolution of programming techniques during the last few decades tends to favor more advanced but more complex ways to handle technical solutions, which often creates an additional burden in the authoring process. For example, it is acceptable for an author that entering a picture in a system requires putting a given file at a given place, with a given name. This solution may seem quite out-of-date for a modern developer, as it is not error-free, insecure, etc. However, not only does this solution require less computing effort (making the project more iterative) but it also enables the content to be immediately taken into account. Conversely, a clean, secure, modern way to proceed, with a content-management interface for example, may require some longer procedure to have the image used in the runtime system.

It is also very often the case that information systems refuse incomplete information: if some fields are not filled, the work cannot be executed at all. As a result, the author cannot test partial content. The solution is often to build intermediate systems that accept incomplete data, or even erroneous data, and make some corrections (e.g., use defaults values). This is rarely considered in specifications, in favor of a clean solution to enter content. In addition, a system of default variables requires finalized models and design patterns of the possible content, all of which may still be under construction in early phases.

This issue relates to the first issue mentioned above, regarding agility, but it is different: in a research context, the team is targeting, at best, a research prototype, not a product. Therefore, some "dirty" elements may remain for the whole duration of the project. This is something which must be accepted by all members of the project.

Opacity is therefore both a technological and methodological issue. A trade-off between time invested to develop useful testing/debugging tools and the delay such investment may provoke in the project must be found, which is particularly difficult. Therefore, it is also valuable to explore cheap methodological solutions, inspired from iterative design methods: paper prototyping, role playing, use of existing mockup interface software (e.g., Figma), etc.

6 Recommendations and Conclusion

Since our listing of 10 authoring issues in IDN back in 2009, has the situation changed? Our main finding is that beyond the observation that most of the 2009 issues remain—albeit depending on the nature of the projects—they are particularly visible in the form of issues in communication within an interdisciplinary team. Technological advances are of course beneficial to the field (new interactive devices available, such as augmented reality, better prototyping software, more advanced 3D animation systems, etc.), but at the same time these advances are a threat, because they complicate the system architecture and the content it handles. For example, progresses in security, reliability, and scalability have changed the way databases are accessed in web architectures, and made it more complex.

The collaborative issues discussed in this chapter lead us to propose three general recommendations for experimental IDN projects:

1. **Team building**. This is of course a very general aspect of project management, but it seems that it is particularly crucial in IDN. In order to share a common vision of the product, each project member needs to understand the other's approach and goals. In the end, technical staff is creative too, and creative staff is technical too. If, as mentioned above, IDN blurs the line between authoring and programming, this should be reflected into the project structure. One particular technique that

we recommend is to role play the future product, which meets the double goal of building the team and sharing a vision of the product.

2. **Compromising between sophistication and intuitiveness**. Too often, specific design decisions are made by one disciplinary field, favoring one end of the spectrum between sophisticated design choices that allow for scalable, secure, portable and open code, and intuitive design choices that allow for quick, easy to understand, "just doing the job" functionalities. We recommend that each of these decisions should be negotiated in-group in order to find a suitable compromise.

3. **Developing a culture of uncertainty and change**. While this is at the core of agile methods (see "Responding to change over following a plan" and "Welcome changing requirements" [33]), the motivation here is different. It is not about satisfying the client or improving the reactiveness and efficiency of the development team, but rather about the shared acceptance that the targeted interactive narrative is not, and cannot be, fully specified, and that the specification needs to be discovered on the way, due to the experimental nature of these projects. This is certainly a culture already present in successful game studios, because games share with IDN the fundamental characteristics that, at the end, they only exist as an experience (as concisely stated decades ago: "[play] is not matter" [34]).

Since IDN work has to do with stories, ironically, living through a project is also quite story-like! In this chapter, we have met different characters, a global quest, obstacles, dilemmas, conflicts, hidden agendas, various viewpoints on the same events or props… all of which are elements of stories well documented in our field. Less mentioned in this chapter but nevertheless omnipresent in IDN projects are emotions: hope, fear, challenge, frustration, anger, proudness, curiosity, suspense, etc. Therefore, it is not absurd to believe that IDN technologies and concepts could contribute to the organization and structuring of IDN projects.

References

1. Si M, Marsella SC, Riedl MO (2008) Integrating story-centric and character-centric processes for authoring interactive drama. In: Darken C, Mateas M (eds) Fourth artificial intelligence and interactive digital entertainment conference (AIIDE). AAAI Press, Menlo Park, CA, pp 203–208
2. Spierling U, Grasbon D, Braun N, Iurgel I (2002) Setting the scene: playing digital director in interactive storytelling and creation. Comput Graph 26:31–44
3. Thomas J, Young R (2006) Author in the loop: using mixed-initiative planning to improve interactive narrative. In: AI planning for synthetic characters and computer games, ICAPS 2006 workshop
4. Mateas M, Sengers P (1999) Narrative intelligence—papers from the 1999 AAAI fall symposium—TR FS-99-01. AAAI Press, Menlo Park, California
5. Murray JH (1997) Hamlet on the Holodeck: the future of narrative in cyberspace. Free Press, New York
6. Delany P, Landow GP (eds) (1991) Hypermedia and literary studies. MIT Press, Cambridge, MA

7. Charles F, Lozano M, Mead SJ, Fornes Bisquerra A, Cavazza M (2003) Planning formalisms and authoring in interactive storytelling. In: Göbel S, Braun N, Spierling U, Dechau J, Diener H (eds) Proceedings of the technologies for interactive digital storytelling and entertainment (TIDSE) conference. Fraunhofer IRB, Darmstadt, pp 216–225

8. Szilas N, Marty O, Réty JJ-H (2003) Authoring highly generative interactive drama. In: Balet O, Subsol G, Torguet P (eds) Virtual storytelling, second international conference (ICVS 2003). Lecture notes in computer science, vol 2897. Springer, Heidelberg, pp 37–46

9. Spierling U, Iurgel I (2006) Pre-conference demo workshop "Little Red Cap": the authoring process in interactive storytelling. Technologies for interactive digital storytelling and entertainment. Springer, Berlin, Heidelberg, pp 193–194

10. Spierling U, Szilas N (2009) Authoring issues beyond tools. In: Iurgel I, Zagalo N, Petta P (eds) Second joint international conference on interactive digital storytelling (ICIDS 2009). Lecture notes in computer science, vol 5915. Springer, Heidelberg, pp 50–61

11. Evans R, Short E (2014) Versu—a simulationist storytelling system. IEEE Trans Comput Intell AI Games 6:113–130

12. Ryan J (2018) Curating simulated storyworlds. UC Santa Cruz. ProQuest ID: Ryan_ucsc_0036E_11714. Merritt ID: ark:/13030/m5xw9h7g. Retrieved from https://eschol arship.org/uc/item/1340j5h2

13. Snow CP (1963) The two cultures and a second look: an expanded version of the two cultures and the scientific revolution. Cambridge University Press

14. Crawford C (2015) Crawford lecture at ICIDS. https://www.youtube.com/watch?v=xb8KWs y5OSM

15. Stern A (2001) Deeper conversations with interactive art: or why artists must program. Convergence 7:17–24

16. Szilas N (2005) The future of interactive drama. In: Proceedings of the second Australian conference on interactive entertainment, pp 193–199

17. Szilas N (2015) Re-considering the role of AI in interactive digital narrative. In: Koenitz H, Ferri G, Haahr M, Sezen D, Ibrahim Sezen T (eds) Interactive digital narrative—history, theory and practice. Routledge, New York, NY, pp 136–149

18. Mateas M, Stern A (2004) A behavior language: joint action and behavioral idioms. In: Prendinger H, Ishizuka M (eds) Life-like characters: tools, affective functions and applications. Springer, Cognitive Technologies, Heidelberg, pp 135–162

19. Spierling U, Szilas N, Hoffmann S, Richle U (2010) Tutorial: introduction to interactive story creation. In: Aylett R, Lim MY, Louchart S, Petta P, Riedl MO (eds) 3rd international conference on international digital storytelling (ICIDS 2010). Lecture notes in computer science, vol 6432. Springer, Heidelberg, pp 299–300

20. Spierling U, Mitchell (2014) Story modeling and authoring. In: 7th international conference on international digital storytelling (ICIDS 2014), pp 262–263

21. Chen F, Kampa A, Mitchell A, Spierling U, Szilas N, Wingate S (2016) Exploring new approaches to narrative modeling and authoring. In: 9th international conference on international digital storytelling (ICIDS 2016), pp 464–465

22. Hargood C, Mitchell A, Millard DE, Spierling U (2017) Authoring for interactive storytelling workshop. In: 10th international conference on international digital storytelling (ICIDS 2017), pp 405–408

23. Mitchell A, Spierling U, Hargood C, Millard D (2018) Authoring for interactive storytelling. When, why, and do we actually need authoring tools? In: 11th international conference on international digital storytelling (ICIDS 2018), pp 544–547

24. Hargood C, Mitchell A, Millard D, Spierling U (2020) Authoring for interactive storytelling 2020. http://narrativeandplay.org/ais/2020/

25. Mateas M, Stern A (2005) Build it to understand it: ludology meets narratology in game design space. In: DiGRA conference, pp 16–20

26. Brooker C, Slade D (2018) Bandersnatch

27. Spierling U, Coors V (2014) SPIRIT—entertaining encounters with ancient history. In: Klein R, Santos P (eds) Proceedings of 12th EUROGRAPHICS workshops on graphics and cultural heritage. Eurographics Digital Library

28. Szilas N, Chauveau L, Andkjaer K, Luiu AL, Bétrancourt M, Ehrler F (2019) Virtual patient interaction via communicative acts. In: 19th ACM international conference on intelligent virtual agents. ACM Press, New York, pp 91–93
29. Szilas N (2007) A computational model of an intelligent narrator for interactive narratives. Appl Artif Intell 21:753–801
30. Duchamp M (1957) The creative act. Writings Marcel Duchamp, New York Da Capo, pp 138–140
31. Szilas N, Wang J, Axelrad M (2008) Towards minimalism and expressiveness in interactive drama. In: DIMEA 08 Proceedings of 3rd international conference on digital interactive media entertainment and arts, pp 385–392
32. Kampa A, Stöbener K, Spierling U (2016) User interface prototyping for handheld mobile augmented reality applications. In: Wallner G, Kriglstein S, Hlavacs H, Rainer M, Lugmayr A, Yang H-S (eds) Entertainment computing, Proceedings of ICEC 2016, Lecture notes in computer science, vol 9926. Springer International Publishing, pp 229–234
33. Manifesto for Agile Software Development. https://agilemanifesto.org/
34. Huizinga J (1951) Homo ludens Essai sur la fonction sociale du jeu. Gallimard, Paris

The Authoring Tool Evaluation Problem

Charlie Hargood and Daniel Green

Abstract Authoring tools, the software used to create, edit, and develop Interactive Digital Narrative (IDN), are a critical part of both IDN authorship and research. These tools, their features, interface paradigms, visualisations, and user experience (UX) can impact the authoring process and the resulting works, and consequently must inform our wider understanding of IDN context. While IDN research has widely explored data models for authoring tools, feature sets, and demonstrated a variety of developed tools for a range of IDN forms, it has done comparatively very little to evaluate and study the UX of these tools and their impact on authors and their works. In this chapter, we survey the existing work on authoring tools and explore the scale of this problem, the reasons for it, how the community has documented this issue, and how we might begin to tackle it. We conclude that the existing methods for the study of UX are poorly suited for the study of authoring tools, and that as well as making the study of tool UX a priority, we must also develop new methods of evaluation.

We shape our tools and thereafter our tools shape us—John Culkin

Interactive Digital Narrative (IDN) is crafted by writers and narrative designers (hereafter simply referred to collectively as "authors") using a myriad of tools and technologies. These technologies are writing tools, domain specific languages and story logic compilers; they vary from roughly hewn in-house tools to polished commercial products, and from research prototypes to proprietary studio software. Collectively, we can call this collection of technologies "Authoring Tools". There is some debate as to what exactly fits within this definition [22, 61]—but for the purpose of this chapter, we will be adopting Green's definition [22] of tools created specifically for the purpose of creating or designing the story component of an IDN rather than those that merely could be used.

C. Hargood (✉) · D. Green
Bournemouth University, Poole, UK
e-mail: chargood@bournemouth.ac.uk

D. Green
e-mail: dgreen@bournemouth.ac.uk

© The Author(s), under exclusive license to Springer Nature Switzerland AG 2022
C. Hargood et al. (eds.), *The Authoring Problem*, Human–Computer Interaction Series,
https://doi.org/10.1007/978-3-031-05214-9_19

These tools are critical to IDN—they are the interface through which the ideas and designs of the author are filtered into the work. The vast majority of works of Hypertext fiction or game narrative or electronic literature was, at one point or another, pushed through the aperture of an authoring tool, and it cannot be overstated how the design of that tool may have shaped the resulting work. The tool itself may contain functions or interfaces that lend themselves not only to one style of storytelling or form of interaction over another, but also the User eXperience (UX) of that technology may have an effect on the author such that it changes their workflow or creative thinking, which, in turn, changes their work. Furthermore, the usability of these tools might even impact whether works are created at all, a new author tempted by the medium might be dissuaded by a difficult tool or persuaded by an accessible tool—their works may or may not come to pass because of the design of the tools of our domain. It is for all these reasons that the design of authoring tools is critical to the field of IDN and remains a frequent grand challenge, and topic of debate, within the space of relevant conferences such as ICIDS[1] or workshops such as NHT[2] and AIS[3]. Over a decade ago, Spierling and Szilas explained "Authoring is still considered a bottleneck in successful Interactive Storytelling" [67], and further back still Adams [1] was highlighting the challenges in multimedia authoring tool design—these bottlenecks and challenges remain.

UX research is a substantial part of HCI within computer science, concerning itself with understanding how users interact with technology and the impact of design decisions on their use, usability, and user satisfaction. This is critical for both understanding the value of these tools and the impact of their application. As a substantial field, UX research is well documented not only in books such as those by Goodman et al. [19] and conferences such as ACM CHI,[4] but also in domain specific publications such as the work of Drachen et al. [11] and ACM CHIPlay[5] for games UX. However, while a substantial part of the wider technology world recognises the importance and value in UX research, in our own field of IDN, its application is limited to understanding "the reader experience" through the evaluation of works and experiences (such as those called for by O'Flynn [53] or reviewed by Revi [57]) and less "the author experience"—where authoring tools often go unevaluated. There are some discussions of the general challenges in IDN authorship [37, 67], and Emily Short is a significant voice in the community reviewing these tools [62], however, these do not amount to a formal study of the UX of authoring tools. This is a claim that suggests we do not understand the tools on which the work in our field relies upon, but it is also a claim that demands explanation.

---

[1] https://ardin.online/conferences/icids-interactive-storytelling/ as of 24/01/22.

[2] http://nht.ecs.soton.ac.uk/ as of 24/01/22.

[3] http://narrativeandplay.org/ais/ as of 24/01/22.

[4] https://sigchi.org/conferences/conference-history/chi/ as of 25/01/2022.

[5] https://sigchi.org/conferences/conference-history/chiplay/ as of 25/01/2022.

Table 1 Authoring tools in three evaluation groups: example, partial, evaluated

Example		Partial	Evaluated
StoryPlaces [26, 47]	StorySpace [5, 6]	Mímisbrunnur [68, 69]	SVC [79]
Villanelle [42]	ASAPs [39, 40]	CANVAS [33–35]	SWB [55, 56]
DraMachina [10]	EmoEmma/DSL4MAS [8]	StoryTec [16, 17]	GHOST [25]
FAtiMA [41]	GAIA [36]	IDtension [70]	Deig [12, 13]
HyperDyn [49]	Scenejo [15, 77]		Inform 7 [51]
ABL [43]	ICT Story Manager [20]		Quest [76]
VHE [18]	NSL [73, 74]		Articy:Draft [2]
Twine [38]	Scribe [44]		
Art-E-Fact [30, 65]	Cyranus [31, 32]		
Generator [54]	Creactor [32]		
INSCAPE [3]	TADS [58]		
ADRIFT [78]	Inklewriter [29]		
Ren'Py [59]	Timeline [63]		

1 Problem

As discussed above, there are a myriad of IDN authoring tools [22, 61]. Some of these tools are proprietary, or remain sealed in their studios beyond scrutiny, meaning it is impossible to tell if UX studies of these tools have been conducted or what the results of those studies might be. However, a great many are open source, freely available research prototypes, or otherwise accessible and yet we do not see a wealth of UX understanding of these tools. A survey of authoring tools from wider IDN community as listed in Table 1 reveals that a significant majority have not been studied with regards to their user experience, and even for those that have, the level of evaluation is somewhat modest. It should be noted that our survey excludes tools that might be used for a small part of the authoring process, but not for the creation of the story proper, such as Story Validator [75] (which is used in IDN analysis) or procedural generators such as PaSSAGE [72] or SPHINX [50]. While tools for procedural systems or emergent narrative are not included here, that is, not to say their UX is any less important or that IDN research should not aspire to explore this space (emergent narrative is addressed in another chapter in this section)—these are, however, fundamentally very different forms with a different concept of authorship that we do not complicate our initial survey with. We categorise the current state of evaluation of these tools into three groups:

- **Example**: Presentation of tool with examples of use and function.
- **Partial**: Some form of evaluation but does not fully consider the UX.
- **Evaluated**: Those who undergo an evaluation that does explore the UX.

It is important to note that the genealogy of these technologies is such that one technology is often based on the advances developed in another, and where this happens, we consider evaluations to be transitive forward, but not backward. For example, if system B was based on an earlier system A, then we would consider an evaluation of A relevant in part to B, but not vica versa, and we are careful to explain below where we feel an evaluation is transitive or not.

Furthermore, it is also important at this stage to stress that it is not our intention to shame any of the scholars, developers, or creators behind these tools (indeed, one of this chapters authors own tools is top of this list). Many of these works have contributed immeasurably to IDN research and practice and there are often good reasons for the absence of evaluation which we will explore later in this chapter. However, first, we need to continue to explore the current state of understanding and evaluation in these three groups of tools.

1.1   Example Group

This group includes the majority of authoring tools in our survey, including some of the arguably most significant tools (in that they are commonly discussed), such as Twine [38] and Inklewriter [29]. Tools in this group are presented without any form of evaluation beyond examples of their use and functionality (thus the label 'example'). They are commonly presented as a discussion of the tool presenting its functionality and design, such as in work by Bernstein [5, 6] or Mitchell [49], and in some cases an example of a story created in the tool is presented as a case study as seen in Martens' work [42], or work by Kim [36]. In some cases, the tools are presented separately from case studies demonstrating their use, such as Weiss's work presenting Scenejo [77] and Glock's examples [15]. Even a tool used as widely as Twine [38] does not appear to have had its UX studied beyond some anecdotal personal experiences of working with the tool as seen in the works of Miles [46] and Schlauch [60], or use in non-UX evaluations in other domains such as Sørensen et al.'s work [64] on Inklewriter [29] in education.

This approach is less an attempt of evaluation and more one of demonstration—the authors do not claim to evaluate the tools, but do wish to clarify their functionality and potential through an example. While we learn much about the potential of the technology from this approach, and in some cases exciting new developments in authoring paradigms, we do not learn anything about the author experience of using such tools, their usability, or how the design of these tools and their innovations might influence authorship or resulting works.

In some cases, these works were formative and built upon in later systems that were partially evaluated, such as in how INSCAPE [3] and VHE [18] led to Story-Tec [17] (which is discussed in the partial group below). However, there is enough difference between these systems that we cannot see such an evaluation as transitive. Furthermore, in other cases, it is worth noting that the reader experience of the resulting stories has been later evaluated, such as for StoryPlaces[6] [48] or Art-E-Fact [27], but again this is the UX of the story not the tool, and this speaks to a fundamental problem in the field of the scholarly attention prioritising reader experience over author experience.

1.2 Partial Group

Some tools do go beyond just exampling functionality and features, and evaluate their tools. However, in the case of the tools in this group they stop short of might what be called a full UX study of the author experience, often just measuring one part of it or exploring a single limited aspect.

Stefnisson in their work on Mimisbrunner [68] conducts an evaluation of the tool [69] using the Creativity Support Index (CSI) [9] in order to show their tool is more supportive than directly programming an experience. While a quantitative measure of support for creativity such as CSI is undeniably valuable, it does not give us a full picture of the user experience, how the design impacted the authors, or how it affected their workflow. Consequently, while quantitative measures provide valuable indicators of potential issues, affordances, or phenomena it is difficult to learn from such an evaluation the reason for, or explanation of, any impact. Indeed, in this case, it limits our conclusions merely to the fact that the tool supports creativity more than pure programming.

StoryTec [17], like the group above, demonstrates its functionality through an example in the 80 days work [16] but its original publication does also include a usability evaluation. This evaluation draws an impressive number of participants (n = 86) but does not go beyond a simple self-report quantitative measure of usefulness and a couple of user quotes. While we can draw some conclusions from this as to the usability of this particular system, we again are unable to learn anything of substance about the details of the author experience or the impact of the tool.

We see a similar approach in Kapadia's work on CANVAS and their IBT projects. The original IBT work is evaluated in terms of the users "difficulty" in using the tool via a self-report 1–5 difficult rating and the clicks/time to create a story [35] but again while we might learn a limited impression of the usability of this tool, we are no wiser as to why or the specifics of the author experience of using IBTs here. Kapadia's further work using this in CANVAS [33] and elsewhere [34] relies upon this earlier evaluation of IBTs being transitive and does not further evaluate the user experience of the authoring tool. However, CANVAS later formed part of SWB [56] which was more extensively evaluated and is discussed below [55].

Finally, we have Szilas' seminal work on IDtension [70, 71], a complicated technology framework that is part procedural generator but also includes authorship components.For the most part, IDtension fits within the prior group, in that the work on it communicates functionality and examples, however, Szilas' work with Marty does go beyond this into collaboration with an author that explores the author expe-

---

[6] It is to be noted that, at the time of writing, a project with a UX evaluation of StoryPlaces' authoring tool has begun but is not yet complete.

rience. This evaluation is somewhat informal, includes a single author, and falls short of a rigorous UX study, but there is some consideration for the experience here that can help us learn about the impact of the tool's design, such as the resulting systematic and fractal method of writing.

Consequently, in this group, we can see some studies adopting an approach to tool evaluation—demonstrating relative ease of use in a limited quantitative fashion. But, from these studies, we do not learn about the specifics of the author experience or how the tools design might impact their use or results in a way that could inform the creation of future tools or our understanding of their use.

1.3   Evaluated Group

In some cases, authoring tools have been more substantially evaluated in a way that explores the author experience, as seen with the tools in this group. The majority of this work comes from three teams of researchers: the Zurich team of Zund and Poulakos et al., the Skovde team of Engstrom et al., and the authors of this chapter (Hargood and Green of Bournemouth).

Beginning with our own work this is atypical in that it is not evaluating our own tools but the tools of others, specifically Inform 7 [51], Quest [76], and Articy:Draft [2]. This study [23] was motivated in part by the very problem that we are presenting in this chapter, and all of these tools which would have otherwise fallen into the example group without evaluations beyond examples of their use. This makes this study somewhat less typical (all others being evaluations of the developers' own tools) and we will discuss it (and our observational and interview approach) later in this chapter.

The Zurich team, alongside Kapadia (whose work on CANVAS we cover in the previous section), have completed evaluations of their Story Version Control (SVC) [79] and Story World Builder (SWB) [55, 56] systems. Their evaluations rely on the System Usability Scale (SUS) [7]—a well-established, and long used, survey from the UX research world. While SUS only provides a quantitative measure of usability (similar to the quantitative approaches in the partial group above), Zund and Poulakos do go beyond this to explore the author experience through interviews and discussion, drawing conclusions on how authors' practice was impacted (such as reusing content) and the usability of paradigms (such as graphs). However, even here the evaluation and analysis of the data is still somewhat brief, and the evidence provided amounts to no more than a couple of pages of discussion rather than a full qualitative dissection of the experience and its explanation. Consequently, while we absolutely can learn about the author experience from these studies, our understanding remains incomplete.

Engstrom's work on Deig [13] and the Deig Writing Companion [12] is significantly more extensive. Here we see a longitudinal study where a substantial group of writers (n = 19) spend an extended period writing using the tool (5 days) in the case of Deig [13] and partial use through a full game development project and three writers in the case of Deig Writing Companion [12]. The result is a rich collection of evidence on the author experience, usability, intuitiveness, and structure for the Deig tools that represents the gold standard in author experience studies. While the results here are exceptional, so too are the costs—UX research is built upon a foundation of pragmatism and the necessity of keeping methods achievable [11, 19], and not all research projects have the resources or the opportunities for longitudinal studies— such that insisting on such an approach would do nothing to address the problems discussed in this chapter. This does not diminish the impressive results of Engstrom's work, but it does mean that his approach is not necessarily a solution for the problem.

Finally, outside of the publications of these three teams, there is one other tool that fits this group: GHOST and the work by Guarneri et al. [25]. Their survey and interview method goes beyond the quantitatively focused work in the partial group exploring author experience issues such as complexity and speed. However, it is still an extremely brief discussion appended to the presentation of the tool, and participants were only reporting on a 15 minute experience with the technology making the conclusions based only on the very start of a project. This makes this study informative but still of limited value in terms of fully understanding the author experience.

2 Explanation

So we have a problem in IDN research. Authoring tools are an essential part of our practice, UX is an essential part of understanding technology and its impact, but only a tiny handful of tools have been through any form of UX evaluation—and for most of those it is brief and/or does not explore the author experience. We are wielding hammers that may be shaping us and our work in ways we don't understand. Why?

While the authors of this chapter do not pretend to have interviewed every IDN academic on the reasons for this issue, from the work discussed above, we can infer four potential reasons for this issue:

2.1 Collaboration Between Research and Authors Is Hard

UX evaluation demands users, and for authoring tools that means authors. This is a skilled and limited participant set. Participant recruitment always raises challenges for any user study, even when the participants may belong to broad demographics, but when we constrain potential participants to a limited group of skilled individuals who already have access to similar tools to those that you are offering access to finding suitable participants becomes a genuine problem. This was something identified as a key challenge for IDN research in Spierling and Szilas' seminal work on IDN authorship [67] where they also point out that authors that are attracted to the project are often direct collaborators, co-designers, or even developers whose proximity makes them unsuitable as a UX evaluation participant. Consequently, faced with the challenge of finding authors, there is a temptation to focus on the reader instead where participants are much less limited. This may explain why we see many more reader experience evaluations [57] than author experience evaluations, bringing us neatly to our next explanation.

2.2 Reader Focus

A lot of IDN work focuses on the reader rather than the author. This is not without reason; the reader experience is to some extent the ultimate outcome of a IDN project, and what impacts their understanding and experience is undeniably important. IDN is also a research field that explores a broad range of mediums from Hypertext to parser fiction, to 3D worlds, to VR, AR, and locative narrative—and the field's understanding of this range of storytelling mediums and their impact on the reader is far from complete and undeniably important. Consequently, a significant proportion of IDN projects may consider authors, and authoring tools, as merely a means to an end—a step along the road to a particular piece of work or story deployment, and that any evaluation will seek to evaluate those stories rather than the tools used along the way. This may also be why, in our survey above, the most common form of authoring tool evaluation is "example"—stories created in the tools as proof of its functionality, but lacking scrutiny of their UX or authorial impact.

2.3 UX Is Not a Priority

IDN research covers a range of questions and areas of study far beyond UX, and in exploring these mediums, poetics, and technologies, as discussed above, it is possible authoring tools are often created as a means to an end towards answering these other questions. Given the limited resources of a research project, and the cost of running user studies, we might postulate that a motivation for not exploring the UX of tools is their cost, given that they don't represent the priority for the project. There are two issues at play here—the first is the author experience as a priority (something this chapter is trying to address) but also the cost of UX. As discussed earlier, UX research often highlights the importance of pragmatism in methods [11, 19], and UX researchers in other parts of the digital creative industries such as Medlock [45] and Huguenin [28] often stress the need for pragmatic approaches that recognise limited resources and "quick and dirty" UX methods in a world that potentially recognises the value of UX but does not necessarily prioritise it. Consequently, difficult and/or expensive methods such as the longitudinal studies presented by Engstrom [12, 13] cannot be the sole answer to this problem at scale. While these types of studies provide invaluable insight, we also need the "quick and dirty" methods seen elsewhere in UX research to make studies as accessible and pragmatic as possible. This brings us to our final explanation.

2.4 UX Methods Are Poorly Suited to the Study of Authoring Tools

Modern UX and HCI research has been criticised for being overly dogmatic. Greenberg and Buxton highlighted this in their seminal work [24] and also called for UX research to develop new methods custom—suited to the focus of their study rather than always adopting established protocols. Established UX study best practice often focuses on task-based usability tests [19]—have a user use your product as it is supposed to be used in a number of set tasks and record their performance, response, and experience. This may work fine if you are developing a car or a shopping website, where the common usage is clear and achievable in a short period of time. But what are the common tasks for IDN authorship? And how long do they last? Were we to use this standard approach with an authoring tool we might face the problem of telling an author to sit down and create an IDN, which might take days or even years. It is for this reason, we see some works like Engstrom's [12, 13] using longitudinal methods, and also why studies such as Guarneri et al.'s [25] are problematic as a typical short task method means your participants only barely begin to create their stories when that early set up is not typical of a substantial part of the writing process. Breaking authorship down into sub tasks comes with the challenge of identifying representative tasks for something as wide reaching and varied as a creative work. Even were we to achieve that we are still faced with the problem that all of those tasks put together is still a study that lasts the length of the creative process and beyond the resources of most researchers. Such long studies also hinder the application of many of a UX researchers most useful tools—methods such as the verbal protocol, described as "the single most valuable usability engineering method" by the UX pioneer Jakob Nielsen [52], become impossible to apply over such exercises robbing us of the valuable experience data they might provide. There are other solutions to longitudinal studies like this in UX, such as the diary study method [19], but these are very expensive as they effectively demand commissioning a full writing project— limiting the study to very a small n and failing to provide the pragmatism demanded above.

This absence of pragmatic user experience evaluation methods combined with the availability of short quantitative approaches such as SUS [7] and CSI [9] potentially leads researchers into relying on these brief measures of usability instead, such as we saw above in many of the works of our survey's "partial" group. It is to be noted that survey-based quantitative measures play a valuable role in UX evaluation, helping to identify phenomena for study and form broad initial observations. However, used alone, they leave us with a relative number confirming relative usability but not an in-depth understanding of the authoring experience or the impact of the tool.

Consequently, established UX methods have not only failed to serve the author experience evaluation, but they also have arguably laid a quantitative baited trap potentially tempting researchers into avoiding its qualitative challenges.

3   Solutions

The nature of this chapter, indeed this book, is to highlight unsolved problems and unanswered questions. Consequently, the authors of this chapter do not claim to have a solution. However, that doesn't mean we cannot discuss potential ways forward to begin to address this issue.

3.1   We Need New Methods

As described above, there are a number of problems with the application of established UX methods on authoring tools:

- It is challenging to break down a complex creative process such as IDN authorship for task-based usability tests
- Authorship is a lengthy process
- Shortening IDN authorship risks only evaluating story set up, which isn't typical of the full authoring process
- Longitudinal studies lose access to some evidence and are not always pragmatic
- Quantitative measures are useful but insufficient by themselves to fully understand the author experience

Consequently, in the spirit of Greenberg and Buxton [24], we need to develop new bespoke methods for authoring tool evaluation. These methods should seek to provide insight into traditional UX concepts such as usability, accessibility, and performance—but also the impact of the author experience on the author workflow and practice, and the impact on the work itself. Furthermore, these methods should tackle not just the impact of the interface paradigms, but also authoring tool features and functionality, and the impact of underlying models and structures. All of these variables are important to understand the impact of our tools, and that impact can come from all of these design sources.

While we don't have a solution to all of this yet, the authors of this chapter have been working towards some new methods in this space to address this problem, and we call on the community to assist in these efforts. We have developed [23], and continue to refine [21], a new method for understanding the author experience of IDN authoring tools. This method aims to both be pragmatic in being deliverable in a 1–2 hour study, but still target a representative sample of the authoring process, and gather quality data on the author experience.

The underlying principle of our method is completing an incomplete story. The participant will be given an authoring tool with an IDN story that is part written but missing a significant part of the story. They will then be asked to complete this missing part with guidance notes on what it should include, but creative freedom to interpret those as they see fit. In summary, the protocol is as follows:

1. Participants complete a brief pre-study demographic survey
2. Participants are given a short video and notes training them in basic use of the authoring tool.
3. Participants are given the authoring tool with a recognisable story that is partially complete but missing a section in the middle
4. Participants are given guidance on what this section should include but given creative freedom to complete the work.
5. While completing the work, the participant thinks aloud (verbal protocol), their screen is recorded to log interactions, and the researcher documents their behaviour, response, and attitude.
6. Following the exercise, the participant is interviewed on their experience targeting the impact of different parts of the tool design and their process.
7. Study closes. Data gathered includes the demographic survey, resulting story, screen recording of the exercise, audio recording of think aloud and interview, and researcher notes on behaviour during the study.

The specifics of the story selected (for our studies we deployed the often used "Little Red Riding Hood" and selected scenes from "Mass Effect" for different studies) and specific interview questions can vary depending on study—but this is the outline of the method we have been developing. There is a benefit to using a story with which participants are familiar in order to avoid a further training burden of familiarising them with the story, but there is also a benefit in controlling the content of the story to be representative of the form of IDN being explored. "Little Red Riding Hood" has previously been used as a staple test story IDN by the research community [66], and the interactive fiction community has similarly made use of Cloak of Darkness [14] in a similar way. Benchmarking, and the role of stories such as Little Red or Cloak of Darkness as standard stories to test in evaluations (and their suitability), is naturally a research topic in its own right, and while expanding on that here is outside the scope of this chapter that does not make it any less an important, and further work there would be valuable. We have explored this method, and variations of it, on a set of authoring tools which (prior to our studies) were both prominent and unevaluated beyond examples of use: Inform 7 [51], Quest [76], and Articy:Draft [2] have all been evaluated using the method [23]. We have also applied iterations of the method to prototype interfaces we have been working on for new tools [21]. These studies have not only shown our method to be effective, returning a wealth of useful authoring experience data, but also reveal the weaknesses within the method as well.

In terms of weaknesses, there are two key issues here. The method still requires tool training, and this is both time-consuming and a problem in terms of what is sufficient training for a genuine test. This problem could be avoided by recruiting prior users—but this would not help for new tools, and we were keen to target the author recruitment problem discussed in the previous section by targeting as broad a section of participants as possible. As such, we recruited people with a professional interest in IDN (and as such would at least be comfortable with the concepts involved) but still trained them in individual tools. Only about 14% of our participants felt that the training was insufficient for the exercise [21]—but this remains a constraint of the method that might influence results. The second weakness is the tension between structure and creativity. In attempting to retain the consistency of task-based usability methods, we wanted to try to have authors complete a repeatable and representative part of the story. To do this, while avoiding the problem of participants only setting up their story, we developed an approach that had participants complete a middle section of a partially complete story that guided them in terms of its content to ensure representative IDN content was explored, such as introducing characters, dialogue, exploring a space, and other common patterns. However, early feedback on the methodology criticised the artificial nature of the exercise in being too constrained given the inherent free form creativity involved in writing, so, consequently, we adjusted our content instructions to be mere suggestions, and while we kept these suggestions, participants were given more creative freedom. This is a tension in the methodology that is as yet unresolved—guidance ensures evaluation consistency and repeatable exercises but constrains the fundamental creativity in genuine authorship. Similarly, the more we give participants creative freedom the more genuine the exercise but the more exercises diverge, and the less we can be sure of representative content.

In terms of strengths, we are pleased that "completing a partially completed story" approach keeps the study length modest, and that by training participants we can recruit broadly. Both of these ensure a pragmatic approach to the method often called for in UX evaluation. At the same time, our studies have shown this method can return rich author experience data from which we were able to detect impacts on the authors' workflow, impacts on their resulting stories, and impact on their attitudes and experience [21, 23]. Furthermore, the story-finishing approach helps to ensure the exercises are more representative of the writing process by avoiding an exercise that is a story set up only, and guiding the content to a representative patterns (although as discussed above there is a tension in this part of the method design). Finally, the rich array of qualitative data gathered—from recordings of use, to the verbal protocol, to the interview—meant we were able to explore a range of areas of impact such as interface paradigms, functionality, and underlying models. As we continued to use this method, we tweaked the story content being completed, or the interview questions, to focus on the parts of the tool most in need of scrutiny—for example, in a later study, we focused part of our protocol on story testing functions in order to better impact the author experience impact there [21]. Not only was our work enlightening in terms of the author experience of the tools we explored, but we were able to use it to draw together a set of principles for future authoring tool design [21].

Ultimately, we do not pretend this is "one method to rule them all"—the approach shows promise, but has weaknesses, and needs further refinement. Furthermore, to attempt to establish a new author UX evaluation orthodoxy would be contrary to the very call to action that inspired us to develop new methods [24]. Indeed, while pragmatic qualitative methods, such as those we propose, are part of the way forward there are other paths that also demand attention—such as quantitative methods, and model evaluations. Furthermore, pragmatic lighter methods such as ours do not replace the qualitative value of larger scale free writing longitudinal studies, such as those demonstrated by Engstrom [12, 13]—which are more genuine, and less artificial, than what we propose here (if significantly more expensive). However, our method does represent an example of the beginnings of a potential approach to address part of the problem this chapter explores. There will be a need for other bespoke methods that address this problem, and different mediums will demand their own bespoke methods. As previously mentioned, evaluating a procedural tool is very different from the more conventional authoring tools explored in this chapter—and bespoke methods for different forms is at the heart of both Greenburg's motivating work [24] and our intent.

As noted, the approach we describe here is principally qualitative, however, as stated above, quantitative measures also have an important role to play. While long established methods in this area such as SUS [7] already provide valuable instruments, here we may further develop these into bespoke quantitative measures for authorial experience—indeed, the previously mentioned CSI [9] is such a development, and might be explored further.

Finally, it is also important to confront the assumption of what is being evaluated—a tool, such as interface paradigms and functionality, or underlying models, such as how that tool understands the components and connections of an IDN. One model (such as caligraphic hypertext [4]) could be used by many tools (such as Twine [38], Storyspace [6], and others). No authoring tool evaluation is completely divorced from either the tool or the model—as the author must experience both in order to create. However, another gap in our field lies in the development of new methods to explore specifically the impact of one or the other on the author experience through direct comparison.

3.2 The Author Experience Needs to Become a Priority

It is possible that, despite recognising the value of understanding the author experience, the absence of tool evaluations of depth is not just due to the challenges of those studies and their methods, but also due to the priority of challenges and questions to the research community. Consequently, while we feel methodological challenges represent a big part of this problem (as discussed above), all the methods in the world won't help if answering the question of the author experience is not a priority for the community. Consequently, if this chapter does anything beyond highlighting the problems of authoring tool evaluation, it is to call the community to action to address this problem. As we have laid out here authoring tools are a critical part of IDN and our understanding of them, and how they impact authors and their works, is lacking. Consequently, beyond our call for new methods above, we conclude this chapter with three grand challenges to the community:

1. **Study new tools**: As the community continues to develop new tools, we need to make understanding the author experience of these technologies a priority and a part of research plans that include tool development. We should be developing new methods to do this, and iterating on prior methods, to improve our understanding of the consequences of new technology.
2. **Study old tools**: Understanding the author experience needs not only to be part of projects that include tool development, but also something that concerns itself with the unevaluated tools of the past, particularly those widely used and adopted by the community. Furthermore, as these studies begin to appear, we should, as good scientists, be repeating those studies to confirm, refute, and modify our findings and understanding. Understanding the author experience cannot just be a part of research that happens to include a tool for another focus—it needs to become a priority in its own right.
3. **Study the impact on both author and work**: We need to broaden our approach to the author experience beyond mere usability. This does not mean to disregard usability, it remains a critical issue, but to go beyond it to understand how the workflow and practice of authors is affected in their UX more broadly. While some studies we have discussed here have begun to do this, we also need to go beyond even this to explore the impact on resulting works and explore how stories are changed by the tools that develop them.

This is not to suggest that this should be the only priority for IDN research, but rather that it should be a priority, and current work in the field (as laid out in this chapter) does not support that it is. This chapter also lays out why we feel it should be a priority, in that the author experience of tools has direct impact on the works created and the accessibility of the field. Consequently, author experience not only influences reader experience, but also the existence of works, structural designs, and styles of writing in our medium as a whole.

Authorship, and authoring tools, remain a critical part of IDN research [67], and UX remains a critical part of the study of technology [19], creating a combined challenge in our field. Our understanding of our tools needs to go beyond examples of their use, and our approach to UX needs to mature beyond a simple metric of usability. We need a richer understanding of the author experience, how we shape our tools, and how they shape us.

References

1. Adams B, Venkatesh S (2004) Authoring multimedia authoring tools. IEEE Multimed 11(3):1–6
2. Articy-software: Articy:draft. https://www.articy.com/en/
3. Balet O (2007) Inscape an authoring platform for interactive storytelling. In: International conference on virtual storytelling. Springer, pp 176–177
4. Bernstein M (2001) Card shark and thespis: exotic tools for hypertext narrative. In: Proceedings of the 12th ACM conference on hypertext and hypermedia, pp 41–50
5. Bernstein M (2002) Storyspace 1. In: Proceedings of the thirteenth ACM conference on hypertext and hypermedia, pp 172–181
6. Bernstein M (2016) Storyspace 3. In: Proceedings of the 27th ACM conference on hypertext and social media, New York, NY, USA, pp 201–206
7. Brooke J et al (1996) SUS: A 'Quick and Dirty' Usability Scale. Usability Evaluation Ind 189(194):4–7
8. Charles F, Pizzi D, Cavazza M, Vogt T, André E (2009) EmoEmma: emotional speech input for interactive storytelling. In: Proceedings of the 8th international conference on autonomous agents and multiagent systems, vol 2, pp 1381–1382
9. Cherry E, Latulipe C (2014) Quantifying the creativity support of digital tools through the creativity support index. ACM Trans Comput-Hum Interact (TOCHI) 21(4):1–25
10. Donikian S, Portugal JN (2004) Writing interactive fiction scenarii with DraMachina. In: International conference on technologies for interactive digital storytelling and entertainment. Springer, pp 101–112
11. Drachen A, Mirza-Babaei P, Nacke LE (2018) Games user research. Oxford University Press
12. Engström H (2019) I have a different kind of brain—a script-centric approach to interactive narratives in games. Digit Creat 30(1):1–22
13. Engström H, Brusk J, Erlandsson P (2018) Prototyping tools for game writers. Comput Games J 7(3):153–172
14. Firth R (2022) Cloak of darkness. IF Wiki. https://www.ifwiki.org/Cloak_of_Darkness
15. Glock F, Junker A, Kraus M, Lehrian C, Schäfer A, Hoffmann S, Spierling U (2011) "Office Brawl": a conversational storytelling game and its creation process. In: Proceedings of the 8th international conference on advances in computer entertainment technology, pp 1–2
16. Göbel S, Mehm F, Radke S, Steinmetz R (2009) 80 days: adaptive digital storytelling for digital educational games. In: Proceedings of the 2nd international workshop on story-telling and educational games (STEG'09), vol 498
17. Göbel S, Salvatore L, Konrad R (2008) Storytec: a digital storytelling platform for the authoring and experiencing of interactive and non-linear stories. In: 2008 international conference on automated solutions for cross media content and multi-channel distribution. IEEE, pp 103–110
18. Göbel S, Schneider O, Iurgel I, Feix A, Knöpfle C, Rettig A (2004) Virtual human: storytelling and computer graphics for a virtual human platform. In: International conference on technologies for interactive digital storytelling and entertainment. Springer, pp 79–88
19. Goodman E, Kuniavsky M (2012) Observing the user experience: a practitioner's guide to user research. Elsevier
20. Gordon A, van Lent M, Van Velsen M, Carpenter P, Jhala A (2004) Branching storylines in virtual reality environments for leadership development. In: Proceedings of the national conference on artificial intelligence, pp 844–851. Menlo Park, CA; Cambridge, MA; London; AAAI Press; MIT Press
21. Green D (2021) Don't forget to save! the impact of user experience design on effectiveness of authoring video game narratives. PhD thesis
22. Green D, Hargood C, Charles F (2018) Define authoring tool: a survey of interactive narrative authoring tools. In: Authoring for interactive storytelling workshop (2018)
23. Green, D., Hargood, C., Charles, F.: Use of tools: UX principles for interactive narrative authoring tools. Journal on Computing and Cultural Heritage (JOCCH) 14(3), 1–25 (2021)

24. Greenberg S, Buxton B (2008) Usability evaluation considered harmful (some of the time). In: Proceedings of the SIGCHI conference on human factors in computing systems, pp 111–120
25. Guarneri A, Ripamonti LA, Tissoni F, Trubian M, Maggiorini D, Gadia D (2017) Ghost: a ghost story-writer. In: Proceedings of the 12th biannual conference on italian SIGCHI chapter, pp 1–9
26. Hargood C, Weal MJ, Millard DE (2018) The storyplaces platform: building a web-based locative hypertext system. In: Proceedings of the 29th on hypertext and social media, pp 128–135
27. Hassenzahl M, Ullrich D (2007) To do or not to do: differences in user experience and retrospective judgments depending on the presence or absence of instrumental goals. Interact Comput 19(4):429–437
28. Huguenin J (2018) Running user tests with limited resources and experience. In: Games user research. Oxford University Press
29. Ingold J (2022) Inklewriter. https://www.inklestudios.com/inklewriter/
30. Iurgel I (2004) From another point of view: art-e-fact. In: International conference on technologies for interactive digital storytelling and entertainment. Springer, pp 26–35
31. Iurgel IA (2006) Cyranus—an authoring tool for interactive edutainment applications. In: International conference on technologies for e-learning and digital entertainment. Springer, pp 577–580
32. Iurgel IA (2008) An authoring framework for interactive narrative with virtual characters. PhD thesis, Technische Universität
33. Kapadia M, Frey S, Shoulson A, Sumner RW, Gross MH (2016) CANVAS: computer-assisted narrative animation synthesis. In: Symposium on computer animation, pp 199–209
34. Kapadia M, Shoulson A, Steimer C, Oberholzer S, Sumner RW, Gross M (2016) An event-centric approach to authoring stories in crowds. In: Proceedings of the 9th international conference on motion in games, pp 15–24
35. Kapadia M, Zünd F, Falk J, Marti M, Sumner RW, Gross M (2015) Evaluating the authoring complexity of interactive narratives with interactive behaviour trees. Found Digit Games
36. Kim S, Moon S, Han S, Chan J (2011) Programming the story: interactive storytelling system. Informatica 35(2) (2011)
37. Kitromili S, Jordan J, Millard DE (2020) What authors think about hypertext authoring. In: Proceedings of the 31st ACM conference on hypertext and social media, pp 9–16
38. Klimas C. Twine. https://twinery.org/. Accessed 25 Jan 2022
39. Koenitz H (2011) Extensible tools for practical experiments in IDN: the advanced stories authoring and presentation system. In: International conference on interactive digital storytelling. Springer, pp 79–84
40. Koenitz H, Chen KJ (2012) Genres, structures and strategies in interactive digital narratives–analyzing a body of works created in ASAPS. In: International conference on interactive digital storytelling. Springer, pp 84–95
41. Kriegel M, Aylett R, Dias J, Paiva A (2007) An authoring tool for an emergent narrative storytelling system. In: AAAI fall symposium: intelligent narrative technologies, pp 55–62
42. Martens C, Iqbal O (2019) Villanelle: an authoring tool for autonomous characters in interactive fiction. In: International conference on interactive digital storytelling. Springer, pp 290–303
43. Mateas M, Stern A (2002) A behavior language for story-based believable agents. IEEE Intell Syst 17(4):39–47
44. Medler B, Magerko B (2006) Scribe: a tool for authoring event driven interactive drama. In: International conference on technologies for interactive digital storytelling and entertainment. Springer, pp 139–150
45. Medlock MC, Wixon D, Terrano M, Romero R, Fulton B (2002) Using the rite method to improve products: a definition and a case study. Usability Prof Assoc 51
46. Miles AP, Jenkins K (2017) (Re)born digital-trans-affirming research, curriculum, and pedagogy: an interactive multimodal story using twine. Vis Arts Res 43(1):43–49
47. Millard D, Hargood C, Howard Y, Packer H (2017) The storyplaces authoring tool: pattern centric authoring. In: Authoring for interactive storytelling workshop

48. Millard DE, Packer H, Howard Y, Hargood C (2020) The balance of attention: the challenges of creating locative cultural storytelling experiences. J Comput Cult Herit 13(4)

49. Mitchell A, McGee K (2012) The HypeDyn hypertext fiction authoring tool. In: Proceedings of the 2nd workshop on narrative and hypertext, pp 19–22

50. Morgan L, Haahr M (2020) Honey, I'm home: an adventure game with procedurally generated narrative puzzles. In: International conference on interactive digital storytelling. Springer, pp 335–338

51. Nelson G (2006) Natural language, semantic analysis and interactive fiction. IF Theory Reader 141:99–104

52. Nielsen J (1994) Usability engineering. Morgan Kaufmann

53. O'Flynn S (2019) Media fluid and media fluent, e-literature in the era of experience design. Hyperrhiz 20

54. Pope J. Generator. https://genarrator.org/. Accessed 25 Jan 2022

55. Poulakos S, Kapadia M, Maiga GM, Zünd F, Gross M, Sumner RW (2016) Evaluating accessible graphical interfaces for building story worlds. In: International conference on interactive digital storytelling. Springer, pp 184–196

56. Poulakos S, Kapadia M, Schüpfer A, Zünd F, Sumner RW, Gross M (2015) Towards an accessible interface for story world building. In: Eleventh artificial intelligence and interactive digital entertainment conference

57. Revi AT, Millard DE, Middleton SE (2020) A systematic analysis of user experience dimensions for interactive digital narratives. In: International conference on interactive digital storytelling. Springer, pp 58–74

58. Roberts M. Tads. https://www.tads.org/. Accessed 25 Jan 2022

59. Rothamel T. Ren'py. https://www.renpy.org/. Accessed 31 May 2022

60. Schlauch M (2021) The unlucky Hans. The difficulties of adapting fairy tales as text-based games for young readers. Gamevironments 15

61. Shibolet Y, Knoller N, Koenitz H (2018) A framework for classifying and describing authoring tools for interactive digital narrative. In: International conference on interactive digital storytelling. Springer, pp 523–533

62. Short E (2014) Writing in collaboration with the system. https://emshort.blog/2014/10/29/writing-in-collaboration-with-the-system/

63. Silva P, Gao S, Nayak S, Ramirez M, Stricklin C, Murray J (2021) Timeline: an authoring platform for parameterized stories. In: ACM international conference on interactive media experiences, IMX'21. Association for Computing Machinery. New York, NY, USA, pp 280–283

64. Sørensen BH, Levinsen KT (2015) Evaluation as a powerful practice in digital learning processes. Electron J E-learn 13(4):290–300

65. Spierling U, Iurgel I (2003) Just talking about art—creating virtual storytelling experiences in mixed reality. In: International conference on virtual storytelling. Springer, pp 179–188

66. Spierling U, Iurgel I, Richle U, Szilas N (2009) Workshop on authoring methods and conception in interactive storytelling. In: Joint international conference on interactive digital storytelling. Springer, pp 356–357

67. Spierling U, Szilas N (2009) Authoring issues beyond tools. In: Joint international conference on interactive digital storytelling, pp 50–61. Springer

68. Stefnisson I, Thue D (2018) Mimisbrunnur: AI-assisted authoring for interactive storytelling. In: Proceedings of the AAAI conference on artificial intelligence and interactive digital entertainment, vol 14

69. Stefnisson IS (2018) Mímisbrunnur: a mixed-initiative authoring tool for interactive storytelling. PhD thesis

70. Szilas N (2003) IDtension: a narrative engine for interactive drama. In: Proceedings of the technologies for interactive digital storytelling and entertainment (TIDSE) conference, vol 3, pp 1–11

71. Szilas N, Marty O, Réty JH (2003) Authoring highly generative interactive drama. In: International conference on virtual storytelling. Springer, pp 37–46

72. Thue D, Bulitko V, Spetch M, Wasylishen E (2007) Interactive storytelling: a player modelling approach. In: AIIDE, pp 43–48
73. Ursu MF, Zsombori V, Wyver J, Conrad L, Kegel I, Williams D (2009) Interactive documentaries: a golden age. Comput Entertain 7(3)
74. Ursu MF, Cook JJ, Zsombori V, Kegel I (2007) A genre-independent approach to producing interactive screen media narratives. In: AAAI fall symposium: intelligent narrative technologies, p 174
75. Veloso C, Prada R (2021) Validating the plot of interactive narrative games. In: 2021 IEEE Conference on Games (CoG), pp 01–08
76. Warren A. Quest. http://textadventures.co.uk/quest. Accessed 25 Jan 2022
77. Weiss S, Müller W, Spierling U, Steimle F (2005) Scenejo—an interactive storytelling platform. In: International conference on virtual storytelling. Springer, pp 77–80
78. Wild C (2022) Adrift. https://www.adrift.co/
79. Zünd F, Poulakos S, Kapadia M, Sumner RW (2017) Story version control and graphical visualization for collaborative story authoring. In: Proceedings of the 14th European conference on visual media production (CVMP 2017), pp 1–10

Quantitative Analysis of Emergent Narratives

Quinn Kybartas

Abstract Emergent narratives model the process of storytelling through the use of simulation. The complexity and breadth of possible outcomes from a playthrough of an emergent narrative pose a number of unique challenges to authors. In this chapter, we survey the application of quantitative evaluations of emergent and narrativistic behaviours, examining how they may be used to provide feedback throughout the development process of an emergent narrative work. Four analysis techniques are also presented, which make use of quantitative analysis, benchmarking, comparisons, verification and classification.

1 Introduction

Emergent narratives [EN] are a subgenre of interactive digital narratives [IDN] typically focused on modelling the process of story creation through the use of simulation. EN simulations are often agent-based, with individual agents acting as characters in a virtual storyworld that affords certain actions. The interaction between agents and the world forms a *trace* of events, which, in certain cases, embodies a type of narrativity. A narrative trace is thus viewed as an emergent event resulting from the process of running, and having interactors interact with, a complex simulation.

From an authoring standpoint, the creation of an emergent narrative occurs in multiple manners. On the one hand, there is the authorship of the simulation itself, including the rules, actions, behaviours and other systemic content that drives the work. There is also, arguably, authorship on behalf of the interactor, whose experience of an emergent narrative work is also an act of storytelling within the confines of the work's system. In this chapter, we concern ourselves with the first form of authorship, that of the creator of the simulation itself, and the resulting challenges of building such a complex system. Further, the particular problem the chapter discusses surrounds the problem of *author assistance*, and specifically of understanding the complex behaviours of the emergent narrative, and how these are formed by the content being

Q. Kybartas (✉)
McGill University, Montréal, QC, Canada
e-mail: qkybartas@gmail.com

authored. This is of particular concern in emergent narratives, where the desired experience of the work is not provided directly through authored narrative structures, but rather through a possibility space defined by rules and systems [1].

Author assistance in many IDN works is often provided through the use of *tools*, which reduce the complexity of creating specific content for work. As an example, branching narrative works are often represented using a directed graph, and authoring tools such as TWINE [2] and STORYSPACE [3] use a graph visualization to show the high-level branching structure of the work being created. Typically, these authoring tools are evaluated according to the user experience of using the tool [4], and how it simplifies the process of understanding the work being created [5].

One advantage to using a graph representation is that it enables certain forms of *quantitative analysis*. We define a quantitative analysis as an approach to evaluating narrative works according to a certain set of qualities, which can be reduced to a specific value or model. In branching narratives, quantitative analysis has been used to conclude certain narrative qualities from the structure of the graph, such as the average nodes visited in a given trace, the number of possible choices afforded to the interactor, and the overall impact on the game world [6, 7].

Emergent narratives, by their nature, seem to resist the kind of simple, efficient tools prized in other forms of authorship. This is due, in part, to the fact that the content in an emergent narrative often has a much less fixed, predictable underlying structure in relation to more traditional works. What drives emergent works is often sets of rules or character actions, and during simulations these rules are decided based on the current state of the simulation. While the burden of rule authorship can be reduced, this does not allow an author to understand how a rule interacts and modifies the overall *possible narratives* that may emerge through runs of the simulation [8]. As an example, consider the popular EN work "The Sims" [9], which uses a form of *utility-based AI* in which each character has a set of needs that decay over time, and need to ideally be kept as high as possible (e.g. hunger and energy). Actions are selected predominantly by their overall ability to raise a character's needs, with priorities given to the needs required to survive. While the high-level description of "The Sims" sounds straightforward, during the actual act of authoring actions, the overall behaviour of the system is reduced down to a number of *parameters*. The rate at which needs decay, the amount of needs filled or drained for a certain action, the weighting of importance of certain needs, are all a vast series of numbers that the developers must specify. The end goal is to have a certain amount of stability and predictable character behaviours, but also a subversive element of instability and conflict needed to produce more interesting stories. The experience of playing "The Sims", however, gives an impression of behaviours that are far from sensical. The characters will run through fires to get food or go swimming instead of going to work. The unpredictable behaviours in "The Sims" are so common that they have become an iconic part of the franchise. Though, from a content authoring perspective, all of "The Sims" possible actions are grounded in real-world logic, the low-level behaviours created by the parameters are simply too numerous and complex for the game's developers to fully understand and design around.

In the past, I was fortunate to work as a designer on a moderately sized emergent narrative game, and less fortunate in that it never saw release; however, it made clear many of the unique authoring challenges of ENs. Bug reports would almost always list occurrences of strange behaviours, which would result in a return to the large table of parameters for each action and tweak values to find a solution. As the project progressed and got more complex, authoring and bug-fixing became more fragile and tedious. Would lowering the need decay of hunger from 5.5 units/day to 5.45 units/day make characters eat more regularly? Would it work for a few days and then slowly drift until characters would eat at three in the morning? Would adding the option to have a snack stop characters from ever eating dinner, since it is faster and more convenient to snack throughout the day? Though these behaviours are not impossible, and could easily define normal human behaviour, in the intended experience of the work they were undesirable. Furthermore, it seemed to identify a gap in the understanding and support of authorship for EN works, that of creating an "understanding" of the simulation and how changes in the rules change the possible narratives which might emerge from the simulation.

In this chapter, we survey works that attempt to understand, analyze and classify the behaviour of complex systems. This survey is split into three sections. First, we survey approaches to the analysis of the rules and content underpinning the simulation itself, and how the potential behaviour of these rules can be understood. The second section looks specifically at the simulation itself, both in how it is modelled, and how extracting traces or systems behaviour can reveal insight into the broader behavioural patterns present in the simulation. Lastly, we explore how interactor behaviour and experience of the game can be used by authors to aid in authorship and understand the way interactors engage with the work. Its noteworthy that the field of EN is quite broad, and as such the types of analysis needed are often dependent on the type of EN being developed. A game like "Dwarf Fortress" is radically different than "The Sims", and as such, we can't expect the same approaches to work between games. Likewise, we will also draw examples of research more generally positioned in IDN or games research but discuss its potential overlap within the field of EN.

As a quick note on terminology, in this chapter, we use the term "work" or "game" interchangeably to describe a specific instance of an EN. We use a "trace" to describe a set of output from the EN simulation and "play trace" in the instance when the trace comes from a interactor's interaction with the system.

2   Analyzing the Rules

Long before there is full, playable, or even testable EN, there is likely a large portion of development based entirely on the authoring of low-level system behaviours. These can be actions in games like "The Sims", narrative content in storylet focused games such as "King of Chicago" [10], the social or norm rules in works made with the *Comme-Il-Faut* [11] and *Versu* [12] engine, and so forth. Though the broader experience of the EN will be influenced by surface elements such as the graphics, audio and text, the behaviour of the system will be strictly defined through the rules and their implicit behaviour.

Emergent narrative often gets described in a fuzzy sense as having a form of "narrative possibility space". There are multiple ways we can more formally define the "possibility space" of an EN. One approach is to define a possibility space as every possible playthrough of a system, i.e. the accumulation of all possible traces. The narrative possibility space, then, is a subset of the possibility space consisting of traces which may be classified as a narrative, as containing a narrative, or as containing a certain sense of narrativity. This is what is most commonly assumed to be the "narrative possibility space" but it is still based upon determining a classification for "narrativity". This is by no means a dead-end. Ryan approaches "narrativity" instead from the perspective of tellability and how it relates to the possible alternate worlds which might have occurred in the narrative [13]. Likewise work on EN *curationism* allows authors to provide a definition of different types of narrative traces, and the classification procedure can explicitly find instances of these traces among the broader traces of the simulation.

An alternate approach to analyzing for narrativity is to instead focus on a specific *quality* of narrative and map the possibility space of this particular quality. In the procedural generation community, *expressive range analysis* is often used to evaluate the content of a set of generative methods according to a set of numerical qualities, which can be inferred from the content created by the system [14]. The "space" of qualities is mapped visually, by varying specific parameters of the generative methods and seeing how the resulting space changes. To be applicable to emergent narrative, the qualities defined need to relate specifically to narrative or IDN. One particular quality of narrative which has received attention is *conflict*, as most, but not all [15], types of narrative are said to possess a number of conflicts and an overall progression defined by the encountering and resolution of said conflicts. In work from Ware et al. [16], narrative conflict is broken down into a set of quantitative metrics, treating a conflict as a form of complication or hindrance in the *goals* of a particular character. The metrics allow for conflicts to be detected and valued in the traces of a provided narrative generation system. Other formalizations of narrative properties include work on surprise [17], tellability [18], reincorporation [19] and impact [20].

Though most of these works explore ways to evaluate traces of an IDN system analytically, the formalisms provided can instead be the focus of authorship and evaluation. This approach to authorship was examined in the work of Szilas, who first provided a formal definition of "dramatic conflicts" according to paradoxical relations between the goals of one or more characters [21]. Since the work used fixed goals, the total number of conflicts possible within the works can be known, and the Szilas further provided an authoring tool and IDN model specifically designed for authoring these dramatic conflicts. One of the interesting results from this work is that, simply through the design of character goals and actions, all possible conflicts of the system can be understood, irrespective of the specific experience of interactors. Later work from Szilas et al. looked at how the conflicts present in an author's work can be automatically detected and clustered, giving authors a quick overview of the overall structure and style of the underlying work [22]. In my own work, I've looked at how, by applying a formal metric of goal-based conflict, the overall space of conflict in an emergent narrative work can be presented visually and analyzed [23]. One of the advantages to trying to understand EN simulation through specific qualities is that we are effectively able to reduce the overall fuzziness surrounding the term "narrative possibility space", and "narrativity", and more specifically study which the narrative qualities we are interested in seeing emerge, and the way the content and rules of the work support or hinder this quality.

Though a quality-focused analysis is one possibility for re-framing systemic behaviour, it is also possible to evaluate the system in terms of fixed metrics that have no particular relation to narrative quality but are nonetheless critically important for the EN work. In Garbe et al.'s work on the design and implementation of the IDN work "Ice-Bound", a particular focus was placed upon the design of authorship assistance tools for content [24]. "Ice-Bound" is a work that requires a significant amount of text to be authored for many possible variants of interactor choice. Given the breadth of choices, it would be very easy to miss or under develop certain patterns of interactor behaviours. The tools designed then examined different combinations of potential interactor choices and classified which of those were lacking in supporting content. This made it easier to concentrate authorship on areas needing further development. "Ice-Bound" was a *storylet* style of EN work, and storylet works often require a significant amount of content development for each specific storylet, and so comparatively to rule-based EN works, focus the analysis on content over behaviour is reasonable. Storylet ENs do, however, depend on the behaviour of the underlying system, what Kreminski and Wardrip-Fruin define as the *content selection architecture* [25], and as such even storylet works can benefit from behavioural and quality-based analysis.

In some cases, the overall format of an EN work allows certain properties to be understood using existing methods and verification techniques. The progression of a simulation over time can in a sense be *predicted* by looking at which particular rules might be applied at different states of the simulation. As an example, in Maher's historical retrospective on the "King of Chicago", it is noted that the game's designer was uncertain if all the game's storylets were *accessible* to interactors. Essentially, "King of Chicago" kept track of interactor variables over time, which acted as the "state" of the game. Each storylet had a precondition that indicated in which state of the game the storylet would be most likely, and several postconditions that would change the state in the game. Storylets then were selected at each stage by choosing the storylet whose precondition most closely matches that of the game state. So the accessibility concern the designer spoke of boils down to the idea that certain game states could never be reached regardless of the choices made by the interactor, meaning the selection procedure would never select storylets, which required an impossible state as precondition. *Accessibility* is often a concern in EN design, in which content can easily be made inaccessible as the development of the work proceeds. In the case of "King of Chicago", and similar storylet designs, the solution is quite simply to reduce the accessibility concern down to a pathing problem, and, since the storylets in "King of Chicago" can only appear once per run, if is quite simple to perform a check to see if there is a path from the starting state of the game to each of the storylets. This can similarly be used to check the accessibility of rules in a simulation and can be extended to look at features such as the *coverage* of certain groups of content, the probability of content being experienced by the interactor, etc. Accessibility is a particular type of narrative quality, that, rather than being estimated or broadly understood, can be formally understood and proven. A deeper form of proving and understanding IDN works was taken by Pickett et al. and involved *transforming* an existing IDN format, in this case interaction fiction, into a different model through which formal qualities can be proven, in this case Petri-Nets [26]. The work attempted specifically to look at progression problems in IDN, such as whether certain endings were accessible, if there were dead-ends where the interactor was unable to progress, etc., which could not easily be understood from the existing interactive fiction model.

3   Analyzing the Simulation

While authoring tools, content analysis and quality analysis can serve an important role in authorship, they can also be expensive. The tools and methodology must always be adapted to any major changes in the formatting or implementation of the simulation and its content. Furthermore, it may simply be the case that the author's preferred authoring style is indifferent to the highly quantified and low-level approach enabled by tools and analysis. For many authors, the creation of content is done holistically, with an overall estimation of how the rules will modify the overall experience. The approach taken by Adams for "Dwarf Fortress" highlights this [27]. For Adams, the simulation is iteratively grown with new systems added to allow for specific narrative experiences, of which the first step is to write a sample story of one desirable narrative the author wishes to see in the work. Adams then determines which systems may produce different elements of the sample story, and in turn expands these systems with additional parameters so that variants or new versions of the sample story may appear. This style of authorship can be said to be heavily dependent on what Mateas terms *procedural literacy*, a skill that enables, among other things, an ability to translate media effects to procedural code, and understand how the code can, through procedural process, create the media effect in turn [28]. In these cases, the author's estimations and intended results are tested by rigorously testing the simulation itself, using different starting states and parameters, to attempt to understand if the new systems are behaving correctly and providing the intended result.

As with any approach, there are both advantages and disadvantages to adopting a procedural literacy auteur position. Adams' approach, for example, focuses on the continual development and implementation of new systems, resulting in the extremely long development time of "Dwarf Fortress". For many authors, this approach is simply too intensive and expensive as a development approach to IDN works. It may also blind the author to quicker or more efficient approaches, and ways to reuse existing systems. Lastly, it can result in systems that perform a specific role for a specific narrative, but in practice have little to no use in the broader simulation or are not engaged with by the majority of interactors. More broadly though, procedural literacy is an extremely difficult skill to build and hone, and lacks a larger community of practitioners, practices and references. To approach a more formal and analytical style of procedural literacy, it helps to look outside of IDN and games research and into the broader field of the analysis of complex systems and emergent behaviour.

Similar to the Petri-Net modelling work of Pickett et al., the understanding of complex systems often occurs by transforming or reducing the behaviour to a specific, understandable and evaluable framework. Holland proposes such a framework for generalized complex adaptive systems, based upon the idea of signal processing, and treating the behaviour of complex systems as signals operating within boundaries that define certain types of emergent behaviour [29]. In Holland's model, the agent and simulation itself send out *signals*, and these signals can be classified within certain boundaries, based on these boundaries, the agents will process the signal into something new, which may occasionally permeate the existing boundary into a new one, where it can be processed again. As a simple example, we can imagine the signals that might result in a kiss between two characters becoming an affair story. First, the agents act within their own interpersonal boundaries and might process a romantic signal between each other and transform it into an action, i.e. a kiss. The kiss is itself a behavioural signal, and if boundaries are defined to classify relationship types, a kiss signal, coupled with signals that both characters are married to other characters, can transform into a new signal, representing that an affair behaviour has occurred. This behaviour can then form a signal in the boundary of narrative types, and with a number of other signals (discovery, fallout, etc.) form an affair narrative. It is important to note that this in no way might be the formal way the system is developed, rather, Holland presents it as model for understanding how the resulting system works and produces certain behaviours. Holland approaches this model from a number of perspectives, such as how to classify boundaries, how to define the permeation between boundaries, etc., as well as exploring how this model can be understood probabilistically and used to understand the emergent behaviours resulting from each system.

Though one of the more highly detailed works on complex systems, Holland's framework is a challenging system to understand, and to my knowledge, there are no particular authoring tools or formal approaches to using this framework. A simpler alternative might be found in the work of Osborn et al.'s PLAYSPECS, which approaches the task of understanding emergent system behaviour by first converting the system into regular expressions, and then using software verification techniques to prove the properties about system behaviour. As with Holland, analyzing an EN work with this method involves transforming the existing simulation to a different format, which is time intensive and costly, but in turn can provide a type of formal analysis of the overall system behaviour.

An alternate approach to analyzing complex system behaviour, described by Mitchell, involves visually mapping the progression of the state of a simulation over time with a particular set of rules, and then looking for particular patterns in the results and how those relate to high-level system behaviour [30]. In the example provided by Mitchell, the state of simulation is reduced to a list of bits, which are assigned a white pixel for true and black for false. At each timestep, the new state of the system is drawn in a new row of the visualization, resulting in an image that shows the changes in simulation over time. Mitchell's visualization approach, in some sense, has similarity to the aforementioned *expressive range analysis*, and I explored a similar type of visualization of conflict patterns in my own work [31]. Visualizations such as these can form an interesting avenue for procedural literacy, focused on discovering and understanding patterns in a simplified model of the simulation trace. Visualizations, however, are highly dependent on being able to fully run the simulation, and extract the traces in the form a visual pattern, meaning that this particular form of analysis would typically be more applicable at mature state of development of the EN work. Visualizations also depend on having the ability to interpret the results from what may be a significant amount of data. The challenge of interpretation has been approached in some works by finding techniques to automatically extract the interpretation from traces of the system itself. Moncion et al., provide a form of behaviour analysis that focuses on modelling an *interaction network* of the interaction of agents over time in a simulation. The authors propose that the emergent behaviour in complex systems is entirely dependent on the interactions between agents and entities and the system, and explicitly chart each interaction as part of an interaction network, that evolves over the course of the simulation. Following this, the authors use network analysis techniques to extract information about the larger patterns and properties found in the interactions between agents [32].

4 Analyzing the Interactor's Experience

Ideally, an EN work will eventually be experienced by an audience. This occurs after the release of the work but can also occur during the development in the form of play-testing, through which the authors of the work can fix or modify the EN based on interactor's feedback. Play-testing often loosely takes the form of a *user study*, in which the interactor's experience in the game is surveyed at the end of the test, allowing authors to assign quantitative values to certain qualities of the EN work. User studies also feature prominently in IDN research and their works, typically focusing on the specific affordances of interaction, and its impact on the overall experience [33]. EN works again, however, are difficult to evaluate using user studies or play-testing, for the same reasons that they are hard to author. Specifically, the amount of possible experiences in an EN is significantly broader than traditional games or works, and these experiences tend to vary more between interesting and boring results. One particular issue I faced in practice was that the complexity of the EN work we were making was growing so radically, that play-testers were no longer able to fully explore the new content added to the system since the last play-test, meaning that increasingly we were receiving less actionable feedback over time. A common approach for authors of larger scale ENs is to use a form of *early access* model, where interactors understand they are buying an incomplete game and typically given a space to voice their feedback in forums or other types of social media.

A unique approach to understanding the user experience in EN works, and in turn to evaluate the larger system, is by examining interactor *re-tellings*. As proposed by Eladhari, many interactors tend to share certain exciting or interesting experiences within the game, and share these experiences as a narrative, often adding a significant amount of ornamentation not present in the underlying simulation [34]. For Eladhari, the ability of a system to encourage these re-tellings can be understood as a measure of quality for the system, since the overall goal of these systems is that their users have an experience which feels narrativistic. Eladhari's re-tellings specifically describe a story which is told after the user's experience, but this same analysis would work on Ryan's concept of *emplotment* [35]. Ryan proposes an alternate way in which narratives are constructed from complex behaviours, specifically that the viewer of the work is actively attempting to construct possible narratives from the behaviours they see, adapting and dropping different potential narratives based on whether later behaviour in the system supports or invalidates that particular narrative (Ryan uses sportscasting as an example type of emplotment). A criticism to Eladhari's approach is taken by Sych, who points out that a large body of re-tellings are humorous, and present criticisms of the overall inability for the system to produce interesting narratives, one which is shared with a public audience for scrutiny [36]. As such, it is harder to perform critical analysis on re-tellings, and it is more the burden of the author or the critique to determine exactly what the re-telling might be saying about the simulation that created it.

Analytic approaches to evaluating the interactor's experience in a work often forgo subjective elements such as enjoyment and instead attempt to measure and analyze the specific actions taken by the interactors in their testing of the work, which is often called a *play trace*. Play traces provide a more direct understanding of how the interactor interacted with the system itself, irrespective of their enjoyment of the narrative, or presentation of the work, etc. In McCoy et al.'s evaluation of "Prom Week", an evaluation was performed to test if the work encouraged a large diversity of interactor experiences [11]. The evaluation was performed by collecting the play traces of a number interactors and then creating a graph of the actions taken overtime, and the number of interactors who took each action at each point in time. The evaluation showed that the graph branched outward extremely quickly, meaning that in just a few steps interactors would be taking entirely different actions, and thus having a different experience. Later work from Antoun et al. attempted to instead use textual narratives to evaluate play traces, which involved developing a process by which the play trace would be converted to a natural language text defining each step in the trace [37]. Antoun et al.'s approach is, in some sense, an automation of Eladhari's re-tellings but instead leaves the judgement of the narratives to the authors.

There can be said to be a potential here for the automated analysis of re-tellings, either written or generated. While detailed re-tellings are more sparse, generating re-tellings for every single interactor of an EN work may lead to an absurd amount of content for the author to evaluate. The evaluation is also subjective, since in a re-telling the experience of interactors is already in the form of a narrative, and often contains far more depth than was actually represented by the system. There are certain broad features that can be analyzed in text, such as using sentiment analysis to determine the particular emotional impact of the work, and the broader field of textual analysis is far to large to survey here. Franzosi, in writing on the quantitative analysis of narratives, also opts for representing the narrative in an alternate format, specifically linguistic formats such as syntax tree or grammar, and then evaluates certain properties of narrative quality present in these formats [38].

5   Analysis Techniques for Authoring

One of the lingering questions about applying quantitative analysis to the authorship of ENs is exactly when and how this analysis should be used. The works surveyed in this chapter vary significantly, as does their process for analyzing emergent behaviours. Certain analysis techniques are much more work intensive, such as user tests or the transformation of the work into a different format, while others can be used quickly and steadily throughout development. In this section, we briefly discuss a rough framework for how quantitative analysis can relate and work alongside the authorship process. In particular, we identify four main ways in which analytical data can be used, for *benchmarks*, *comparisons*, *verification* and *classification*.

5.1   Benchmarks

Benchmarks refer to the ability to quantify certain qualities of the overall EN system. Many quantitative analysis techniques reduce certain properties of the EN system down to a particular set of values, and these values can be seen as a baseline of the work's performance at the current state of development. This could be, for example, the amount of conflicts, the content completed, or the number of issues within the simulation such as inaccessible content or dead-ends. This could also include the results of user studies, play traces or other trace analysis of the system.

5.2   Comparisons

We define comparisons as the ability to compare the behaviour of an EN system between stages in its development. If benchmarking is used, then one approach to comparison is to observe the difference between benchmarks of different instances of the EN work. Fast benchmarks, such as those provided by automated processes, can be used throughout development, even at the point of tuning particular values on a rule. Others are more difficult, such as player analysis, where new benchmarks may only be possible in long intervals.

Comparisons can also be done between the output presented by visual or abstract representations of the system. With a significant amount of procedural literacy, an author can observe changes in the patterns and behaviours of the system. Although harder to understand initially, such representations can represent a significant amount of system behaviour that is hidden when reduced to single values or probabilities.

Comparisons can also be done in a more qualitative sense by the author in examining player reactions in user studies, sample runs of the system, or re-tellings. These sorts of comparisons are very common in existing practices of EN. While this survey wished to look at alternate forms of evaluation, it is nonetheless still an essential method of understanding an EN work.

5.3 Verification

Verification refers to the process of proving certain features of an EN system are true. Using the above benchmarking method, we can set a certain benchmark as a goal and require the system to meet that goal, taking comparisons as a way of evaluating if changes to the EN work have been beneficial towards reaching the goal benchmark. For example, if we want a certain number of conflicts then we can keep track of the current number of conflicts in the system and how close we are to achieving that particular goal. This can serve the purpose of seeing if a certain change to the system is "good" according to the desires of the author.

Verification can also be done formally, by transforming the system into a different representation, such as Playspecs or Petri-Nets, or reducing particular problems to existing problems, such as using path-finding for accessibility or detecting content gaps. Transformation approaches tend to require more effort in that the EN work must be transformed correctly into the new representation, before any meaningful results can be gleaned. Such approaches tend to benefit from authoring tools that can keep track of multiple representations of the work while only presenting the simplest representation to the author.

5.4 Classification

Classification involves the extraction and labelling of patterns or behaviours from the broader functioning of the EN system. For visualization, this process is typically done by the author, who visually discovers the patterns in the work itself. Alternatively, the use of pattern detection can automatically perform classification, such as the analysis of interaction networks.

Classifications are used in a number of analysis approaches, where formal models of narrative qualities are used to classify instances of a quality in a given trace.

Classifications are also at the core of some EN approaches, such as curationism, which specifically classifies narrative instances in traces. Behaviours are also classified in complex systems analysis, such as the signal and boundary model.

Classifications can also be used to group certain re-tellings, or play-test results. In particular, classifying certain player experiences as good/bad, fun/boring, complicated, etc. are all feedback that can be specifically gleaned by observing player behaviour. Play traces can also be classified, such as by determining if a given play trace is unique or possesses certain qualities of its own.

6 Conclusion

Emergent narratives are an exciting, but daunting work to face as an author. They are plagued by long, ambiguous development times, strange behaviours, ample bugs and significant content authoring, but at the same time, EN games are often highly praised and beloved, even in spite of these quirks, for the broad and unique experiences they offer.

Taking a quantitative approach to understanding EN authorship may feel reductive or too technical, it is also impossible to say that EN works are not highly dependent on this low-level behaviour, regardless of whether the author is aware of it or not. In some sense, the author of an EN work needs to be equally competent at working at the technical, low level of development as they are at the higher and surface-level features of the work. Though we are nowhere near close to solving the authoring problem of emergent narratives, there are a number of approaches and techniques that can at least shed some light into the complexity hiding within each simulation.

While a quantitative evaluation does not directly represent the quality of either the emergent narrative work or a specific narrative instance, it nonetheless provides quick feedback that can easily be acted upon by the author of a given work. It could easily form a part of an authoring tool or be used to help model and design rules during pre-production. In this way, quantitative analysis tools can be considered a valuable addition to authoring tools for complex narrative models.

Acknowledgements This research was funded with the support of the Natural Sciences and Engineering Research Council of Canada (NSERC), [funding reference number: CGSD2-534211-2019].

References

1. Koenitz H, Louchart S (2015) Practicalities and ideologies, (re)-considering the interactive digital narrative authoring paradigm. In: Li B, Nelson M (eds) Proceedings of the fifth international conference on the foundations of digital games, Asilomar, CA
2. Klimas C (2013). Twine. http://twinery.org/
3. Bernstein M (2002) Storyspace 1. In: Proceedings of the thirteenth ACM conference on hypertext and hypermedia. ACM, New York, NY, USA, pp 172–181

4. Green D, Hargood C, Charles F (2021) Use of tools: UX principles for interactive narrative authoring tools. J Comput Cult Herit 14(3)
5. Spierling U (2018) Tools and principles for creation in interactive storytelling: the issue of evaluation. Author Interact Storytell 6
6. Kybartas Q (2013) Design and analysis of ReGEN. A narrative generation tool. Master's thesis, McGill University, Montréal, Canada
7. Partlan N, Carstensdottir E, Snodgrass S, Kleinman E, Smith G, Harteveld C, El-Nasr MS (2018) Exploratory automated analysis of structural features of interactive narrative. In: Rowe J, Smith G (eds) Proceedings of the 14th AAAI conference on artificial intelligence and interactive digital entertainment. The AAAI Press, Edmonton, Alberta, CA, pp 88–94
8. Louchart S, Truesdale J, Suttie N, Aylett R (2015) Interactive digital narrative. In: Chapter emergent narrative, past, present and future of an interactive storytelling approach. Routledge Studies in European Communication Research and Education. Routledge, United Kingdom, pp 185–199
9. Maxis. The Sims. Electronic Arts
10. Cinemaware (1986) The king of Chicago. Cinemaware (Adventure Game)
11. McCoy J, Treanor M, Samuel B, Reed AA, Mateas M, Wardrip-Fruin N (2014) Social story worlds with Comme il Faut. IEEE Trans Comput Intell AI Games
12. Evans R, Short E (2014) Versu—a simulationist storytelling system. IEEE Trans Comput Intell AI Games 6(2):113–130
13. Ryan M-L (1991) Possible worlds, artificial intelligence, and narrative theory. Indiana University Press, Bloomington, IN, USA
14. Smith G, Whitehead J (2010) Analyzing the expressive range of a level generator. In: Proceedings of the 2010 workshop on procedural content generation in games. ACM
15. Koenitz H, Pastena AD, Jansen D, de Lint B, Moss A (2018) The myth of 'universal' narrative models. In: Rouse R, Koenitz H, Haahr M (eds) Interactive storytelling. Springer International Publishing, Cham, pp 107–120
16. Ware SG, Michael Young R, Harrison B, Roberts DL (2012) Four quantitative metrics describing narrative conflict. In: Oyarzun D, Peinado F, Michael Young R, Elizalde A, Mendez G (eds) Interactive storytelling, LNCS, vol 7648. Springer Berlin Heidelberg, pp 18–29
17. Bae B-C, Young RM (2014) A computational model of narrative generation for surprise arousal. IEEE Tran Comput Intell AI Games 6(2):131–143
18. Berov L (2017) Towards a computational measure of plot tellability. The AAAI Press, In Intelligent Narrative Technologies
19. Tomaszewski Z (2011) On the use of reincorporation in interactive drama. In: Intelligent narrative technologies IV. Papers from the 2011 AIIDE workshop, pp 84–91
20. Kybartas Q, Verbrugge C (2014) Analysis of ReGEN as a graph-rewriting system for quest generation. IEEE Trans Comput Intell AI Games 6(2):228–242
21. Szilas N (2016) Modeling and representing dramatic situations as paradoxical structures. Digit Sch Humanit 32(2):403–422
22. Szilas N, Estupiñán S, Richle U (2018) Automatic detection of conflicts in complex narrative structures. In: Rouse R, Koenitz H, Haahr M (eds) Interactive storytelling. Springer International Publishing, Cham, pp 415–427
23. Kybartas Q, Verbrugge C, Lessard J (2020) A sketch-based tool for authoring and analyzing emergent narratives. Proceed AAAI Conf Artif Intell Interact Digit Entertain 16(1):319–321
24. Garbe J, Reed AA, Dickinson M, Wardrip-Fruin N, Mateas M (2014) Author assistance visualizations for ice-bound, a combinatorial narrative. In: Proceedings of FDG 2014—ninth international conference on the foundations of digital games
25. Kreminski M, Wardrip-Fruin N (2018) Sketching a map of the storylets design space. In: Rouse R, Koenitz H, Haahr M (eds) Interactive storytelling. Springer International Publishing, Cham, pp 160–164
26. Pickett CJF, Verbrugge C, Martineau F (2005) (P)NFG: a language and runtime system for structured computer narratives. In: Proceedings of the 1st annual North American game-on conference (GameOn'NA 2005). Eurosis, Montréal, Canada, pp 23–32

27. Adams T (2019). Emergent narrative in Dwarf Fortress. In: Short TX, Adams T (eds) Procedural storytelling in game design. Taylor & Francis Ltd, pp 149–158
28. Mateas M (2005) Procedural literacy: educating the new media practitioner. On Horiz (Special Issue). Future Games, Simul Interact Med Learn Contexts 13(1)
29. Holland J (2012) Signals and boundaries: building blocks for complex adaptive systems. MIT Press, Cambridge, Mass
30. Mitchell M (2009) Complexity: a guided tour. Oxford University Press
31. Kybartas Q, Verbrugge C, Lessard J (2021) Tension space analysis for emergent narrative. IEEE Trans Games 13(2):146–159
32. Moncion T, Amar P, Hutzler G (2010) Automatic characterization of emergent phenomena in complex systems. J Biol Phys Chem 10:16–23
33. Roth C, Koenitz H (2016) Evaluating the user experience of interactive digital narrative. In: Proceedings of the 1st international workshop on multimedia alternate realities. ACM
34. Eladhari MP (2018) Re-tellings: the fourth layer of narrative as an instrument for critique. In: Rouse R, Koenitz H, Haahr M (eds) Interactive storytelling, pp 65–78. Springer International Publishing, Cham
35. Ryan M-L (2006) Avatars of story. University of Minnesota Press
36. Sych S (2020) When the fourth layer meets the fourth wall: the case for critical game retellings. In: Bosser A-G, Millard DE, Hargood C (eds) Interactive storytelling, pp 203–211. Springer International Publishing, Cham
37. Antoun C, Antoun M, Ryan JO, Samuel B, Swanson R, Walker MA (2015) Generating natural language retellings from prom week play traces. In: Proceedings of the FDG workshop on procedural content generation in games
38. Franzosi R (2009) Quantitative narrative analysis. In: Quantitative applications in the social sciences. SAGE Publications

An Ethics Framework for Interactive Digital Narrative Authoring

Hartmut Koenitz, Jonathan Barbara, and Agnes Karolina Bakk

Abstract Interactive Digital Narrative (IDN) provides expressive opportunities that can be applied to many serious and non-fiction topics. Such applications, in particular, but also fictional IDN, have an ethical dimension, an aspect in need of increased attention as IDN matures and is more widely deployed. In this chapter, we identify aspects of IDN ethics with a particular concern for IDN authoring, taking into account earlier efforts in related areas, such as more generalized perspectives on ethics in computer sciences and considerations pertaining to video games. We use IDN for cultural heritage as a frame for discussing ethical aspects in IDN, since this application area is particularly prone to issues in this regard. Furthermore, we put a focus on VR, as a topic that most fully divorces audiences from the outside world during the IDN experience and thus poses particular ethical challenges for authoring. Throughout the discussion, we identify questions that an IDN ethics framework needs to address. Then, we introduce such a framework with 12 rules and briefly discuss their application. The IDN ethics framework is meant to be as a first edition, to be further developed by the community.

H. Koenitz (✉)
Södertörn University, Huddinge, Sweden
e-mail: hartmut.koenitz@sh.se

J. Barbara
Saint Martin's Institute of Higher Education, Hamrun, Malta
e-mail: jbarbara@stmartins.edu

A. K. Bakk
Moholy-Nagy University of Art and Design, Budapest, Hungary
e-mail: bakk@mome.hu

C. Hargood et al. (eds.), *The Authoring Problem*, Human–Computer Interaction Series,
https://doi.org/10.1007/978-3-031-05214-9_21

1   Introduction

Interactive Digital Narrative (IDN[1]) provide expressive opportunities that can be applied to many serious and non-fiction topics. Such applications, but also fictional topics, have an ethical dimension, an aspect in need of increased attention as IDN matures [1] and is more widely deployed. Ethics frameworks are well developed in journalism [2] and education [3], and are increasingly a concern in other areas such as governance [4]. In general, IDNs are media products and therefore it is tempting to assume that ethics frameworks for other media products might be applicable. However, due to their dynamic and systemic nature, IDN differ considerably from earlier fixed forms of narration and thus require a specific theoretical perspective, such as Koenitz' SPP model [5], that is, independent of the legacy perspective that earlier media bring with it. Similarly, we have to reframe the ethical dimensions explored within the academic field of IDN study and design. The impact of the specific characteristics of IDN as dynamic artifacts, as well as the changed role of the audience as interactors who participate in shaping their experience, needs to be carefully considered in this regard. The question is which aspects of earlier ethics frameworks can be applied to IDN and whether there are aspects which require specific approaches that might still need to be developed further.

In this chapter, we identify dimension of ethics pertinent to IDN authoring, taking into account earlier efforts in related areas. We will use the example of cultural heritage and virtual reality (VR) to identify and discuss these issues in more depth, as these area applications are particularly challenging when it comes to aspects of ethics. On that basis, we propose a general IDN ethics framework, applicable to a broad range of IDN forms and both "serious" and "non-serious" uses, to be further developed by the community.

2   Interactive Ethics

In general, ethics can be defined as

> [...] the discipline concerned with what is morally good and bad and morally right and wrong. The term is also applied to any system or theory of moral values or principles.[2]

In the present chapter, we understand ethics in the second sense, as a system of moral values applicable in the context of IDN authoring. Such a system exists concretely, for example, in journalism in the form of codes of conduct or handbooks, for example, the "Handbook on Ethical Journalism" by the New York Times [2]. Yet, this type of codification depends on the author/reader binary of immutable,

---

[1] We use the singular "Interactive digital narrative" to mean the category and "IDNs" to mean individual works.

[2] Singer, P. "ethics". Encyclopedia Britannica, December 15, 2021. https://www.britannica.com/topic/ethics-philosophy.

static forms of narrative. With IDN, conditions have changed. Because of the specific affordances and aesthetic qualities of IDN [6], its dynamic and interactive nature, IDN in principle do not create a fixed product with an associated meaning, but rather experiences facilitated by the possibility space of the protostory [7], which often contains a multiplicity of meanings to afford a systemic understanding. This does not mean to say that non-interactive narrative works always have easy to identify and understand meanings nor that multiplicity of interpretation is exclusive to IDN. However, the fact remains that with IDN, the actual artifact can be transformed, in principle, and choices by the audience, who are no longer readers, but interactors, can result in both different paths and outcomes. Furthermore, IDN offers replay and thus the opportunity to revisit and reconsider prior choices. In some cases, IDN works even facilitate co-creation (e.g., in works such as *The Sims* or in RPG games with emergent narratives such as *World of Warcraft* [8]). Conversely, IDN adds further levels of complexity to the already difficult questions of meaning-making (by creators) and sense-making (by authors). Perspectives concerned with these questions in non-interactive mediated expressions are therefore insufficient to cover IDN.

With the move to IDN from earlier, static forms of narrative like print literature and film, comes a profound change in responsibility. This is true in principle even if the extent of agency, the ability to make meaningful decisions [6] and thus impact the experience varies between different works. The specific potential of IDN is in the creation of a broadly conceived intended understanding experience reached via a range of interactions. Under these circumstances, the interactor's actions as well as their consequences become a shared responsibility, a new type of implicit contract between creator and an audience, which is no longer in the role of receivers as readers/viewers, but instead interactors involved in "active creation of belief" [6].

and moral behavior becomes a conscious choice by the interactor, as the work is no longer fixed. The infamous raid on a virtual funeral in the MMORPG *World of Warcraft* in 2006 required planning and coordination [9]. Similarly, "harvesting" the little sisters in Bioshock [10] or treating customers nicely in Neo Cab [11] is conscious decision. Indeed, some IDN center around difficult moral decisions, such as in *We, the Revolution* [12], which puts the interactor in the role of a judge during the French Revolution. And even in exploratory-type IDN [13], e.g., interactive documentaries where choice is restricted to one of selections between different perspectives, this decision is still one with ethical implications—do I want to listen more to the pirate's perspective in *The Last Hijack Interactive* [14] or to the one by the hijacked captain?

Yet, "shared responsibility" is an incomplete way to describe the ethical dimension of IDN creation. There is still a power differential between creator and interactor—it is the creator who defines the rules, relationships, and spaces of an IDN system. Consequently, the IDN creator retains a larger share of moral responsibility for the entire possibility space of a given work and what happens in it. Will Wright might not have intended for interactors to torture the virtual creatures in *The Sims* [15], but his procedural system also enables this kind of behavior.

Consequently, we might talk about an *ethical paradox* of IDN authoring: procedural systems on the one hand enable independent decisions which are the responsibility of interactors, yet, if such decisions are morally reprehensible, the system creator can still be understood as sharing responsibility for it, as it was their system facilitating the problematic behavior. The question remains if and where a boundary condition exists that clearly delimitates creator and interactor responsibility. An ethics framework for IDN needs to address these issues, the questions of individual and shared responsibility and moral behavior under interactive conditions.

2.1 Related Work

In line with our own questions, James H. Moore already in 1985 defines "computer ethics" as the "consideration of both personal and social policies for the ethical use of computer technology" [16]. Ever since, the topic has been further investigated and discussed in the context of particular areas of the digital medium.

In the related field of video games, the question of ethics has been approached before, for example, by Sicart [17], who points out that players/interactors bring an understanding of ethical values from outside the work to the interactive experience, something we have not considered so far. Sicart sees interactors as subjects who are capable of their own ethical decisions within the interactive experiences, as long as the work in questions enables such decisions and allows for reflection. This criterion can be used as value judgement for authoring, Sicart argues—good game design facilitates reflection, bad game design does not. In our given context, we can see the aspect of reflection as an important consideration when it comes to ethical IDN authoring.

In 2010, a group of computer scientists created five rules pertaining to the "Moral Responsibility for Computing Artifacts". The rules are as follows:

Rule 1: The people who design, develop, or deploy a computing artifact are morally responsible for that artifact, and for the foreseeable effects of that artifact. This responsibility is shared with other people who design, develop, deploy, or knowingly use the artifact as part of a sociotechnical system.

Rule 2: The shared responsibility of computing artifacts is not a zero-sum game. The responsibility of an individual is not reduced simply because more people become involved in designing, developing, deploying, or using the artifact. Instead, a person's responsibility includes being answerable for the behaviors of the artifact and for the artifact's effects after deployment, to the degree to which these effects are reasonably foreseeable by that person.

Rule 3: People who knowingly use a particular computing artifact are morally responsible for that use.

Rule 4: People who knowingly design, develop, deploy, or use a computing artifact can do so responsibly only when they make a reasonable effort to take into account the sociotechnical systems in which the artifact is embedded.

Rule 5: People who design, develop, deploy, promote, or evaluate a computing artifact should not explicitly or implicitly deceive users about the artifact or its foreseeable effects, or about the sociotechnical systems in which the artifact is embedded [18].

These rules mirror not only our own considerations in terms of shared responsibility, but also add several useful aspects to our discussion. In terms of the creator's responsibility for an artifact after deployment, the authors restrict it to the degree in which any effects of it "are reasonably foreseeable by that person" (ibid). Conversely, the rules point out the interactor's responsibility for the "knowingly use" of a computational artifact. Yet, this statement opens the question what "knowing usage" consists of and how a creator can facilitate it.

Echoing Sicart's insight about external aspects, "the rules" add the dimension of context to an ethics framework, more precisely the impact of the surrounding "sociotechnical systems"—the society in which the artifact is embedded including the technical systems used for authoring, distribution, and consumption—on the use and interpretation of computational artifacts such as IDN. We understand this aspect also as an awareness of a digital divide and the resulting questions of access. Many members of society are being precluded from or restricted in their participation in both authoring of and interacting with IDN by intersectional regimes of oppression based on categorical distinctions, such as gender, race, origin, sexual orientation, and religion.

A further dimension raised by Miller et al. is the potential for deception by creators. This is an important concern, especially when we consider the role non-interactive narratives have played as underpinnings of ideologically motivated discrimination, atrocities, and genocides.

In 2017, Charles Ess argued that Digital Media Ethics (DME)—"ethical challenges and issues that arise in conjunction with our everyday use of… digital media" [19]—are informed not only by philosophy and applied ethics but also by ethical insights of professionals working in information and computing as well as the community of end users of digital media.

Even more recently, in a chapter concerned with digital media ethics in the context of museums, Kidd [20] introduces four areas of concern faced by museums when using interactive digital media: valuing user contributions, managing its risks, mixing fact with fiction, and the negotiation of power. User contributions are part of a shared authoring process and something we have not explicitly considered so far. Sometimes discussed under the heading of "user-generated content", such contributions are often problematic, especially in a museum context, where they are not in line with the objective, impartial, or impolitical perspective intended by the museum, and their moderation raises ethical issues of ownership and emotional impact. Another aspect is the risk of misuse and copyright breaches: such as unacknowledged repurposing or distortion brought about by online access to museum works. Kidd asks: "What ethical responsibilities users or visitors might reasonably be expected to uphold?" [20], yet this is also a question for creators regarding what kinds of interactor behaviors they facilitate. A more direct question for authoring in this context is the mixture of archaeological fact with speculative fiction, which is in conflict with the ethical obligation of museums to present only facts. And yet, such a combination is often used in museum-related IDN to fill in gaps in the narrative due to unavailable evidence and the need to make the story comprehensible. In addition, while this aspect can be controlled more easily in the physical museum space, moderating it in the digital realm, inclusive of social media spaces and taking its affordance for multiple perspectives into account, is a challenge in managing the public's perception of the museum's stance on speculation [21].

In the context of immersive journalism, Uskali et al. discuss the issue of age appropriateness and suggest recommended age ratings [22]. In addition, the same authors issue a warning about the increasing sophistication of manipulation and disinformation campaigns, an aspect that journalist and other creators have an ethical obligation to take into account in the age of deep fakes and bot-driven Twitter accounts.

3   Ethics in Cultural Heritage IDN

As we have shown in the last section, the question of ethics under interactive considerations has been considered before. Conversely, a number of open questions exists which we will identify throughout this paper (marked in bold). We will now use the topic of cultural heritage representation to better understand moral issues arising in IDN authoring on a concrete backdrop and identify the particular concerns an ethics framework needs to address in terms of concrete guidelines for creators.

Cultural heritage may refer to sites (excavated or built), artifacts, as well as practices and customs that one or more individuals consider to be worthy of being preserved [23] and socially transmitted [24, 25]. Moreover, a key aspect of cultural heritage is one's relationship with it: the use of the past for the purpose of the present [26, 27]. This subjective evaluation of what is considered heritage opens up a multiperspective consideration that makes it a fitting subject for IDN. Simultaneously, ethical aspects (what to represent, how to represent, how to give access, who to attribute ownership to, who to give access) are front and center in Cultural Heritage. Thus, this area of application is particularly fitting to discuss ethical aspects of IDN authoring, for example, in regard to misrepresentation, contested histories, and power structures (cf. [28]).

The traditional way of representing cultural heritage is an official top-down perspective determined by established authorities and institutions in the form of museums and monuments. Such institutions are normally led by professionals whose ethical responsibilities include conservation, restoration, and stewardship [29]. One such international authority is UNESCO, whose World Heritage List identifies aspects of the past as worthy of remembrance and preservation. In contrast, a bottom-up approach toward cultural heritage identifies relationships that individuals or groups of people have with the past that may be misaligned or in contest with official heritage. Examples of such unrecognized [30] variants of cultural heritage are local folklore and traditions, specialized private museums, and heritage brought by immigrants to a host nation [26]. Tension may arise between top-down and bottom-up approaches when these result in opposing views. Key criteria used in cultural heritage evaluation, such as authenticity, cannot be judged only against fixed criteria, but also need to take into account the subjective cultural context [31]. In addition, there is often an element of uncertainty (e.g., due to the lack of records) and together these aspects can lead to wrong judgements in terms of authenticity and purpose, which, if exposed, can diminish trust in institutions and information sources [32].

IDNs can be used to present consequential ethics: allowing the interactor to discover the consequence of their actions in dealing with ethical issues of cultural heritage. But in this chapter we focus on deontological ethics, an ethical theory that uses rules to distinguish right from wrong [33].

In the next section, we will first analyze ethical issues arising in IDN cultural heritage projects in general, then consider established strategies in mitigating ethical issues in representing cultural heritage and what IDN authoring can learn from such strategies and finally explore further ethical aspects introduced by the VR platform.

3.1 Ethical Considerations of Tangible and Intangible Cultural Heritage

Tangible cultural heritage, such as historic sites and artifacts, are associated with a range of ethical concerns even outside the framing of IDN authoring. A first example is the question of ownership, including ownership of interpretation (see [34] for an extended discussion of this aspect for IDN authoring in a European context, and also the work on decolonization of games). *Who owns the past and its interpretation?* is an ethical concern that IDN authors need to address. The archaeological profession has reacted to this concern with the concept of *stewardship*: a site or an artifact is not owned but rather guarded while under their care. Consequently, questions arise as to *what exactly should be stewarded*, for the sake of *whom*, and *why*? [35] An alternative approach is the concept of *cultural ownership*: artifacts can be the property of a cultural group which suggests collective, rather than individual, rights concerning ownership, accessibility, and use. However, the concept of "cultural property" itself is problematic as it might come from a place of oppression, e.g., by conquests in war or by means of colonialization [35]. IDNs can serve as a representation of these different perspectives toward cultural property, allowing for perspective-taking, particularly those which are different from one's own point of view. This means an ethics framework need to guide the IDN author in answering the following questions: **How can we make the existence of intersectional regimes of oppression transparent to the interactor, especially their effects on perspective-taking and representation?**

In addition, property suggests something that is fixed while culture itself is of a dynamic nature [36]. Therefore, it is difficult to determine who, at a given point in time, belongs to the group that created the object of heritage—"cultural insiders"—and those who do not—"cultural outsiders" [24, 37]. These questions are pertinent to IDN authoring as they problematize the starting situation, rule systems, and role we give to interactors in a given work [6]. With regard to the latter, we need to be aware that there are limits to "scripting the interactor" [6], casting the audience in a specific role. It is questionable whether we can successfully impose a "cultural insider" role on "outsiders". Even the most skillful scripting of the interactor by the author cannot replace years of cultural development and personal immersion that ascribe meaning to artifacts and sites. The challenge here is the presentation of a contextualized situation that bears a cultural insider's perspective without trivializing the values attributed to the elements of such a representation. The guiding question here is: **How can IDN ethically convey contextual "cultural insider" information to an interactor and prevent the danger of disconnecting representation and context?**

Further ethical considerations arise with intangible cultural heritage [38], where value is assigned to human behavior, skills, activities, rituals, and ceremonies. These are carried out in an actual space and might include the use of artifacts as tools or props. Their intangibility makes them immune to outright ownership, but liable to appropriation [39]. When such activities are reproduced digitally, especially by IDN authors as cultural outsiders, the question arises whose interests are represented and whose are unduly favored. Are the interests of the "cultural insiders" who gave rise to such behavior being given their due importance, or are they being eschewed in favor of the interests of "cultural outsiders" (e.g., former colonizing nations) who, maybe due to hidden political agendas, are attracting attention unto themselves? [37, 39]. This discussion leads us to the following question: **How can IDN be ethical in portraying the cultural insider's perspective?**

More concretely in regard to authoring, these considerations translate into questions of representation and contextual information. The lack of the latter is an important issue to consider for ethical IDN authoring. For example, recordings of global south tribal dances on YouTube [37] which are lacking the tradition and experience of "cultural insiders" are ethically problematic, especially considering the wide availability of the platform across the global north to audiences of different abilities and experiences. And while the full range of this kind of information might be inaccessible to outsiders in principle, an ethical approach still needs to aim for conveying contextual information whenever possible. Therefore, we ask: **How can IDN design accommodate interactors with different levels of abilities, experience with interactive artifacts and prior knowledge regarding the topic of the artifact?**

The aspect of representation is also connected to difficult choices for authoring in terms of realistic depiction and believability aided by plausible speculation, which is often necessary to create a more complete experience, yet the separation between fact and fiction must be made evident [32]. The question is: **How can evidenced and speculative perspectives be represented fairly and responsibly in an IDN?**

Using IDN to represent intangible cultural heritage brings a particular challenge for authoring when the interactor is expected to participate in its re-enactment. How do we "teach" the skills and proper cultural behavior necessary for participation to the interactor? In rewarding the interactor who succeeds in re-enacting the behavior, are we rewarding cultural appropriation? How faithfully must the behavior be re-enacted for it to be successful? In simplifying a behavior's complexity for the sake of a smooth experience, are we trivializing the original ritual and thereby offending the cultural insiders to whom it belongs? The question here is: **How can we prevent undue simplification and trivialization of a complex behavior and situations in an IDN?**

If we only concentrate on the "outer form"—the movements, the actions, we are not conveying the full meaning of the behavior, and what it represents. The process behind the red ochre spiral paintings adorning the ceiling of the Hal-Saflieni Hypogeum can be faithfully represented but the meaning attributed to such symbols by their creators is as yet unknown. Therefore, the challenge for ethical IDN authoring is to convey that meaning—as fully as possible—developed over generations, through all means available in an IDN (contextual information, scripting into a role, onboarding functions that take different knowledge levels into account, etc.).

3.2 Addressing Shortcomings of Digital Cultural Heritage Representations

The London Charter [40] presents a *modus operandi* on how digital representations of cultural heritage can be ethical, by, for example, considering more than one alternative option, ensuring the veracity and authenticity of information sources, documenting methodology and decisions taken, identifying uncertainties, and ensuring sustainability of the digital representation across time. However, Thompson [37] identifies four elements that are often left out of digital representations of cultural heritage:

1. The absence of believably realistic representations of characters belonging to the "cultural insiders" group, often due to budgetary or technological limitations, may suggest that the space is uninhabited and open to exploitation.
2. The fixed or pre-determined point of view taken by the lens limits the alternate viewing of a given scene with interactive viewing being deemed to be also limited by financial or technological limitations.
3. The passage of time over a layered landscape is often omitted from digital representations of the past as they are depicted either in their present situation or in an imagined state of relevance to its use.
4. When a multitude of options are available, the choice of the single representation excludes the other choices—a choice often made subjectively according to the values of the decision-maker rather than objectively according to the object's or site's meaning.

In designing a digital experience of the past, be it tangible or intangible, making a choice is unavoidable, and every choice brings with it problems as most often there is no "right" choice. This makes IDN an attractive medium through which cultural heritage can be represented. The narrative legacy of IDN implies the presence of characters, both as NPC and as the interactor character, and this helps address Thompson's first concern. However, more attention needs to be paid to make sure that "cultural insiders" are represented, and this representation happens in an ethical manner. Nevertheless, the major advantage of using IDN to represent cultural heritage is that different perspectives or interpretations can be built right into the actual artifact addressing the rest of Thompson's concerns, be they points of view, time-dependent, or choice-dependent perspectives. Therefore: **How can the creator's perspective-taking be conveyed transparently?** Besides, an IDN has to allow interactors to make choices between them within single playthroughs, and also replays, to experience more content and form their own perspectives, develop unique and synthesized value judgements [41], and gain a systemic understanding [42]. The question here is: **How can we create multi-perspectives in a way that each perspective is given a fair and responsible treatment in accordance with established rules of democratic discourse and international laws?**

Forms of IDN which focus on embodiment such as Augmented Reality (AR) [34] and Virtual Reality (VR) technology [43] are particularly adept in representing cultural heritage. Likewise, other application areas for IDN may have their own suitable platform, with their own ethical issues. In the following discussion, we will concentrate on VR, as this form presents particular ethical challenges for IDN authoring, when designing an experience which is both embodied and removed from the outside world. An ethical framework for IDN authoring needs to be able to also address these aspects.

Virtual Reality—"the sum of the hardware and software systems that seek to perfect an all-inclusive, sensory illusion of being present in another environment" [44] is a platform of choice for over two decades in the digital conservation of heritage sites [43]. The use of a head-mounted device for VR representation minimizes the perceived "hypermediated" [45] presence of technology and creates a sense of embodiment [46], of presence through self-location. This type of experience can also help the interactor understand perspectives other than their own, but almost literally putting them into another body [47]. However, these capabilities of VR, affecting perception and bodily phenomenology, put interactors in a potentially problematic situation, as they are removed from the real-world context, and are asked to trust a virtual environment which has the possibility to trick the senses to the point where they might even encounter physical health issues such as nausea. Madary and Metzinger explored ethical concerns raised by such experiences and suggested a possible code of conduct for authors and consumers of VR experiences [48]. The authors argue that VR's illusion of embodiment may have a manipulative effect, especially if "illusions of embodiment are misused" [48]. This means, we need to ask: **How do we avoid deceiving interactors? Are there situations when deception can be a legitimate means to convey an understanding?** Furthermore, Madary and Metzinger emphasize the importance of informing the audience about potentially lasting psychological effects of VR. Another potential danger is in excessive usage, which can lead to a condition where VR users could "experience the real world and their real bodies as unreal, effectively shifting their sense of reality exclusively to the virtual environment" [48]. The following question is therefore crucial: **How do we warn of interactors of possible health dangers arising from the use of specific platform chosen to deliver the IDN?**

With the proliferation of immersive journalism and VR documentaries [49–52], the question of perspective has become more important, both in a literal sense, as the question where the gaze is pointed at, and in terms of the overall representation. In this regard, creators should clearly position their work as a designed representation of a "unique aspect of their reality" [53].

Having explored ethical issues arising from the subject matter (i.e., cultural heritage) as well as platform (i.e., virtual reality) in order to identify ethical questions for authoring IDN of cultural heritage in VR, we are now ready to discuss the topic in relation to IDN authoring in general.

4 Ethics for IDN Authoring

What drives an artist to create interactive narrative works? And what effects do they intend to achieve in their audiences? The question of the effects of mediated products on their audiences has been studied for a considerable time. Walter Benjamin in his 1936 analysis of the work of art turned mass media product [54] observes the loss of the authority of the unique art piece, yet at the same time identifies a democratization that makes art accessible to much larger audiences. The Frankfurt School warns of the dangers of a manipulating and manipulated "cultural industry" [55] in part influenced by their observations of the role of media in the rise of Nazism and as a propaganda instrument in the hands of the Nazi government. In contrast, Habermas [56] emphasizes the crucial function of the media to inform citizens in democratic societies and consequently alerts us of the considerable responsibilities of media producers. During the last decade, the use of IDN by public broadcasters like Arte (France/Germany) [57], VPRO (the Netherlands) [58, 59], and the BBC (UK) [60] increased, and more recently private streaming producer Netflix has entered the field with Bandersnatch [61]. Continuing in this vein the European COST research network INDCOR (Interactive Narrative Design for COmplexity Representations)[3] investigates the use of IDN for representing complex topics with the aim to increase the application and understanding of IDN even further.

A crucial prerequisite to all discussions of ethical questions in IDN design is an understanding of its specific qualities in contrast to fixed narrative forms. IDN as dynamic, systemic forms are principally open to unexpected consequences and unintended uses (cf. [62]) and this central aspect shifts a part of the responsibility to the audience as interactors. Certainly, the IDN designer should take all reasonable measures to keep the interactor focused on the intended understanding. However, just as taking "happy selfies" in a concentration camp monument is not the fault of the monument's administrators, but that of the selfie-takers themselves, suggesting that there is a limit to the designer's responsibility. If no deviation of any kind from a fixed experience is intended, IDN might just not be the right means and thus fixed forms of narration should be preferred. With this central aspect in mind, we can proceed with a framework of ethical rules which IDN creators should consider before and during the design process.

---

[3] https://indcor.eu.

4.1   An Ethics Framework for IDN Authoring

The following rules are developed in reaction to the challenges identified throughout Sect. 3 where cultural heritage and VR serve as a frame, as this application area and platform are particularly challenging in terms of ethical aspects of IDN authoring. Our framework complements existing efforts (e.g., Rouse's process-focused perspective [28]) and should be seen as a starting point for further discussion and revisions.

1. Creators and interactors share the responsibility for the effects of IDN systems, provided that

   a. Creators are responsible for all effects of an IDN system that can reasonably be foreseen.
   b. Creators are responsible for taking reasonable measures to inform interactors of their role within an IDN experience as well as what opportunities they have for interaction.
   c. Interactors are responsible for their actions when experiencing IDN, as long as they understand their role and how they can interact.

2. Creators should not deceive interactors about their role or opportunities for interaction; exceptions require specific artistic or educational purposes.
3. Creators need to inform interactors about potential health risks.
4. Accessibility needs to be assured in IDN design. IDN need to accommodate interactors with different levels of abilities and prior experience with interactive artifacts.
5. Creators need to be transparent about their perspective-taking.
6. IDN representations need to responsibly represent intersectional regimes of oppression, including those based on gender and fixed gender roles, sexual orientation, origin, appearance, and neurodiversity. IDN provide specific opportunities to expose such regimes of oppression.
7. IDN featuring multiple perspectives should assure that each perspective is treated fairly and responsibly.
8. A given work should take advantage of the multifaceted representation capabilities of IDN and should portrait complex situations accordingly. Undue simplification and trivialization of complex situations should be avoided.
9. Creators need to take the context a work is placed in, the surrounding society and available infrastructure into consideration.
10. Creators should accommodate interactors with different levels of prior knowledge regarding the topic of the respective work.
11. An IDN needs to scaffold the experience for the interactor so that they arrive at an understanding of how their actions have resulted in the outcome.
12. When content is represented which includes "insider knowledge" (e.g., "cultural insiders", specific societal groups, or national customs), IDN creators need to provide a reasonable amount of context so that the content can also be understood as best as possible by an audience of "outsiders".

4.2 Applying the Ethical Framework

We will now consider some examples to show how the ethics framework can be applied to analyze the design choices in existing works and what we can learn from this application.

In the case of a VR IDN in Cultural Heritage, the choices of interactor role, navigation and agency are important factors with ethical implications. In *The Last Goodbye* [63], the interactor is a visitor taken on a guided tour accompanying the main protagonist Pinchas Gutter on a tour of the Majdanek concentration camp, with limited agency provided only in terms of gaze direction. From the perspective of our framework, the representation can be qualified as ethical—the interactor is clearly cast in a role (rule 1b), which would also provide limited agency in real life. *The Last Goodbye* presents the monument and the genocide that happened there (rule 6) in a responsible manner, through the perspective of a guide (rule 5), an insider who explains what happened (rule 12). The main issue with the title (a problematic perspective for a walking experience, due to the use of a drone for recording, leading to a limited experience of embodiment) is not of an ethical nature, but rather of design choices.

The *Stanley Parable* [64] is a narrative game, which puts the interactor on a journey through a Kafkaesque world, an office building from which there seems to be no escape. Here, the interactor is purposefully given misleading information and thus deceived. However, this deception is transparent (e.g., when the narrator's instructions and commentary are at odds with what the interactor can do) and serves a clear artistic goal as a parable about free will and therefore qualifies as ethical (rule 2).

A further example, *The Book of Distance* [65], exposes ethical problems. In this VR work, the interactor experiences the memories of a Canadian Japanese family and the trauma of internment during WW2. The interactor serves as a sidekick to whoever is currently leading the narrative. As the interactor's actions visibly affect the state of the space around them, there is self-location, agency, body ownership, indeed embodiment [46]. The player not only learns how to do these actions but visually sees the result of them, e.g., photos appear as the result of the camera button being pressed, sown strawberry seeds flourish, are harvested, and the fruits presented at the table. These positive aspects are however marred by the ethically problematic design choice of not providing a fixed role to the VR interactor [66]. At times, the interactor serves as sidekick to Onezo the protagonist, Randall the narrator, or even the Canadian military, without clear indication why these changes happen, violating rule 1b. A particular problematic design choice is when the interactor's only option to progress the narrative is pressing a lever which results in Onezo being detained in an internment camp, turning the interactor from the protagonist's sidekick into an oppressor. This is a deceitful role change violating rule 2, but also affecting rules 6, 7, and 8, as the IDN here fails to provide room for an explanation of why the role change happened or how this oppressive measure was motivated. We can speculate that the design intention here was to make the interactor complicit in the internment but forcing the interactor into this new role without any preparation, warning or post-factum explanation is unethical. What makes this aspect unethical is neither to overarching intention, nor the forced action, but the lack of context and motivation. Another issue here is regarding rule 11, as there is no causal connection and no explanation how the interactor's prior actions have led to this situation. An ethical way to present this aspect would be to focus on the role of outside forces earlier.

A similarly problematic and deceptive role change happens in the narrative game *A Way Out* [67]. Here, the interactor is initially cast in the role of one part of a duo of runaway criminals, only to learn at the very end of the experience that they are actually an undercover cop and are forced to shoot the runaway companion, violating rules 1b, 2 and 11. Again, the interactor is forced into a new role without preparation or prior warning while the time invested acting in what seems to be the actual role is essentially invalidated. An important element missing here is any identifiable purpose, any lesson that could be learned, also because the situation is both unrealistic (impossible in the real world) unbelievable (does not make sense within the fiction).

5   Conclusion

In this paper, we have considered the question of ethics in IDN authoring. We discussed a general perspective and drew the connection to existing work on ethics in the digital, computational medium. We take a bottom-up approach to our investigation rooted in an analysis of ethical considerations arising from applications of IDN in Cultural Heritage, taking into account the particular challenges arising from the use of virtual reality technology. We used this approach to identify ethical questions for IDN design, and finally answering to these challenges, developed an ethics framework containing a set of foundational rules to guide IDN authoring. To show how these rules can be used to critically evaluate IDN design, a select number of example IDN experiences are described in terms of their abiding by, or failing to abide be, these foundational rules. The framework is meant as a starting point, to be further discussed and developed by the academic and professional communities, for example, the questions under what conditions deception of the interaction might be considered ethical.

Acknowledgements The authors would like to acknowledge the support of the EU COST Action CA 18230 INDCOR (Interactive Narrative Design for COmplexity Representations) in the creation of this work.

References

1. Koenitz H (2018) Thoughts on a discipline for the study of interactive digital narratives. In: Rouse R, Koenitz H, Haahr M (eds) Interactive storytelling: 11th international conference for interactive digital storytelling, ICIDS 2018. The 3rd international conference for interactive digital storytelling, Cham, pp 36–49
2. The New York Times: Ethical Journalism. https://www.nytimes.com/editorial-standards/eth ical-journalism.html
3. National Education Association: Code of Ethics for Educators. https://www.nea.org/resource-library/code-ethics-educators
4. Wieland J (2001) The ethics of governance. Bus Ethics Q 11:73–87
5. Koenitz H (2015) Towards a specific theory of interactive digital narrative. In: Koenitz H, Ferri G, Haahr M, Sezen TI (eds) Interactive digital narrative. Routledge, New York, pp 91–105
6. Murray JH (1997) Hamlet on the Holodeck: the future of narrative in cyberspace. Free Press, New York
7. Koenitz H (2015) Towards a specific theory of interactive digital narrative. In: Interactive digital narrative: history, theory, and practice. New York
8. Blizzard Entertainment (2004) World of Warcraft [Virtual Game World]
9. Gibbs MR, Carter M, Arnold M, Nansen B (2013) Serenity now bombs a world of warcraft funeral: negotiating the morality, reality and taste of online gaming practices. Presented at the AoIR Selected Papers of Internet Research
10. 2K Games (2007) BioShock
11. Chance Agency (2019) Neo Cab
12. Polyslash (2019) We. The Revolution
13. Ryan M-L (2006) Avatars of story. University of Minnesota Press, Minneapolis
14. Submarine Channel (2014) Last Hijack Interactive. Submarine Channel
15. Wright W (2000) The Sims [video game]
16. Moor JH (1985) What is computer ethics? Metaphilosophy 16:266–275
17. Sicart (2009) The ethics of computer games 1–273
18. Miller KW (2011) Moral responsibility for computing artifacts: "the rules"
19. Ess C (2017) Digital media ethics. In: Oxford research encyclopedia of communication. Oxford University Press, Oxford
20. Kidd J (2019) Digital media ethics and museum communication. In: The Routledge handbook of museums, media and communication, pp 193–204
21. Palombini A (2017) Storytelling and telling history. J Cult Heritage 134–139
22. Uskali T, Ikonen P (2021) The impact of emotions in immersive journalism. In: Us-kali T, Gynnild A, Jones S, Sirkkunen E (eds) Immersive journalism as storytelling. Ethics, production and design. Routledge, London
23. Kersel MM, Luke C (2015) Diplomacy and neo-imperialism. Global Heritage Reader 70–93
24. Appiah A (1994) Race, culture, identity: misunderstood connections, The Tanner Lectures on Human Values. Delivered at University of California, San Diego
25. Scheffler S (2009) Immigration and the significance of culture. In: Nationalism and multiculturalism in a world of immigration, pp 119–150
26. Harrison R (2012) Heritage: critical approaches
27. Smith L (2006) Uses of heritage
28. Rouse R (2019) Someone else's story: an ethical approach to interactive narrative design for cultural heritage. In: Cardona-Rivera RE, Sullivan A, Young RM (eds) Interactive storytelling: 12th international conference on interactive digital storytelling, ICIDS 2019. Springer Nature, pp 47–60
29. Ireland T, Schofield J, Ireland T, Schofield J (eds) (2015) The ethics of cultural heritage. Springer, New York, NY
30. Harrison R (2010) What is heritage? In: Understanding the politics of heritage
31. ICOMOS (1994) Nara Document on Authenticity

32. Colley S (2015) Ethics and digital heritage. In: Ireland T, Schofield J, Ireland T, Schofield J (eds) The ethics of cultural heritage. Springer, New York, NY, pp 13–32
33. Alexander L, Moore M (2007) Deontological ethics. In: Zalta EN (ed) The Stanford encyclopedia of philosophy (Winter edn)
34. Koenitz H (2021) Reflecting in space on time: augmented reality interactive digital narratives to explore complex histories. In: Fisher JA (ed) Augmented and mixed reality for communities. CRC Press, Boca Raton, FL, pp 183–198
35. Matthes EH (2018) The ethics of cultural heritage. In: Zalta EN (ed) The Stanford encyclopedia of philosophy (Fall 2018 edn). Stanford, CA
36. Mezey N (2007) The paradoxes of cultural property. Colum L Rev 107:2004
37. Thompson EL (2017) Legal and ethical considerations for digital recreations of cultural heritage 26
38. UNESCO (2003) Convention for the safeguarding of the intangible cultural heritage. UNESCO, Paris
39. Sherman SR (2008) Who owns culture and who decides?: ethics, film methodology, and intangible cultural heritage protection. West Folk 67:223–236
40. Beacham R, Niccolucci F, Denard H (2009) The London Charter. For computer-based visualization of cultural heritage
41. Lean J, Moizer J, Towler M, Abbey C (2006) Simulations and games: use and barriers in higher education. Act Learn High Educ 7:227–242
42. Rejeski D, Chaplin H, Olson R, Scholars, for Woodrow Wilson International Center (2015) Addressing complexity with playable models
43. Ch'ng E, Cai Y, Thwaites H (2018) Special issue on VR for culture and heritage: the experience of cultural heritage with virtual reality: guest editors' introduction. Presence Teleoperators Virtual Environ 26:iii–vi
44. Biocca F, Delaney B (1995) Immersive virtual reality technology. Commun Age Virtual Reality 15:10–5555
45. Bolter JD, Grusin R (2000) Remediation: understanding new media. MIT Press, Cambridge, MA
46. Kilteni K, Groten R, Slater M (2012) The sense of embodiment in virtual reality. Presence Teleoperators Virtual Environ 21:373–387
47. la Peña de N, Weil P, Llobera J, Spanlang B, Friedman D, Sanchez-Vives MV, Slater M (2010) Immersive journalism: immersive virtual reality for the first-person experience of news. Presence 19:291–301
48. Madary M, Metzinger TK (2016) Recommendations for good scientific practice and the consumers of VR-technology. Front Robot AI
49. la Peña de N (2014) Project Syria
50. Arora G, Pousman B, Milk C (2015) Clouds over Sidra. https://www.unicefusa.org/stories/clo uds-over-sidra-award-winning-virtual-reality-experience/29675
51. Ex Nihilo (2016) Notes on Blindness
52. Williams RR (2019) Traveling While Black
53. Fisher JA (2019) Empathic actualities: toward a taxonomy of empathy in virtual reality. In: Cardona-Rivera RE, Sullivan A, Young RM (eds) Interactive storytelling: 12th international conference on interactive digital storytelling, ICIDS 2019. Springer Nature, Cham, pp 233–244
54. Benjamin W (1963) Das Kunstwerk im Zeitalter seiner technischen Reproduzierbarkeit. Surhkamp, Frankfurt/Main
55. Horkheimer M, Adorno TW (2006) The culture industry: enlightenment as mass deception. In: Media and cultural studies: keyworks, pp 41–72
56. Habermas J (1989) The structural transformation of the public sphere. Polity Press/MIT Press, Cambridge, MAS
57. Dufresne D (2013) Fort McMoney. http://www.fortmcmoney.com
58. Duijn M, Wolting F, Co-Director Documentary, Pallotta T, Co-Director Documentary (2014) The Last Hijack Interactive
59. Duijn M, Interactive Director (2018) The Industry. https://theindustryinteractive.com/

60. Ursu MF, Zsombori V, Wyver J, Conrad L, Kegel I, Williams D (2009) Interactive documentaries: a golden age. Comput Entertainment (CIE) 7
61. Bandersnatch (2019)
62. Koenitz H, Eladhari MP (2021) The paradigm of game system building. ToDIGRA 5
63. Arora G, Palitz A (2017) Last Goodbye
64. Wreden D (2013) The Stanley Parable [Video Game]
65. Okita R (2020) The Book of Distance
66. Oppenheim D, Okita RL (2020) The Book of Distance: Personal Storytelling in VR. Presented at the ACM SIGGRAPH 2020 Immersive Pavilion, Virtual Event USA
67. Hazelight Studios (2013) A Way Out